Competitive Struggle

America's
Western Fur Trading Posts,
1764–1865

Competitive Struggle

America's Western Fur Trading Posts, 1764–1865

by
R.G. Robertson

Photos by Karen A. Robertson

tamarack books, inc.

First Edition: May, 1999
10 9 8 7 6 5 4 3 2 1

ISBN 1–886609–19–5

The cover features a photograph of the Southwest Bastion of Fort Union in North Dakota.

Published by:
Tamarack Books, Inc.
PO Box 190313
Boise, ID 83719-0313
1-800-962-6657

Printed in the United States of America

Dedication

To Karen,

who shares my love of history
and my passion
for exploring America's West

73384

Table
of
Contents

Part I
America's Wealth: Beaver and Buffalo

Part II
Forts, Factories, and Posts of America's Fur Trade

Acknowledgments

I am deeply indebted to Kathy Gaudry of Tamarack Books for her constructive criticism and encouragement, without which *Competitive Struggle* would never have been written. More than my publisher, Kathy is a mentor and friend.

For answers to my many questions, I thank Geoffrey Bahr, interpretive specialist for Jackson County, Missouri, Parks and Recreation at Fort Osage; Mike Bailey of the Pembina, North Dakota, State Museum; Chan Biggs of the Lewistown, Montana, BLM office; Sue "Turtle Dove" Barker of the Fort Buenaventura replica in Ogden, Utah; Jean Brainerd of the Wyoming State Archives; Diane Brotemarkle, Historian at the Fort Vasquez Museum; Bob Clark of the Montana State Historical Society Library; Dan Deuter, Curator of the Fort Uncompahgre replica; Peggy Ford of the City of Greeley, Colorado, Museum; RoxAnn Grabowski of the Old Fort Madison replica; James Hanson, Curator of the Museum of the Fur Trade; Susan Hoskinson, Director of the Fort Vasquez Museum; Susan Juza and John Slader of the Fort Atkinson State Historical Park; George Knapp of the Fort Connah Restoration Society; Scott Langford, National Park Service Ranger at the Fort Vancouver National Historic Site; Rebecca Lintz of the Colorado State Historical Society; Richard Mackie, author of *Trading Beyond the Mountains: The British Fur Trade on the Pacific, 1793–1843;* Mike McGuire, Education Programmer at the Fort Nisqually Historic Site; Ed Maddox,

ix

Historian at the Fort Uncompahgre replica; Anna Nielsen of the North Platte Valley Historical Association; Evelyn Partner of the Utah State Historical Society; Jim Potter of the Nebraska State Historical Society; Rick Read of the Oregon State Historical Society; John Vinsen, President of the Parma, Idaho, Historical Society; and Joy Werlink of the Washington State Historical Society.

I am also grateful to the rangers and staff at the following locations: the Fort Benton Museum; Bent's "Old" Fort National Historic Site; Fort Boisé replica; Fort Bridger, Wyoming, State Historic Site; Champoeg, Oregon, State Heritage Visitor Center; Fort Clatsop National Memorial; Fort Hall replica; Fort Laramie National Historic Site; Fort Mandan replica and Lewis and Clark Foundation; Museum of the Fur Trade; Museum of the Mountain Man; Fort Nisqually replica; Fort Uncompahgre replica; Fort Union National Historic Site; and Fort Vancouver National Historic Site.

For help in obtaining the many references that I used in researching this book, I thank the staff at the Ketchum, Idaho, Community Library. I also thank Tom and Connie Thomsen of the Wild Hare Ranch in Aurora, Oregon, for chauffeuring me over the backroads of the Willamette Valley.

For developing the book's detailed maps, I thank Evelyn Phillips of Typographics, and for fact-checking and helping me "get the words right," I thank Dale Gray, Maggie Chenore, and Gail Ward.

Finally, I am beholden to my wife, Karen Robertson, for reading my manuscript, for suggesting improvements and corrections, and, especially, for photographing the trading post replicas.

R.G. Robertson

Introduction

My purpose in writing this book was to compile a record of America's western fur trading posts. Rather than merely producing a sterile list of dates and locations, I wanted to recount the history of the beaver plew and buffalo robe trade through the forts, Indian factories and trading houses of that era.

I chose *Competitive Struggle* as the title because ruthless competition pervaded every level of the fur trade, from national governments to the lowest ranking laborers. Leading the vanguard of this contest were the traders—resourceful men such as John Evans and René Jusseaume—who went head-to-head thousands of miles beyond the rule of law. Behind the traders stood the fur companies. Whether they were state-sanctioned monopolies such as the Hudson's Bay Company, moneyed partnerships like John Jacob Astor's American Fur Company, or shoestring outfits akin to Larpenteur & Smith, each of them battled its rivals with an intensity that often verged on warfare. Some of these firms were managed by gentlemen in ruffled shirts and frock coats; others were run by frontiersmen in muslin and moccasins. Counted among their ranks were patricians, bastards, and scoundrels—men typified by Pierre Chouteau, Jr., Sir George Simpson, and Alexander Harvey. Yet no matter their breeding and refinement, all shared a keen business sense. Each of them sought to ruin his competitors, both on the prairie with liquor and cutthroat prices, and in the corridors of Congress with favors and bribes. Native American tribes such as the Blackfeet and Crows also entered the fray, warring among themselves for access to the traders' bounty, as well as with the trapping brigades that wantonly trespassed on Indian land.

More than a mere commercial rivalry among companies, the struggle to dominate the fur trade was an extension of a much larger contest among governments. From the mid-eighteenth century through the next one hundred years, six nations vied to control what is today the western continental United States. Spain, France, Great Britain, Russia, and Mexico: all staked claims on various tracts between the Mississippi River and Pacific Ocean. By 1848, each of those claims had fallen victim to Manifest Destiny and the competitive zeal of the American people. During the same period of time, the global lust for beaver pelts that had ignited this mercantile fervor evaporated under the changing whims of fashion. Recreating itself, the fur trade survived another two decades, fueled by an expanding demand for buffalo robes. But just as public taste for beaver hats had waned, the appetite for buffalo robes also proved fleeting. By the end of America's Civil War, the fur trading era was dead.

To tell this story of America's fur trade, I divided the book into two parts. Part One presents an overview of the trade's parallel branches: beaver and buffalo. In this section, I outline the evolution of the beaver trade from its early reliance on Indian trappers, through its use of large, company-owned trapping brigades, to its demise. I also describe the rise of the buffalo robe trade and its reliance on Indian producers, a riverine transportation system, and fixed trading sites. Finally, I trace the trading cycle and sketch what it was like to have lived in a remote trading post.

Part Two recounts the history of individual trading houses and, through them, the saga of the fur trade. I list them alphabetically rather than by geographic region, owner, or time period because I feel these other categories are just as arbitrary. For the repetition that is sometimes necessary to allow each fort's story to stand alone, I ask the reader's forbearance. Several long sections, including *Fort Astoria, Flathead Post, The Osages, Mandan Villages,* and *Pembina,* provide continuity by giving an overview of events that happened across many years. I also cover military forts, such as Fort Leavenworth and Fort Atkinson, that were important to the fur trade. Those that were not, such as Fort Gibson, Fort Smith, and Fort Kearny, I have excluded. In cases where the Army named its garrisons after old fur trading posts, as in Fort Hall and Fort Spokane, I give the location of the Army facilities in order to avoid confusion if the reader has heard of one, but not the other.

Where possible, I pinpoint the exact location of historical sites. The position of trading posts and Indian towns such as Fort Union and the Mandan's *Matootonha Village* are well established; however, the whereabouts of smaller, less well-known trading houses, like Juan Munier's Ponca Post, are more difficult to determine. Many tribes, including the Poncas, lived in fixed communities when not off hunting, often moving their towns to be closer to game or abandoning old sites that had become unsanitary. When a tribe relocated, its trader usually followed. Although the Poncas called the country around the confluence of the Missouri and Niobrara rivers their homeland, they shifted their village many times over the years. Needing to stay near his customers, the Poncas' trader had to rebuild his trading post as well. Because the location of every seasonal trading cabin is unknown, I refer to many sites as "near the confluence of" or "in the vicinity of."

Adding to the difficulty of pinpointing certain forts, early fur traders measured distances in leagues which were anywhere from 2.4 to 4.6 statute miles long. Since travel was most often by water, early surveys followed the meandering turns of rivers such as the Missouri and Osage. The measurement problem is further compounded by the nature of rivers, which—because of erosion—are continually reducing their lengths. Today, the Missouri from its mouth to the Three Forks in western Montana is many miles shorter than it was when Lewis and Clark made their measurements nearly two hundred years ago.

When writing about rivers, I sometimes refer to their left or right sides rather than using a compass direction. This is especially helpful when a river meanders, say from north to south, while generally flowing from west to east. A left or right reference assumes the reader is facing the direction of flow—that is, looking downstream.

When discussing fur partnerships as a single business entity, I connect the partners' names with "&," as in Smith, Jackson & Sublette or Frost & Todd. When mentioning the partners as individuals, I use "and," as in Fontenelle and Drips.

I have included flowcharts of my own design, showing the evolution of the major fur companies and their competitors. I hope the diagrams will eliminate the confusion brought on by so many firms being named after partners who changed their affiliations as often as a rattlesnake sheds its skin. When writing about the American Fur Company's successors—Pratte, Chouteau & Company and Pierre Chouteau, Jr., & Company—I use the legal titles even though the traders and trappers continued calling them the American Fur Company.

Although I include posts (such as Fort Bridger and Fort John II) that primarily catered to the Oregon- and California-bound emigrant wagon trains, all posts dealt, to some extent, in beaver pelts and buffalo robes. Needing to limit the book's scope, I purposely left out the Russians. They never were major participants in the beaver trade, and, with the exception of Fort Ross on the northern California coast, their efforts focused on Alaska. Students of the fur era will undoubtedly notice minor trading houses that I have excluded. In my defense, I offer the observation of a National Park Service ranger-historian when I explained the goal of my research: "Fixing the location of every single trading post—man, that's like trying to describe individual trees in a forest fire. You're bound to miss a few."

Finally, I have included a list of replica and reproduction trading posts that are open to the public. Some, like Fort Union and Fort Vancouver, have been reconstructed on their original sites. Others, such as Fort Hall and Fort Nisqually, have been built in more convenient locations. For the sake of simplicity, I call all of these posts replicas, even those that are not exact copies of the originals. All are well worth a visit.

RGR

Major Fur Companies of North America

Canadian Fur Companies

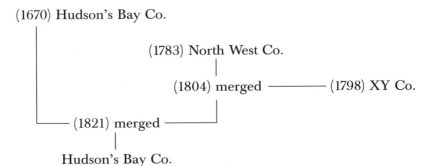

(1670) Hudson's Bay Co.

(1783) North West Co.

(1804) merged —————— (1798) XY Co.

(1821) merged

Hudson's Bay Co.

Early St. Louis Fur Companies

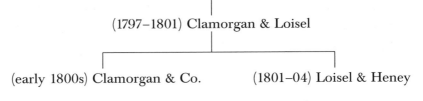

(1793–97) Co. of Discoverers & Explorers of the Missouri River

(1797–1801) Clamorgan & Loisel

(early 1800s) Clamorgan & Co.   (1801–04) Loisel & Heney

Evolution of the Missouri Fur Company

(1802–06) Manuel Lisa, Benoît & Co.

|

(1807–09) Lisa, Menard, Morrison & Co.

|

(1809–12) St. Louis Missouri Fur Co.

|

(1812–14) Missouri Fur Co.

|

(1814–18) Manuel Lisa

|

(1818) Cabanné & Co.

|

(1819–25) Missouri Fur Co.

|

(1825–28) Pilcher & Co.

Major Fur Partnerships of the Chouteau Family

(1760s) Max: Maxent, Lacléde & Co.

|

(1770s–early 1800s) Auguste & Pierre Chouteau, Sr.

|

(1813–21) Pierre Chouteau, Jr., & Bartholomew Berthold

|

(1821–23) Berthold, Chouteau & Pratte

|

(1823–34) Bernard Pratte & Co.

|

(1834–38) Pratte, Chouteau & Co.

|

(1839–65) Pierre Chouteau, Jr., & Co.

Evolution of John Jacob Astor's American Fur Company

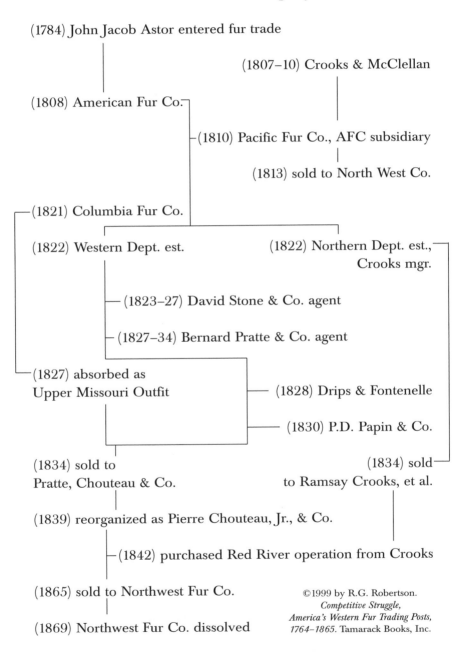

(1784) John Jacob Astor entered fur trade

(1807–10) Crooks & McClellan

(1808) American Fur Co.

(1810) Pacific Fur Co., AFC subsidiary

(1813) sold to North West Co.

(1821) Columbia Fur Co.

(1822) Western Dept. est.

(1822) Northern Dept. est., Crooks mgr.

(1823–27) David Stone & Co. agent

(1827–34) Bernard Pratte & Co. agent

(1827) absorbed as Upper Missouri Outfit

(1828) Drips & Fontenelle

(1830) P.D. Papin & Co.

(1834) sold to Pratte, Chouteau & Co.

(1834) sold to Ramsay Crooks, et al.

(1839) reorganized as Pierre Chouteau, Jr., & Co.

(1842) purchased Red River operation from Crooks

(1865) sold to Northwest Fur Co.

(1869) Northwest Fur Co. dissolved

Evolution of the Rocky Mountain Fur Company

(1821–24) Ashley & Henry
|
(1824–25) Ashley
|
(1825–26) Ashley & Smith
|
(1826) sold to Smith, Jackson & Sublette

(1830) sold to Rocky Mountain Fur Co.

(1831) Sublette & Jackson supplier
|
(1832–33) Sublette supplier
|
(1833–34) Sublette & Campbell supplier

(1828) Drips & Fontenelle

(1834) Fitzpatrick, [Milton] Sublette & Bridger
|
(1834) Fontenelle, ——————— Pratte, Chouteau & Co.
Fitzpatrick & Co. supplier

(1836) dissolved; partners hired by Pratte, Chouteau & Co.

Opposition Firms to Pierre Chouteau, Jr., & Company

(1842–45) Union Fur Co.
    backed by Bolton, Fox, Livingston & Co.

(1846–54) Harvey, Primeau & Co.
    backed by Robert Campbell

(1854–56) J. Picotte & Co.
    backed by Robert Campbell

(1856–59) Frost, Todd & Co.
    backed by Robert Campbell

(1859–60) Clark, Primeau & Co.

(1860) Larpenteur, Smith & Co.
    Larpenteur backed by Robert Campbell

(1861) Larpenteur & Lemon
    backed by Robert Campbell

(1861–63) Bruguier & Booge

(1861–65) La Barge, Harkness & Co.
    Robert Campbell fur broker

Evolution of Bent, St. Vrain & Company

(1828) Charles Bent left the bankrupt Pilcher & Co.
|
(1828–29) Charles & William Bent
|
(1830) [Charles] Bent, St. Vrain & Co.
|
(1831) William Bent joined Bent, St. Vrain & Co.
|
(1847) Charles Bent murdered
|
(1849) Bent, St. Vrain & Co. dissolved
|
(1849–69) William Bent & Co.

Opposition Firms to Bent, St. Vrain & Company

(1830–34) Gantt & Blackwell

(1835–40) Vasquez & [Andrew] Sublette

(1841–42) Lock, Randolph & Co.

(1836–42) Lancaster P. Lupton

(1841–43) Sibille, Adams & Co.

(1843–45) Bernard Pratte, Jr., & John Cabanné, Jr.

Other Fur Partnerships

(1820s) Sibley, Baillio & Boggs

(1823–25) Baillio & "Old Bill" Williams

(1832–35) Benjamin Bonneville

(1832–36) Nathaniel Wyeth

(early 1800s–1860s) various Robidoux brothers and sons

(1837–38) Fraeb & [Peter] Sarpy

(1840–41) Fraeb & Bridger

(1842–53) Bridger & Vasquez

(early 1840s–49 and 1850s) Joseph Bissonette

(1849–50) Bordeaux & Bissonette

(1850–68) James Bordeaux & Son

Part I

America's Wealth: Beaver and Buffalo

America's Fur Trading Century

Between the founding of St. Louis in early 1764 and the end of the Civil War 101 years later, the Great Plains, Rocky Mountains, and Pacific Northwest witnessed a competitive struggle for fur that had ramifications far beyond the country's beaver ponds and buffalo wallows. At its pinnacle, America's western fur trade reached from the Mississippi River to the lower Columbia, and from the Arkansas and Gila to the Milk. Its tentacles stretched from mountain streams and sweetgrass prairies to St. Louis and Montreal, and on to New York, Boston, London, Paris, and Canton. The traffic in animal skins employed, not only Kentucky- and Virginia-born trappers, but also Arikara warriors and Assiniboine wives; French-Canadian traders and mixed-blood voyageurs; Scottish clerks and Creole merchants; Wall Street financiers and New England sea captains; British hatters, Dutch furriers, and Chinese coolies.

During the 101 years that it was centered in the western United States, the fur trade embroiled two vastly different civilizations in a contest that eventually doomed a way of life. Seeds of the Native Americans' defeat were sown during the raucous heyday of the mountain men and robe traders, when the tribes became dependent on white-made goods. The commerce in fur gave Indians the fire steels, needles, and brass kettles that eased their physical labor, but it did so at a terrible cost. The price of progress included smallpox, cholera, venereal disease, and alcoholism.[1]

The later bloody slaughters by the US Cavalry at Bear River, Sand Creek, and Wounded Knee were merely a tragic finale to a war that had long been lost.

Citing these heart-rending consequences of the beaver and buffalo trade, revisionist historians paint the fur companies as evil, preaching that they shamelessly exploited the Indians for profit. To the extent that the companies used liquor to cheat their native customers, they were indeed corrupt. But in terms of exploitation, there was far less than the revisionists would have us believe. Like all commerce, the fur trade was based on comparative advantage. During the eighteenth and early nineteenth centuries, the beaver, buffalo, and other game that the Indians used for shelter, clothing, and food were so plentiful the tribes regarded them as nearly worthless when compared with manufactured wonders such as mirrors, fusils, and fishhooks. In contrast, well-heeled Europeans, Chinese, and Americans prized the pelts of certain animals as though they were worth a king's ransom. Standing between the Indians and the white and Asian consumers were the fur companies, eager to provide each side what it desired.

Until the mid-1830s, beaver pelts dominated the North American fur trade, their demand fueled by men's hat styles and by a physical property of the beaver's barbed under-hair that made it suitable for felting—the process by which hats were made. Before the expansion of the large trapping brigades in the 1820s, white trappers brought to market only a limited number of pelts. The lion's share of the supply came from Indian hunters who bartered their plews to roving traders, particularly those of the North West Company of Montreal. For a few months every year, Nor'West traders would visit the various tribes, swapping vermilion, metal arrowheads, awls, and other trade items for dressed animal skins. Although these early traders bought otter, ermine, fox, wolf, and other pelts, they paid the highest prices for beaver.

Nor'West traders and those of their fierce Canadian competitor, the Hudson's Bay Company, operated from fixed forts, often called factories. While functioning as a home base for the traders, these posts also provided the Indians an alternative place to barter their furs. Before the two firms merged in 1821, the

4

Hudson's Bay Company was restricted by its charter to the rivers and streams draining into Hudson Bay, a covenant the company often violated. The North West Company had no such constraint. Its traders roamed at will across southern Canada, and routinely invaded the upper Missouri plain. Over the years, the Nor'Westers extended their line of forts until they stretched from their supply depot at Lachine (on the St. Lawrence River, near Montreal, Quebec) to the Oregon coast.

By the late eighteenth century, American traders had begun to challenge the Nor'Westers around the Great Lakes. Beyond the Mississippi, a few Spanish and French traders operated on the lower Missouri River, but few dared venture as far north as the Mandans (in North Dakota). The Louisiana Purchase and its subsequent exploration by Meriwether Lewis and William Clark opened the upper Missouri and Oregon country to the Americans.

During the early 1800s, St. Louis merchants scrambled to form partnerships; they were determined to garner a piece of the exploding fur trade. Lacking a better model, they patterned their businesses after those of the North West and Hudson's Bay companies. However, unlike the British firms, which chiefly relied on Indians for their furs, American trading companies increasingly allowed whites to supplant native trappers. By the late 1820s, brigades of mountain men were the main providers of beaver pelts below the forty-ninth parallel. The newly amalgamated Hudson's Bay Company countered with its own trapping brigades, although it did so primarily in the Snake River drainage (Idaho).

American fur partnerships, such as Smith, Jackson & Sublette, dominated the central Rocky Mountains. Pack trains regularly hauled supplies from St. Louis, up the Platte River, and across South Pass to the festive summer trade fairs or rendezvous, where trappers exchanged their plews for a few quarts of water-diluted alcohol and another year's outfit. Even in the beaver trade's best days, few trappers struck it rich. Because hard money was scarce, beaver pelts served as collateral, their value arbitrarily set by the fur companies—usually at three dollars per pound for top quality plews. Using last year's catch of fur or a credit against the

catch of the coming year, the trappers bought equipment and supplies—gunpowder, bar lead, nipple caps, a mainspring or some
other part needed to repair a damaged rifle, a new trap or two to
replace those that had been stolen or lost—required to survive
another season in the wild. After purchasing the necessities, most
trappers spent their remaining furs on luxuries such as tobacco,
liquor, sugar, cotton shirts, coffee beans, raisins, and *foofuraw*—the
beads, ribbons, cloth, bells, and other gewgaws needed to keep an
Indian wife smiling or to buy sexual favors from some warrior's
daughter. Knowing that they might die before the next rendezvous, the trappers turned each year's fair into a drunken spree,
unconcerned that they were purchasing goods the fur companies
had marked up five hundred, one thousand, or even two thousand
percent.

During this time, a separate but parallel fur industry was
spreading up the Missouri River and its tributaries. Based on buffalo robes, this parallel fur trade was dominated by John Jacob
Astor's well-capitalized American Fur Company. Unlike the
Rocky Mountain beaver trade which relied on mobile brigades of
white and mixed-blood trappers, the robe trade depended on
Indians, particularly Indian women who transformed the raw buffalo hides into soft, warm robes. Indian men killed the buffalo, but
the backbreaking work of butchering, fletching, and curing was
done by women. Nevertheless, the women's labor belonged to
their fathers and husbands, who, more often than not, decided
what to buy at the fur companies' trading posts.

The American Fur Company organized its western trading
empire to accommodate its native customers. Like spokes of a
wheel, supply lines reached out from large depots, such as Fort
Union and Fort Pierre, to smaller regional posts, like Fort
McKenzie and Fort Van Buren.[2] The regional posts then supported smaller trading houses, many of which were tepees or crude log
cabins intended to last but a single winter. Because these outlying
houses could be quickly and inexpensively built, the traders were
able to follow the nomadic tribes when they switched hunting
grounds. Such an operation required a substantial commitment of
capital and personnel. A headquarters post such as Fort Union

employed upwards of one hundred men as *engagés* (laborers), craftsmen (cooks, blacksmiths, carpenters, coopers, and the like), hunters, traders, and clerks—all commanded by a *bourgeois*. A regional post employed fifteen or twenty men having similar skills, whereas a temporary post made do with one or two traders and a couple of *engagés*. In the early 1830s, the American Fur Company also used its headquarters posts as distribution centers for the pack trains that supplied its trapping brigades at the annual rendezvous. Then in the 1840s and 1850s, British and American trading posts along the Oregon Trail catered to thousands of weary emigrants heading for the rich farmland of Oregon's Willamette Valley or the California goldfields.

Except when debauched with liquor, Indians bargained hard, demanding well-made merchandise—meaning European-manufactured merchandise. American-made products were generally of inferior quality, particularly in the 1820s and early 1830s. Robes and furs were bartered for muskets, flints, gunpowder, lead, knives, metal arrow and spear points, tomahawk pipes, vermilion, copper kettles, tobacco, blankets, ribbons, cloth, brass bracelets, glass beads, fire steels, fishhooks, awls, mirrors, whiskey—in the eyes of the Indians, a wealth of goods they could not produce themselves.

Unlike the supply lines for the Rocky Mountain beaver trade which used mule and horse pack trains, the buffalo trade depended on rivers. Early on, the fur companies employed keelboats and mackinaws, which required human muscle to drag them upstream against the spring currents. Then, in the 1830s, steamboats began churning up the Missouri, gradually extending their range to Fort Tecumseh in 1831, Fort Union the following year, and finally, Fort Benton in 1860. Where the steamers could not go, the fur companies continued relying on dugouts, pirogues, mackinaws, and keelboats.

According to historian Hiram M. Chittenden, during the peak years of America's beaver trade from 1807–43, over 150 forts, posts, and factories were constructed in the plains and mountains west of St. Louis.[3] Because the US Army closeted its dragoons in stockades on the lower Missouri River, the mid- and upper

Missouri trading forts of the fur companies projected American authority, what little of it there was. Many of these posts, such as Fort Raymond at the confluence of the Bighorn and Yellowstone rivers, lasted but a season or two. Others acted like lodestones, drawing the farmers, preachers, storekeepers, and blacksmiths needed to establish towns such as St. Joseph, Missouri, which grew up around Joseph Robidoux's Blacksnake Hills Trading Post.[4]

The summer of 1833 marked the first time the American Fur Company's shipments of buffalo robes exceeded those of beaver pelts. It also marked the beginning of a decline in the beaver trade, a decline that eventually doomed the large trapping brigades and, ultimately, the mountain men's way of life. After the final rendezvous in 1840, some white trappers continued hunting beaver, working in small teams instead of large brigades. But the death of the rendezvous supply system forced these diehards to sell their catches at the fur companies' trading posts. Even then, the trappers earned scant profit. Continuing a slide that had begun in the 1830s, St. Louis beaver prices fell throughout the 1840s, reaching seventy-five cents per pound by the decade's end.[5]

The sagging market for beaver was offset by a rising demand for buffalo robes, which in turn spurred the American Fur Company's second successor, Pierre Chouteau, Jr., & Company, to enlarge its network of fixed posts. Seeing a chance for gain, other firms sprang up, attempting to carve out their own piece of the trade. Over the years, a series of these opposition companies dashed themselves against the Chouteau empire. Each entity strived to compete, even as they suffocated beneath a growing mountain of debt. One after another they failed. None of them could best Pierre Chouteau, Jr., and his son, Charles.

During the peak years of the buffalo trade—the 1850s—the Chouteaus annually shipped one hundred thousand robes east. Unlike the demand for beaver pelts which had been international, the market for buffalo robes ended at the Atlantic seaboard. A few robes were sold in London but, for the most part, Europeans preferred making their coats and lap covers from locally-produced sheepskins that were far less expensive than imported buffalo hides.

Buffalo robes that could be bought in trade goods from the Indians at $1.35 each, fetched $3.00 to $6.00 in St. Louis.[6] However, transportation pushed up their cost, dictating a volume business if a company hoped to show a profit.

All this commerce had a devastating effect on the buffalo. In the decades before the robe trade, the spreading use of horses had enabled Indians to hunt more efficiently. Rather than randomly killing bulls and cows at buffalo jumps, as their ancestors had done, mounted warriors in the nineteenth century could take only cows. Their meat was more tender than a bull's and their thinner hides were far easier to tan. Though the buffalo numbered in the tens of millions, this selective hunting slowly eroded the sexual equilibrium of the herds. Because horses enabled the Indians to find game more easily, the tribes naturally accumulated more and more horses. These, in turn, competed with the buffalo for grass, further upsetting the ecological balance.

The notion that Indians used every part of the buffalo, wasting nothing, is a myth. When the herds were plentiful, the Indians, as did the mountain men, butchered the humps, livers, tongues, and other delicacies, leaving the remainder of the carcasses to the wolves.[7] As a result of these factors, by the early 1840s the herds west of the Continental Divide had been all but wiped out.

During the 1840s and 1850s, the trade in robes accelerated the buffalo's extinction east of the Rocky Mountains. At the same time, the Oregon Trail divided the Great Plains herd in two, and encroaching settlements reduced available forage and introduced the buffalo to brucellosis and other deadly cattle diseases.[8] White hunters, such as Buffalo Bill Cody, and visiting eastern and European "sportsmen," like Sir St. George Gore, added to the carnage by introducing a methodical efficiency to the slaughter.

In the 1850s, white migration into Minnesota and Iowa pushed increasing numbers of Sioux onto the upper Missouri where epidemics of smallpox and measles had destroyed the ability of indigenous tribes to resist the white invasion. The dwindling buffalo herds and continued white encroachment ignited Sioux hostility, which prompted the white settlers to demand military protection. The Army purchased old trading posts from the fur companies and built new forts to house its troops. The presence of soldiers and the opportunity for "free" land, especially after Congress passed the Homestead Act in 1862, encouraged more whites to emigrate, which in turn inflamed more Sioux war parties.

By the end of the Civil War, the fur trade was all but finished. While tribes such as the Sioux, Cheyenne, and Arapaho struggled to retain their freedom, most of the others accepted their fate and began moving onto government reservations. The remnants of once mighty buffalo herds scoured the prairie for grass and water, awaiting the final onslaught of white buffalo skinners. The few fur trading posts still in existence resembled an old pack mule—too weary to take another step and too stubborn to die. As America embraced the new age of industrialization, the 101-year era of the western fur trade faded into memory.

Perseverance: The Life of a Fur Trader

The coat of arms of Canada's North West Company proclaimed a motto that was as apropos to the Nor'Westers as it was to every other fur company employee in North America: "Perseverance"–the will to continue without regard to storms, loneliness, fatigue, or fear.

Perseverance defined the men who worked for the fur companies, no matter which side of the forty-ninth parallel they called home. It characterized the firms' managing partners, whether in Montreal or St. Louis; it embodied French-Canadian voyageurs manning *canots du nord* (freight canoes), as well as those straining against keelboat setting-poles; it coursed through the veins of the lowest-ranking mixed-blood *engagé* toiling away at a primitive, log trading house in the midst of the Blackfoot Confederation. No matter what other traits these men had–whether courage, strength, stamina, wisdom, or just plain spunk–above all else, they had perseverance.

A fraternity existed among these men who ran the fur companies' supply lines and trading houses. Initiation into this fraternity required prospective members to spend at least one winter in the wilderness. Those who did were forever known as *hivernans* or winterers, a title that set them apart from the *mangeurs de lard,* the "eaters of pork" as the greenhorns were called.[1] Being an *hivernan* gave a man swagger and a confidence that came only through personal trial. To have endured a winter beyond the settlements was a badge of honor, much like that of a soldier who has braved combat. It was during a winter of blizzards, bitter cold, and mind-numbing boredom that a man learned the meaning of perseverance.

A Place to Trade

Post, fort, house, and factory referred to a fixed trading establishment where Indians and trappers swapped their buffalo robes and furs for manufactured necessities, trinkets, and whiskey. When naming their trading posts, the British fur companies used these terms interchangeably, whereas the American firms favored fort, although they also used post and, occasionally, house. What differentiated a post from a fort or factory or house was not its name but rather its primary function. Headquarters posts, such as the American Fur Company's Fort Union and Fort Pierre, served as supply depots supporting outlying regional posts, such as Fort Piegan or Fort Berthold. In turn, the regional posts provisioned roving traders who wintered among the tribes, often conducting their barter from log shacks that they abandoned in the spring when the Indians renewed their nomadic migration. Because many tribes made their winter camps in the same valleys year after year, certain sites became customary trading places. Some of the more important ones included the confluence of the Belle Fourche and Big Cheyenne rivers and the mouths of the Grand and Moreau rivers (all in South Dakota).

The typical post was made from local trees, usually cottonwood. Whether square or rectangular, most stockades were designed on the same pattern, especially early on. Log pickets, set on end so they extended twelve to twenty-five feet above the ground, provided the main defense. Two log blockhouses (Fort Union's were made from stone) with cannon and rifle ports occupied diagonal corners of the stockade, enabling guns to cover all sides of the fort in case of attack. At some posts a wooden catwalk circled the inside of the pickets, about four or five feet from the top. Although intended for defense, the walkway more often served as a promenade for the residents and their Indian wives. Occasionally, *engagés* whitewashed the buildings and pickets at larger establishments, such as Fort Clark among the Mandans.[2]

Some trading posts (i.e., Bent's "Old" Fort) were constructed from Spanish-style adobe bricks, called doughboys. Because adobe was fire-resistant and less apt to rot, in the 1840s and 1850s a few wooden posts (such as Fort Benton near the Falls of the Missouri and Fort William at the mouth of the Yellowstone) were rebuilt from doughboy bricks. Better insulators than logs, they kept adobe forts cooler than wooden ones in the summer and easier to heat in the winter.

The interior of a large trading post typically contained at least one warehouse, cooper and carpenter shops, a blacksmith shed, kitchen, dining hall, gunpowder magazine, quarters for the *engagés,* craftsmen, and clerks, and a home for the *bourgeois,* usually the most elegant structure within the stockade. Whereas trading normally took place in a secure room that barred access to the central courtyard, at the Hudson's Bay Company's Fort Vancouver, Indians entered the trade room from the interior of the stockade. If a sizable band came to a post, the *bourgeois* allowed eight or ten Indians in the trading room at one time, keeping the remainder of the party awaiting its turn outside the main gate. During periods of unrest, merchandise and furs were passed through a wicket in the stockade. Because animal skins were shipped in packs (sixty beaver pelts or ten buffalo robes per ninety-pound pack), every post needed a fur press, typically a wedge or pole press at a small trading house or a heavy iron screw press at a headquarters fort.

At nearly every post, *engagés* planted a vegetable garden in order to add variety to the diet and reduce the expense of importing food. Located in the temperate and fertile Columbia River Valley, Fort Vancouver had extensive gardens and orchards; in contrast, at Fort McKenzie on the upper Missouri, all attempts at agriculture failed. Sandy soil and infrequent summer rains on the western Montana plain made farming risky, at best.

Unless stables had been built outside the palisades, the interior of a post looked and smelled more like a barnyard than a trading factory. Each evening, *engagés* locked the fort's horses, goats, and milk cows inside the stockade to prevent their theft. Depending on how long it had been since the last rain, the ground was either a dusty dunghill or a muddy dung stew. Occasionally, workmen laid plank walkways among the buildings in order to protect their shoes and moccasins from the mire, but for the most part everyone took the filth in stride, especially since the streets of America's towns and cities were no different. A fort's hard-used courtyard received a meager reprieve on the days a guard escorted the stock onto the prairie to graze.

Trading Post Organization

Trading post personnel were organized in a hierarchy similar to that of the military. Although a caste system segregated the levels, the fur companies often promoted from within, which allowed a diligent individual who could read and write to move up the ranks. In American trading forts the commander was called the *bourgeois,* pronounced "boosh-way" by uneducated trappers. The Hudson's Bay and North West companies designated the senior officials at their posts as factors. The title chief factor was used when a factor managed an entire region. For example, Chief Factor Dr. John McLoughlin, during his tenure as Fort Vancouver's superintendent, oversaw the Hudson's Bay Company's Columbia Department which encompassed the Oregon country and parts of southwestern Canada. Likewise, American *bourgeois* of headquarters forts also directed trading operations within a larger sphere. While having charge of Fort Union, Kenneth McKenzie supervised the Upper Missouri Outfit of the American Fur Company, which took in the country from the forty-ninth parallel to the mouth of the Big Sioux River (near Sioux City, Iowa).[3]

Bourgeois and factors, many of whom were company partners, not only managed upwards of one hundred employees, but they also had to stay on friendly terms with the various Indian bands that traded at their forts. Theirs was a skill that could not be learned from books; its lessons required many years on the frontier. A *bourgeois* or factor had to know when to welcome a visiting tribe and when to lock the gates, when to threaten a belligerent war chief and when to cajole. Akin to a ship's captain on the high seas, a fort commander ran his trading post by rules that permitted him to deal with the unforeseen; and, like a ship's captain, he was expected to enforce those rules in a realm where no legal structure existed.

As was the case with a British factor, an American *bourgeois* and his family always lived in the fanciest building in the stockade. At larger posts, the commander's home equaled the better houses in the downriver settlements, particularly after steamboats began pushing up the Missouri. As the steamers reduced transportation costs, the *bourgeois* imported more and more luxuries from St. Louis, Cincinnati and New Orleans. When Kenneth McKenzie had charge of Fort Union in the 1830s, he occupied a one-story house that boasted eight glass windows. By 1851, succeeding *bourgeois* had added a second floor and balcony, along with a "widow's walk" atop the roof.[4]

Next in command, behind the *bourgeois* and factor, were the clerks. Although small trading houses had only one clerk, larger posts, such as Fort Pierre, had several, their rankings determined by their seniority within the company. When the *bourgeois* left his post, the senior clerk took over his responsibilities and even moved into his house if the *bourgeois* was expected to be gone for some time. Whereas a *bourgeois* made twelve hundred dollars a year or as much as twenty-five hundred dollars if he was a partner, clerks earned from five hundred to eight hundred dollars depending on their experience. Clerks occasionally became minor shareholders in their companies but not so often as the *bourgeois* and factors.

The ability to read and write, as well as have some knowledge of arithmetic, were the basic requisites for all clerks since they had charge of the ledgers and kept track of every beaver plew, buffalo robe, and glass trade bead that moved in and out of the fort. Beyond that, they supervised lower level employees, acting in many ways like junior officers at an Army barracks. Unmarried clerks shared quarters that were separate from those of the lower ranking employees.

Most clerks dressed in the same manner as the *bourgeois*, wearing white ruffled shirts, their high collars tied with black cravats. Except in the hottest weather, they also wore waistcoats and black frock coats. When Charles Larpenteur joined Fort Union as a junior clerk in 1834, he had to borrow a coat before he could eat because Kenneth McKenzie required him to come to the table properly attired. James Archdale Hamilton, the fort's senior clerk at the time, bathed and donned a fresh shirt every day, habits that marked him as fastidious as any New York City banker.[5]

Next in line behind the clerks were the traders, although at smaller posts the head trader sometimes served as clerk and commander. Earning between four hundred and six hundred dollars per year—a bit more if they also worked as interpreters—traders bartered with the tribes, swapping knives, twists of tobacco, and hanks of ribbon for beaver and muskrat pelts, tanned deer skins, and buffalo robes. At a headquarters or regional post, the senior trader often dressed like the clerks and enjoyed some of the same privileges, such as dining at the *bourgeois's* table.

Trading posts also employed hunters. Major establishments, such as Fort Union, annually consumed eight hundred buffalo, not to mention elk, deer, pronghorn, geese, and ducks. Maintaining an adequate stock of food was a full-time job. In the early 1840s before gaining fame as John Frémont's guide, the trapper Christopher "Kit" Carson hunted for Bent's Fort on the Arkansas River, earning one dollar a day.[6]

Standing on a par with the hunters were the trading post craftsmen—blacksmiths, carpenters, cooks, coopers, and the like—the men who shoed horses and repaired traps, pounded together mackinaw boats and added rooms to the *bourgeois's* house, baked bread and roasted hump ribs, and built barrels and kegs. Although the pay of craftsmen was low, three hundred or four hundred dollars a year, the fur companies fed them and provided a roof over their heads.

Least among the posts' employees were the *engagés*, the manual laborers who chopped wood, sawed planks, pressed robes, unloaded keelboats, made charcoal, guarded the remuda, gathered prairie hay, and dug graves. Many were French-Canadian or mixed-blood, often scorned by their superiors and seldom appreciated. For an annual wage of $150 to $200, *engagés* performed the dull, backbreaking chores upon which the fur trade depended.

Trading Post Life

At the larger trading posts such as Fort Pierre and Fort Union, cooks prepared everyone's food in the fort kitchen, the menu dictated by what was in season, as well as by the skill of the hunters. Usually, two meals per day were served: breakfast around mid-morning and supper in the late afternoon. Fur company personnel took their meals together in the dining hall, where seating and diet were determined by rank. Distinguished visitors, clerks, and, sometimes, a favorite trader ate at the *bourgeois's* table. These fortunate few dined on the best the kitchen could offer: buffalo tongue, roasted hump, trout, geese, fresh vegetables, bread, butter, pie, and creamed coffee, occasionally rounded off with Madeira or brandy.

The craftsmen, hunters, and lower level traders sat apart from the *bourgeois* and his party. For these second class employees, the cooks typically served boiled buffalo, biscuits—if there was plenty of flour, otherwise pilot bread (hardtack)—hominy (corn soaked in lye to remove the hulls), and black coffee.

At the bottom of the hierarchy, the *engagés* subsisted on food that was hardscrabble when compared with the delicacies served at the *bourgeois's* table. The cooks boiled the poorest cuts of buffalo in a large kettle, then placed the cauldron on the dining hall floor beside communal pots of hominy mush and rendered fat (tallow). When the dinner bell rang, the *engagés* gathered round the containers and speared the meat with their knives, gulping it down among mouthfuls of mush, tallow, and river water.[7] In contrast, at smaller, satellite posts with only a handful of men, everyone usually ate the same fare.

When the buffalo herds were scarce and the larder ran low on jerked meat, everyone from the *bourgeois* to the *engagés* lived on pemmican. Most trading posts stocked this staple of the prairie. As

17

with buffalo robes, Indian women also produced pemmican, and their menfolk traded it to the fur companies, where it was stored for lean times. Although recipes varied, pemmican was made from powdered meat (buffalo jerky that had been pounded to a pulp), fresh or dried berries, and melted tallow which the women mixed together and put up in large skin bags that held fifty or sixty pounds. Nutritious and filling, the confection could safely be stored for months.

To ease the tedium of post life, the *bourgeois* often hosted entertainments where fort musicians played their bagpipes, Jew's harps, and fiddles for Scottish reels and cavorting jigs. The men danced with one another while their Indian wives and sweethearts gathered on the periphery, bobbing and swaying to the music.

Often a *bourgeois* would host a dance to amuse a distinguished visitor. During the fur trading era, company partners, naturalists, artists, and wealthy European adventurers occasionally journeyed up the Missouri, stopping at this fort and that, perhaps for a day or a month. In 1832, the painter George Catlin accompanied Pierre Chouteau, Jr., on the riverboat *Yellow Stone* during the first steamed voyage to Fort Union. Chouteau was a partner in the American Fur Company and head of its Western Department. While staying at the fort, Catlin worked on sketches in one of its stone bastions, using a cannon as his seat. A year later, the German nobleman Alexander Philipp Maximilian, Prince of Wied-Nuwied, attended by his artist, Karl Bodmer, also traveled to Fort Union aboard a steamer.[8] After their visit, they continued up the Missouri via keelboat to spend the summer at Fort McKenzie before dropping down to Fort Clark at the Mandan villages for the winter.[9] Similarly, the famous naturalist John James Audubon made a trip to Fort Union in 1843 when he was over sixty years old, bringing with him a four-man entourage of fellow bird watchers.

Despite the visitors and dances, boredom overhung the trading posts like a shroud. Low morale was epidemic, especially in winter.[10] Although the fur trade attracted men who could abide isolation, few could handle it well. Some of those who could afford the companies' high prices sought relief with whiskey, but liquor alone could not fill all the empty hours. Much of the monotony found its way into the trading posts' logbooks where the *bourgeois* and clerks laced their entries with "dull," "lonesome," and "gloomy." These pages held the daily chronicles of bored minds noting the most mundane details as if they were matters of state. Nothing so typifies the weary sameness of post life than the journal entries of Francis Chardon. During each month of his five years as *bourgeois* of Fort Clark, Chardon doggedly recorded the number of rats he had killed. On April 30, 1839, the count reached 3,729.[11]

The majority of men found relief from the tedium in the arms of Indian maidens. Many of these affairs were brief liaisons fostered by tribal cultures that permitted husbands and fathers to share the sexual favors of their women. Indian men often sold their wives and daughters for a few fishhooks, a knife, or a couple of cups of mountain whiskey. It was the unusual company man who resisted such temptations, whether he was an *engagé,* blacksmith, clerk, or *bourgeois.* Even high ranking fur company partners partook. Until he married his cousin, George Simpson, the North American governor of the Hudson's Bay Company, was legendary for dallying with native women. When he was old and distinguished, a few of his contemporaries thought his informal title, "Father of the fur trade," came less from his managerial skills than from the many children he had sired during his numerous inspection tours of the Hudson's Bay trading posts.[12]

Still, not all encounters among the fur company men and Indian women were fleeting. A number of fort employees married into native families, both for companionship and to strengthen their ties with a particular tribe. An Indian wife proved especially helpful when a trader did not speak her people's language. Fur companies on both sides of the forty-ninth parallel encouraged these "country marriages," as the British called them, thinking they were good for business. Polygamy was also condoned. Traders regularly took wives for a season or two to cement a relationship with one tribe, then wed another woman when they went to trade with a different band.

The reward for native women was the white man's riches: a brass pot for boiling water instead of a pouch made from a buffalo's stomach; a metal sewing needle rather than a bone awl; bolts of muslin and flannel in lieu of animal skins. Many of the sons from these marriages—particularly those of company partners—were educated by their fathers and then hired by the fur companies as traders, interpreters, and clerks.

Even *bourgeois* sometimes had more than one wife. During his years as commander of Fort Union, Edwin Denig kept two, calling one "the younger" and the other "the older." He eventually married Deer Little Woman ("the younger") in a Christian ceremony and moved with her to Canada after he retired in 1856.

Alexander Culbertson, a long-standing employee and partner in the American Fur Company's successors, wed Medicine Snake Woman (Natawischicksina),[13] the daughter of a Blackfoot chief. In addition to being a loving wife and mother, she was an invaluable interpreter when Culbertson parleyed with the upper Missouri tribes. In the late 1850s after he retired to a farm near Peoria, Illinois, he built her a grand home called "Locust Grove," and further humored her by erecting a tepee in the front yard.

No matter what a post's employees did to pass their nights, their days were filled with work. In late summer, *engagés* spent endless hours hand-cutting the longstem plains grasses, then storing this prairie hay for winter when the snow would prevent the horses and other livestock from grazing. Despite the *engagés'* efforts, the fodder often ran short in February and early March, requiring the men to feed their horses shaved cottonwood bark.

Engagés also devoted much of their time to chopping wood for cooking and heating. Since the trees closest to a fort were the first to be harvested, ensuing seasons required that the men venture farther afield to locate fresh sources of timber. This problem was particularly taxing on the eastern plains, away from the mountains, where work details often needed to travel ten or twenty miles to reach an uncut grove.

The combination of boredom, loneliness, and hard physical labor ensured that the turnover in trading post personnel was high. The careers of most *bourgeois* ran but fifteen years, whereas the tenure of non-partner clerks and traders averaged a bit over six, and that of *engagés* lasted less than half as long.[14]

The Cycle of Trade

Spring in the fur country was a time of awakening and renewal; of melting snow and rushing streams; of nesting birds and budding cottonwoods. At trading posts from the Arkansas to the Columbia, everyone from the *bourgeois* to the lowest-ranking *engagé* cast off his winter lethargy in anticipation of the coming supply boats and pack trains. In Indian camps on the Yellowstone, the Big Cheyenne, the South Platte, and a myriad of other rivers and creeks, native women struck their tepees, loaded their children and belongings on travois, and prepared to follow their husbands on the annual migration to the summer hunting grounds. Traders who had wintered among the tribes bundled their robes and furs, bid good-bye to their customers and friends, and headed for Fort Berthold, Spokane House, or some other post.

Upon arriving at their home forts, the traders handed their bounty to *engagés* who cleaned, aired, and pressed the skins into packs, combining them with the robes and pelts acquired by the forts' in-house traders. At Fort Hall on the unnavigable Snake River, everything had to be transported overland, at first by horse and mule pack trains and then by wagons. Throughout most of the fur country, however, rivers dictated movement of merchandise to market or of supplies to the outlying posts. Missouri River trading houses such as Fort Clark and Fort Benton floated their furs downstream on mackinaws that were built by resident carpenters.

During the 1830s and 1840s, dozens of these flat-bottom boats descended the Missouri on each spring rise, their holds bursting with cargo that included, not only dressed hides, but also salted buffalo tongues. In the early years of the fur trade, the mackinaws ended their journeys in St. Louis; however, from the late 1840s on, most of them had their lading transferred to steam packets at Council Bluffs (near Omaha, Nebraska), which then ferried the payloads on downstream.

The notion of using steamboats on the upper Missouri originated with Kenneth McKenzie. In 1830, he began pressuring his fellow American Fur Company partners, Pierre Chouteau, Jr., and Ramsay Crooks, to send a steamer to Fort Union.[1] At McKenzie's insistence, Chouteau and Crooks eventually purchased the 130-foot side-wheeler, *Yellow Stone,* which ascended the Missouri to Fort Tecumseh in 1831. A year later the boat reached Fort Union at the mouth of the Yellowstone. The following spring, the company bought the stern-wheeler *Assiniboine;* however, she burned a couple of years afterwards, persuading Chouteau that it would be less risky to charter steamers rather than own them outright.

In the 1840s, shipwrights designed steamboats with wider beams and shallower drafts so they could more readily negotiate the Missouri, where sandbars were especially troublesome. When a boat caught on one, its passengers and often its cargo had to be unloaded in order to float it free. In another innovation, stern-wheels replaced side-wheels, which were easily damaged by sawyers, *embarras,* or small floating islands of detached riverbank that were hurled down on the spring floods.[2] Steamer usage gradually increased over the years, as did the boats' range. Nevertheless, the fur trading era was nearly finished before the first steamboat landed at Fort Benton below the Falls of the Missouri in 1860.

At each trading post on the upper Missouri, nothing was more anticipated than the arrival of the annual supply boat, its holds and decks piled high with boxes and casks. The entire fort usually turned out to welcome the steamer's pilot and crew. Indians came too, often hundreds of them from the tepee village invariably located just outside the stockade. Women, children, warriors, and weathered old men lined the bank, staring at the wealth of trade goods being off-loaded by the boat hands and *engagés*. Meanwhile, clerks checked the inventory against the manifest, ensuring that the post received its proper allotment. Everyone worked quickly so the steamboat could complete its journey before the river fell. Summers on the upper Missouri were a continual battle against time.

After the steamer departed, clerks allocated the stores for the satellite posts beyond the vessel's range, directing *engagés* to load the merchandise on a mackinaw or keelboat. Voyageurs then sailed but more often rowed, pushed, and *cordelled*–pulled using a long rope called a *cordelle* that was fastened to the boat's single mast–these sluggish craft to the next link in the supply chain. Reaching the more remote posts usually took until late October. At every fort, clerks set aside a share of the provisions for the post's own Indian trade, portioning out the balance to the traders who would spend the coming winter camped with individual tribes. Hurrying to beat the snow, these traders dispersed to their assigned locations, hauling their horde of trade goods by pack mule or canoe. Traders often worked in pairs and, if they were lucky, enjoyed the assistance of an *engagé* or two. Upon reaching the trading site, the men built a tiny cabin or repaired one they had used before. In some cases they offered merchandise on credit, allowing Indian men to pledge the expected robe production of their wives and daughters as collateral. The traders remained with their designated bands until spring, when the cycle of commerce began anew.

Hides from cows and young bulls made the best robes, especially if the animals were killed between November and February when their hair was thick. Indian men did the hunting, but the skinning, butchering, and tanning fell to their womenfolk. After the meat and fresh hides had been packed to camp, the women cut the meat into long, inch-thick strips, hanging them to dry on a wattle of cottonwood branches and willows. The lattice needed to be suspended high in the air to prevent the tribe's numerous dogs from helping themselves to a tasty meal.

The work of turning a raw buffalo hide into a velvety robe

began by laying the hide on the ground, flesh-side up, and pegging down its edges. Kneeling with her legs and feet tucked beneath her, an Indian woman scraped away the fat and sinew until the hide consisted of skin and hair. Although recipes varied, a typical tanning solution was made from either buffalo brains or human urine, which the woman kneaded into the hide with her fingers, an effort that usually took several hours. Afterwards, she again staked out the hide or draped it over a cord. Depending on the sun and clouds, drying required two to four days, which enabled the woman to work on four or five hides at a time. Once the tanning mixture had dried, she enlisted a female relative or friend to help draw the stiffened skin back and forth across a taut cord–usually made from braided rawhide–transforming it into a soft, pliable robe. Most women could dress twenty robes during a tribe's winter camp.

Not all robes were sold to the fur companies; many were needed for bedding, tepees, and clothing. However, excess robes belonged to a woman's husband or, if she was unmarried, to her father, who bartered them to the traders. As the demand for robes increased in the eastern United States, Indian men recognized the economic advantage in having multiple wives. Polygamy had always been accepted by Plains Indian cultures, but the buffalo robe trade encouraged its spread.

Throughout the winter, traders bargained for the finished robes, storing them inside their tiny quarters until the spring thaw. If a tribe had no trader, it would sell its robes at the closest fort.

Seeing a band of Indians approach his trading post, the *bourgeois* welcomed it with a cannon salute followed by gifts of food and sweetened coffee. Seeking to put the Indians in a good humor, post traders gave them tobacco, then smoked with them, and listened as they recounted past coups. In April 1837, Francis Chardon, the *bourgeois* at Fort Clark, greeted a village of Arikaras who had come to trade by running up the American flag and firing ten volleys from the stockade cannon. Afterwards, the Indians hosted a feast in his honor, serving him a tribal delicacy: boiled puppy. Chardon reciprocated, giving his guests ten pots of corn. Both meals were followed by long speeches, proclaiming friendship.[3]

Many times during these greeting ceremonies, the traders primed their customers with liquor, hoping it would induce the Indians to swap their robes and furs for another drink. Far too often the ploy succeeded. In contrast with their drunken brethren, sober Indians bargained keenly, savoring the trading process and taking as long as possible to strike their deals.

The Fur Trade Market

Except for occasional dips during economic downturns, the world market for beaver fur had prospered for several hundred years before traders in any great numbers began penetrating the country west of the Mississippi. Fueling this demand were men's hats. Through the centuries styles changed, sometimes dramatically—such as when the bolivar replaced the tricorn—but the beaver's under-hair remained the hatters' preferred felting material.

By the mid-1820s, beaver pelts fetched nearly six dollars per pound in St. Louis. Lured by such prices, scores of young men flocked to the fur companies' trapping brigades. From the Sangre de Cristo Mountains north of Santa Fe, to the headwaters of the Green River west of the Continental Divide, trappers harvested beaver by the tens of thousands. Then, in the early 1830s, when overtrapping threatened to annihilate North America's largest rodent, the increasing use of inexpensive nutria fur from South America[4] and a change in hat fashions plunged the price of beaver pelts into a downward spiral from which it never recovered. Silk replaced beaver in the hats of style-conscious gentlemen in the eastern United States and Europe. Anticipating that other men would follow the trendsetters' lead, John Jacob Astor sold his majority interest in the American Fur Company in June 1834. As the decade ended, the price of beaver approached two dollars per pound, making the large, company-owned trapping brigades no longer economical. Male vanity and cheap nutria pelts had tolled the death knell for the fur brigades and the rendezvous supply system they had engendered. By 1841, the glory days of the mountain men were finished.

Companies like the Rocky Mountain Fur Company, whose life's blood was the beaver market, perished. Other firms, such as Pierre Chouteau, Jr., & Company and Bent, St. Vrain & Company, adapted by exploiting the expanding market in buffalo robes.

In contrast with beaver, the demand for buffalo robes started low, then climbed. The American Fur Company's out-of-pocket cost for the trade goods required to purchase a single buffalo robe was $1.35. However, the direct labor (men and boats) and overhead (the expense of maintaining the trading posts and running the rest of the distribution system) needed to transport the trade goods to the Indians and ship the buffalo robes to market, ballooned each robe's cost to $2.55. Although the wholesale price for buffalo gradually increased, raising the profit per hide from forty-five cents in the early 1820s to more than seven times that by the late 1830s, the robe trade dictated a volume production in order to make economic sense. Accordingly, the American Fur Company and its successors (Pratte, Chouteau & Company in 1834 followed by Pierre Chouteau, Jr., & Company in 1839) steadily expanded their network of forts and traders, boosting the annual output of buffalo robes from twenty-five thousand in the late 1820s to one hundred thousand in the 1850s.[5] As an adjunct to the robe trade, the companies earned extra profit by satisfying an eastern appetite for salted buffalo tongues.

Although buffalo robes gave the fur trade an additional quarter century of life, their market, like that of beaver, eventually fell victim to change. By the mid-1860s, white migration, dwindling buffalo herds, Indian unrest, and the Civil War spelled the end of the robe market. When Charles Chouteau sold Pierre Chouteau, Jr., & Company's trading posts in 1865, the era of America's western fur trade closed.

Liquor and the Fur Trade

The greatest blot on the fur companies was their use of liquor to sway, cheat, and ultimately debauch America's Indians. To varying degrees every firm dispensed it, justifying the practice as a competitive necessity.[6] As more and more tribes developed an alcoholic craving, the companies' rationalization became self-fulfilling. After all, if a trader at Bent's Fort declined giving his Cheyenne customers a quart or two of whiskey, they had only to visit the traders at nearby Fort Pueblo. Similarly, clerk Charles Larpenteur plied Fort Union's Assiniboine patrons with drink nightly, to prevent them from going to Hudson's Bay Company posts above the forty-ninth parallel.[7]

Laws against offering liquor to the Indians had been in existence since the 1700s. Article Twelve of the Spanish regulations for the fur trade authorized a fine of one hundred *piastres* for anyone caught selling or giving away alcohol to Indians in the Missouri country.[8] Yet traders regularly ignored the rule. In later years, wealthy fur men such as Pierre Chouteau, Jr., and Sir George Simpson publicly lamented the terrible effects of alcohol on native culture, but so long as their rivals tapped a keg, they authorized their traders to respond in kind. For the owners of small firms, such as Harvey, Primeau & Company or Frost & Todd, liquor was the sole lever by which they could pry their way in among the giants.[9]

Although for years it had been illegal for American traders to sell whiskey to Indians,[10] in 1832 the United States Congress enacted a new statute designed to give teeth to the prohibition. The effort was futile. Fur company riverboats continued smuggling spirits past the government inspectors at Fort Leavenworth and Council Bluffs,[11] and the annual rendezvous supply caravans always packed copious quantities of pure grain alcohol in oak kegs—or as the Indians called them, "hollow woods." As much as the eastern politicians and missionary societies sought to keep the tribes away from "demon rum," in reality, they could do little besides wring their hands and rail.

Before starting to dicker over the robes and furs of their Indian customers, traders often offered them a cup of liquor "on the prairie"—free—to dull their wits and, perhaps, induce them into giving away their wives' labor for another sip of mountain whiskey—two hundred-proof alcohol diluted with water and flavored with spices. Should the whiskey make the Indians unruly, there was always laudanum. A few drops of the opiate derivative in a cup of spirits invariably pacified the most bellicose warrior.[12]

After the Indians became drunk, traders often added more water to the alcohol, reducing its potency and saving the fur company money. An Indian who suspected such deceit would spit a mouthful of the whiskey in a fire to test whether it would burn. If diluted with too much water, the liquor would drown the flames. This practice gave rise to the term "firewater."

Other tricks used by the traders included filling the bottom third of a cup with candle wax or draping a thumb inside a cup as the liquor was being poured. Both ploys ensured that the cup held less than a full measure.

Once the Indians had acquired a taste for whiskey, many of them demanded it as a condition for their trade. The subsequent effect on the tribes was devastating. Besotted Indian men sold their wives and daughters for more drink. At posts such as Fort Sarpy I on the Yellowstone River, drunkenness and prostitution were rampant. Stabbings and eye-gougings were as commonplace as sour stomachs and pounding hangover-headaches. Shootings, however, were rare since the traders usually locked away the Indians' guns before uncorking a jug. Although not all Indians fell prey to alcoholism, those who did saw their lives sink into a sea of depravity, starvation, and death. And for that, the fur trade bears the guilt.

Part II

Forts, Factories, and Posts of America's Fur Trade

1-8 designates the map where the fort is located

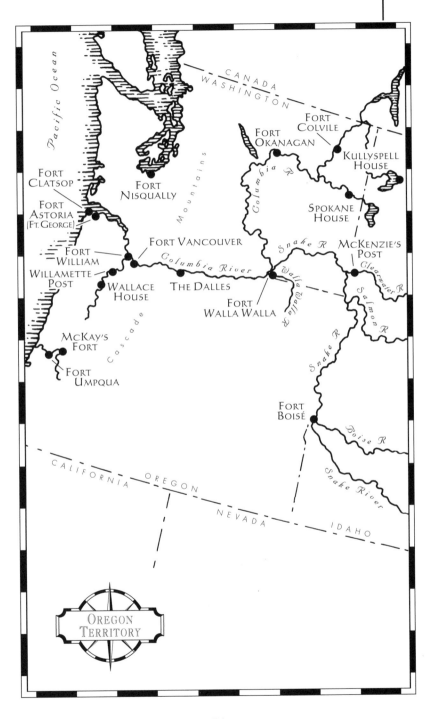

Oregon Territory

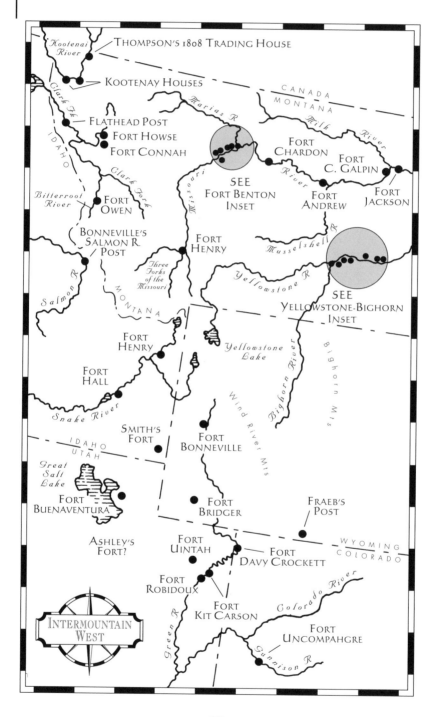

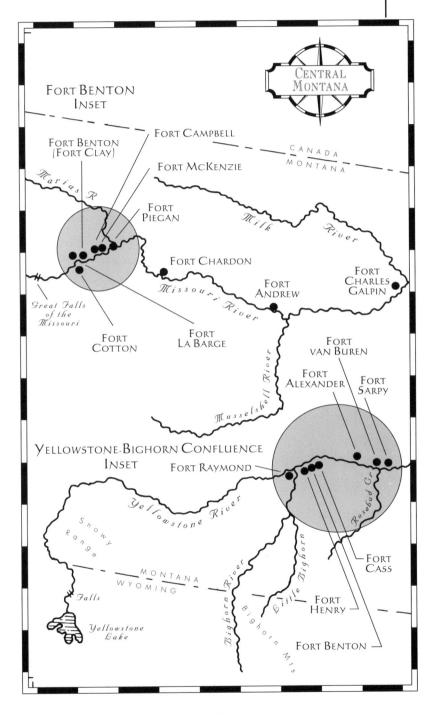

FORT BENTON
INSET

CENTRAL
MONTANA

FORT CAMPBELL

FORT BENTON
(FORT CLAY)

C A N A D A
M O N T A N A

FORT McKENZIE

Marias R.

FORT
PIEGAN

Milk

River

FORT CHARDON

FORT
ANDREW

FORT
CHARLES
GALPIN

Great Falls
of the
Missouri

Missouri River

FORT
COTTON

FORT
LA BARGE

Musselshell River

FORT
VAN BUREN

FORT
ALEXANDER

FORT
SARPY

YELLOWSTONE-BIGHORN CONFLUENCE
INSET

FORT RAYMOND

Yellowstone River

Snowy

Range

M O N T A N A
W Y O M I N G

Rosebud Cr.

FORT
CASS

Falls

Yellowstone
Lake

Bighorn River

Little Bighorn

FORT
HENRY

Bighorn Mts.

FORT BENTON

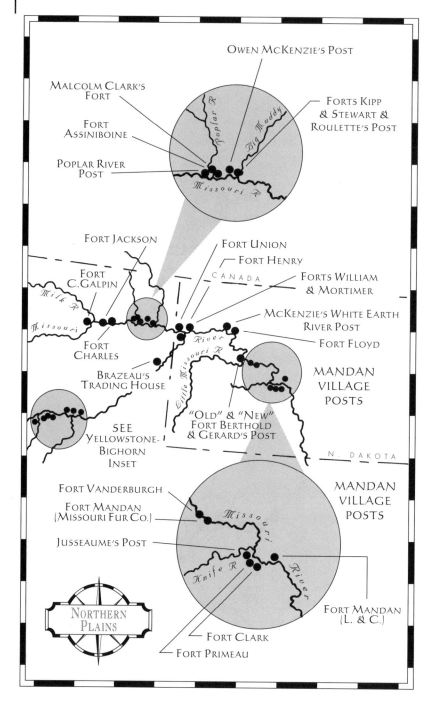

OWEN MCKENZIE'S POST

MALCOLM CLARK'S
FORT

FORTS KIPP
& STEWART &
ROULETTE'S POST

FORT
ASSINIBOINE

POPLAR RIVER
POST

Poplar R

Big Muddy

Missouri R

FORT JACKSON

FORT UNION

FORT HENRY

C A N A D A

FORT
C. GALPIN

FORTS WILLIAM
& MORTIMER

Milk R

MCKENZIE'S WHITE EARTH
RIVER POST

Missouri

FORT FLOYD

FORT
CHARLES

River

MANDAN
VILLAGE
POSTS

BRAZEAU'S
TRADING HOUSE

Little Missouri R

SEE
YELLOWSTONE-
BIGHORN
INSET

"OLD" & "NEW"
FORT BERTHOLD
& GERARD'S POST

N. DAKOTA

FORT VANDERBURGH

MANDAN
VILLAGE
POSTS

FORT MANDAN
(MISSOURI FUR CO.)

Missouri

JUSSEAUME'S POST

Knife R

River

NORTHERN
PLAINS

FORT MANDAN
(L. & C.)

FORT CLARK

FORT PRIMEAU

PEMBINA-RED CONFLUENCE POSTS

HENRY'S PEMBINA POST

XY POST

HUDSON'S BAY POST

GRANT'S POST

FORT DAER

FORT PAUBNA

Lake Winnipegosis

Lake Winnipeg

Lake Manitoba

Assiniboine River

CANADA

Lake of the Woods

Rainy Lake

GINGRAS'S TR. POST

PEMBINA POSTS

CANADA
N. DAKOTA

Pembina R.

Red River

Mississippi River

KITTSON'S POST

PARK RIVER POST

FOREST R. POST

RED LAKE POST

TURTLE RIVER POST

GRANDES FOURCHES POST

MANDAN VILLAGE POSTS

Missouri R.

FORT MANUEL

Grand R.

TABEAU'S ARIKARA POST

N. DAK
S. DAK

James R.

Big Sioux R.

ARIKARA VILLAGES

Cheyenne R.

Missouri R.

SEE PIERRE INSET

LECLERC'S POST

MINNESOTA

IOWA

Bad R.

White R.

HANDY'S POST

FORT MITCHELL

VERMILION POST

BIG SIOUX POST

TRUTEAU'S WINTER POST

Niobrara R.

FORT CHARLES

COLIN CAMPBELL'S HOUSE

PONCA POSTS

DICKSON'S POST

Council Bluffs

SEE C. BLUFFS INSET

CENTRAL PLAINS

Platte R.

NEBRASKA

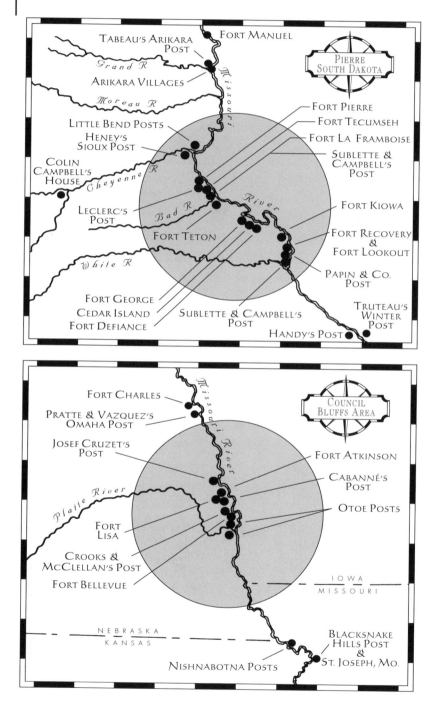

FORT MANUEL

TABEAU'S ARIKARA POST

Grand R

ARIKARA VILLAGES

Moreau R

LITTLE BEND POSTS

HENEY'S SIOUX POST

COLIN CAMPBELL'S HOUSE

Cheyenne R

LECLERC'S POST

Bad R

FORT TETON

White R

FORT GEORGE
CEDAR ISLAND
FORT DEFIANCE

SUBLETTE & CAMPBELL'S POST

HANDY'S POST

PIERRE SOUTH DAKOTA

FORT PIERRE
FORT TECUMSEH
FORT LA FRAMBOISE

SUBLETTE & CAMPBELL'S POST

FORT KIOWA

FORT RECOVERY & FORT LOOKOUT

PAPIN & CO. POST

TRUTEAU'S WINTER POST

FORT CHARLES

PRATTE & VAZQUEZ'S OMAHA POST

JOSEF CRUZET'S POST

Platte River

FORT LISA

CROOKS & McCLELLAN'S POST

FORT BELLEVUE

Missouri River

COUNCIL BLUFFS AREA

FORT ATKINSON

CABANNÉ'S POST

OTOE POSTS

IOWA
MISSOURI

NEBRASKA
KANSAS

NISHNABOTNA POSTS

BLACKSNAKE HILLS POST & ST. JOSEPH, MO.

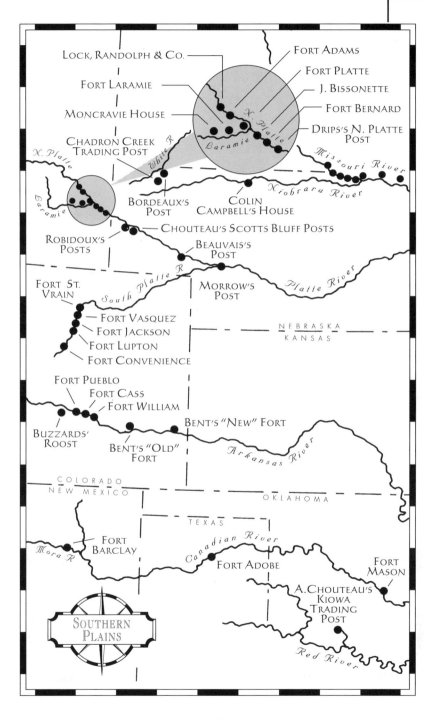

LOCK, RANDOLPH & CO.

FORT ADAMS

FORT PLATTE

FORT LARAMIE

J. BISSONETTE

MONCRAVIE HOUSE

FORT BERNARD

CHADRON CREEK
TRADING POST

DRIPS'S N. PLATTE
POST

N. Platte

White R.

Laramie

N. Platte

Missouri River

Laramie

Niobrara River

BORDEAUX'S
POST

COLIN
CAMPBELL'S HOUSE

ROBIDOUX'S
POSTS

CHOUTEAU'S SCOTTS BLUFF POSTS

BEAUVAIS'S
POST

South Platte R.

Platte River

FORT ST.
VRAIN

MORROW'S
POST

FORT VASQUEZ

FORT JACKSON

NEBRASKA

FORT LUPTON

KANSAS

FORT CONVENIENCE

FORT PUEBLO

FORT CASS

FORT WILLIAM

BUZZARDS'
ROOST

BENT'S "NEW" FORT

BENT'S "OLD"
FORT

Arkansas River

COLORADO

NEW MEXICO

OKLAHOMA

TEXAS

Canadian River

FORT
BARCLAY

Mora R.

FORT ADOBE

FORT
MASON

A. CHOUTEAU'S
KIOWA
TRADING
POST

SOUTHERN
PLAINS

Red River

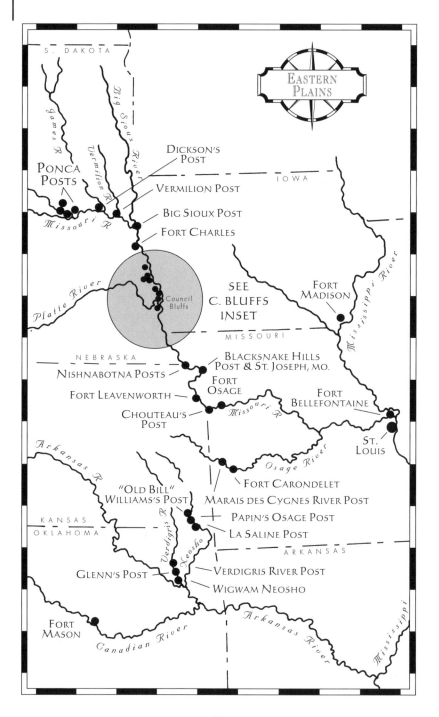

Fort Adams through Fort Atkinson

7 **Fort Adams:** In 1841 Sibille, Adams & Company of Missouri built a cottonwood trading post dubbed Fort Adams near the confluence of the Laramie and North Platte rivers (between Guernsey and Lingle, Wyoming).[1] The partnership abandoned the post the following spring after buying nearby Fort Platte.

7 **Fort Adobe:** William Bent and his partner, Ceran St. Vrain, probably traded along the central Canadian River as early as 1842, no doubt erecting the occasional temporary cabin near an Indian winter camp. In 1845, they and their Santa Fe partner, Charles Bent–William's older brother–decided their firm, Bent, St. Vrain & Company, needed something more permanent. That winter St. Vrain, perhaps with William Bent's assistance, directed the construction of an adobe trading post on the Canadian, giving it a name befitting its architecture, Fort Adobe (in the Texas panhandle; via road, twenty-eight miles northeast of Stinnett).[2]

Kiowa and Comanche hostility soon forced the fort's abandonment. In 1848, William Bent attempted to reopen the post but changed his mind after a war party killed some of his stock. Rather than see Fort Adobe commandeered by Indians or their Comanchero allies, he burned its interior late that year or early 1849. Thereafter, its remains were known as Adobe Walls.[3]

In November 1864, a punitive Army expedition–led by the former mountain man, Kit Carson–fought several thousand Comanches and Kiowas at the site.[4] Although Carson's troops were as outnumbered as George Custer's would be twelve years later at the Little Bighorn, Carson escaped with his command intact, having inflicted heavier casualties on the Indians than they did on him.[5] Ten years after Carson's engagement, Adobe Walls witnessed another battle when twenty-eight buffalo hunters took shelter behind the fort's crumbling ramparts as they repelled seven hundred Comanche and Cheyenne warriors.[6]

3 **Fort Alexander:** In 1842, Alexander Culbertson decided that Pierre Chouteau, Jr., & Company should shift its Yellowstone operation upriver in order to oppose a trading house that the Union Fur Company had opened at the mouth of the Little Bighorn (in south-central Montana; see forts George and Mortimer for more about the Union Fur Company). Culbertson was the manager of the Chouteau firm's Upper Missouri Outfit and *bourgeois* of Fort Union. That fall Culbertson ordered clerk, Charles Larpenteur, to burn the company's Fort Van Buren across from the mouth of Rosebud Creek (near Cartersville, Montana) and build its replacement twenty miles upstream (a bit west of Forsyth). When the post was completed, Larpenteur christened it Fort Alexander in Culbertson's honor.[7]

Instead of making Larpenteur the *bourgeois* of the new establishment, Culbertson ordered him downriver to Fort Union where he was urgently needed to handle the whiskey trade. Being a teetotaler, Larpenteur was one of the few employees Culbertson could trust to remain sober while dispensing liquor to the Indians.[8] In 1849, Larpenteur was finally offered command of Fort Alexander but declined because of ill health and the desire to move his family to a farm. He also may have been concerned about his family's safety, since at the time Crow hostility made Fort Alexander the company's most hazardous post.[9]

After the construction of Fort Sarpy below the mouth of the Rosebud in the summer of 1850, Fort Alexander was abandoned.[10]

3 **Fort Alexander Sarpy** (aka Fort Alexander): See Fort Sarpy.

2,3 **Fort Andrew** (aka Fort Andrew Dawson): In late 1862, workmen for Pierre Chouteau, Jr., & Company erected Fort Andrew on the Missouri River, about fifteen miles upstream from its confluence with the Musselshell (now beneath the upper reaches of Montana's Fort Peck Lake).[11] The aging Pierre Chouteau, Jr., and his son, Charles, hoped the fort would bolster their firm's trading position vis-à-vis the newly formed La Barge, Harkness & Company. (See Fort Charles Galpin for more about the competition between the two firms.)

5,6 **Arikara Posts:** During the mid-eighteenth century the Arikaras numbered about seventy-five hundred people and lived in fixed villages along the Missouri River above its confluence with the Bad[12] (upstream from Pierre, South Dakota). French traders had been visiting the tribe for years, creating an appetite for European goods.[13] Meanwhile, the better-armed Ojibwas (Chippewas) around Lake Superior stepped up attacks on their Sioux neighbors along the upper Mississippi River. Bowing to the Ojibwas' muskets, the Sioux began a multiyear exodus from their Minnesota homeland and invaded the territory of their traditional, village-dwelling enemies along the Missouri. In the early 1780s, smallpox swept the central Missouri, reducing the Arikaras by four-fifths.[14] In 1794, Sioux war parties drove the disease-weakened Arikaras up the Missouri to the mouth of the Grand River (the vicinity of Mobridge, South Dakota).[15] Unable to defeat the more numerous Sioux, the Arikaras had little choice but to accept their exile.

In the summer of 1795, expedition leader, Jean Baptiste Truteau of the Company of the Discoverers and Explorers of the Missouri River came to the Arikaras nearly destitute, having been robbed the previous year by the Sioux and over the winter by the Omahas (see Mandan Villages for details about Truteau's travails). Although he probably traded with the Arikaras and most likely built a small cabin, it is doubtful that he established the fort envisioned by the company's managing partner, Jacques Clamorgan, in the comfort of his St. Louis counting room.[16] Truteau intended to stay with the tribe until a relief party arrived in the autumn of 1796; however, that May, Sioux warriors again attacked the Arikaras, propelling them into headlong flight. Abandoning all but their rifles and the clothes on their backs, Truteau and his handful of men fled down the Missouri, praying their scalps would not end up decorating Sioux lances. Upon reaching the Omahas, Truteau paused at his company's Fort Charles (south of Omadi, Nebraska), then continued on to St. Louis, arriving early that summer.[17]

Soon after the turn of the century other St. Louis traders pushed up the Missouri, opening tiny, often fleeting trading houses in the Arikaras' villages. In 1802, smallpox again devastated the Arikaras, reducing their number to about two thousand. In October 1804, Lewis and Clark found them living in three villages four miles upriver—one on a three-mile-long island near the mouth of the Grand and the other two on the Missouri's right bank.[18]

Manuel Lisa established a small trading house for the tribe in 1809; it operated for four years until he rebuilt it twelve miles upriver (see Fort Manuel).[19] Then in the early 1820s, a trader named Citoleux ran an Arikara post for Berthold & Chouteau.[20] By the time William Ashley came up the Missouri in 1823, the tribe was living in two villages a few miles above the mouth of the Grand (just north of Mobridge, South Dakota, on the Standing Rock Indian Reservation).[21]

2 **Ashley's Fort:** Perhaps as early as autumn 1825, but more likely sometime during the following year, trappers working for William Ashley and Jedediah Smith built a small trading fort near the Great Salt Lake. The post's precise location is unknown. A few historians place it in the vicinity of Utah Lake (south of Salt Lake City), while others suggest somewhere on the Sevier River. Hudson's Bay Company brigade commander, Peter Skene Ogden wrote about the post in 1827 and again in 1828.[22]

1 **Fort Astoria** (renamed Fort George, December 1813, after being purchased by the North West Company of Montreal): Fort Astoria was the brainchild of John Jacob Astor, a German emigrant who arrived in the United States in early 1784, six months shy of his twenty-first birthday. A born merchant, Astor no sooner stepped on the shore of his adopted home than he entered the fur trade. Carrying a pack of wampum—for which he had paid almost nothing—he bartered the strings of beads to the Iroquois of upper New York state, receiving in payment beaver and otter pelts that brought him a handsome return when he sold them for hard money. Within a few years he hired his own traders and began brokering their furs to London. By 1800, he had accumulated a tidy fortune and, in the process, had become America's preeminent fur baron. Managed from New York City, Astor's expanding empire successfully competed with the North West Company of Montreal in its own backyard, the Great Lakes.[23]

As the new century began, Astor widened his business environs to include the Far East. Each year a substantial portion of the pelts exported from North America to Great Britain was transshipped to Canton, trading center of the South China Sea (now Guangzhou, China). The Chinese fur market was huge and lucrative. Deciding to bypass the London merchants and send his furs to Canton directly from the United States, Astor chartered a ship and loaded it with over thirty thousand pelts. The venture was a resounding success, earning him profits so large, he acquired an entire fleet.[24]

While Astor was busy enlarging his international trade, the 1803 Louisiana Purchase electrified every fur merchant from the Atlantic seaboard to the Mississippi River. Three years later, the completed exploration of Lewis and Clark confirmed everyone's hope. The Missouri plains and Rocky Mountains were overrun with beaver. In St. Louis and in Kaskaskia, Illinois, fur traders began forming partnerships (in those days it was the principal way to obtain capital) as they plotted strategies for penetrating the continent's western interior. In New York City, John Jacob Astor also gazed west, grasping that an expansion of his empire to the Pacific coast would be a complement to his China trade. Although the Louisiana Purchase included only the land in the western Mississippi River watershed (the entire purchase lay east of the Continental Divide), the United States felt it had just as valid a claim to the Oregon Territory as any other nation, especially since the Columbia River had been discovered by Robert Gray, an American sea captain.[25]

In April 1808, Astor formed the American Fur Company,[26] allowing him to consolidate his various trading ventures in a single, more manageable concern. Over the next two years he developed an elaborate plan to meld his North American fur operations with his burgeoning China trade. Astor intended building a large fort at the mouth of the Columbia River that would serve as a supply depot for a series of inland trading posts. As he envisioned it, these posts would eventually extend from the Oregon coast over the Continental Divide, and down the Missouri River to the Mississippi. Astor's ships would take aboard trade goods and other provisions at eastern ports, sail around Cape Horn, and off-load their cargoes at Fort Astoria—the name chosen for his Pacific headquarters. The ships could then be filled with furs that had been sent downriver from the inland trading posts. The vessels would sail to China, exchange the furs for silk, nankeen, tea, and other Oriental treasures, and return to New York.[27]

Taking his idea to Montreal, Astor tried interesting the governors of the North West Company in the venture. Although it made economic sense, the governors rejected it.[28] At the time, the North West Company's supply line stretched from Montreal up the Ottawa River to Lake Nipissing, down the French River to Georgian Bay, past Sault Sainte Marie and across Lake Superior, then along a labyrinth of more rivers and lakes that were connected by countless portages, making it over three thousand miles to the most distant point. The company replenished its trading posts using large freight canoes, paddled by as many as a dozen French-Canadian voyageurs. Every year, well over one hundred birchbark canoes—*canots de maître,* each of which were thirty-six to forty feet long with a beam of five feet, paddled by ten *milieux* (rowers who knelt two abreast), in addition to an *avant* (bowsman), and *gouvernail* (steersman), and capable of holding three tons of cargo—were dispatched from the company's warehouses to the inland waterways. Because of weather and the vast distances between Montreal and the firm's far-flung forts, a single cycle of commerce (£-trade good-beaver pelt-£) often took two and a half years to complete.[29]

The Nor'West governors knew that if Astor achieved his plan, his overhead would be a fraction of theirs, and as a result, he would be able to undercut the price at which they sold their furs in the world market. They were already in a desperate struggle with the rival Hudson's Bay Company and did not relish seeing another formidable competitor gaining strength on their southern flank. Yet if Astor's scheme would work for him, they saw no reason why, with slight modification, it would not also do for them. A supply line running from a northwest coastal seaport up the Columbia River into Canada would be less costly than the one they currently employed. Accordingly, the governors sent word to David Thompson, their most able cartographer, to descend the Columbia River and claim the country at its mouth for Great Britain.[30]

Meanwhile, after having his plan spurned by the Nor'Westers, Astor decided to implement it on his own. In June 1810, he established the Pacific Fur Company as a subsidiary of his American Fur Company subscribing to half of the new firm's shares himself, and reserving the rest for a group of junior partner-employees.[31] Needing men with experience in the fur trade, Astor recruited most of the Pacific Fur Company's stockholders, clerks, and *engagés* from the North West Company, which meant that they were British subjects. However, to serve as the enterprise's senior partner, Astor chose a twenty-six-year-old American merchant named Wilson Price Hunt.

The logistics of Astor's plan required two expeditions. Lieutenant Jonathan Thorn, on leave from the US Navy, was to sail the 290-ton *Tonquin* around Cape Horn while Hunt led a sixty-man force overland from St. Louis. Upon reaching the mouth of the Columbia, Thorn was to unload supplies and the thirty-three men who would construct Fort Astoria. It was hoped that the post would be completed by the time Hunt's party arrived. Meantime, Lieutenant Thorn would sail north and trade for furs at the Russian settlements along the Alaskan coast.[32]

The *Tonquin* departed New York on September 6, 1810.[33] From the moment the sheets caught the wind, Lieutenant Thorn treated his passengers in a manner that was both harsh and bizarre. Having been trained on a man-of-war, he saw no difference between the discipline required aboard a thirty-six-gun frigate and the discipline needed on a merchant ship. As the *Tonquin's* captain, he deemed his word law and countenanced no dissent.

Naturally, the Pacific Fur Company's partners and *engagés*, most of whom had never before been to sea, chafed under Thorn's autocratic rules, especially his demand that all candles be extinguished at eight o'clock in the evening.[34] Anyone caught disobeying felt the muzzle of Thorn's cocked pistol pressed against his forehead and heard the captain promise to clap the offender in irons.

After putting in for stores at the Falkland Islands in the south Atlantic, Thorn sailed away, stranding a tardy shore party of company shareholders who frantically tried catching up in a longboat. He would have deserted them had not Robert Stuart, another of the partners, pulled a pistol and threatened to paint the quarterdeck with the captain's blood.[35] During a stop at the Hawaiian Islands, Thorn severely beat a crewman who was late returning to the ship. Not satisfied that he had punished the hapless sailor enough, the captain tossed him overboard.[36]

When the *Tonquin* reached the mouth of the Columbia River on March 22, 1811, a large sandbar (Peacock Bar) blocked the entrance. Despite heavy waves and an approaching squall, Thorn ordered a five-man boat crew to sound a route past the bar. The crew's skiff swamped, drowning all hands. The next day the seas were still running high. Determined to enter the estuary on the ebbing tide, Thorn sent another crew to locate a channel. As the rowers pulled against the river's outflowing current, a powerful wave caught their boat, carrying it into the open ocean where it capsized, sending two more men to a watery grave.[37]

A couple of nights later, a following wind cooperated with the tide, enabling the *Tonquin* to sneak past the sandbar and anchor in the Columbia River estuary. During the ensuing weeks Pacific Fur Company *engagés* felled trees and constructed cabins and warehouses on the peninsula between Youngs Bay and the estuary (where the city of Astoria, Oregon, now sits). Eager to carry out his trading mission to Alaska, Lieutenant Thorn set sail on June 1 but was forced to stand off the sandbar, awaiting a favorable wind that would propel the *Tonquin* into the open sea. Five frustrating days later, the ship finally eased into the Pacific and headed up the coast.[38]

At Nootka Sound on the west side of Vancouver Island, Thorn paused to trade for sea otter pelts with the local Indians. While the captain bartered with a chief, a misunderstanding between them escalated into a full-blown argument. Consumed by his temper, Thorn hurled a fur in the chief's face and demanded that he and his people leave the ship. Alexander McKay, one of the Pacific Fur stockholders who had gone with the *Tonquin* to supervise the trading, told Thorn that the insult could have dire repercussions, but the haughty captain dismissed the warning with a sneer. Over the next few days the Indians continued swapping their otter skins for beads, mirrors, and other trinkets, acting as if the affront to their chief had been forgotten. But beneath their smiles, they seethed for revenge.[39]

Early one morning while McKay and Thorn were in their cabins, nearly two dozen Indians paddled out to the *Tonquin* and climbed aboard, clamoring to trade. Other Indians followed, so many that the ship's main deck swarmed with warriors. When Thorn came topside, he was pleased to see the barter going well. However, as the crowd of natives continued to grow, he became alarmed and ordered his crew to make preparations to get under way. A moment later one of the chiefs screamed a war whoop. As Alexander McKay turned toward the signal, he saw the blur from a tomahawk a split second before it smashed the side of his skull. All about the ship Indians fell on the crewmen, clubbing them senseless, then slitting their throats. Lieutenant Thorn attempted to defend himself but was overwhelmed by the slashing knives. Minutes after the attack began, he lay dead in a pool of his own gore.

Several of the crew who had been in the rigging preparing to make sail, climbed down to the main deck, fought their way through the slaughter, and reached the gun locker. Now armed, they forced the Indians from the ship. Too few to sail the *Tonquin*, the survivors decided to take their chances in one of the longboats. With luck they hoped to work their way along the coast to Fort Astoria. The clerk James Lewis listened to their plans, knowing that he would soon die of his wounds. Vowing to kill as many of the tribe as he could, he had his shipmates help him to the power magazine where he fixed a fuse. That night his four companions rowed away, hidden by a black, overcast sky.

Just after dawn the following morning, the Indians again clambered onto the ship. Below decks in the powder magazine, Lewis waited, his hands holding a fire steel and flint, his ears straining at the noise from above. Hearing the warriors start down the ladders into the lower compartments, Lewis leaned forward and struck steel to flint. The *Tonquin* exploded in an orange ball of fire, splintered wood, and dismembered bodies.

The remainder of the tribe soon captured the four crewmen who had escaped in the longboat. They were taken to the main village where they suffered a slow, painful death. The *Tonquin's* fate would never have been known had not the ship's native interpreter, Lamazee, jumped into the bay during the initial assault. Some of the Indians had protected him, allowing him to talk to the captive crewmen before they were killed. In time he returned to Fort Astoria and relayed the terrible story.[40]

Like the crew of the *Tonquin,* Astor's overland expedition to the mouth of the Columbia also faced hardships. On September 3, 1810, three days before the *Tonquin* had sailed from New York, Wilson Price Hunt arrived in St. Louis with a party of hunters and voyageurs he had enlisted in Montreal and the Great Lakes' fur trading center, Michilimackinac (Mackinac Island, Michigan).[41] During the next six weeks he collected more men from the grog shops and wharves of the young river town, then escorted them up the Missouri to a winter camp at the mouth of the Nodaway River (just above St. Joseph, Missouri) to await the spring thaw.[42] In January, Hunt returned to St. Louis to recruit more men and purchase additional supplies for the coming journey.

Hunt's task of finding keelboat crews and hunters was made doubly expensive because Manuel Lisa was also combing the town for men to join his St. Louis Missouri Fur Company, which planned to expand its trapping forays into the Yellowstone and Three Forks country.[43] Although Hunt's destination was the Oregon coast, Lisa correctly suspicioned that Astor and his American and Pacific Fur companies also had designs on the upper Missouri. Over the following weeks, as Hunt and Lisa scrambled to sign up every frontiersman capable of drawing breath, relations between them slid from cool to frigid.

On March 12, 1811, Hunt ushered his latest recruits onto keelboats and ordered his voyageurs to cast off the mooring lines.[44] Upstream from St. Louis, the Mississippi flowed as if it were two rivers divided by a pane of glass. In the eastern half, the forest-green water coursed with a lazy indifference that camouflaged its underlying power, but to the west where Hunt's voyageurs strained at their oars, it ran swift with the color of creamed coffee. A few miles north of St. Louis, the Missouri surged into the Mississippi like a thick-necked street brawler elbowing its way into a genteel crowd of passersby. Here the Missouri's five-mile-per-hour current roiled with trees and miniature islands of riverbank that had been ripped free by late winter floods. Below the confluence, the Mississippi River needed many miles to dilute the Missouri's rawboned exuberance.

Three weeks after Hunt set out, Manuel Lisa followed in his wake, leaving from the growing river town of St. Charles (about twenty miles above the Missouri's mouth). Lisa was going upstream with provisions for the St. Louis Missouri Fur Company's trading posts. Because of the hostility between his firm and the Pacific Fur Company, he worried lest Hunt incite the Sioux to attack him, a concern that Hunt also had, should Lisa gain the lead.[45] Consequently, Lisa determined to catch Hunt who had a 240-mile head start, before either of them reached Sioux country. What occurred was the greatest keelboat race in the annals of riverine history.

On April 17, Hunt stopped at the Nodaway camp where he had left his early recruits to spend the winter. Four days later the entire expedition cast off.[46] From dawn till dusk the men toiled against the Missouri's muddy current. During the few occasions when the wind and river cooperated, the voyageurs hoisted a sail, but most of the time they endured the backbreaking toil of poling, pulling, and rowing their four keelboats against the spring tide.

Downriver, Lisa pushed his twenty-man crew relentlessly, driving his lone keelboat with will as well as muscle. Upon reaching Fort Osage (near Sibley, Missouri) on April 25, he was cheered to learn that he had shaved one hundred miles off Hunt's lead.[47] Like Hunt's voyageurs ahead of them, Lisa's boatmen subsisted on fatback and corn mush mixed with tallow. The diet was bland, but it packed energy.

In May when the rivals passed the Omaha villages (north of Decatur, Nebraska), Lisa had trimmed Hunt's advantage to four days. Growing more anxious about possible Sioux war parties up ahead, Lisa sent Toussaint Charbonneau cross-country to ask Hunt to wait so they could travel together. Charbonneau and his wife, Sacajawea, had gained fame with Lewis and Clark and were now journeying with Lisa to the Mandans. Charbonneau caught the Pacific Fur Company expedition near the Niobrara River (on the Nebraska-South Dakota border). Although Hunt promised to stop among the nearby Poncas and allow Lisa to catch up, in truth, he had no intention of giving Lisa a chance to capture the lead.[48]

On May 23, Lisa saw Francis Benoît rowing downstream with a canoe-load of pelts from the St. Louis Missouri Fur Company's trading post among the Mandans. Hearing from Benoît that the Sioux were indeed on the warpath, Lisa pressed his voyageurs to redouble their efforts. Three days later Charbonneau returned, saying that Hunt had consented to wait. But Hunt was not waiting. The same day Charbonneau gave his report, Hunt picked up three St. Louis Missouri Fur Company trappers who agreed to guide his expedition across the Continental Divide. John Hoback, Edward Robinson, and Jacob Reznor (sometimes spelled Rezner) were returning from the Snake River country where they had wintered with Andrew Henry (for more about their adventures see Fort Boisé and Fort Henry on Henry's Fork of the Snake River).[49]

When Lisa reached the Ponca village (just above the mouth of the Niobrara River near the Nebraska-South Dakota state line) on May 27, he learned that Hunt had broken his word and gone ahead. Although the Pacific Fur Company was still in front, Lisa had shrunk its lead to three days. Ordering his men back to the *cordelle,* he vowed to catch Hunt or die trying. Now each day's labor lasted long into the night, exhaustion being the voyageurs' only reward. During one twenty-four-hour period, an upriver wind allowed Lisa to cover nearly seventy-five miles, an unheard-of distance when a good day's travel was usually counted in the high teens.[50]

On May 30, the Pacific Fur expedition halted before a band of Sioux, who demanded that it leave them a trader. Hunt bluffed his way past, telling the warriors that another party of white men would soon arrive to build the tribe a trading fort. Two days later the Sioux stopped Lisa, who gained his freedom to continue by promising to open a post for them at Cedar Island (above the Missouri's Grand Detour) when he returned from the Mandans.[51]

The next morning, June 2, Lisa finally caught Hunt. Their keelboat race up the Missouri River had covered 1,100 miles in just two months, a feat that has never been equaled. Exhausted by their contest, the rivals slackened their pace and continued the journey, keeping each other in sight.

By June 12, when they reached the Arikara villages above the mouth of the Grand River[52] (north of Mobridge, South Dakota), the parties had become, if not friendly, at least civil. On the advice of Hoback, Robinson, and Reznor, Hunt decided to abandon the Missouri and push due west, thereby avoiding the Blackfeet. Lisa purchased the Pacific Fur Company's keelboats, paying for them with horses he had bartered from the Arikaras and Mandans.[53]

On July 18, Hunt, Marie Dorion—the pregnant Indian wife of interpreter Pierre Dorion—her two children, and sixty-one more men left the Arikara villages. Hunt, four other company partners, and Pierre Dorion rode; everyone else, including Marie Dorion, walked. Most of the expedition's eighty-two horses were needed for packing.[54] Over the next three months the party crossed the Black Hills and southern Bighorn Mountains, crested the Continental Divide at Union Pass (west of Dubois, Wyoming), and dropped into the upper Green River drainage. They then followed the Hoback River until it emptied into the Snake (south of Jackson, Wyoming). Led by its three guides, the expedition climbed Teton Pass and descended into Pierre's Hole (Teton Basin near Driggs, Idaho). On October 8, Hunt and his men reached Egin Bench on the North Fork of the Snake River (near Rexburg, Idaho), where the party's three guides—Hoback, Robinson, and Reznor—had spent the previous winter with Andrew Henry and a brigade of St. Louis Missouri Fur Company trappers.[55] Hunt moved his people into the brigade's abandoned quarters, naming the North Fork and deserted cabins in Andrew Henry's honor.

Hoping to make better time by boat, Hunt had his woodsmen hew fifteen dugouts from cottonwood logs. Hoback, Robinson, Reznor, and two more men decided to forgo the rest of the journey, opting instead to trap the Snake River country (Idaho). Days earlier, four other trappers had remained behind to hunt beaver along the Hoback and Snake headwaters (in western Wyoming).[56] On October 19, after leaving the horses with some friendly Shoshones, the expedition loaded into its cottonwood canoes and set off down the newly christened Henry's Fork.[57]

A few miles later, Henry's Fork skirted around two old burned-out volcanoes (Idaho's Menan Buttes) and merged with the Snake's South Fork. At American Falls the men portaged. Some distance below, where the river had carved a deep canyon, a dugout glanced off a boulder and capsized, drowning the voyageur Antoine Clappine.[58] Four others in the canoe, including company stockholder, Ramsay Crooks, felt lucky to escape with their lives.

Ahead the current frothed with rapids. Towering hundreds of feet above both sides of the river, the volcanic canyon walls loomed dark and sheer. Just beyond where Crooks and Clappine's canoe had overturned, the basalt blocks that defined the Snake's course squeezed the stream into a raging flume. Here the river plunged over a cataract, then plunged again. Bubbling like a witch's brew, the water seethed with pale green boils. Eventually, this narrowest and most southern point on the Snake River would come to be named Caldron Linn.[59]

Needing to know whether the river was navigable below the falls, Hunt sent scouts to reconnoiter. A few days later they reported that it was impassable; to try would be suicide. After dispatching Crooks and a small detail to retrieve their horses from the Shoshones, Hunt allowed several men to strike for Fort Astoria on foot. Crooks soon returned to the camp near Caldron Linn, worried that winter would close in before he could retrieve the herd. Hunt now had no choice but to cache the equipment that could not be carried, and walk to Fort Astoria. He prayed he would make it before snow blocked the passes.

On November 9 Crooks and eighteen men started along the Snake's left bank while Hunt and the remainder of the force followed the right. During the next month, the parties shivered across the central Snake River Plain. Starving and desperately in need of horses, Hunt finally turned away from the river. For mile upon dreary mile, his detail trekked northwest over the desolate wasteland. As Hunt encountered isolated Indian camps, he bartered for a bit of dried salmon, sometimes a dog—for the cookpot—and occasionally, a horse. Eventually returning to the Snake in early December, he reunited with Ramsay Crooks and his emaciated company, which was in even worse shape than Hunt's. Reducing their meager rations to almost nothing, Hunt and his men shared the meat from a recently butchered horse.[60]

The following day the two groups continued their march, striving to keep each other in sight as they lurched along either side of the Snake River. Over every weary mile, hunger gnawed at their strength. As the parties stretched out along the two shorelines, each step became an act of will. To quit walking was to die. Leading the right-hand procession, Hunt and a few men surprised a small Shoshone camp. Frightened, the half dozen Indians ran, abandoning their five ponies. The Astorians quickly slaughtered one of the animals and roasted its flesh. Hunt ordered the remaining four horses to be taken along as food.

Ill and continually falling behind, Ramsay Crooks and hunter John Day straggled after their companions as they continued down the Snake. Another horse was butchered and eaten. Then the expedition's luck changed. Hunt found a Shoshone village and enlisted the aid of three guides. Crooks, Day, and the others who were too weary to go on remained among the friendly tribe while Hunt and the rest of the overlanders turned away from the Snake River and trudged west. On December 30, Pierre

Dorion and his family remained in camp while the rest of the Astorians pressed ahead. Sometime that day Marie Dorion gave birth. The next morning the Dorions and their new baby caught up to the main body. A week later, the child died.

After enduring knee-deep snow, freezing rain, and bone-chilling wind, the feeble expedition–including Marie Dorion–reached the Columbia River on January 21, 1812; however, the current was too rough for the party to chance using dugouts until it was below The Dalles. Half-dead from hunger and exposure, the overlanders stumbled into Fort Astoria on February 15, a month behind the men Hunt had allowed to leave Caldron Linn on their own.[61]

By the time Hunt reached Fort Astoria, the *engagés* who had come aboard the *Tonquin* had nearly completed the post's construction. Much had happened at the Pacific Fur Company's western headquarters while the overland expedition was sweating its way up the Missouri River and over the Continental Divide. In mid-June 1811, while workmen were still cutting timber for the

Fort Astoria Blockhouse

fort's buildings, Indians brought word that the North West Company had established a trading post on the Spokane River (see Spokane House). Knowing they must counter it, the partners at Astoria began planning to send fellow-shareholder David Stuart to open competing posts in the vicinity.[62]

Four weeks later, Stuart was nearly ready to set off when a large canoe came around Tongue Point, flying the Union Jack. In it rode David Thompson and eight Nor'West voyageurs. Thompson's arrival at Fort Astoria completed the first full-length reconnaissance of the Columbia River (he had discovered its headwaters in 1807[63]), but Thompson could not carry out his orders to raise the British flag on the Oregon coast and claim the land for Great Britain. The Pacific Fur Company had beaten him there by four months.

On July 23, Stuart started up the Columbia to establish a trading presence in opposition to the North West Company. Thompson accompanied him for a ways before turning off for Spokane House. That fall, while Stuart constructed Fort Okanagan just above the mouth of the Okanogan River[64] (east of Brewster, Washington), and She-Whaps Post on the South Thompson River near its confluence with the North (at Kamloops, British Columbia),[65] rumors of the *Tonquin's* destruction filtered down to Astoria via the Indian "telegraph."

In May 1812, three months after Wilson Hunt and the main body of overlanders had reached Fort Astoria, Ramsay Crooks and John Day arrived. Crooks and Day had regained their strength among the Snake River Shoshones, then lost it again when striking for the coast. The two men would have most likely died if David Stuart and his party had not stumbled across them while returning to Fort Astoria from Fort Okanagan.

That spring, while Crooks and Day convalesced, Astor's ship *Beaver* sailed into the Columbia estuary and unloaded much-needed supplies as well as more clerks, *engagés,* and another company shareholder, John Clarke.[66] With sufficient personnel now on hand, the Pacific Fur partners felt ready to open more inland forts and wrest the Indian trade away from the Nor'Westers. Yet unbeknownst to the men at Astoria, matters were coming to a head in

Washington, DC, and London that would eventually shatter their dreams. On June 19, 1812, the United States declared war on Great Britain.

While the British and American navies began raiding each other's ocean-going commerce, the Astorians established trading posts on the Willamette, Spokane, Clark Fork, and Clearwater rivers (see Wallace House, Spokane House, Flathead Post, and McKenzie's Post). Robert Stuart, who had come out on the *Tonquin,* and a few men—including Ramsay Crooks and Robert McClellan—returned east, carrying news of the enterprise to John Jacob Astor in New York. Hunt sailed up the Pacific coast on the *Beaver,* trading for sea otter and seal pelts at Russian outposts in Alaska, then continued to Hawaii to await another Astor supply ship that would convey him back to Fort Astoria.[67]

Word of the war between the United States and Great Britain first reached the Astorians at their Spokane River trading house in December 1812. Two Nor'West employees burst into the fort, boasting that a British frigate would soon sail into the Columbia estuary and exact Astoria's surrender. The news threw a number of the Pacific Fur Company's partners into a panic. Donald McKenzie, who had built a fort above the mouth of the Clearwater (near Lewiston, Idaho), dashed back to his post, cached its trade goods, and fled to Astoria. Upon arriving, McKenzie soon persuaded Duncan McDougal, Astoria's *bourgeois,* that their position was futile. McKenzie reasoned that the only sane course was to gather everyone from the outlying forts and return to St. Louis via Hunt's overland route. After receiving McDougal's permission, McKenzie and two clerks left in March to alert Fort Okanagan and the company's post on the Spokane River.

On June 14, 1813, all of the Pacific Fur Company's available partners gathered at the mouth of the Columbia to debate McKenzie's proposal to abandon Fort Astoria. The *Beaver* had not arrived on schedule, leading to the conclusion that it had probably sunk or been taken captive. (Unbeknownst to the men at Astoria, the *Beaver's* captain had deposited Wilson Hunt in Hawaii in early December 1812, then gone to China to sell his cargo of Alaskan fur. Upon learning about the war, he decided to wait it out in Canton.) Without resupply, the Pacific Fur shareholders knew their enterprise would be hard-pressed to survive, even if a British man-of-war did not blast Astoria apart with its cannons. Seeing no alternative, the partners agreed to stay in the Oregon country until the following spring, then go home via Hunt's overland route, leaving the firm's trading posts to the British.[68] Soon after the decision was made, Nor'Wester John George McTavish and a platoon of Canadian trappers set up camp in the shadow of Astoria's palisades in case it should become necessary to bring the fort under siege. That fall the Astorians and Nor'Westers visited back and forth, treating one another more like friends than enemies.

While his partners were resolving to surrender their trading venture, Wilson Hunt counted the passing days in Hawaii, eager to return to the Oregon coast. He planned to secure passage to Fort Astoria on the *Lark,* another of Astor's ships, that was expected to arrive soon from New York. Hunt was unaware that the *Lark* had been wrecked by a Pacific storm, and that the British Royal Navy had blockaded Astor's other supply ships on the Atlantic seaboard. On June 20, 1813, the sailing vessel *Albatross* arrived from China bringing word of the war. Hunt's vexation at frittering away his time immediately degenerated into full-fledged alarm. Drawing on Astor's credit, Hunt hired the *Albatross* to ferry him, and all the supplies he could put his hands on, across the Pacific to the mouth of the Columbia.[69]

On August 20 when Hunt landed at Fort Astoria, he saw that events had slipped beyond his control. Rather than counter his partners' plan to desert the Oregon country, he accepted their decision. Sailing again on the *Albatross,* which had other commitments and could not be chartered to salvage Astoria's one hundred thousand dollar-inventory of fur, Hunt returned to Hawaii, hopeful of finding another ship. However, that ambition evaporated during a stopover at the Marquesas Islands when he heard that the twenty-six-gun sloop HMS *Raccoon* was bound for the Columbia estuary.[70]

That fall, John Clarke sold the Spokane River trading post to the North West Company. Three of his clerks, including

Alexander Ross, elected to join the Montreal firm rather than return with Clarke to the United States. At Fort Astoria, McDougal decided to sell the Pacific Fur Company's remaining forts and their inventory of pelts and other stores to the Nor'Westers rather than wait for Hunt to return with a chartered ship. McTavish, the Nor'West commander who was still encamped just beyond the fort's stockade, could hardly refuse since McDougal offered the furs at a fraction of their value. Besides, McTavish knew that if he did not accept, the North West Company would lose everything when the HMS *Raccoon* arrived and its captain captured the Pacific Fur Company's property as a spoil of war. As a condition of the exchange, McTavish allowed McDougal and any other Astorian shareholder who wished it to join the North West Company as partners.[71] Many, including Donald McKenzie, did.

McDougal and McTavish signed the bill of sale on October 23, 1813, but the final details of the transfer dragged on until November 12. One month later, HMS *Raccoon* dropped anchor in the Columbia River estuary. Peeved that Fort Astoria's furs had slipped through his fingers, the sloop's captain, William Black, hoisted the Union Jack and formally claimed the post for Great Britain, renaming it Fort George.[72]

In February 1814, the brig *Pedler* brought Hunt back to Fort Astoria. After taking aboard all the Pacific Fur Company hands who wanted to go with him, he sailed away,[73] bitter that his efforts of the last four years had come to naught.

The sale of Fort Astoria spelled the death of the Pacific Fur Company; however, the following year when the Treaty of Ghent—ending the War of 1812—required the return of all land captured under arms, Captain Black's annexation of the post looked as though it would unravel. But despite being ordered by the American and British governments to give Astoria—now Fort George—back to Astor, the North West Company's partners refused, claiming they had legally purchased the post prior to Captain Black's ceremonial seizure. It was a legal technicality, but since the Americans had no desire to start another war over the matter, Fort George remained firmly in the Nor'Westers' grip.[74]

In 1818, the United States and Great Britain agreed to joint occupancy of the Oregon country, and the case was laid to rest pending the establishment of a permanent international boundary between the United States and western Canada. Then in 1821, the Nor'Westers merged with the Hudson's Bay Company, and title to the fort passed once again. Three years afterward, George Simpson–at the time, governor of the Hudson's Bay Company's Northern Department–ordered a new trading post built one hundred miles east on the Columbia River's north bank (see Fort Vancouver), lest the company lose Fort George when the border between the United States and Canada was finally settled. With the completion of Fort Vancouver (opposite Portland, Oregon), Fort George was abandoned on June 7, 1825. After a couple of years the harsh coastal climate rotted its log pickets. In 1829, the Hudson's Bay Company rebuilt the post on a smaller scale and used it to monitor American sailing ships.

4   Fort Assiniboine: During the early summer of 1834, Pratte, Chouteau & Company's riverboat *Assiniboine* attempted the first steamed voyage up the Missouri beyond Fort Union.[75] The risky excursion ended in near-disaster when the boat became trapped by low water at the mouth of the Poplar River (near Poplar, Montana).[76] Needing to guard the marooned vessel until the spring rise, Kenneth McKenzie, head of the firm's Upper Missouri Outfit, sent Lewis Crawford to construct a trading post on the left bank. McKenzie figured that if men had to be there for the winter anyway, they might as well spend their time trading with the Assiniboines and Crees.

The following March, after the resurgent Missouri lifted the craft off the sandy riverbed, the steamer descended to Fort Union, picked up a cargo of buffalo robes, and proceeded downstream. Near the Missouri's confluence with the White Earth River (in western North Dakota), the *Assiniboine* again ran aground[77] and once more had to await the runoff from western storms to float it free. At Fort Clark (near the town of Fort Clark, North Dakota), the boat took on more buffalo robes and numerous specimens of birds and mammals that had been collected by Alexander Philipp Maximilian, Prince of Wied-Nuwied, during his scientific excursion up-country. Near the mouth of the Little Heart River at the upper end of Sibley Island (close to Bismarck, North Dakota), the ill-fated *Assiniboine* met its final disaster, catching fire and burning to the waterline. Everything on board was destroyed, including Prince Maximilian's collection and company buffalo robes valued between sixty thousand and eighty thousand dollars, all of it uninsured.[78]

Company traders used Fort Assiniboine during the winter of 1835–6, after which it was probably abandoned.[79] In 1879, the US Army established a fort of the same name about ten miles southwest of Havre, Montana. Intended for Sioux and Blackfoot control, the post lasted until 1911.[80]

4   **Fort Atkinson** (aka "New" Fort Berthold): See "New" Fort Berthold.

6   **Fort Atkinson** (US Army): In the autumn of 1819, Colonel Henry Atkinson supervised the construction of a military fortifica-

Fort Atkinson West Barracks

tion on the west side of the Missouri River, about one mile from Council Bluffs (nine miles north of Omaha, Nebraska, in the Fort Atkinson State Historical Park, near the town of Fort Calhoun). Originally called Cantonment Missouri, the fort had the distinction of being the western-most military facility in the United States.[81]

The name Council Bluffs stemmed from the exploration of Lewis and Clark who had camped there in early August 1804, and parleyed with members of the Otoe and Missouri tribes. During the fur trapping era, traders referred to the entire region as Council Bluffs.[82]

In June 1820, flooding on the Missouri prompted the Army to relocate to higher ground, about a mile and a half south of the original stockade. The new facility measured 455 feet by 468 feet

Right: **Fort Atkinson Powder Magazine**

Below: **Powder Magazine & Barracks at Fort Atkinson**

and was eventually garrisoned by one thousand soldiers. The following January, the post was renamed Fort Atkinson in honor of its founder. During the early days of the fur trade, the outpost was an important stopping place for keelboats traveling the Missouri River. In the summer of 1823, Colonel Henry Leavenworth used the fort from which to launch an inept campaign against the Arikaras (for details, see Fort Henry at the confluence of the Missouri and Yellowstone rivers), and in 1824, the trapper Tom Fitzpatrick and two companions walked seven hundred miles to Fort Atkinson after their bull boat capsized in rapids on the North Platte River (in central Wyoming).[83] In the mid-1820s, the expanding trade between St. Louis and New Mexico prompted the Army to move closer to the Santa Fe Trail. Fort Atkinson was closed in June 1827, and replaced by Fort Leavenworth (in eastern Kansas).[84]

Fort Barclay through Buzzards' Roost

7 **Fort Barclay:** In 1848, six years after they had established Fort Pueblo (the site of Pueblo, Colorado), Alexander Barclay (sometimes spelled Barkley or Barklay) and Joseph Doyle built a trading post on the right side of the Mora River, about a mile upstream from its confluence with the Sapello (a bit west of Watrous, New Mexico). The post's location was strategic, since it sat astride the Santa Fe Trail.[1]

7 **Beauvais's Post:** Around 1850, a trader named Beauvais nailed together a tiny cabin on the right side of the North Platte River at Ash Hollow (south of Lewellen, Nebraska). Most likely established for the Oregon- and California-bound emigrant traffic rather than buffalo robes, the dilapidated-looking trading post closed in 1853.[2]

8 **Fort Bellefontaine:** On November 3, 1804, the Sauk and Fox Indians who occupied the country bordering the Illinois, Des

Moines, Rock, and central Mississippi rivers (northeastern Missouri, eastern Iowa, northern Illinois, and southern Wisconsin), ceded fifteen million acres of their land to the US Government. In return for this birthright, the tribes were allowed to live in their own country until it could be sold to white farmers. For its part, the American government promised to give the Indians one thousand dollars worth of annuities per year and provide them with a licensed trader.

In 1805, the US Army established Fort Bellefontaine on the south bank of the Missouri River, four miles above its confluence with the Mississippi (in the bottomland north of the Spanish Lake-suburb of St. Louis, Missouri). The fort was America's first military post and government Indian factory west of the Mississippi River. Although the Office of Indian Trade in Georgetown, DC, which administered the factory system, assumed that Bellefontaine would satisfy the terms of the Sauk and Fox treaty, the Indians found its location inconvenient. In 1808, the Army built them a new factory trading house above the Des Moines Rapids (see Fort Madison– aka Fort Bellevue) and transferred Bellefontaine's factory to the newly opened Fort Osage (see Osage Posts and Fort Osage). Fort Bellefontaine remained a military post only.

Because of flooding along the Missouri River, soldiers relocated Fort Bellefontaine atop Belle Mont in 1810. In July 1826, the post's garrison moved to Jefferson Barracks (a new facility just south of St. Louis). The Army used Bellefontaine as a warehouse until 1834 when it was abandoned.[3]

8   **Fort Bellevue** (aka Fort Madison): See Fort Madison.

6   **Fort Bellevue** (in later years known as Sarpy's Trading Post): In the spring or early summer of 1823, Missouri Fur Company *engagés* built Fort Bellevue for the Omaha trade, locating the post on the west side of the Missouri River (at Bellevue, Nebraska), nine miles above the mouth of the Platte and about thirty miles south of Fort Atkinson and Council Bluffs.[4]

By 1825, Indian attacks and competition with other trading firms had reduced the Missouri Fur Company to little more than a shell of its former self. Hoping to resuscitate their dying partnership, the owners reorganized as Pilcher & Company.[5] Using Fort Bellevue as their forward base, they again sent their traders among the Sioux, Omahas, Mandans, and other tribes of the central and upper Missouri. For two years Pilcher & Company struggled against competitors that were far better capitalized, but by 1827 the partners knew they were waging a losing war. That fall, in a final attempt to save their floundering firm, Joshua Pilcher, Lucien Fontenelle, Andrew Drips, William Vanderburgh, and Charles Bent took a trapping brigade to the mountains. When their hunt proved unsuccessful, the partners called it quits.[6]

Fontenelle and Drips soon formed a new trading partnership backed by the American Fur Company. In 1829, Fontenelle returned to Fort Bellevue, constructed a few buildings and strengthened the trading operation. He and Drips had probably obtained title to the post during the breakup of Pilcher & Company.[7]

For the next several years, Lucien Fontenelle and Andrew Drips led trapping brigades and rendezvous supply caravans for the American Fur Company. Although, legally, their partnership was separate from John Jacob Astor's company, for all practical purposes they conducted business as if they were its employees.[8] The Fontenelle & Drips partnership may well have continued to own Bellevue; however, Pierre Chouteau, Jr., who managed the American Fur Company's Western Department, treated the fort as if it were another of the firm's many trading houses. When Fontenelle's Omaha wife and children were not traveling with him, they usually stayed at Fort Bellevue, which they considered home. Always fond of his liquor, Fontenelle began to drink more heavily as his business ventures soured in the mid-1830s.[9] Nearly broke, he returned to his family at Bellevue in 1838 and died there two years later.[10]

During the 1840s, Fort Bellevue earned far more profit catering to the wagon trains bound for California, Oregon, or the Mormon enclaves around the Great Salt Lake than it did from furs and buffalo robes. In the early 1850s, the current *bourgeois,* Peter

Sarpy, added a ferry across the Missouri River, thereby funneling more traffic past the fort.[11] By the early 1860s, a town had grown around the old post and the buffalo robe trade was little more than a faint recollection.

3 **Fort Benton** (formerly known as Fort Clay): In the late fall of 1845, Alexander Culbertson established a Blackfoot trading post for Pierre Chouteau, Jr., & Company some distance below the Falls of the Missouri (about five miles above today's Fort Benton, Montana). Built in the bottomland on the Missouri's right side, the post was named Fort Lewis in honor of Meriwether Lewis, co-commander of the Corps of Discovery, and replaced Fort Chardon at the mouth of the Judith (in central Montana).[12]

Because there was no suitable ford near Fort Lewis, Indians on the west side of the Missouri had difficulty crossing over to trade. In the spring of 1847, the company relocated the trading post a few miles downstream on the river's left bank

Fort Benton Warehouse

65

(now the town of Fort Benton, Montana),[13] a place the traders hoped would be more convenient for their Blackfoot customers. The new post was named Fort Clay, although many people called it Fort Lewis after its predecessor. Three years after Fort Clay opened, *engagés* began rebuilding its cottonwood structures from adobe, a chore that lasted the decade.[14] On Christmas Day 1850, Alexander Culbertson rechristened the post Fort Benton, honoring Missouri's Senator Thomas Hart Benton, a longtime friend of the American Fur Company and Pierre Chouteau, Jr.

Between June 1859, and August 1860, Lieutenant John Mullan built a military road connecting the Army's Fort Walla Walla (near Walla Walla, Washington and not to be confused with the Hudson's Bay Company's Fort Walla Walla) with Fort Benton.[15] On July 2, one month before the "Mullan Road" reached the Missouri River, two Chouteau steamboats–the *Chippewa* and *Key West No. 2*–landed three hundred soldiers at Fort Benton, making it the first time steamboats had ascended so far up the

Keelboat at Fort Benton

Missouri. A rock shelf in the riverbed just above the trading post prevented steamers from continuing upstream.[16]

On June 19, 1866, Pierre Chouteau, Jr., & Company sold the post to the Northwest Fur Company (no affiliation with the North West Company of Montreal), which allowed it to fall into disrepair.[17] Following the breakup of the Northwest Fur Company in 1869, its former partners leased the decaying fort to the US Army, which used it as a freight depot until the mid-1870s.

3 **Fort Benton** (Missouri Fur Company): Named for Missouri's Senator Thomas Hart Benton, the Missouri Fur Company's Fort Benton was located near the confluence of the Bighorn and Yellowstone rivers (about sixty miles east of Billings, Montana). The post's founding and even its building site are clouded in uncertainty. The best guess places it on the Yellowstone, two or three miles below the mouth of the Bighorn. Fort Benton was constructed either in the fall of 1821 by Missouri Fur Company *partisans* (trapping brigade commanders), Michael Immell and Robert Jones, or in the fall of 1822.[18]

The deaths of Immell and Jones at the hands of the Blackfeet in the spring of 1823 compelled Joshua Pilcher, the Missouri Fur Company's field manager, to withdraw his trappers from the upper Missouri and Yellowstone, leaving Fort Benton to rot.

7 **Bent's "Old" Fort** (known officially as Fort William): During the years 1833–34, William Bent constructed Bent, St. Vrain & Company's most famous trading post, locating it on the north bank of the Arkansas River approximately twelve miles upstream from the mouth of the Purgatoire (between La Junta and Las Animas, Colorado). The fort's adobe structure replaced a log stockade that Bent had built near the mouth of Fountain Creek, probably in late 1831 (in the vicinity of Pueblo, Colorado; see Fort William–Bent's log stockade–endnote 10). In size and importance, Bent's adobe fort rivaled the American Fur Company's forts Union and Pierre. Bent, St. Vrain & Company dissolved in early 1849,[19] with William Bent retaining ownership of the Arkansas

Bent's "Old" Fort

Bent's
"Old" Fort

Trade
Goods
at Bent's
"Old" Fort

Screw Fur Press
at Bent's
"Old" Fort

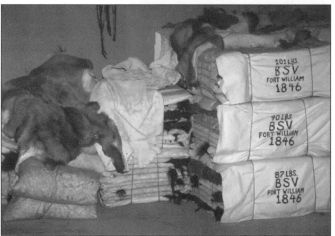

Buffalo
Robe Packs
at Bent's
"Old" Fort

River post. That summer a cholera epidemic killed half of the Southern Cheyennes who were Bent's friends and primary customers. Disheartened, William Bent removed all the trade goods and other stores from his fort and, in August 1849, blew it to smithereens.[20]

7 **Bent's "New" Fort:** During the summer and early autumn of 1853, William Bent established a new trading post on the Arkansas, building it on the river's north bank in a wooded bottomland known as Big Timbers (nine miles west of Lamar, Colorado). Made from sandstone, Bent's "New" Fort was slightly smaller than his old adobe fort, whose charred ruins sat about thirty miles upstream.[21] Because the new post was never profitable, Bent rented it to the US Army in July 1857, replacing it with a small trading stockade near the mouth of the Purgatoire River (east of Las Animas, Colorado). Later that year, the Army returned the sandstone fort to Bent, who again staffed it with traders although he spent little time there. In February 1860, Bent offered to sell the post to the Army for twelve thousand dollars but his offer was refused. In early September the Army again rented the fort–for sixty-five dollars a month–using it as a storage facility.[22] That autumn, crews constructed military barracks around the outside of the stone stockade. Originally called Fort Fauntleroy, the facility was soon renamed Fort Wise after Virginia's Governor Henry Wise; in June 1862, after Virginia seceded from the Union, the Army switched the name to Fort Lyon in honor of deceased Brigadier General Nathaniel Lyon.[23]

In July of that year, William Bent again tried enticing the Army to buy his stone fort. Once more the War Department declined, this time claiming that the land belonged not to Bent but to the Indians.[24] For the next several years Bent repeatedly attempted either to sell his fort to the government or have it returned to him; however, his pleas were continually rebuffed. Flooding by the Arkansas River prompted the Army to abandon Fort Lyon in June 1867, after building its replacement–also called Fort Lyon–about twenty-five miles upstream (the site of the Fort

Lyon Veterans Hospital, near Las Animas, Colorado).[25] Now worthless, Bent's sandstone fort was left deserted.

7 **Fort Bernard and the Sarpy's Point Posts:** In 1837, Peter Sarpy[26] founded the first trading post at this North Platte River site that sat eight miles east of Pratte, Chouteau & Company's Fort Lucien (see Fort Laramie for the many names by which the Laramie River post was known; Sarpy's North Platte trading house, sometimes called Fort Sarpy, was located about four miles northwest of Lingle, Wyoming). Unable to compete with Fort Lucien, Peter Sarpy abandoned his venture within the year.[27]

In 1845, John Richard (or Richards) constructed a small log post at Sarpy's Point, naming it Fort Bernard for the trading firm of Bernard Pratte, Jr., and John Cabanné, Jr. Like nearby Fort Platte, which it replaced, Fort Bernard was intended to compete with Pierre Chouteau, Jr., & Company's Laramie River trading post—formerly Fort Lucien, now rebuilt and renamed Fort John (Pratte, Chouteau & Company had become Pierre Chouteau, Jr., & Company in 1839).[28] Discouraged that they could do little more than be a thorn in the side of Fort John, Bernard Pratte, Jr., and John Cabanné, Jr., soon ended their partnership, leaving Fort Bernard to its *bourgeois,* John Richard.[29] The new owner enjoyed little success, for in late 1846, a fire reduced his trading house to ashes.[30]

In late 1849 or early 1850, James Bordeaux and Joseph Bissonette built yet another small trading post at Sarpy's Point. Their partnership splintered after one year with Bissonette moving three miles up the North Platte to the fort (or what was left of it) that he had owned before joining Bordeaux.[31] Bordeaux retained the Sarpy's Point post and continued operating it for a number of years (for more about James Bordeaux see Bordeaux's Post).[32]

4 **"Old" Fort Berthold** (aka Fort James): Following the upper Missouri smallpox scourge of 1837, the Hidatsas and a handful of surviving Mandans deserted their Knife River villages near Fort Clark, relocating forty-two miles up the Missouri at Fishhook Bend (now under Lake Sakakawea in west-central North Dakota).[33]

Eager to again secure the tribes' loyalty, Pierre Chouteau, Jr., & Company sent James Kipp and Francis Chardon, in the fall of 1845, to establish a trading post. The men built the stockade on the left side of the Missouri near the Indians' Like-A-Fishhook Village.[34]

First called Fort James after James Kipp, the post was soon renamed Fort Berthold in honor of either Pierre or Frederick Berthold, cousins and long-standing associates of Pierre Chouteau, Jr. In 1862, Sioux warriors set fire to the fort, destroying many of its buildings[35] and prompting Chouteau's traders to move into nearby Fort Atkinson (not to be confused with the Army's Fort Atkinson at Council Bluffs) which had been abandoned after its owners sold out to Pierre Chouteau, Jr., & Company two years before (see "New" Fort Berthold—formerly known as Fort Atkinson—and Fort Defiance for details).

4 **"New" Fort Berthold** (formerly known as Fort Atkinson): In the summer of 1858, Frost, Todd & Company—a consortium of investors backed by former mountain man Robert Campbell—built a trading post on the left side of the Missouri near Fishhook Bend, separated from the Chouteau company's Fort Berthold by Like-A-Fishhook Village of the Hidatsas and Mandans (now covered by North Dakota's Lake Sakakawea). The Frost & Todd owners named their post Fort Atkinson after resident partner Edward Atkinson.[36]

In November 1859, Frost, Todd & Company dissolved, passing Fort Atkinson to Charles Primeau and Malcolm Clark. After Robert Campbell declined to finance them, the two partners struggled to compete with Fort Berthold but soon admitted defeat. In 1860, they sold out to Pierre Chouteau, Jr., and his son, Charles.[37] Though larger than nearby Fort Berthold, Fort Atkinson remained empty for two years until a fire at the older post forced its traders to shift their operation. Fort Atkinson was then renamed Fort Berthold.

Sioux unrest brought the Sixth Iowa Cavalry to the region in the summer of 1864. The following winter the troops constructed quarters just beyond the fort's palisades.[38] As the spring of 1865 began, the Chouteaus sold the old trading post to the recently organized Northwest Fur Company.[39] In June 1867, the Army withdrew. Surviving the breakup of the Northwest Fur Company in 1869, Fort Berthold served as a trading post and Indian agency until 1874, the year it finally closed.[40]

2 **Big Timbers Trading Post:** See Smith's Fort.

6 **Bijou's Post:** See Cedar Island.

7 **Joseph Bissonette's North Platte Post:** In late 1843 or early 1844, Joseph Bissonette constructed a tiny, log trading cabin beside the North Platte River, a few miles downstream from the mouth of the Laramie (in the vicinity of Lingle, Wyoming).[41] Bissonette had worked for the American Fur Company and its successors before joining Sibille, Adams & Company in the early 1840s. When that partnership folded in 1843, he opted to remain on the North Platte as an independent trader. Following the sale of Fort John (aka Fort Laramie) to the US Army in June 1849, Bissonette formed a short-lived partnership with James Bordeaux who had been the senior trader at the Laramie River post. The two men erected a trading house at Sarpy's Point, about eight miles east of Fort John.[42] After the partners had a falling-out, Bordeaux kept the Sarpy's Point post and Bissonette moved three miles upstream and, either reoccupied his old North Platte post, or built a replacement. In time Bissonette expanded his operation to include small posts near the confluence of the North Platte and Deer Creek (Glenrock, Wyoming) and on La Bonte Creek (south of Douglas, Wyoming).

6,8 **Blacksnake Hills Post:** Around 1825, Joseph Robidoux III built the Blacksnake Hills Post on the left bank of the Missouri, downstream from its confluence with the Nodaway River. In 1843, this eldest of the Robidoux brothers platted a town around his trading house, naming it in honor of his patron saint. Within five years St. Joseph, Missouri, boasted eighteen hundred residents, and twelve months later, hucksters were proclaiming it the premier starting point for forty-niners rushing to the California goldfields.[43]

1 **Fort Boisé** (aka Snake Fort and Big Wood Fort) **and other Boise River Posts:** In August 1813, Astorian John Reed (or Reid) erected the first trading post near the confluence of the Snake and Boise rivers (via road, about five miles northwest of Parma, Idaho). While his trappers dispersed to hunt beaver, Reed traded for horses with the neighboring tribes. War between the United States and Great Britain had thrown the Pacific Fur Company's partners into a panic. Because most of them wanted to abandon the Oregon country and return to St. Louis, horses were needed for the overland trek.

Just after the New Year, Shoshone warriors of the Dog Rib band attacked Pierre Dorion, Jacob Reznor, and Giles Leclerc who were working some streams about five-days' march from Reed's trading house. Though mortally wounded, Leclerc crawled to the trappers' nearby cabin and told Marie Dorion, the Indian wife of Pierre Dorion, that her husband and Reznor were dead. Knowing

Fort Boisé

**Fort Boisé
Hudson's Bay
Marker**

that the Shoshones would likely come to kill her, Marie helped Leclerc and her two children onto a horse and started for Reed's post. Midway there, Leclerc died. Two days later the woman arrived at the mouth of the Boise River and discovered Reed and all of his *engagés* lying in their own blood. Counted among the victims were Edward Robinson and John Hoback.

Desperate to save her children, Marie Dorion pointed her pony west, determined to reach Fort Astoria and safety. Winter caught her in the Blue Mountains (in central Oregon), killing her emaciated horse. Fighting to survive, the young woman built a shelter against the cold and snow, then settled in to await the spring thaw, her only food being stringy horse meat, pine nuts, and the few rabbits she could snare. Half-dead from starvation by the time she was able to continue, Marie bundled up her children and struggled to the Columbia River where they were rescued by a North West Company trapping party.[44]

In 1819, Nor'Wester–and former Astorian–Donald McKenzie founded the second trading house near the mouth of the Boise; however, Indian attacks soon forced its abandonment.[45]

In the autumn of 1834, Thomas McKay established the third post near the confluence of the Boise and Snake rivers.[46] Owned by the Hudson's Bay Company, McKay's Fort Boisé was intended to counter Nathaniel Wyeth's Fort Hall, three hundred miles to the east. Subsequent factors François Payette and James Craigie replaced Fort Boisé's original cottonwood logs with sun-dried adobe bricks. After the decline of the fur trade, the post became an important stop for travelers on the Oregon Trail. Then in 1853, flooding changed the Snake's channel, destroyed the fort's stockade, and forced company *engagés* to move the outbuildings to higher ground. Three years later when Indian hostility and declining emigration made Fort Boisé unprofitable, the Hudson's Bay Company locked its gates and withdrew.[47]

In 1863, the US Army established a garrison forty-three miles upstream from the mouth of the Boise River (Boise, Idaho), also naming it Fort Boise. This garrison became Boise Barracks in 1879. The fort housed troops until 1913 when it was closed. Since then, the Army has reopened it several times.

2 **Fort Bonneville** (aka Fort Nonsense and Bonneville's Folly): In 1831, Captain Benjamin Louis Eulalie de Bonneville secured a two-year leave from the US Army in order to try his hand at the fur trade. After obtaining the financial support of Alfred Seton, a wealthy New York merchant and former clerk at John Jacob Astor's Fort Astoria, Bonneville went to Missouri and began implementing his plan. Using Fort Osage (near Sibley, Missouri) as his staging point, Bonneville spent the winter assembling the trading goods, supplies, weapons, wagons, horses, mules, oxen, and 110 trappers he needed to launch his expedition. Ready at last, Bonneville's large brigade lumbered west from the Army fort on May Day 1832.[48]

After traveling up the Platte, North Platte, and Sweetwater rivers, Bonneville crossed the Continental Divide at South Pass on July 24,[49] then built a trading post on the high plains within sight of the Wind River Mountains. He located his fort three hundred yards west of the Green River, five miles above its confluence with Horse Creek (about fifteen miles west of Pinedale, Wyoming).[50] Most experienced trappers thought the site foolish because it was uninhabitable during the region's severe winters. As a result, they alternately dubbed it "Fort Nonsense" and "Bonneville's Folly."[51] For the next three years, Bonneville used the fort as his headquarters when not in the field with his brigades. Competition from the American and Rocky Mountain Fur companies eventually bankrupted Bonneville's operation. In 1835, two years past his authorized leave, he returned east and learned that the Army had dropped him from its rolls. Although he had sent a letter from the mountains asking for an extension to his leave, his request had been misplaced. During the next eight months while he sought reinstatement, Bonneville wrote about his western travels, eventually selling the unpolished manuscript to Washington Irving.[52] The noted author rewrote the book and published it as *The Rocky Mountains; or Scenes, Incidents and Adventures in the Far West*. Later Irving re-titled it *The Adventures of Captain Bonneville*. By then the Army had returned Bonneville to active duty.

Benjamin Bonneville enjoyed a distinguished Army career, seeing service in Florida's Second Seminole War and the Mexican War. In the latter conflict he was wounded by grapeshot at Churubusco. Too old for a battle command during the Civil War, he supervised recruit training at Benton Barracks in St. Louis. Shortly before his assassination, Abraham Lincoln signed Bonneville's promotion to brevet brigadier general. The former mountain man and venerable soldier died at the age of eighty-two on June 12, 1878.

2 **Bonneville's Salmon River Post:** Benjamin Bonneville erected a short-lived trading house at the western foot of the

Bitterroot Mountains in early autumn 1832, a few weeks after leaving his newly established "Fort Nonsense" (see Fort Bonneville– aka Fort Nonsense and Bonneville's Folly). Located on the left side of the Salmon River, five miles below its confluence with the Lemhi (downstream from Salmon, Idaho, and across from Carmen), the post was little more than a collection of primitive log cabins from which the Army-captain-turned-mountain-man traded with the visiting Nez Perces and Flatheads.[53] Bonneville had hoped to winter here, but in mid-November, shortages of game and grass forced him to relocate his camp about a day's march down (north) the Salmon. The next month he again switched sites, moving along the Salmon to its confluence with the North Fork, then up this tributary to a narrow, protected valley.[54] Just before the first of the year, he left his latest camp and rode up the Salmon to the Pahsimeroi Valley, then turned southwest, eventually reaching the Snake River Plain where he searched for one of his brigades that was overdue.

7 **Bordeaux's Post:** Perhaps as early as 1833 and definitely by 1837, American Fur Company traders from Fort Pierre (across

Cargo Bound for St. Louis
(Bordeaux's Post)

Bordeaux's Post

from Pierre, South Dakota) established a small, seasonal trading house for the Brulé Sioux on Bordeaux Creek, a tributary of the White River (about three miles east of Chadron, Nebraska).[55] During the 1840s, James Bordeaux–from whom the post and near-by creek took their names–operated the outlet as a winter trading house or satellite of Pierre Chouteau, Jr., & Company's Fort John (aka Fort Laramie). Marie Huntkalutawin, Bordeaux's Corn Band Brulé wife, helped ensure the Sioux's friendship and the post's success.[56] When not at Bordeaux Creek, Bordeaux worked as a clerk and trader at Fort John, occasionally taking command when the *bourgeois* was absent.[57]

Bordeaux quit the Chouteau company shortly after it sold Fort John to the US Army in 1849, and began competing with his former employer between the North Platte and White rivers. From 1850 to 1868, Bordeaux used his post on Bordeaux Creek as a headquarters to support his far-flung trading ventures, which included posts on Rawhide Creek near Rawhide Butte (now called

Pole Fur Press at
Bordeaux's Post

Rawhide Mountain, the butte is located about twelve miles south of Lusk, Wyoming; the trading post's location is unknown), and another at Sarpy's Point, overlooking the North Platte (about four miles northwest of Lingle, Wyoming).[58]

After Bordeaux and Marie moved to the Dakotas in the late 1860s, their son, Louis, intermittently operated the Bordeaux Creek post for another four years, eventually turning it over to Francis Boucher. The new owner brought down the wrath of the Army by selling repeating rifles to the Sioux. Soldiers from nearby Fort Robinson (located a few miles west of Crawford, Nebraska) evicted Boucher from Bordeaux's old trading house in 1876.[59]

6 **Fort Bouis:** See Fort Defiance.

6 **Brazeau's or Brassaux's Fort** (aka Fort Lookout): See Fort Kiowa.

4 **Brazeau's Trading Houses:** In the years leading up to 1820, Joseph Brazeau, Jr., built several small, temporary trading forts on the north side of the Yellowstone River, about fifty miles above its confluence with the Missouri.[60]

2 **Fort Bridger:** Between the summers of 1842 and 1843, Jim Bridger and Louis Vasquez–with backing from Pierre Chouteau, Jr., & Company–built Fort Bridger on the left bank of Black's Fork of the Green River (in southwest Wyoming, about thirty miles east of Evanston).[61]

Although Bridger and Vasquez traded with visiting Indian tribes, their primary customers were the Oregon-bound families who needed to repair their wagons and replenish their dwindling supplies. Sitting at the intersection of the Oregon and Cherokee trails (the Cherokee Trail connected Bent's Fort and Fort Pueblo

Entrance to Fort Bridger

Fur Press & Interior of Fort Bridger

on the Arkansas River with Sacramento, California), the fort was the first trading post established specifically to serve America's westward migration.[62] During its early years Fort Bridger was the only place between Fort John (aka Fort Laramie in eastern Wyoming) and Fort Hall (in southeastern Idaho) where an emigrant could fatten his oxen on good grass while a blacksmith replaced a damaged tire on his wagon. Many historians mark the end of the mountain man era with Fort Bridger's formal opening in 1843. Because Jim Bridger could never shed his wanderlust, the day-to-day operation of the trading post fell to his partner, Louis Vasquez. Bridger preferred trapping and guiding for the Army or for wealthy Europeans who wanted a taste of the frontier.

Soon after the Mormons began settling the Salt Lake Valley in 1847, friction heated between their leader, Brigham Young, and Bridger. By the early 1850s, Mormon distrust of the US Government, coupled with the Latter Day Saints' desire to supply the Oregon-bound emigrants, led Young to pressure Bridger and

Vasquez to sell their fort. When Bridger resisted, a rumor that he was furnishing lead and gunpowder to the Indians and urging them to massacre Mormon settlers gave Young the pretext to confiscate his adversary's property.[63] In 1853, a Mormon posse raided the Black's Fork trading post but missed capturing Bridger who had ridden off after being forewarned. Brigham Young's agents

Above:
Bourgeois's
Quarters at Fort
Bridger

Right:
Exterior Wall
of Lodgings at
Fort Bridger

took possession of Fort Bridger, claiming they had bought it from Vasquez.[64] If Louis Vasquez agreed to sell, he most likely did so while staring down the barrel of a Mormon rifle. The following spring the Utah Territorial Legislature annexed Fort Bridger into the newly created Green River County. Over the next three years, while Mormon traders at Bridger's fort catered to the passing emigrant wagons, relations between the Latter Day Saints and Washington, DC, steadily deteriorated.

In 1857, the US Government initiated the so-called "Mormon War," dispatching Colonel Albert Sidney Johnston to prevent Brigham Young and his followers from establishing an independent nation. That September, Army detachments from Fort Leavenworth set up Camp Winfield on Ham's Fork of the Green River, about thirty-five miles northeast of Fort Bridger and near the site of the 1834 mountain man rendezvous. When armed Mormon units from Fort Bridger began harassing Johnston's troops, the colonel ordered his men to march on Black's Fork. Knowing that they were too few to defend Bridger's former trading post, the Mormons burned it before retreating to strongholds near Salt Lake City. Johnston left his supply train at the ruined fort, then went into winter camp farther up Black's Fork, intending to carry the battle to the Mormons in the spring.[65] Hoping to recoup the losses he had suffered when Brigham Young misappropriated Fort Bridger in 1853, Jim Bridger leased the charred remains to the Army for six hundred dollars per year. In early 1858, a mediator from Washington stepped into the fray and negotiated a truce; the Mormon War ended without ever really starting. The Army retained Fort Bridger, replacing the scorched stockade with new buildings. Because Jim Bridger could not provide clear title to the fort's land, the government refused to make the lease payments or to buy the old trading post from him; however, years later after Bridger had died, the Army did pay his heirs six thousand dollars for the original ten-year lease.[66] Except for a two-year hiatus (1878–80), the Army occupied Fort Bridger until 1890.[67]

3 **Fort Brulé:** See Fort McKenzie.

2 **Fort Buenaventura** (aka Brown's Fort): In 1836, nineteen-year-old Miles Goodyear hired on with the Whitman-Spalding missionary party as it prepared to journey to the Oregon country and convert the Cayuse and Nez Perce Indians to Christianity. (For more about Dr. Marcus Whitman, the Reverend Henry Spalding, and their wives, see Fort Walla Walla–formerly called Fort Nez

Right:
Fort
Buenaventura

Below:
Interior of Fort
Buenaventura

Perces.) Although Goodyear worked diligently at his chores, his interest lay not in spreading the Word of God but in becoming a mountain man. That summer, when the party reached Fort Hall on the Snake River (north of Pocatello, Idaho), Goodyear bid the missionaries good-bye and turned his energy to the fur trade.[68] Over the next four years as the price of beaver slid toward oblivion, Goodyear lived his dream of being a trapper.

In 1840, the mountain men celebrated their final rendezvous, a pitiful affair really, especially when compared with the raucous galas of years past. Thereafter, the diehards who clung to the trapper's way of life had to peddle their pelts at fur company trading houses. Even then there was little money in it. Before long, many trappers drifted away from the beaver ponds, either returning to family farms in Missouri or Tennessee, or heading west to take up the plow in Oregon's Willamette Valley. A few became hunters, furnishing meat for tables at posts such as Bent's Fort or Fort Union. And some, like Miles Goodyear, tried horse trading.

After Jim Bridger and Louis Vasquez established Fort Bridger to cater to traffic on the Oregon Trail, Goodyear herded his horses to the Black's Fork post (in southwestern Wyoming) and swapped them to the passing emigrants. Seeing the success his friends were having at their fort, Goodyear rode to the east side of the Great Salt Lake in 1845 and, with the help of his Ute Indian wife, Pomona, built a log trading post on the Weber River, about two miles upstream from its confluence with the Ogden (in Ogden, Utah). A promoter named Lansford Hasting had published a book recommending a shortcut to California—Hasting's Cutoff. The route followed the Weber River through a constricted canyon that emptied at Goodyear's doorstep. In 1846, the Donner party heeded Hasting's advice and wasted precious weeks hacking its way through the difficult terrain. Because of the delay, the Donners were marooned by blizzards in the Sierra Nevada Mountains and resorted to cannibalism. After the Donner disaster, few other wagon trains were willing to give the canyon a try.

With trade at Fort Buenaventura nearly nonexistent, Miles Goodyear sold the post in 1847 to an early Mormon settler, James Brown. While Goodyear and Pomona traveled west to a new life in California, Brown moved his family inside the Buenaventura stockade and renamed it Brown's Fort. Eventually the countryside surrounding the post attracted a host of Latter Day Saints and grew into a thriving town.[69]

7 **Buzzards' Roost:** Around 1842, Maurice LeDuc, William LeBlanc, and a few more French-Canadian trappers built a small, adobe trading post, nicknamed Buzzards' Roost, on the east side of the Wet Mountains beside Adobe Creek (about four or five miles south of Florence, Colorado). Intended for the Utes, Buzzards' Roost was marginally profitable, at best, since the tribe rarely came by to trade. Two years after the post opened, Hardscrabble–a settlement of traders, scratch farmers, and ruffians–sprang up on the nearby creek of the same name. Buzzards' Roost and the fledgling town were abandoned in the late 1840s.[70]

Cabanné's Post through Cruzet's Post

6 **Cabanné's Post:** In 1822 or early 1823, John Cabanné, Sr., established a trading post for Berthold, Chouteau & Pratte,[1] locating it on the west side of the Missouri River, eight miles below Council Bluffs (on the northern outskirts of Omaha, Nebraska).[2] Known as Cabanné's Post, the fort competed with nearby Fort Bellevue for the Omaha trade.

    After Bernard Pratte & Company (formerly Berthold, Chouteau & Pratte) joined the American Fur Company in 1827, Cabanné continued running the Council Bluffs trading house for another six years. In 1833, Joshua Pilcher succeeded Cabanné as *bourgeois* (for the reason, see Leclerc's Posts). Some years later the post was abandoned, and its stores were transferred to Fort Bellevue.[3]

3 **Fort Campbell:** During the late fall and early winter of 1846, Alexander Harvey, managing partner of Harvey, Primeau &

Company, built a small trading post on the left side of the Missouri (between Fort Benton, Montana, and the mouth of the Marias River), a bit downstream from Pierre Chouteau, Jr., & Company's Fort Lewis.[4] Harvey named his post Fort Campbell in honor of his firm's underwriter, Robert Campbell. From the time it opened until 1860, Fort Campbell passed through various partnerships that attempted to challenge the Chouteau empire (see Fort Defiance–aka Fort Bouis–for more about Harvey, Primeau & Company). As America approached the beginning of the Civil War, the Chouteaus bought out their last major competitor and took possession of the rival post. Trading operations were transferred to Fort Benton, and the Fort Campbell stockade was turned over to Catholic missionaries.[5]

5,6,7 **Colin Campbell's Houses:** A quarter-blood Sioux, Colin Campbell worked as a trader for the American Fur Company and its successors from the 1820s until the mid- to late 1850s. During these years he built numerous temporary trading posts for the Sioux, including one at the confluence of the Niobrara and Snake rivers (about twenty-five miles southwest of Valentine, Nebraska)[6], and another at the Forks of the Cheyenne River (in western South Dakota).[7] In the 1840s, he ran a small post for Pierre Chouteau, Jr., & Company at the mouth of Crow Creek, downstream from the Missouri's Grand Detour (near Shelby, South Dakota, on the Crow Creek Indian Reservation).[8]

8 **Fort Carondelet:** Between 1794 and 1795, Auguste Chouteau and his half brother, Pierre, Sr., constructed Fort Carondelet on a limestone bluff on the south side of the Osage River, downstream from the Great Osage village and a little above Panther Creek (in eastern Vernon County, Missouri).[9] The post was named for François Luis Hector Carondelet, the Spanish governor-general of Louisiana. (For more about the Osage Indian trade see Osage Posts and Fort Osage.)

2 **Fort Kit Carson** (known by local Indians as Carson's Houses): A fort in name only, these log huts on the Green River a bit south of its confluence with the Duchesne (about one mile south of Ouray, Utah) housed a company of trappers led by Kit Carson during the winter of 1833–4. The cottonwood-lined bottomland between the Duchesne confluence and that of the White River, which fed into the Green two miles below, had provided shelter to trappers as far back as 1824, when Etienne Provost's brigade also wintered here.[10]

3 **Fort Cass** (aka Tulloch's Fort): In the autumn of 1832, Samuel Tulloch of the American Fur Company built a 130- by 130-foot, cottonwood trading post on the right bank of the Yellowstone River, two or three miles below the mouth of the Bighorn (about sixty miles northeast of Billings, Montana).[11] Although some trappers referred to the post as Tulloch's Fort, its official name was Fort Cass, in honor of Lewis Cass, Secretary of War.

Before the fort was even finished, Tulloch sent the infamous mountain man James Beckwourth to induce the Crows to shift their allegiance and trade from the rival Rocky Mountain Fur Company to the American Fur Company. Beckwourth's success at winning the loyalty of the tribe was demonstrated in the autumn of 1833, when Crow warriors—most likely at Beckwourth's urging—robbed the Rocky Mountain Fur Company brigade of Tom Fitzpatrick. The Indians traded Fitzpatrick's pelts to Tulloch, who forwarded them to Fort Union. When Fitzpatrick protested to the US Government, Kenneth McKenzie, the *bourgeois* of Fort Union, offered to sell him back his own furs with a healthy markup for storage and handling. Fitzpatrick declined the purchase.[12]

Fort Cass was abandoned in 1835, replaced by Fort Van Buren (east of Cartersville, Montana).[13]

7 **Fort Cass** (aka Gantt's Fort): In the fall of 1832, John Gantt established his first trading house on the Arkansas River, locating it on the north bank, most likely near the mouth of Fountain Creek (in Pueblo, Colorado). Called Gantt's Fort, the post consisted of several log cabins protected by a cottonwood stockade.[14]

Kit Carson spent the winter of 1832–3 at Gantt's Fort, as did John Gantt and a number of his trappers. Gantt and his partner,

Jefferson Blackwell, hoped to garner the fur and buffalo robe trade from the neighboring tribes, a venture that put them in direct competition with Bent, St. Vrain & Company.

In May 1834, John Gantt rebuilt his old post with one made from adobe, placing it three miles away from the log fort of Bent, St. Vrain & Company (see Fort William–Bent's log stockade–endnote 10 for the controversy over where these posts were located). As befitting a new establishment, Gantt gave his trading post a fresh name, calling it Fort Cass after Lewis Cass, President Jackson's Secretary of War; nevertheless, many people continued referring to it as Gantt's Fort.

Soon after Fort Cass opened, William Bent became convinced that a band of Shoshones–they were a long way from home–had stolen some mules from his brother, Charles. On July 29, William raided the tribe's camp beside Fort Cass, killing three warriors and driving off the rest. Gantt & Blackwell's employees watched the skirmish from inside their palisades, never coming to the Indians' aid. Because the Shoshones had been visiting Fort Cass, Indian mores dictated that Gantt & Blackwell should have given them its protection. The incident showed Bent, St. Vrain & Company to be the stronger firm, prompting the local Cheyennes and Arapahos to shift their trade from Fort Cass to the new adobe fort (Bent's "New" Fort) that William Bent had opened a few months earlier. Having lost its customers, Gantt & Blackwell folded in late 1834, and its partners abandoned Fort Cass.[15]

6   **Cedar Fort** (aka Fort aux Cédres): See Fort Recovery.

6   **Cedar Island:** In the late 1700s, the trader Régis Loisel quit the North West Company and immigrated to St. Louis. In 1796 or 1797, he became a partner with Jacques Clamorgan during the demise of Clamorgan's Company of the Discoverers and Explorers of the Missouri River (for more about Clamorgan's firm see Mandan Villages). A few years later Loisel ended his association with Clamorgan and, in 1801, formed a partnership with another former Nor'West trader, Hugh Heney.[16]

Although the record is murky about the date, around the

time the two men became partners, Loisel established a trading fort on the south side of a one-and-one-half-mile-long, cedar-covered island—not surprisingly called Cedar Island—above the Missouri River's Grand Detour (on the Lower Brulé Indian Reservation, about thirty-five miles below Pierre, South Dakota).[17] Known as Loisel's Fort and Fort aux Cédres, the trading post was intended for the Sioux. Soon after founding the fort, Loisel sent Heney to open a satellite post at the mouth of the Cheyenne River (see Heney's Sioux Post). During the winter of 1803–4, the Sioux so abused Loisel that he decided to abandon Cedar Island and return to St. Louis.[18] Not wanting to forfeit the Missouri entirely, he sent his clerk, Pierre-Antoine Tabeau, upriver to trade with the Arikaras (see Tabeau's Arikara Post). Hugh Heney, no doubt, suffered the same rough treatment as his partner, since he deserted his Cheyenne River post and skedaddled back to Canada and the North West Company, thereby ending his relationship with Loisel. On September 22, 1804, during the Corps of Discovery's journey up the Missouri, and during the return two years later, Lewis and Clark stopped by the Cedar Island fort, reporting its buildings in good condition.

In 1809, the St. Louis Missouri Fur Company opened a trading post in Loisel's abandoned fort. The next spring, a fire destroyed the stockade and a fur inventory valued between twelve thousand and fifteen thousand dollars.[19] In the fall of 1811, the company repaired the fort and, again, traded with the Sioux.

During the summer of 1812, Manuel Lisa—now managing partner of the newly organized Missouri Fur Company—ordered the Cedar Island post to be rebuilt, appointing Louis Bijou its *bourgeois* and giving him four thousand dollars worth of goods.[20] Soon afterwards, the War of 1812 raised British influence among the Plains tribes, making the river hazardous for American traders. Although the Missouri Fur Company abandoned most of its posts, Bijou managed to operate his trading house and hang onto his scalp. Despite his effort, the Cedar Island fort could not keep the Missouri Fur Company afloat. The pelts Bijou shipped to St. Louis were too few to pull the firm's ledgers into the black, especially with the war driving the price of beaver below $2.50 per pound.

In the fall of 1813, the partners auctioned off the company's property and, shortly after the New Year, dissolved their partnership. Lisa retained Bijou's post along with a fort at Council Bluffs (see Fort Lisa) and continued to run them during and after the war.[21]

Around 1819, Joseph Brazeau, Jr., opened a trading post near a cedar island for Berthold & Chouteau; it lasted for at least two years, perhaps longer.[22] The record is unclear whether this was Loisel's Cedar Island above the Grand Detour or another one downstream.

6 **Fort aux Cédres** (aka Cedar Fort): See Cedar Island and Fort Recovery.

6 **Cerré's Establishment** (aka Teton Post, Papin's House, and the French Post): See Fort Teton.

7 **Chadron Creek Trading Post** (aka Chartran Trading Post): In 1841, *engagés* working for Lancaster P. Lupton erected a small trading house on Chadron Creek, several miles upstream from its confluence with the White River (about six miles south of Chadron, Nebraska; for more about Lupton see Fort Platte). The post was intended to compete for the Sioux traffic with Pierre Chouteau, Jr., & Company's nearby Bordeaux Post.

A year later Lupton sold his trading business to Sibille, Adams & Company, which installed Louis B. Chartran as *bourgeois* of the Chadron Creek Post.[23] In 1843, Sibille & Adams sold out to Bernard Pratte, Jr., and John Cabanné, Jr., who continued employing Chartran until their partnership dissolved two years later. The Chadron Creek Post probably closed soon thereafter.[24]

2,3 **Fort Chardon** (aka Fort F.A.C.): In early 1844, Francis Chardon, *bourgeois* of Pierre Chouteau, Jr., & Company's Fort McKenzie, and his senior trader, Alexander Harvey, revenged the killing of a black bondman by murdering a party of Blackfeet who had come to the upper Missouri post to trade (see Fort McKenzie for the massacre's details; the post was located several miles downriver from Fort Benton, Montana). The tribe retaliated, boycotting

Fort McKenzie and making the surrounding prairie unsafe for Chouteau traders. Wanting to escape the Indian hostility and hoping that a new post would entice the Blackfeet to resume their commerce, Chardon burned Fort McKenzie and, that spring, began constructing its replacement. Naming the post for himself, he built it on the left side of the Missouri River, a bit below its confluence with the Judith (near the Chouteau-Fergus county line in central Montana). The ploy failed. The Blackfeet continued attacking Chouteau traders and spurned the new fort, bartering their robes at the Union Fur Company's Fort Cotton instead (five miles above Fort Benton, Montana).[25]

In the spring of 1845, the financial backers of the Union Fur Company decided to end their money-losing venture by selling their trading posts to their competitor, Pierre Chouteau, Jr. That summer Alexander Culbertson, head of the Chouteau operation on the upper Missouri, relieved Francis Chardon as *bourgeois* of Fort Chardon.[26] Determined to regain the Blackfoot trade, Culbertson stripped the post of its merchandise and equipment, taking everything upriver. In the bottomland near the now deserted Fort Cotton, he constructed Fort Lewis. With the Union Fur Company no longer operating on the upper Missouri, the Blackfeet had no choice—other than a long ride to a Hudson's Bay Company post— but to renew their trade with Pierre Chouteau, Jr., & Company. Culbertson burned Fort Chardon, but it is unclear whether he set it ablaze in the fall of 1845, or the following spring when he returned to Fort Union (the company's headquarters post near the mouth of the Yellowstone) with his winter's take of robes.[27]

4 **Fort Charles** (Bruguier & Booge): In the autumn of 1861, the trading firm of Bruguier & Booge built Fort Charles on the left side of the Missouri River near the mouth of Prairie Elk Creek (on the Fort Peck Indian Reservation, close to Oswego, Montana). After unsuccessfully competing with Pierre Chouteau, Jr., & Company for a couple of years, Bruguier & Booge abandoned the post, ordering its people downriver. In late 1863, Robert Meldrum claimed the deserted fort for the Chouteaus and re-established its trade.[28]

5,6 **Fort Charles** (James Mackay): In the late fall of 1795, James Mackay of the Company of the Discoverers and Explorers of the Missouri River built Fort Charles on the west side of the Missouri, between the river and the Omaha villages (on the Omaha Indian Reservation, six miles downstream from Omadi, Nebraska; for details see Mandan Villages). The trading post was abandoned in the spring of 1797.[29]

7 **Chartran Trading Post:** See Chadron Creek Trading Post.

7 **Auguste Chouteau's Post** (Canadian River): See Fort Mason (aka Camp Holmes).

8 **Chouteau's Post** (aka Kansas Post): By the early 1790s, Pierre Chouteau, Sr., and his half brother, Auguste, had begun trading with the Kansas Indians near the confluence of the Kansas and Missouri rivers.[30] In 1798, the Spanish government of Louisiana granted John Cabanné, Sr., and Gregory Sarpy a trading license for the tribe, and the two partners soon opened a small post (probably in the vicinity of Kansas City, Missouri).[31] The governor-general renewed their license for the next three years, but in 1802, Jacques Clamorgan persuaded a new governor-general to give him all the Missouri trade except for the Pawnees and Osages. The assignment of licenses remained more or less the same in 1803, the year the United States purchased the Louisiana Territory.[32]

With the American government now administering the licenses, the Chouteau brothers regained the Kansas trade. Soon afterwards, Pierre, Sr.'s second oldest son, Pierre, Jr., entered the family fur business as a teenager, serving first as a clerk and then as a trader.[33]

In 1813, Pierre, Jr., formed a partnership with his brother-in-law, Bartholomew Berthold, and on May 1 opened a store in St. Louis. Although the shop did a profitable business in dry goods and crockery, the lure of beaver was too strong for the young men to ignore, especially Pierre Chouteau, Jr., who had been born to the fur trade the way a naval officer's son is born to the sea. A year after becoming partners, Chouteau and Berthold began sending their own traders to the lower Missouri. Then sometime before 1819, François Chouteau, the half brother of Pierre, Jr., and one or more of the Cerré brothers opened a Berthold & Chouteau trading house for the Kansas Indians. Known as both Chouteau's Post and Kansas Post, it sat on an island in the Missouri River, three miles below the mouth of the Kansas (in Kansas City, Missouri). After floods destroyed the post in 1826, workmen rebuilt it on the south side of the Kansas River, thirteen miles west of the original site (in Kansas City, Kansas).[34] In the late 1830s, the post was managed by Cyprian Chouteau, another of Pierre, Jr.'s many brothers.[35]

4 **Fort Clark** (American Fur Company): In the spring or summer of 1831, James Kipp built an American Fur Company trading post atop a high bank on the right side of the Missouri River, eight miles downstream from the mouth of the Knife (near Fort Clark, North Dakota, about fifty-five miles northwest of Bismarck). Kipp named the 120- by 160-foot fort after William Clark of Lewis and Clark fame.[36] Three years later, John Jacob Astor unloaded his majority interest in the American Fur Company, and its Upper Missouri Outfit and Western Department passed to Pratte, Chouteau & Company.

On June 19, 1837, Pratte & Chouteau's steamboat *St. Peter's* stopped at Fort Clark, delivering the annual stock of trade goods and supplies.[37] In addition to the usual gunpowder, blankets, and beads that the crewmen off-loaded, they also brought ashore smallpox, unleashing an epidemic that eventually spread death across the entire upper Missouri. Among the nearby Mandans, it destroyed over ninety percent of the tribe; by some estimates, fewer than 140 members escaped.[38] All who did wore pockmark brands for the remainder of their lives. After the disease ran its course, the surviving Hidatsas and Mandans migrated forty-two miles upriver to Fishhook Bend (see "Old" Fort Berthold). Arikaras, who had been visiting the Mandans and had also suffered from the smallpox, appropriated their hosts' deserted lodges near Fort Clark, giving the post a reason to remain open.[39]

In the late 1840s, Harvey, Primeau & Company built Fort

Primeau about three hundred yards from Fort Clark. This competing post passed through the hands of several firms before the last one folded in 1860 (see Fort Defiance for details about Chouteau opposition). Shortly afterwards, fire destroyed a portion of Fort Clark, prompting its traders to annex the abandoned Fort Primeau.[40] When the Arikaras moved upriver the following year to join the Hidatsas and Mandans at Like-A-Fishhook Village, Pierre Chouteau, Jr., and his son, Charles, closed Fort Primeau and what remained of Fort Clark, consolidating their trade in "New" Fort Berthold at Fishhook Bend.[41]

8 **Fort Clark** (US Army) (aka Fort Sibley and Fiery Prairie Fort): See Osage Posts and Fort Osage.

4 **Malcolm Clark's Fort:** In the late fall of 1860, Malcolm Clark, *bourgeois* of Pierre Chouteau, Jr., & Company's Fort Union, ordered his workmen to construct a trading house at the confluence of the Missouri and Poplar rivers (near Poplar, Montana). That winter, Clark's traders began the cutthroat competition that eventually drove the rival firm of Charles Larpenteur and Robert Lemon into bankruptcy (see Poplar River Post for details).[42]

1 **Fort Clatsop:** After reaching the Oregon coast in late 1805, Lewis and Clark's Corps of Discovery erected Fort Clatsop as its winter quarters, locating it on the west side of the Lewis and Clark River (formerly the Netul River) about three miles upstream from its entry into Youngs Bay (near Astoria, Oregon).[43] Although Lewis and Clark never intended the fort to be a formal trading post, it immediately became a magnet for the neighboring Clatsops, who bartered dried salmon, elk, seal, and roots to supplement the meager fare brought in by the expedition's hunters. After food, the most coveted assets the tribe had to offer were the sexual favors of its wives and daughters.[44]

Fort Clatsop consisted of two facing log buildings that were separated by a tiny, rectangular parade ground, its ends secured by gates and vertical pickets. The buildings were divided into a storage locker, orderly room, and living compartments. Cramped,

Fort Clatsop
1805–6 Winter Quarters for the Corps of Discovery

damp—during its three-month stay, the Corps had rain eight days out of every nine—and infested with fleas, Fort Clatsop was nothing short of miserable.[45]

Although the Corps of Discovery was a military undertaking, its mission was firmly rooted in the fur trade. In addition to ordering the exploration of the uncharted Louisiana and Oregon territories, President Thomas Jefferson, who fathered the venture, had charged Lewis and Clark to evaluate the country's potential for trapping. Eager to win the upper Missouri and Columbia River Indians away from the North West and Hudson's Bay companies, the President had pressed the two captains to maintain peace with the western tribes and promise them that American traders would soon follow in the expedition's wake.[46]

The Corps of Discovery had begun its exploration up the Missouri on May 14, 1804, traveling in a keelboat and two pirogues. Five months and sixteen hundred miles later, Lewis and Clark reached the Mandans, where they spent the winter (see

Fort Clatsop

Mandan Villages). After sending a portion of their party back to St. Louis, the captains renewed their journey the following April, taking with them the mixed-blood interpreter Toussaint Charbonneau, Sacajawea, his Shoshone wife, and her new-born son. From the headwaters of the Missouri River, the Corps crested the Continental Divide and descended the Clearwater, Snake, and Columbia rivers, reaching the Pacific Ocean in November 1805. Early the next month, the party crossed the Columbia estuary and began chopping logs for Fort Clatsop; construction was completed on December 30.

Winter on the Oregon coast consisted of pouring rain, misty rain, and more rain. Food and clothing rotted in the damp cold, and nearly everyone took sick. Lewis and Clark wrote in their journals while their men stood guard, hunted, dallied with native women, and wished away the hours. When the Corps bid farewell to Fort Clatsop on March 23, 1806, no one shed a tear.[47]

3 **Fort Clay:** See Fort Benton (formerly known as Fort Clay).

1 **Clearwater Post:** See McKenzie's Post.

1 **Fort Colvile:** In 1826, the Hudson's Bay Company established Fort Colvile on the left side of the Columbia River, a bit below Kettle Falls (about ten miles west of Colville–spelled correctly–Washington).[48] Named for Hudson's Bay partner Andrew Colvile, Fort Colvile replaced Spokane House, furnishing grains, potatoes, cattle, pigs, poultry, and horses to the firm's other inland forts.

During the spring of 1829, American *partisan* Jedediah Smith and a companion traveled by canoe from Fort Vancouver to Fort Colvile, then switched to horses as they made their way to David Jackson's winter camp on the Flathead River (in western Montana; Smith and Jackson were partners in Smith, Jackson & Sublette).[49]

In June 1859, the US Army began constructing Harney Depot on Mill Creek, about thirteen miles east of Kettle Falls. A few years later the depot's name was changed to Fort Colville (spelled with three l's) in honor of the Fort Colvile trading post. The Hudson's Bay Company operated its Fort Colvile until the late 1860s. The military abandoned its Fort Colville in 1883 after opening Fort Spokane (not to be confused with the Spokane House trading post) at the confluence of the Spokane and Columbia rivers.[50]

2 **Fort Connah:** With the expanding importance of the robe market in the mid-1840s, the Hudson's Bay Company needed a trading house closer to the buffalo herds than its Flathead Post on the Clark Fork River (in western Montana). East of the Continental Divide, Pierre Chouteau, Jr., & Company dominated trade along the Missouri, offering a strong inducement for the Flathead Indians to sell their robes at Chouteau's newly constructed Fort Lewis (a few miles upstream from Fort Benton, Montana; see Fort Benton–formerly known as Fort Clay). The buffalo roamed the upper Missouri plain, compelling the tribe to range far from its Flathead River Valley in order to hunt. The Hudson's Bay Company wanted to open a trading facility closer to the Flathead's homeland, lest the Fort Lewis *bourgeois* persuade the Indians to move east of the Divide.

In 1846, Neil McArthur came to the Flathead Valley and built a Hudson's Bay trading house beside a stream that soon became known as Post Creek (about two miles southeast of the Ninepipe Reservoir, between St. Ignatius, Montana, and Flathead Lake). Located fifty miles west of old Flathead Post, the new installation consisted of a few log cabins, a corral for the stock, and a small bastion. The following year, Angus McDonald took command of the trading house, naming it after the Connen River in his native Scotland. Because an Indian friend of McDonald's had

Fort Connah

difficulty pronouncing Connen, the factor shortened it to Connah. The abbreviation was not universally accepted, for throughout the fort's existence, Hudson's Bay officials often referred to it as Flathead Post in company correspondence.[51]

The Hudson's Bay Company operated Fort Connah until 1871, when changing government policy forced the concern to abandon its properties below the forty-ninth parallel.[52]

7 **Fort Convenience:** In the early 1830s, Louis Vasquez erected Fort Convenience near the confluence of Clear Creek and the South Platte River (in north Denver, Colorado). Vasquez's trading post operated intermittently at that location until around 1836, when it may have been rebuilt about six miles farther down the South Platte.[53]

3 **Fort Cotton:** During the winter of 1842–3 or early the following spring, the Union Fur Company opened Fort Cotton on the right side of the Missouri, some distance below the river's famous waterfalls (about five miles above Fort Benton, Montana; see forts George and Mortimer for the firm's history). When the Union Fur Company failed in May 1845, its underwriters sold Fort Cotton to Pierre Chouteau, Jr., & Company. That fall, Chouteau-partner Alexander Culbertson stripped the post and constructed Fort Lewis in its shadow.[54]

5 **John Crébassa's Trading House:** See Pembina Posts.

2 **Fort Davy Crockett** (aka Fort de Misère): In 1837, Philip Thompson, William Craig, and Prewitt Sinclair[55] constructed a cottonwood and adobe trading post in Brown's Hole. Named after the legendary self-promoter Davy Crockett, the fort sat on the left side of the Green River, a bit upstream from the mouth of Vermilion Creek (in Brown's Park National Wildlife Refuge just east of the Utah-Colorado border). During the late 1830s and early 1840s, a number of mountain men, including Kit Carson, used the post as a gathering place, especially during the region's harsh winters. Even by the standards of the time, Fort Davy Crockett was a shabby establishment, hence its derisive nickname, Fort de Misère. By 1844, it lay in ruin.[56]

6 **Crooks's and McClellan's Post:** After forming their partnership in early 1807, fur traders Ramsay Crooks and Robert McClellan ascended the Missouri with eighty men, intending to go at least as far as the Yellowstone. A small military force commanded by Ensign Nathaniel Pryor, a former member of the Corps of Discovery, had preceded them on the river, escorting Chief Shahaka to the Mandans. Shahaka had come down from the Mandan villages with Lewis and Clark in 1806, to visit the eastern United States and President Jefferson. In order to induce the chief to make the trip, the government had promised to see him safely back to his people. As Pryor's boats came even with the Arikaras, the tribe attacked, killing four of the party but missing Shahaka. Abandoning the mission, Pryor turned tail for St. Louis. While descending the Missouri, he met Crooks and McClellan coming upstream and warned them that the Arikaras were on the warpath. The traders immediately scuttled their plans for the Yellowstone and dropped below Council Bluffs, where they constructed a post for the Omaha trade on the west side of the Missouri, a bit upstream from the entrance of Papillon Creek (near Bellevue, Nebraska).[57]

In 1809, a large flotilla of keelboats and mackinaws belonging to the St. Louis Missouri Fur Company sailed past the post of Crooks and McClellan, prompting the traders to hastily assemble a forty-man force aboard their own keelboat and follow. Some miles upstream, Crooks and McClellan were stopped by a large band of Sioux warriors who demanded that the traders build them a post. Knowing it would be folly to argue, Crooks and McClellan ordered their *engagés* to begin cutting logs for the palisades. While the work was going on, the Sioux raced to their camp to collect their supply of furs and buffalo robes. As soon as the Indians were out of sight, Crooks and McClellan gathered their men on their boat and retreated downriver to their fort near Council Bluffs. Although it was never proven, the two traders blamed Manuel Lisa, the St. Louis Missouri Fur Company's managing partner, for inciting the Sioux.[58]

Early in 1810, Crooks and McClellan closed their Missouri River post and terminated their partnership. That June, Crooks journeyed to Michilimackinac[59] (Mackinac Island atop Michigan's Lower Peninsula) where he met Wilson Price Hunt, who was hiring trappers for an overland trek to the Oregon coast. Hunt recruited Crooks to the Astorian venture by offering him a share in the Pacific Fur Company, a subsidiary of John Jacob Astor's American Fur Company.[60] During the winter of 1810–11, the Astorians camped at the confluence of the Nodaway and Missouri rivers (a bit above St. Joseph, Missouri). When McClellan happened by the camp on his way to St. Louis, Crooks talked his former partner into joining the expedition. Eager to have him, Hunt also offered McClellan a share in the enterprise. On April 21, 1811, the Astorians left their winter quarters and began their epic journey to the Pacific.

6 **Cruzet's Post:** See Otoe Posts.

Fort Daer through French Post

5 **Fort Daer:** See Pembina Posts.

1 **The Dalles:** In the late 1820s, an American trader and trapper named Bache, who had formerly worked for the Hudson's Bay Company, built a trading post at The Dalles on the Columbia River (east of Portland, Oregon) to compete with his old employer. Aided by his Nez Perce wife, Bache enjoyed an early success attracting Indians away from the British company's inland posts. However, Dr. John McLoughlin, chief factor of the Hudson's Bay Columbia Department, soon responded to Bache's opposition by sending James Birnie to establish a competing trading post. Birnie ruined Bache by over-bidding him for furs. Seeing his profits dwindle to nothing, Bache closed his operation in 1829 or 1830 and re-enlisted in the Hudson's Bay Company as a trapper.[1]

Dauphin Trading Houses: In the 1830s, the American Fur Company and its successors employed at least four Dauphins on the upper Missouri. Charles, Alexis, and Constant were brothers, while Pierre may or may not have been related.[2] In late 1833, one of them worked at a satellite post that was probably located near the confluence of Cherry Creek and the Little Missouri River (between Watford City, North Dakota, and the Fort Berthold Indian Reservation). The post had been built by the fall of 1832, since the trader Pierre Papin wintered there that year.[3]

During the late 1850s and early 1860s, a Louis Dauphin erected a number of one-room, log trading houses along the upper Missouri, between the mouths of the Poplar and Milk rivers (in Montana). Never intended to last more than a season or two, these posts catered to the nomadic bands of Atsinas and Assiniboines that roamed the northern plains. Hating all fur companies equally, the French-Creole Dauphin worked as a free trader, selling his furs and buffalo robes directly to the merchants and brokers in St. Louis rather than to Pierre Chouteau, Jr., & Company or one of its opposition firms. Louis Dauphin eked out a living until 1865 when he lost his hair to a Sioux war party.[4]

2,3 Fort Andrew Dawson: See Fort Andrew.

6 Fort Defiance (aka Fort Bouis): In 1846, Alexander Harvey, Charles Primeau, Joseph Picotte, and Anthony Bouis, all lifelong fur men and former employees of the American Fur Company and its Chouteau-dominated successors, formed Harvey, Primeau, & Company.[5] Each of them was determined to drive a stake through the heart of Pierre Chouteau, Jr., and his trading empire. Although Harvey & Primeau was capitalized at just over fifteen thousand dollars, its ultimate financial strength came from its St. Louis agent and outfitter, Robert Campbell.[6] Campbell had been an early Ashley man and former partner of William Sublette. In years past, Chouteau had forced Campbell and Sublette from the upper Missouri and Laramie rivers (see Fort Laramie and Fort William–Sublette & Campbell for details), so Campbell now sought revenge by backing Harvey & Primeau.

Alexander Harvey and his partners departed St. Louis in early July 1846 on the steamboat *Clermont No. 2*, which was loaded to the gunwales with fifty thousand dollars worth of stores, most of it bankrolled by Campbell. About six miles above the Missouri's Grand Detour, the boat stopped and partner Joseph Picotte, *engagés*, and traders stepped onto the right shore near the mouth of Medicine Creek, ready to construct Fort Defiance (about forty miles southeast of Pierre, South Dakota).[7] The *Clermont No. 2* continued upriver to the mouth of the Yellowstone. There it deposited Harvey and his entourage at the abandoned Fort Mortimer, which they repaired and renamed Fort William (twenty-two miles southwest of Williston, North Dakota). With the late summer days quickly slipping away, Harvey then pressed his carpenters to assemble a mackinaw and raced the approaching winter up the Missouri into Blackfoot country. As the river was about to freeze, he erected Fort Campbell below Chouteau's Fort Clay (near Fort Benton, Montana).[8]

During the next few years, robe traffic on the upper plains was so profitable that Harvey & Primeau sent traders to the Yellowstone for the Crows, and to the new village of the Hidatsas and Mandans at Fishhook Bend (see "Old" Fort Berthold).

Unable to best Harvey, Primeau & Company competitively, Pierre Chouteau, Jr., (in the winter of 1848–9) approached Alexander Harvey and Robert Campbell about merging, but they declined, feeling certain that the contest was theirs to win.[9] Both sides now resolved to intensify their commercial warfare. Chouteau's company had the better time of it in 1849, its haul of robes and furs far outstripping that of Harvey and his partners who were rumored to be at one another's throats over their dismal returns. Yet Harvey & Primeau hung on.

During the 1850s, government contracts to transport annuities to the upper Missouri tribes induced fierce bidding wars between the two firms. Eager for the business, Chouteau repeatedly undercut the rates proposed by Harvey's partnership. Although Chouteau's profits on the annuities were modest, they did allay the overhead of his company's vast supply line.[10] With each season, Pierre Chouteau, Jr., & Company chipped away at

Harvey & Primeau, slowly but steadily eroding the will of its partners and their ability to compete.

On July 20, 1854, after a brief illness, Alexander Harvey died at Fort William, his partnership's post at the mouth of the Yellowstone. Bereft of his leadership, Harvey, Primeau & Company seemed ready to disintegrate until Robert Campbell pressed the surviving owners into reorganizing as J. Picotte & Company.[11] After three more years of mediocre profits, the partners called it quits. Still aching to break his old nemesis, Pierre Chouteau, Jr., Robert Campbell formed a new alliance with Frost, Todd & Company. Charles Primeau stayed up-country, working as a trader on the firm's behalf. With Campbell's backing, Frost & Todd bought Fort Defiance and J. Picotte & Company's other trading posts. In late May 1857, this latest consortium sent its annual outfits up the Missouri aboard the steamboat *Twilight*.[12]

In the autumn of 1859, the principal shareholders of Frost, Todd & Company decided to bow out of the competition with Chouteau, figuring they could earn more money in land speculation in the Dakotas. On November 4, they ended their partnership, transferring their upper Missouri posts to Charles Primeau and his new partner, Malcolm Clark.[13]

As the next decade began, Robert Campbell realized that Primeau and Clark would never be more than a minor nuisance to Chouteau's empire. Campbell had spent much of his life battling the American Fur Company and Chouteau, but now the old former mountain man knew that he was licked. To finance an outfit for Primeau and Clark would be a waste. With a sigh of regret, he told the two partners that he was withdrawing his support. Having no where else to turn, Primeau and Clark sold out to Pierre Chouteau, Jr., & Company, which hired them as traders and took possession of their upper Missouri posts.[14]

5,8 **Dickson's Post and other trading houses near the mouths of the James and Vermilion rivers:** William Dickson probably began trading around the mouth of the James River (aka Riviére à Jacques, near Yankton, South Dakota) in the early 1820s when he worked for the Columbia Fur Company.[15] Unwilling to

leave the Yankton Sioux trade uncontested, Bernard Pratte &
Company soon opened a nearby post, sending Sylvestre Pratte,
the oldest son of Bernard Pratte, Sr., to manage it during the winter of 1824–5.[16] After absorbing the Bernard Pratte and Columbia
Fur companies a couple of years later, the American Fur Company
consolidated the two former rivals' trading operations among the
Yanktons, giving command to William Dickson. Dickson evidently moved several times over the years, following the camps of the
nomadic Sioux.[17]

In June 1834, Pratte, Chouteau & Company purchased the
Western Department and Upper Missouri Outfit of the American
Fur Company. Pratte & Chouteau's Yankton trade now became
headquartered at Vermilion Post, located on the north side of the
Missouri, immediately below its confluence with the Vermilion
River (the town site of Vermilion, South Dakota).[18] Dickson man-
aged the post until he committed suicide in late 1838.[19]

Between the spring of 1850 and that of 1851, Charles
Larpenteur supervised Vermilion Post to determine whether he
wished to buy it from Pratte & Chouteau's successor, Pierre
Chouteau, Jr., & Company. Despite describing the trade as "not
bad," he passed on the purchase, and the post was soon
abandoned.[20]

In 1857 as the fur trading era was approaching its close,
Frost, Todd & Company, a group of investors backed by Robert
Campbell, became the latest in a long line of firms to establish a
Yankton Sioux post near the mouth of the James.[21] Frost & Todd
lasted but two years.

7   **Drips's North Platte Post:** In 1857, the former mountain
man Andrew Drips, working for Pierre Chouteau, Jr., & Company,
built a trading post beside the North Platte River (near Torrington,
Wyoming), nineteen miles east of Fort Laramie. The post was
intended for the Oregon Trail traffic rather than the fur trade.
Drips ran the North Platte Post intermittently until his death in
September 1860.[22]

2,3   **Fort F.A.C.:** See Fort Chardon.

8　**Fiery Prairie Fort** (aka Fort Clark and Fort Sibley): See Osage Posts and Fort Osage.

2　**Flathead Post** (aka Salish or Saleesh House): In late 1809, the Nor'Wester David Thompson built Salish House, the first trading post on the Clark Fork River, locating it near Thompson Falls (a few miles upstream from the town of Thompson Falls, Montana).[23] That winter, Thompson stayed at the new fort, collecting twenty-eight packs of beaver.

During the fall of 1811, Piegans (one of the three tribes of the Blackfoot Confederation; see Fort Piegan endnote 24) sacked the empty post, killing a number of Kootenay Indians who were camped outside. In mid-November, Thompson returned to Salish House and found the dead Kootenays piled in a tepee. About a week later, John George McTavish came to the wrecked trading post with fifteen *engagés* and twelve hundred pounds of supplies packed on horseback. By December 16, McTavish's men had the post repaired and ready for business.[24]

The following year, Pacific Fur Company *engagés* constructed a competing fort a few miles upriver from the Nor'Westers.[25] In November 1813, the Astorians' post passed to the North West Company when the Pacific Fur partners sold their operations to the British during the War of 1812 (see Fort Astoria). The Nor'Westers most likely stripped the rival post of its supplies and equipment, taking everything that could be carried to Salish House and leaving the Astorian facility to rot. In 1821, Salish House became the property of the Hudson's Bay Company after its merger with the North West Company.

Over the ensuing years, the Hudson's Bay Company constructed a succession of trading houses on the Clark Fork River, referring to them either as Salish House or Flathead Post. Eventually the Flathead name won out.[26]

In 1822, the Hudson's Bay Company's Northern Department governor, George Simpson, decided to resurrect the Snake River trapping brigades that had been led by the Nor'Wester and former Astorian, Donald McKenzie, from 1818 to 1821 (for more about Donald McKenzie, see Fort Walla Walla).

Rather than launch an expedition from a fort on the Columbia River as McKenzie had done, Simpson ordered Michel Bourdon to set out from Flathead Post. Bourdon had accompanied McKenzie's first brigade, and had discovered and named the Bear River (the Bear drains southeastern Idaho, eventually emptying into Utah's Great Salt Lake). The 1822 Snake Expedition crossed the Continental Divide and trapped south to the Blackfoot River (in eastern Idaho). Blackfoot war parties continually harassed Bourdon's trappers, killing two and wounding two others. Fearing for their lives, fourteen of Bourdon's party deserted, scurrying east with their Indian wives and children. In mid-September, the *partisan* brought his depleted brigade to Spokane House for the winter.[27]

The following spring, Bourdon joined Finan McDonald, the top trader at Flathead Post, in another trapping sortie into the Snake River country. Once more the Blackfeet descended, costing Bourdon and McDonald the lives of six men. This time, however, the trappers bested their foes by killing sixty-eight warriors in a single battle. Only seven members of the attacking war party escaped. The brigade returned to Flathead Post with 4,339 beaver pelts, the largest take of any previous expedition.[28]

In 1824, command of the Snake Expedition passed to Alexander Ross. Another former Astorian, Ross had sailed around Cape Horn on the *Tonquin* and had helped build the Pacific Fur Company's fort at the mouth of the Columbia River. That February, Ross led his brigade out from Flathead Post and, in early spring, reached the Snake River drainage. On the Snake River Plain, a dozen or two of his Iroquois trappers split off from the main party in order to work the streams flowing into the Snake from the south. After telling the Iroquois that they should rejoin him in the fall, Ross took the remainder of his brigade to the Boise Mountains (in south-central Idaho).[29]

That summer while Ross's trappers waded the forks of the Boise and Payette rivers, Shoshones pilfered a few of their traps. In reprisal, Ross captured a number of the Indians' ponies, offering to exchange them for the stolen traps. The Shoshones agreed and the switch was made, but the Indians departed intent on revenge. Sometime later—probably in mid-September—they fell on the Hudson's Bay Iroquois, plundering most of their furs. The Iroquois escaped the skirmish after killing a Shoshone chief. Alone and frightened, the Iroquois huddled on the lower Blackfoot River (near Blackfoot, Idaho), awaiting another Shoshone assault and wondering how they would reach the safety of the main brigade.[30]

An unexpected savior soon arrived in the person of Jedediah Smith. Earlier that year, the young American *partisan* and his trapping brigade had harvested a large catch of beaver from the tributaries of the Green River (in Wyoming). After sending his clerk, Tom Fitzpatrick, and two other men to float the furs back to civilization in a bull boat, Smith and the remainder of his party trapped their way west, intending to resupply at Flathead Post. Smith stumbled across the Iroquois by accident.

Although they outnumbered the Americans by better than two to one, the Iroquois pleaded for Smith and his six men to escort them to Alexander Ross and the Hudson's Bay brigade. Smith agreed, accepting in payment the 105 pelts the Shoshones had not stolen.[31] The Americans and Iroquois forded the Snake River, crossed the lava-rippled Snake River Plain, and rode up Birch Creek Valley between the Lemhi and Beaverhead mountains (in eastern Idaho). The combined party traveled slowly, with the Americans setting their trap lines nearly every night. During the latter half of October, Smith at last delivered the Iroquois to Ross, who was heading to Flathead Post with his brigade.

With no way to prevent the Americans from accompanying him, short of murder, Ross consented to having them tag along as he crossed the Continental Divide at Lemhi Pass and then again at Gibbons Pass (both are on the Idaho-Montana border). On November 26, 1824, the two brigades arrived at Flathead Post which was now located on the north side of the Clark Fork, about six miles upstream from the mouth of the Thompson River (at Eddy, Montana, ten miles east of Thompson Falls). At that time the trading post consisted of six crude log cabins covered by a single roof.[32] The British resupplied Smith's men, but only after the *partisan* had agreed to sell his pelts at a fraction of their St. Louis value.

Alexander Ross had returned to the post to find that Peter Skene Ogden was to replace him as leader of the Snake Expedition. Ogden had been in the fur trade since his teens, having formerly served with the North West Company before joining the Hudson's Bay Company two years after the firms merged.[33] Ogden's orders called for him to trap the Snake River country and spend the winter in the field rather than at Flathead Post. The following summer he was to take his furs to Fort George (the former Fort Astoria) on the Pacific coast, from which they would be shipped around Cape Horn to England. Ogden's brigade would refit at Fort George, precluding the necessity of having the stores packed to Flathead Post, Spokane House, or one of the other inland Hudson's Bay forts.

On December 20, 1824, Ogden departed Flathead Post with the Snake Expedition, which numbered fifty-nine men, thirty Indian wives, and thirty-five mixed-blood children. To transport this vast menagerie, the brigade had 268 horses.[34] Jedediah Smith and his trappers followed a couple of days later, catching up with Ogden's force near the end of the month.

In mid-January 1825, the combined brigades plodded through deep snow over Gibbons Pass and descended into Blackfoot country along the Big Hole River (just east of the Continental Divide in Montana). Two weeks later the Blackfeet struck, making off with twenty-four of Ogden's horses. The Hudson's Bay trappers gave chase but recovered fewer than a dozen. On February 11, the brigades crested Lemhi Pass and dropped down to the western valley and river of the same name (near Tendoy, Idaho); however, deep snow prevented them from traversing the high ground that divided the Lemhi from the Birch Creek Valley to the south.

After restlessly waiting beside the Lemhi River for a few weeks, Jedediah Smith and his men forced a trail over the Lemhi Mountains and entered the Little Lost River Valley. From here the route was clear of snow across the Snake River Plain. Determined to keep Smith from trapping the Snake's tributaries unopposed, Ogden followed in his path, overtaking him on April 7 near the confluence of the Snake and Blackfoot rivers.[35] During the next several weeks, the contesting parties scurried to stay ahead of each other as they trapped their way south. All the while the Blackfeet harassed them, not breaking off until the brigades neared the Bear River.

In late April, the adversaries reached Cache Valley (known by the trappers as Willow Valley, this broad basin stretches from southeastern Idaho into northern Utah) and found signs of other white men. Jedediah Smith was certain they belonged to John Weber's brigade, with whom he had wintered among the Crows in 1823–4. Like Smith, Weber also worked for William Ashley.[36]

In early May, Smith and Weber linked up. Hearing that the Hudson's Bay Company had dared to send a trapping brigade onto American soil (actually they were in Mexican territory, but this technicality seems to have escaped notice), a number of Weber's men rode to Ogden's camp and demanded that the British skedaddle. When Ogden refused, the Americans induced half of his free trappers to desert by promising them that William Ashley would pay for their fur in trade goods at the rate of three dollars per pound—eight times what the Hudson's Bay Company offered. The deserters carried over seven hundred prime pelts[37] to the Americans' camp.

Fearing that the rest of his free trappers might also desert, Ogden fled back the way he had come, intent on putting as much distance as he could between his brigade and the Americans. The Hudson's Bay *partisan* ignored his orders to take his remaining furs to Fort George at the mouth of the Columbia River, concerned that the Americans would follow and disrupt trade over the entire Columbia Department. That fall, Ogden and a handful of his trappers retreated to Fort Nez Perces, near the confluence of the Columbia and Walla Walla rivers (in southeastern Washington), while the rest of his men returned to Flathead Post.[38]

Ogden's run-in with the Americans placed the Hudson's Bay Company and Governor George Simpson on the defensive. Worried that Ogden could lose more of his free trappers, Simpson restricted his brigade's future forays to the Snake River country. It was four years before the Hudson's Bay Company again dared to go among the brash Americans, and by then the

American fur companies had the Rocky Mountain beaver trade locked up.

The Hudson's Bay Company operated Flathead Post until around 1846, when it was replaced by Fort Connah about fifty miles to the east (see Fort Connah).

4 **Fort Floyd**[39] (aka White Earth River Post and Kipp's Post): In 1826, James Kipp built a trading post for the Columbia Fur Company on the left side of the Missouri, a bit below its confluence with the White Earth River (now beneath North Dakota's Lake Sakakawea).[40] A year later, after the American Fur Company had absorbed the Columbia Fur Company as its Upper Missouri Outfit, partner Kenneth McKenzie sent a detail up the Missouri to establish a trading site at the mouth of the Yellowstone. Upon reaching the White Earth River, 105 miles below its assigned destination, the party stopped, most likely because of approaching winter. Needing shelter, the men either constructed a new fort or moved into the one Kipp had built in 1826.[41] Calling the post Fort Floyd, the American Fur Company operated the trading house until the establishment of Fort Union above the Missouri-Yellowstone confluence in 1829, when the White Earth River post was abandoned and then burned.[42]

5 **Forest River Post:** In late 1804, Nor'Wester Alexander Henry the Younger built a Pembina satellite post on the Forest River, south of the forty-ninth parallel (in the vicinity of Warsaw, North Dakota).[43] (See Pembina Posts for more about Henry's operation.)

2 **Fraeb's Post:** In 1841, Henry Fraeb and Jim Bridger constructed a trading post near the confluence of Battle Creek and the Little Snake River (a bit west of the Continental Divide and close to the Colorado-Wyoming state line). Around the same time, Bridger and, either Fraeb or Louis Vasquez, also established a short-lived post on the right side of the Green River, a couple of miles downstream from the mouth of the Big Sandy (in Wyoming's Seedskadee National Wildlife Refuge).[44]

Fraeb and Bridger, together with Tom Fitzpatrick, Milton Sublette, and Jean Baptiste Gervais had bought out Smith, Jackson & Sublette in 1830, forming the Rocky Mountain Fur Company. After the firm folded in 1834, Fraeb worked as an independent trapper, eventually becoming partners with Peter Sarpy. In 1837 they opened a trading post on the South Platte River (see Fort Jackson). A year later their backer, Pratte, Chouteau & Company, sold the post to their principal competitor, Bent, St. Vrain & Company, leaving Fraeb and Sarpy standing at the altar like a pair of jilted brides.

Henry Fraeb eventually hitched up with his longtime friend, Jim Bridger, and founded Fraeb's Post. Given Bridger's propensity to wander, it is doubtful that he spent much time at the small log trading house. In August 1841, Sioux warriors attacked Fraeb and a bevy of his companions on Battle Creek, killing Fraeb and four others. Bridger abandoned Fraeb's Post a short time later.

6 **The French Post** (aka Teton Post, Papin's House, and Cerré's Establishment): See Fort Teton.

Fort Galpin through Fort Hunt

6 **Fort Galpin** (aka Galpin's Post): See Fort Pierre Chouteau (usually shortened to Fort Pierre).

2,3,4 **Fort Charles Galpin:** After Larpenteur, Lemon & Company dissolved in early spring 1862 (for the partnership's early history see Poplar River Post), Charles Larpenteur joined La Barge, Harkness & Company, the latest in a string of opposition firms–such as Larpenteur & Lemon–that attempted to compete with Pierre Chouteau, Jr., & Company. For many years Joseph La Barge and his brother, John, had piloted steamboats on the Missouri River, transporting freight to Chouteau trading posts between St. Louis and Fort Benton (in western Montana); in their new firm, the brothers continued operating steamers. Charles Galpin, another of the La Barge & Harkness partners, had also worked for the Chouteaus, both as *bourgeois* and founder of Fort Pierre II (near Pierre, South Dakota).

A few months after hiring on with the La Barge & Harkness enterprise, Charles Larpenteur established Fort Charles Galpin on the left side of the Missouri at Moose Point, about twelve miles above the river's confluence with the Milk (beneath Montana's Fort Peck Lake).[1] Larpenteur worked at the fort for a short time, while Charles Galpin, for whom it had been named, supervised trading between that facility and a small downriver-post near Fort Pierre II. Partner James Harkness ran Fort La Barge, a trading house near Fort Benton, whose primary business was supplying the Montana Territory's gold mines. As he had done for former firms opposing the Chouteau empire, Robert Campbell brokered the La Barge & Harkness pelts and robes in St. Louis.

La Barge & Harkness fared no better competing with Pierre Chouteau, Jr., & Company than any of its predecessors. Within two years of their firm's founding, the La Barge & Harkness shareholders were fighting among themselves, each trying to salvage what he could from the disintegrating partnership before the courts parceled out the pieces to waiting creditors. Paralleling the fortunes of its owner, Fort Charles Galpin closed in 1864, following an attack by an Indian war party.[2]

7 **Gantt's Fort:** See Fort Cass.

1 **Fort George** (Fort Astoria): (renamed Fort George after being purchased by the North West Company of Montreal).

6 **Fort George** (Missouri River): During the early 1840s John Ebbetts enjoyed modest success, spreading his twenty-nine traders among the various Sioux bands that roamed the White, Heart, and Missouri rivers. By freely dispensing liquor, Ebbetts and his men were able to buy robes and furs from under the nose of Pierre Chouteau, Jr., & Company. Feeling certain he could crush the Chouteau trading empire if he had more capital, Ebbetts formed a partnership with Fulton Cutting and Charles Kelsey of New York City in the spring of 1842. They, in turn, secured the backing of Bolton, Fox, Livingston & Company, which operated a line of trading ships in the North Atlantic. The Bolton, Fox & Livingston alliance gave Ebbetts's firm, which was called the Union Fur Company, the financial muscle to go head-to-head with the Chouteau traders.[3]

In the summer of 1842, Ebbetts and his two partners went up the Missouri to erect fixed trading posts to challenge those of Pierre Chouteau, Jr. On the west side of the Missouri, about thirty miles downstream from Fort Pierre, the partners set to work building Fort George (southeast of Pierre, South Dakota). When the post was nearing completion, Ebbetts and Cutting continued upriver, leaving the elderly Charles Kelsey at the new post as *bourgeois*. That fall when Fort George's traders began soliciting buffalo robes from the Sioux, a Chouteau trader named Frank Beeman came down from Fort Pierre, erected a tepee, and started paying the Sioux higher prices. The Union Fur traders responded by destroying Beeman's lodge and threatening his life.[4]

In order to compete with Chouteau, the Union Fur Company had hired some of the most hard-bitten desperadoes on the Missouri. In 1843, they robbed a trader named William May of a keelboat-load of robes. Soon afterwards, the Fort George men began confronting their own *bourgeois,* Charles Kelsey. When four of them moved into a cabin on Simoneau's (or Simineau's) Island, which sat across from Fort George, Kelsey ordered them to leave. They refused. Unwilling to be defied, the old *bourgeois* rowed over to the island with a double brace of pistols. Upon entering the cabin, Kelsey shot one outlaw as he was removing a pot from the fireplace. The man sprawled dead among the burning coals. As the other three bolted out the door, Kelsey fired twice more, wounding one in the shoulder and killing another as he scrambled over a nearby fence. The fourth man escaped. Worried that the authorities at Fort Leavenworth might decide to hang him, Kelsey fled, eventually returning to New York.[5] (See Fort Mortimer for more about the rivalry between the Union Fur Company and Pierre Chouteau, Jr., & Company.)

By the spring of 1845, the competition had worn down the Union Fur partners, and they sold Fort George and their other posts to their nemesis, Pierre Chouteau, Jr., & Company. A party of Sioux occupied Fort George for a time after the Union Fur Company pulled out,[6] but as soon as the Indians departed, Chouteau *engagés* reduced the post to ashes, thereby denying its use to other rogue trading outfits.

7 **Fort George** (South Platte River): See Fort St. Vrain.

4 **Gerard's Post:** Sometime after 1858, independent trader F.F. Gerard built a tiny, short-lived post between "Old" Fort Berthold and Fort Atkinson at Like-A-Fishhook Village (now beneath North Dakota's Lake Sakakawea).[7]

5 **Gingras's Trading Post:** In 1843, independent trader Antoine Gingras opened a trading post on the upper Pembina

Gingras's Trading Post
Photo courtesy of State Historical Society of North Dakota

River, in a region known as the Pembina Mountains (near Walhalla, North Dakota). By doing so, he thrust himself into the midst of a fierce competition between the Pierre Chouteau, Jr., and Hudson's Bay companies (see Pembina Posts). In 1851, flooding near the Pembina-Red River confluence (Pembina, North Dakota) prompted Father George Belcourt to relocate his Catholic mission about a mile west of Gingras's post, near a trading house that Norman Kittson had built for the Chouteaus. The priest called his mission St. Joseph. Gingras prospered by befriending the large Métis population (people of mixed Indian and white ancestry), who produced buffalo robes for the fur companies. After the fur trade ended, Gingras lived long enough to see Scandinavian emigrants turn the former buffalo range into farms.[8]

8   **Glenn's Trading Post:** In July or August 1820, traders Hugh Glenn and Charles Dennis established a small trading house on the Verdigris River, about a mile above its mouth (near Muskogee, Oklahoma). The post operated for at least one year, but probably closed in the fall of 1821 when Glenn and old friend Jacob Fowler led a trapping brigade to the upper Arkansas River and the Sangre de Cristo Mountains.[9]

5   **Peter Grant's Fort:** See Pembina Posts.

2   **Fort Hall** (Nathaniel Jarvis Wyeth): During the early 1830s, stories about the fur trade—especially the money that could be made in it—pervaded the eastern United States. Nearly everyone knew somebody who had heard about so-and-so striking it rich in the Rocky Mountains. That the tales were mostly false did not retard their spread. The streams and ponds were brimming with beaver, "furry bank notes," the rumormongers called them, just waiting for a fellow with gumption to come out and make his fortune.

    Such stories captivated Nathaniel Jarvis Wyeth. He owned a successful ice cutting business in Cambridge, Massachusetts (he harvested and stored winter pond ice, selling it in the summer), and was certain that his Yankee know-how could be applied to the

Fort Hall

fur trade. Like John Jacob Astor before him, Wyeth envisioned establishing a supply line from the Rocky Mountains to the mouth of the Columbia River. As he worked out a plan in his mind, he saw his ships sailing from Boston around South America and off-loading their trade goods on the Oregon coast. During their return voyages, their holds would be filled with furs, sent down from the mountains by Wyeth's traders.

After securing the financial support of eastern investors, Nathaniel Wyeth launched his bold scheme in 1832. While his supply ship sailed around Cape Horn toward the mouth of the Columbia River, the enterprising Yankee and his company of New England recruits journeyed west from St. Louis with William Sublette's rendezvous supply train. For many of the eastern green-horns, the trip proved more arduous than they had envisioned. When the caravan reached the Pierre's Hole rendezvous (near Driggs, Idaho), half of Wyeth's men elected to return home. Undaunted, the former ice cutter continued on to the Oregon

Territory where he learned that his supply ship had sunk in a Pacific storm.[10]

Discouraged, yet confident that he could still earn a profit on his and his underwriters' investment, Wyeth attended the 1833 summer rendezvous and arranged to accompany the Sublette & Campbell pack train to the settlements. When the trade fair ended, Wyeth started east with the furs and Robert Campbell. Milton Sublette, William's younger brother, joined the procession, needing to seek medical treatment for an inflamed foot. Tom Fitzpatrick and his Rocky Mountain Fur Company brigade tagged along for a portion of the trip, planning to trap the drainages of the Bighorn Mountains (in central Wyoming). Upon reaching the Bighorn River, the party paused to make buffalo-hide bull boats in order to float the pelts down the Bighorn to the Yellowstone, and on to the Missouri where William Sublette was waiting with a keelboat to take them to St. Louis. Before bidding Fitzpatrick good-bye, Wyeth contracted with him and Milton Sublette to supply their fur company at the next year's rendezvous.[11] As an inducement, Wyeth offered to undercut the outrageous prices charged by Sublette & Campbell.

When Wyeth reached the mouth of the Yellowstone (in western North Dakota), he found William Sublette constructing Fort William a couple of miles below the American Fur Company's Fort Union. After purchasing a pirogue from Kenneth McKenzie, the *bourgeois* of Fort Union, Wyeth continued down the Missouri, leaving the Sublettes to follow a few days later with the furs.[12] When Milton Sublette told his brother that Wyeth would furnish the Rocky Mountain Fur Company's stores at the next rendezvous, William turned livid. He had supplied the partnership from its inception and had no intention of letting Wyeth edge him aside.

Nathaniel Wyeth arrived in Massachusetts in early November and at once sought out his investors. He was hopeful that his contract to outfit the Rocky Mountain Fur Company would offset his failure during the previous year. To his relief, his backers agreed to furnish more capital. Resurrecting the scheme that had gone awry in his disastrous first trip west, Wyeth hired the

Fort Hall Interior

brig *May Dacre* and loaded it with trade goods and empty barrels. After obtaining the Rocky Mountain Fur Company's pelts at the 1834 rendezvous, he intended to take the plews to the lower Columbia River, meet the *May Dacre,* and fill her holds with beaver and her barrels with salted salmon, which the brig would then ferry around Cape Horn and sell in Boston. Wyeth would remain behind and establish a string of posts from the Pacific Ocean to the mountains, enabling him to supply future rendezvous from the west rather than the east. To carry out this daring venture, Wyeth and his partners formed the Columbia River Fishing & Trading Company. That done, Wyeth journeyed to St. Louis and began organizing the overland portion of his plan.[13]

In late April 1834, Wyeth started his supply caravan on the Platte River route to the mountains. Milton Sublette rode with him for a ways, but soon turned back because of severe pain in his foot. (Although he later had his lower leg amputated, it eventually cost him his life.) Wyeth pushed his men and pack animals relentlessly, aware that William Sublette was hard on his trail. When Wyeth was thirteen days out of Independence, Missouri, Sublette's pack train passed him, capturing a lead that it never relinquished.[14] Upon reaching the rendezvous on Ham's Fork of the Green River (in southwestern Wyoming), Wyeth learned that Fitzpatrick had disavowed their contract, allowing Sublette to corner the trade. In reality, Fitzpatrick had had little choice but to yield to Sublette's demands. Sublette & Campbell held liens against the Rocky Mountain Fur Company that exceeded its brigades' annual harvest of pelts. When William Sublette insisted that the partnership sell him all of its beaver or pay off the notes, Fitzpatrick was forced to break his word to Wyeth.

Steaming with anger, Wyeth stomped into the camp of Tom Fitzpatrick and fellow-partner Jim Bridger, and issued the most famous threat in the annals of the fur trade: "Gentlemen, I will yet roll a stone into your garden that you will never be able to get out."[15]

The 1834 rendezvous marked the end of the Rocky Mountain Fur Company. Before the celebration broke up, Henry Fraeb and Jean Baptiste Gervais quit the partnership. Fitzpatrick, Bridger, and Milton Sublette (in absentia) formed a fresh alliance, then immediately created another with Lucien Fontenelle and Andrew Drips, known as Fontenelle, Fitzpatrick & Company.[16] Fed up with William Sublette's high-handed ways and ruinous prices, the new partners resolved never again to allow Sublette & Campbell to be their supplier. Little did they suspect, as they made their vow, that Nathaniel Wyeth would soon carry through with his promised "stone."

From Ham's Fork Wyeth took his supply caravan to the Snake River, and on July 15 began constructing a log trading post on the left side of the channel, a bit upstream from the mouth of the Portneuf (in Fort Hall Bottoms on the Fort Hall Indian Reservation between Pocatello and Blackfoot, Idaho).[17] Named for Henry Hall, one of Wyeth's investors, Fort Hall was meant to entice Indians and trappers away from Fitzpatrick's partnership; however, the trading post soon became a threat to the Hudson's Bay Company. The British monopoly quickly countered with a post of its own: Fort Boisé. Although Wyeth tried (for more about Wyeth's efforts in the Oregon Territory, see Fort William– Nathaniel Wyeth), he could not compete with the Hudson's Bay Company on one side, and Fontenelle & Fitzpatrick on the other. Bankrupt, he returned to his ice cutting business in 1836 after agreeing to sell Fort Hall to the Hudson's Bay Company. Title formally passed the following year.[18]

Wyeth may have lost Fort Hall, but the trading post became the "stone" that Tom Fitzpatrick could never remove. Like the plucky New Englander, Fontenelle, Fitzpatrick & Company also struggled along until 1836 before going bust. The same year Wyeth retreated to Massachusetts, Fitzpatrick and his partners hired on with Pratte, Chouteau & Company, which had bought the Western Department and Upper Missouri Outfit of the American Fur Company in June 1834.[19]

During the 1840s, Fort Hall became an important rest stop on the Oregon Trail. In the summer of 1843, missionary Dr. Marcus Whitman estimated that passing emigrants annually spent

Wagon Undercarriages at Fort Hall

four thousand dollars at the fort,[20] purchasing blacksmith services, food, and fresh stock. By the end of the decade the stream of over-landers pausing to spend their money had turned into a tide. Then, in the mid-1850s, declining emigration and bypasses such as Hudspeth's Cutoff so reduced the traffic that the fort was no longer profitable. In 1856, the Hudson's Bay Company closed it down.[21]

Over the years, the Fort Hall name has been appended to many establishments in the vicinity of Wyeth's old trading post. In August 1849, the US Army located Cantonment Loring about three miles upstream from the Hudson's Bay stockade. Before the soldiers abandoned it the following spring, many people began calling the encampment Fort Hall.[22] Six years later, Ben Holladay built a relay station for his stage line a bit southeast of the old post; like Wyeth's former facility, Holladay's was also dubbed Fort Hall. When the government opened a reservation between the Snake and Portneuf rivers for the Shoshones and Bannocks in the late 1860s, it, too, caught the Fort Hall name. In May 1870, the Army constructed a permanent garrison on the reservation (about eight miles south of Blackfoot, Idaho), officially christening it Fort Hall in memory of the original trading post. The military abandoned its Fort Hall in 1883.[23] The Fort Hall Indian Reservation is still in existence.

Hamell's Trading Houses: During the 1850s and 1860s, Augustin Hamell built several small, temporary trading houses for Pierre Chouteau, Jr., & Company on the Milk, Marias, and other upper Missouri tributaries (Montana). Located near a Blackfoot or Atsina winter camp or some other tribal gathering place, these rough-hewn cabins rarely lasted more than a few months or a year, at most.[24]

5,6 **Handy's Post:** This tiny trading house, about which little is known, was located on the right side of the Missouri River at Handy's Point (in South Dakota, about four miles below the Fort Randall Dam). In June 1856, the US Army established Fort Randall on the same site.[25]

6 **Heney's Sioux Post:** In 1801, the former Nor'Wester Hugh Heney became partners with St. Louis trader, Régis Loisel. After establishing a trading post on Cedar Island (in South Dakota, upstream from the Missouri's Grand Detour; see Cedar Island endnote 17 for a discussion of the date the fort was founded), Loisel sent Heney to open a satellite post for the Teton Sioux, near the confluence of the Cheyenne and Missouri rivers (near Mission Ridge, South Dakota, the site is probably under Lake Oahe).[26]

During the winter of 1803–4, the Sioux turned belligerent, causing Heney to abandon his post soon after the spring thaw. Rather than join Loisel, who had fled Cedar Island for the same reason, Heney scurried north to Canada's Assiniboine River country and re-enlisted in the North West Company.[27]

2 **Fort Henry** (aka Fort Three Forks): In the spring of 1809, Andrew Henry and Pierre Menard left St. Louis with the first half of a 350-man expedition belonging to the newly organized St. Louis Missouri Fur Company.[28] The ambitious undertaking intended to trap and trade along the tributaries of the upper Missouri. Several miles above the mouth of the Knife River (in central North Dakota), the flotilla of thirteen keelboats and mackinaws stopped to build Fort Mandan. Accompanied by forty men, Henry continued on horseback to Fort Raymond at the confluence of the Bighorn and Yellowstone rivers (northeast of Billings, Montana), leaving Menard to follow with the supply boats.[29]

Using John Colter as their guide, Henry and Menard left Fort Raymond in late February or March 1810, leading a party of trappers to the Three Forks of the Missouri. Upon arriving in early April, the partners set their men to cutting logs for a stockade and cabins that they placed south of the Jefferson River, about two miles upstream from its confluence with the Madison (beside Jefferson Slough near Three Forks, Montana).[30]

Even before the fort was completed, Blackfoot war parties began harassing the company's trappers, eventually killing eight. One of those was George Drouillard, who with John Colter, had first seen this country with Lewis and Clark. Unable to fight the Blackfeet and harvest fur too, Henry and Menard abandoned the trading post after two months. Pierre Menard departed for St. Louis, taking along those men who had also had their fill of Blackfeet. Determined not to go home empty-handed, Andrew Henry sent word with Menard that he would return to the company's post among the Mandans the following summer. Henry and sixty volunteers then crossed the Continental Divide, praying they could enjoy a winter hunt, free from marauding warriors.[31] (For more about Andrew Henry's saga, see Fort Henry on Henry's Fork of the Snake River.)

2 **Fort Henry** (on Henry's Fork of the Snake River): In June 1810, Andrew Henry and a sixty-man trapping party abandoned their stockade at the Three Forks of the Missouri (see Fort Henry—aka Fort Three Forks), hoping to escape the Blackfeet by crossing to the west side of the Continental Divide. Upon reaching the headwaters of the North Fork of the Snake River (Idaho's Henry's Fork), Henry learned that he had not left his Indian problems behind. At a large alpine lake (Henry's Lake) just below the Divide, a band of Crows stole most of his company's horses. With their gear packed on their few remaining mounts, the trappers trudged south, trailing the North Fork. Over the next few days, they descended from the high country to the flat expanse of the Snake River Plain, ever mindful of the advancing winter. Near Egin Bench,[32] a number of the trappers refused to go farther. After advising the troublemakers to erect some shelter, Henry took the remainder of his men into the eastern foothills to trap.

By late December when the beaver ponds froze, Henry's trappers had collected a good catch of pelts. Shortly after the New Year, they returned to Egin Bench where the slackers had constructed a few crude log huts on the left bank of the North Fork River (about six miles north of Rexburg, Idaho).[33]

That winter, a trapper named Archibald Pelton went insane. Leaving the relative comfort of the party's cabins, he endured the cold and snow as though he were an untamed beast. The following spring when the passes cleared, Henry started east with forty packs of fur, allowing his trappers to accompany him or go their own way as they chose. Pelton refused to leave, opting instead to wander the barren wilds of the Snake River Plain.[34]

Rather than go to the Three Forks and down the Missouri to the Mandan villages, Henry swung a wide arc, exploring the country draining into the Yellowstone and evaluating its trapping potential. The route was longer than the one on the Missouri, but it avoided the Blackfeet. As soon as the long march began, Henry's party started splintering into small groups as each man answered his own whims. Among those who broke off were John Hoback, Edward Robinson, and Jacob Reznor.

In March, a Pacific Fur Company expedition had started up the Missouri with several keelboats, intending to cross to the Oregon coast where the sailing ship *Tonquin* would soon be disembarking workmen to construct a fort at the mouth of the Columbia (see Fort Astoria). Wilson Price Hunt commanded the overland force, and was a shareholder in the trading firm which was a subsidiary of John Jacob Astor's American Fur Company. In April, Manuel Lisa followed in the Astorians' wake, carrying supplies to the St. Louis Missouri Fur Company's post among the Mandans (in central North Dakota), where he hoped to meet Andrew Henry.[35]

On May 22, Hunt sighted two of Lisa's up-country trappers paddling a canoe downstream and enlisted them in his Fort Astoria venture. Four days later, he hailed Hoback, Robinson, and Reznor. Turning their backs on the settlements, they, too, joined the Pacific Fur Company, agreeing to guide its expedition across the Rocky Mountains.[36]

On June 2, Lisa overtook Hunt (below Pierre, South Dakota), Lisa's keelboat having averaged eighteen miles per day for two months. Now traveling together, the parties reached the Arikara villages ten days later. Alerted by Hoback, Robinson, and Reznor to the danger from Blackfoot war parties on the upper Missouri, Hunt decided to continue his journey on land and offered to sell his boats to the St. Louis Missouri Fur Company, provided the payment was made in horses. Lisa accepted. While the main Astorian party remained with the Arikaras, a detail went upriver to Fort Mandan, where it received the promised herd.

On July 18, the five dozen Astorians, accompanied by their interpreter's pregnant Indian wife (for more about this courageous woman, see Fort Astoria and Fort Boisé) and her two children, left the Arikaras. In mid-September, they crested the Continental Divide via Union Pass in the Wind River Mountains (Wyoming), and on October 8, reached Andrew Henry's abandoned cabins on Egin Bench beside the North Fork of the Snake River. Before leaving, Hunt christened the river, Henry's Fork, and the cabins, Fort Henry.

4   **Fort Henry** (at the confluence of the Missouri and Yellowstone rivers): After his trapping foray west of the Continental Divide, Andrew Henry met Manuel Lisa at the Mandan villages (in North Dakota) in September 1811, and returned with him to St. Louis a few weeks later.[37] Although the pelts Henry had brought from the Snake River country covered only a fraction of the St. Louis Missouri Fur Company's expenses, they gave the firm's owners hope. In early 1812, Lisa, Henry, and their partners dissolved their old firm, reorganizing as the Missouri Fur Company. The new partnership sent another expedition up the Missouri, but war between the United States and Great Britain spelled its doom. On January 17, 1814, the Missouri Fur investors voted their company's dissolution.[38]

Eager to serve his country during the crisis, Andrew Henry took charge of the First Battalion of the Sixth Regiment of the Washington County Militia, which was under the overall command of his friend, William Ashley.[39] Henry acquired the rank of major, a title he retained for the rest of his life.

After the war, Andrew Henry remained in the settlements with his young wife, working his claims in Missouri's lead mines near the village of Potosi. He and Ashley maintained their friendship, although Ashley's activities increasingly focused on politics. The revival of the Missouri Fur Company in 1819 piqued Ashley's interest in the beaver trade, and he soon persuaded Henry to take another trapping expedition to the Rocky Mountains. In early 1822, Ashley and Henry formed a partnership and, that February, began advertising for "enterprising young men" to go up the

Missouri River and hunt beaver. Among the many recruits who answered the call were Jedediah Smith and Jim Bridger.

On April 3, Henry departed St. Louis with 150 men. Most of the brigade traveled on horseback, happy to avoid the backbreaking labor of cordelling the party's keelboat against the Missouri's strong current. Bridger, who had enlisted as a blacksmith, went with this group, while Smith followed a month later with a second brigade and the keelboat *Enterprize*. Ashley remained in St. Louis. Henry and the lead brigade reached the mouth of the Yellowstone in late summer and constructed Fort Henry on the south side of the Missouri, four hundred yards above the confluence (a few miles inside the western North Dakota state line, about twenty-two miles southwest of Williston). Henry and his party were unaware that the *Enterprize* and its ten thousand dollars worth of stores had fallen prey to the Missouri's treacherous currents. When Ashley received word of the sinking, he quickly secured another boat-load of supplies and rushed to the second brigade's camp, about twenty miles below Fort Osage (near Sibley, Missouri). With Ashley now in command, the brigade continued up the Missouri, arriving at the newly completed Fort Henry on October 1.[40]

After a brief visit with Henry, Ashley returned to St. Louis in order to assemble another outfit for the next year. As soon as Ashley departed, Henry split the men into two trapping brigades and began the fall hunt. He led one unit up the Missouri, while *partisan* John Weber, a former Danish sea captain, took the other up the Yellowstone.[41]

That winter, the forces of Ashley & Henry were spread between Fort Henry and the Musselshell and Powder rivers. By the spring of 1823, most of their horses were either dead from the cold and overwork or stolen by the Crows and Blackfeet. Desperate for more pack animals so the men could trap streams that were too shallow to work from canoes, Henry sent Jedediah Smith down the Missouri with an urgent request for William Ashley to buy horses from the mid-river tribes.

Ashley had started up the Missouri in March, bringing with him two keelboats and about ninety new recruits, including Tom Fitzpatrick and William Sublette. Smith met them below the

Arikara villages (south of Mobridge, South Dakota). The Arikaras had recently attacked some Missouri Fur Company men from Fort Recovery (near Chamberlain, South Dakota), and their friends had retaliated by killing two warriors. Seeing no difference between one fur company and another, the tribe was primed for revenge when Ashley came ashore seeking horses.[42]

Ashley conducted the trade on a sandbar facing the Arikara's lower village. At first all went well, with Ashley acquiring a couple of hundred buffalo robes and nineteen Indian ponies.[43] However, when he refused to swap a chief a rifle and gunpowder, the tribe grew surly and withdrew into its walled town. Leaving Smith in charge of a guard detail looking after the horses, Ashley retired to his keelboats which were anchored in mid-river.

The next morning, a cloudburst drenched the men on the sandbar, and a strong, northwesterly wind strained the keelboats at their moorings. Ashley wanted to depart, but the storm made it impossible. All that day, Smith and the other men guarding the horses sat under a slate-gray sky, watching for trouble. As evening approached, the wind slackened to a breeze, and the dipping sun painted the horizon with orange fire.

That night, the shore party wrapped itself in buffalo robes and prayed it could leave the sandbar come morning. Then, a few hours before dawn, screams and war whoops from the lower village awoke Smith and his men. Moments later, Edward Rose, the brigade's interpreter who had been staying among the Arikaras, dashed to the riverbank and shouted that the tribe had killed a trapper named Aaron Stephens.[44] Unable to go back to sleep, the horse guards whispered together in the darkness, their fingers curled around the cocks on their flintlock rifles.

At the first rays of daylight, Arikara warriors boiled out of the lower village and unleashed their fusils and arrows at the men on the sandbar. Within seconds, Ashley's nineteen horses lay dead, their bodies now providing cover for Smith and his detail. While some of the Indians fired at the guards, others paddled bull boats across the Missouri, then raced along the high bank on the left side to where they could direct their weapons on the keelboats.

Knowing that the only escape was downriver, Ashley sent word for the shore party to swim for the boats.

As soon as the survivors from the sandbar were hauled aboard the keelboats, the voyageurs slipped the moorings, allowing the Missouri to carry the brigade to safety. Counting Aaron Stephens, Ashley had lost thirteen men; in addition, two of the wounded would eventually die.[45]

Hundreds of Arikara warriors now stood between the keelboats and Fort Henry. Ashley knew that the trappers at the trading post needed to be resupplied, but he also knew that if the Arikaras were left unpunished, they might close the Missouri to all of the fur companies. Perhaps if Andrew Henry brought his men down from the Yellowstone, and if the Army dispatched a company of infantry from Fort Atkinson (at Council Bluffs), the Arikaras could be cowed. Needing to send word of the plan to his partner, Ashley asked for two volunteers to go to Fort Henry. Jedediah Smith and a French-Canadian trapper stepped forward.

Having no horses and wanting to keep clear of the Arikaras, Smith and his companion walked up the Grand River Valley, then swung northwest to the Yellowstone and trailed it to its mouth and Fort Henry. They delivered their message without incident. Heeding Ashley's plea for help, Henry assembled his trappers and started downriver in pirogues, leaving behind a handful of men to oversee the fort.

Meanwhile, Ashley dropped down the Missouri to the Cheyenne River. The wounded and those men who had no stomach to face the Arikaras a second time continued on one of the keelboats to Fort Atkinson, reaching the Army post on June 18.[46]

After learning about the Arikaras' attack, the fort commander, Colonel Henry Leavenworth, lacking authorization from his superiors,[47] decided to punish the tribe with a punitive campaign. While his troops prepared to move north, Leavenworth sent an express to the Missouri Fur Company's senior field partner, Joshua Pilcher, whose headquarters at Fort Lisa was a few miles away from Fort Atkinson, requesting that he lend a hand. Pilcher agreed and began gathering his trappers, informing the colonel that he would pick up additional men when he passed Fort Recovery.

Figuring that more is always better, Pilcher dispatched several interpreters to the Sioux, asking them to join the fray. Liking nothing better than an opportunity to raid their perennial enemy, the Sioux painted their faces for war. On June 22, Leavenworth's command started marching up the Missouri River, supported by keelboats carrying supplies and three pieces of artillery.[48]

Andrew Henry, Jedediah Smith, and the other men from Fort Henry arrived at Ashley's camp near the mouth of the Cheyenne River in early July, having paddled past the Arikaras without a shot being fired. Colonel Leavenworth and the Missouri Legion, as he called his expedition, reached Ashley three weeks later, and over seven hundred Sioux warriors showed up two days after that.

On August 9, as the Legion approached the Arikara villages, Leavenworth ordered the Sioux to move ahead as a blocking force in order to prevent the Arikaras from escaping. Unaccustomed to fighting as a cohesive unit, the mounted Sioux charged pell-mell, catching the Arikaras in a cornfield outside the lower village. The ensuing battle was a melee, far too chaotic for Leavenworth to chance launching a coordinated thrust. Rather than attack, the colonel bade his companies to hold their fire. Seeing the soldiers and trappers in the distance, the Arikaras broke off the fight and fled into their walled towns, leaving a dozen of their fallen compatriots to be mutilated by the frenzied Sioux.

The next morning, Leavenworth brought up the Legion's two cannons and howitzer, hoping to pound the Arikaras into surrender. However, the cottonwood palisades that surrounded the villages absorbed the shots, holding casualties to a minimum. As the ineffective cannonade stretched into the afternoon, the Sioux grew bored and began to scatter. Leavenworth's junior officers urged the colonel to storm the towns, but he hesitated, waffling between ordering a frontal assault or not. With his artillery ammunition nearly gone and evening approaching, Leavenworth withdrew his troops from the upper Arikara village, concentrating his forces around the lower one. When he still failed to order an attack, the remaining Sioux warriors deserted the battlefield and headed home, claiming that they had done all the fighting and the

Americans were cowards. Disgusted with Leavenworth's lack of resolve, Ashley's and Pilcher's trappers agreed.

In the early twilight several Arikaras came out of the lower village and asked to parley. Changing his tactics, Leavenworth decided to talk. Accompanied by Joshua Pilcher, the colonel informed the Indians that he would leave them in peace if they would promise to stop raiding American traders, and would return the guns and other traps they had stolen from Ashley's men on the sandbar. Knowing that by saying yes they could avoid further punishment, the Arikaras conceded. Incredulous, Pilcher told Leavenworth that the Indians would consent to anything in order to have the soldiers leave. Still, as rational as Pilcher's argument was, Leavenworth needed to believe the chiefs. He had begun the expedition without authority. If he ended it without further bloodshed, he might escape censure.

Over the next couple of days, the lower villagers gave back a pittance of the property they had taken from Ashley's trappers. The upper villagers refused to contribute anything, claiming they had not harmed Ashley's men. Faced with this affront, Leavenworth again considered storming the towns, but before he could make up his mind, the Arikaras snatched the decision from his hands. During the night of August 13, the entire tribe fled its two villages and disappeared on the plain.[49]

Colonel Leavenworth disbanded the Missouri Legion a short time later, returning to Fort Atkinson with his Army regulars. Pilcher and the Missouri Fur Company's trappers retreated to Fort Recovery, while William Ashley and Andrew Henry took their men to the French Company's Fort Kiowa (northwest of Chamberlain, South Dakota). None of the traders trusted the fickle Arikaras to keep the peace. Further, Leavenworth's botched campaign had shown the Army to be a grizzly without claws. Every tribe on the upper Missouri knew it had nothing to fear from harassing the fur companies. The Missouri River was no longer safe.

Ashley and Henry now had no clear way to support their trading post at the mouth of the Yellowstone. Because the upper Missouri was in a state of siege, they concluded that it would be far less risky if they sent their trappers overland to the central Rocky Mountains, territory controlled by the more friendly Crows and Shoshones.

Ashley divided his trappers into two brigades, one led by Andrew Henry, the other by Jedediah Smith. Henry's brigade departed Fort Kiowa in early September, while Smith's, because of the difficulty in obtaining horses, set out about four weeks later. Although Henry intended wintering among the Crows, he first needed to fetch the men he had left at Fort Henry. Since he had decided to trap the territory south of the Yellowstone River, a trading house on the Missouri was no longer necessary. Henry's brigade reached Fort Henry in late September, cached some unneeded equipment, then closed the post and started southwest for the Bighorn and Wind River country.[50]

3 **Fort Henry** (at the confluence of the Bighorn and Yellowstone rivers): After departing Fort Henry at the mouth of the Yellowstone River in September 1823, Andrew Henry split his brigade, sending a portion of it with the *partisan* John Weber. Weber was to trap his way southwest, then winter with Jedediah Smith's brigade among the Crows. Meanwhile, Henry and his company pushed up the Yellowstone and, in the late fall, constructed yet another Fort Henry, this one near the mouth of the Bighorn River (about sixty miles east of Billings, Montana).[51]

Intended to support Smith's and Weber's brigades, as well as provide a trading house for the Crows, the post lasted until early summer 1824, when Henry abandoned it and the fur trade. Taking the handful of pelts the Indians and his trappers had brought to the fort, he floated down the Yellowstone and Missouri rivers, reaching St. Louis in late August.[52] Soon after Henry arrived, he and Ashley terminated their partnership.

The closing of the last Fort Henry brought a sea change to the fur trade. For years, enterprises from the Pacific Fur Company to the Missouri Fur Company had used fixed trading posts to replenish their trappers. The Snake River brigades of the North West and Hudson's Bay companies regularly retired to forts such as Spokane House and Flathead Post after their trapping tours. No one thought of resupplying them another way. But in the summer of 1825, with his trappers spread across the Rocky Mountains and his trading posts abandoned, William Ashley was compelled to innovate. That July on Henry's Fork of the Green River (in southern Wyoming), Ashley revolutionized the beaver trade by instituting the rendezvous supply system. For the next fifteen years, fur company pack trains brought the stores to the trappers, instead of making the trappers go to the stores. From Ashley's need to resupply his trappers was born the raucous trade fairs that came to epitomize the mountain man era.

7,8 **Camp Holmes:** See Fort Mason and August Chouteau's Post.

2 **Fort Howse:** In late 1810, Joseph Howse built a Hudson's Bay wintering post somewhere in the Flathead River Valley (south of Flathead Lake in western Montana), then abandoned it the following spring.[53]

6 **Fort Hunt:** See Fort Lisa.

Fort Jackson through Fort Lupton

2 **Fort Jackson** (American Fur Company): In December 1833, Francis Chardon established Fort Jackson on the Missouri near its confluence with the Milk River (about eight or ten miles below Montana's Fort Peck Dam), naming it for President Andrew Jackson. The motivation for constructing an American Fur Company satellite trading house so close to Fort Union was to force William Sublette and Robert Campbell—who had recently established Fort William at the mouth of the Yellowstone—to send one of their traders to compete, thereby diluting their resources.[1] (For more about the rivalry between Sublette & Campbell and the

American Fur Company, see Fort Laramie and Fort William–Sublette & Campbell.)

7 **Fort Jackson** (South Platte River): In 1837, Peter Sarpy and Henry Fraeb secured financing from Pratte, Chouteau & Company and built a small trading establishment on the central South Platte River (near Ione, about twelve miles north of Brighton, Colorado). Named Fort Jackson, after President Andrew Jackson, the trading house was one of four rival posts, each separated from its neighbors by five or six miles of prairie. A rider could easily visit all of them in a few hours. From north to south they were Fort St. Vrain, Fort Vasquez, Fort Jackson, and Fort Lupton.[2]

Sarpy and Fraeb proved unable to compete and, by 1838, were suffocating under the mounting interest on their debts. Seeking to cut its losses, Pratte, Chouteau & Company sold Fort Jackson out from under its founders, transferring the post's title to Bent, St. Vrain & Company which owned the rival Fort St. Vrain. As a part of the sales agreement, the two powerful trading firms divided the territory, with Pratte & Chouteau (which became Pierre Chouteau, Jr., & Company in 1839) taking the country north of the confluence of the North and South Platte rivers, and Bent, St. Vrain & Company taking the country to the south. After William Bent removed the supplies and livestock from Fort Jackson, Pratte & Chouteau's *engagés* burned it to the ground.[3]

4 **Fort James:** See "Old" Fort Berthold.

7 **Fort John** (aka Fort William and Fort Lucien): See Fort Laramie.

7 **Fort John II and other Pierre Chouteau, Jr., & Company Scotts Bluff Trading Posts:** After selling Fort John (see Fort Laramie–aka Fort William, Fort Lucien, and Fort John) to the US Army in 1849, Pierre Chouteau, Jr., & Company dispatched Bruce Husband and John B. Moncravie[4] to Scotts Bluff (in western Nebraska), in order to counter the trading post that Joseph

Robidoux III had built on the east-side grade of Robidoux Pass (spelled Roubadeau on modern maps, the pass lies a few miles southwest of the Scotts Bluff National Monument).[5] That fall, Husband and Moncravie hurriedly erected a small trading house on the right side of the North Platte, a few miles northwest of Mitchell Pass (just north of Nebraska County Road L-79G). The next spring the men constructed a more durable post—called Fort John, Scott's Bluff in company correspondence—in Helvas Canyon, eight miles south of Mitchell Pass (in today's Gering Valley). During the late 1840s and through 1850, the bulk of the emigrant traffic used Robidoux Pass; however, in 1851 the preferred route switched to Mitchell Pass (now crossed by Nebraska State Route 92), prompting the Chouteau traders to relocate their post back beside the Platte River, near where they had built their original cabin.[6]

From 1850 to 1857, Andrew Drips served as *bourgeois* at Chouteau's Scotts Bluff post, after which he moved farther up the North Platte River in order to better serve the wagon trains (see Drips's North Platte Post).[7] The post at Scotts Bluff evidently lasted through the end of the decade.[8]

Joseph Juett's Cheyenne River Post: During the late fall of 1831, American Fur Company trader Joseph Juett (or Jewet) constructed a temporary post for the Cheyennes at the tribe's winter camp somewhere along the Cheyenne River (in South Dakota).[9] The post probably lasted no more than a season or two.

7 Junction House: See Morrow's Post.

4 Jusseaume's Post (known later as Fort Makay): In 1794, René Jusseaume (also Jessaume, Jussaume, and Jussome) opened a trading post for the North West Company between the Mandan and Hidatsa villages near the confluence of the Knife and Missouri rivers (close to Stanton, North Dakota).[10] Jusseaume abandoned the post two years later after being ordered off Spanish soil by John Evans, who had come up the Missouri from St. Louis (see Mandan Villages for more about their confrontation). Evans renamed the post, Fort Makay *[sic]* for his boss, James Mackay, and occupied it during the winter of 1796–7.[11]

8 **Kansas Post:** See Chouteau's Post.

6 **Fort Kiowa** (aka Brazeau's or Brassaux's Fort and Fort Lookout): In the autumn of 1822, Joseph Brazeau, Jr., (or Brassaux) established a trading post for Berthold, Chouteau & Pratte–the French Company–on the west side of the Missouri River about twenty-five miles above the mouth of the White (just south of the Crow Creek Indian Reservation and ten miles northwest of Chamberlain, South Dakota).[12]

After the punitive expedition to punish the Arikaras (see Fort Henry at the confluence of the Missouri and Yellowstone rivers), William Ashley dropped down to Fort Kiowa in late August 1823, where he decided to divide his men into two trapping brigades and send them to Crow country. To carry out his plan, he needed horses. Under normal circumstances he could have acquired them from the Sioux; however, the tribe was searching for buffalo, which had been frightened away from the Missouri River by the coming and going of the Army's Missouri Legion. Ashley scoured the countryside for several days before purchasing enough horses to send Andrew Henry's brigade on its way. Even then, Ashley bought so few animals that the trappers had to walk; all of their stock was required for packing.[13]

After wasting another four weeks trying to round up mounts for Jedediah Smith's brigade, Ashley turned to Fort Kiowa's temporary *bourgeois,* John Pierre Cabanné, Sr. Cabanné kindly lent Smith and his men a sufficient number of horses to start them on their journey.[14] Smith eventually found a Cheyenne camp and traded for his own horses, sending the borrowed ones back to Fort Kiowa.

In 1827, Bernard Pratte & Company–a successor to Berthold, Chouteau & Pratte–joined the American Fur Company as its St. Louis agent, and Fort Kiowa became part of the American Fur Company's Western Department. Alexander Philipp Maximilian, Prince of Wied-Nuwied, wrote in his journal about

"Fort Lookout" (Fort Kiowa) during his 1833 trip to the upper Missouri;[15] at the time the fort functioned as a trading post as well as an Indian agency. Fort Kiowa was abandoned sometime in the late 1830s and, in 1840, was appropriated as a wintering post by Joseph La Barge who had put together a small outfit in opposition to Pierre Chouteau, Jr., & Company. A former steamboat pilot for the American Fur Company and its successors, La Barge soon sold out to the Chouteau partnership and re-entered its employ, leaving Fort Kiowa to rot.

7 **Kiowa Trading Post of Auguste Chouteau:** During the summer of 1837, Auguste Pierre Chouteau–the older brother of Pierre, Jr.–established a small, short-lived trading house for the Kiowas on Cache Creek, near the eastern foot of the Wichita Mountains (about three miles south of Oklahoma's Fort Sill Military Reservation; see Osage Posts and Fort Osage for more about Auguste Chouteau's trading ventures).[16]

4 **Fort Kipp:** Needing to challenge Frost, Todd & Company's Fort Stewart, which sat on the north side of the Missouri, five miles above its confluence with Big Muddy Creek (about nine miles west of Culbertson, Montana), James Kipp ordered the construction of a competing post in early 1859. Frost & Todd's traders had captured much of the Assiniboine trade away from Pierre Chouteau, Jr., & Company's Fort Union, and Kipp wanted it back. That spring, Chouteau workmen built a small trading post, christened Fort Kipp, two hundred yards away from Fort Stewart.[17]

Near the end of the year, Frost & Todd dissolved and Fort Stewart passed to Clark, Primeau & Company which sold out to the Chouteau firm the following year. Shortly afterwards, Pierre Chouteau, Jr., & Company abandoned forts Kipp and Stewart, transferring the Assiniboine trade back to Fort Union. Soon after the traders headed downriver, Indians set the deserted posts on fire.

In 1862 and 1863, a Chouteau trader named Joseph Roulette, Jr., re-established a trading presence (see Roulette's Post) on the ruins of Fort Kipp in order to counter nearby Owen McKenzie's Post.[18]

4 **Kipp's Post** (aka White Earth River Post): See Fort Floyd.

2 **Kootenay House** (sometimes spelled Kootenai, Kootanae, Kootanie, and Kutenai): The first Kootenay House—built in July 1807 by David Thompson for the North West Company—was located near the headwaters of the Columbia River, above the forty-ninth parallel, and a bit downstream from Windermere Lake (in southeastern British Columbia).[19] In 1808, Thompson's traders opened a short-lived trading house near the confluence of the Kootenai and Tobacco rivers (a bit west of Eureka, Montana). Then in November that year, Nor'Wester Finan McDonald established another Kootenay post on the Kootenai River near the mouth of Libby Creek (close to Libby, Montana).[20] Three years later, the North West Company rebuilt the McDonald trading post a few miles east, a little above the Kootenai's merger with the Fisher (beneath Lake Koocanusa, Montana; see Kullyspell House for more about David Thompson.)

In 1821, Kootenay House passed to the Hudson's Bay Company when it merged with the North West Company. During the next forty-three years, the trading post saw only intermittent use. Then in 1864, the Hudson's Bay Company abandoned the American site and rebuilt Kootenay House on Canadian soil.

1 **Kullyspell House:** David Thompson emigrated from England to Canada in 1784 at the age of fourteen, already apprenticed to the Hudson's Bay Company. Frustrated that the firm refused to allow him to pursue his interest in cartography, he joined the North West Company in 1797. During the next fifteen years Thompson covered nearly fifty-five thousand miles via foot, horseback, and canoe, eliminating "unexplored" from the maps of North America. In his travels he discovered the headwaters of the Mississippi, made the first complete reconnaissance of the Columbia River (see Fort Astoria), and surveyed most of the eventual western boundary between the United States and Canada.[21]

In September 1809, Thompson came down the Kootenai River (in the panhandle of Idaho) and established Kullyspell House, Salish House, and Spokane House. Intended for the Spokane, Coeur d'Alene, and Flathead Indians, Kullyspell House was located on Memaloose Point, a small peninsula on the northeast side of Lake Pend Oreille (near Hope, Idaho, the original site is now covered by the lake).[22] The post was a single-room log cabin manned by one or two traders. A year after Kullyspell House opened, the North West Company abandoned it because of continual harassment by the Blackfeet.

In 1812, Thompson returned to Montreal and resigned from the North West Company. During most of his remaining years, he continued working as a surveyor, but bad luck dogged him and his fortunes steadily declined. Late in his life, he tried to interest the noted American writer Washington Irving in his adventures, but nothing came of it. With his health and eyesight failing, Thompson was finally reduced to selling his surveying instruments and his winter coat in order to buy food. One of North America's greatest cartographers died February 16, 1857, a forgotten pauper.

Thompson's maps and thirty-nine journals testify to his achievements. One map at Fort William (on the north shore of Lake Superior) was ten feet long and displayed the one and one-half million square miles he had explored. Considered too important to be seen by the North West Company's competitors, it was kept behind a locked door, visible to no one but Nor'West partners.

3 **Fort La Barge:** In the summer of 1862, James Harkness of La Barge, Harkness & Company built an adobe post named Fort La Barge on the left side of the Missouri River, one and one-half miles upstream from Fort Benton (above the town of Fort Benton, Montana).[23] Organized during the winter of 1861–2, the partnership was one in a long line of opposition firms that attempted to challenge Pierre Chouteau, Jr., & Company.

When Fort La Barge was completed, Harkness hurried downriver to St. Louis, refusing to winter on the upper Missouri. Exasperated and desperate for a *bourgeois* to take command of the post, Joseph and John La Barge gave the position to longtime trader Joseph Picotte. However, Picotte was more interested in sampling the fort's whiskey than in seeing to the post's efficient operation. Next, the brothers turned to Robert Lemon (formerly of Larpenteur, Lemon & Company), but he found the fort in such dire straits that in August 1863, he sold its assets to the *bourgeois* of nearby Fort Benton in order to obtain funds to pay Fort La Barge's *engagés* and traders.[24]

By then La Barge & Harkness was in its death throes. For the next two years the territorial court decided the partnership's fate, eventually auctioning off its various pieces to satisfy creditors. Finally, in 1865 the last opposition firm to Pierre Chouteau, Jr., & Company came to an ignoble end.

6 **Fort LaFramboise:** In 1817, French-Canadian trader Joseph LaFramboise built a trading post that he named for himself on the north bank of the Bad River, just above its confluence with the Missouri (inside the town of Fort Pierre, South Dakota; the Bad River was formerly the Teton). Competition from the Columbia Fur Company's Fort Tecumseh, which was located about a mile away, forced the abandonment of Fort LaFramboise in 1822.[25]

In the late 1850s and early 1860s, a François LaFramboise traded among the Sioux as an independent. Then in 1862 or 1863, he joined La Barge & Harkness, which was in competition with Pierre Chouteau, Jr., & Company, and put up a crude hovel that he also dubbed Fort LaFramboise. The post was located three miles upstream from the Chouteau firm's Fort Pierre II (a couple of miles above Pierre, South Dakota).[26]

7 **Fort Lancaster:** See Fort Lupton.

7 **Fort Laramie** (aka Fort William, Fort Lucien, and Fort John): During the autumn and winter of 1833, Robert Campbell—in partnership with William Sublette—managed a trading post at the mouth of the Yellowstone (in western North Dakota; see Fort William–Sublette & Campbell), attempting to compete with the

American Fur Company on its home ground. Kenneth McKenzie, *bourgeois* of nearby Fort Union, ruthlessly bid beaver prices to the moon in an effort to squash Campbell's upstart, Fort William. The tactic showed every sign of success.

Downriver in his St. Louis counting room, William Sublette read Campbell's expresses with frustration. Every letter told how McKenzie was cornering the trade. The few pelts that Campbell had bought cost more than they would fetch at market. Knowing that he and Campbell could never match the American Fur Company's resources, Sublette, during a winter trip to New York City, offered to sell the money-losing Fort William and abandon his plan to seed the Missouri with trading posts. Eager to rid himself of a wily competitor, Pierre Chouteau, Jr., manager of the American Fur Company's Western Department, agreed to the purchase in February 1834. In return he gave Sublette & Campbell free rein to supply the future mountain rendezvous.[27] Later, when William Sublette read over the bill of sale, he must have smiled, for nothing in the contract prevented him from constructing a post on the North Platte.

Fort Laramie Cavalry Barracks

Sublette was well acquainted with the territory around Laramai's Point, which, like the Laramie River, took its name from Jacques Laramie (also spelled Loremy, Laremais, or LaRamee),[28] a French-Canadian trapper who had been killed on its headwaters in 1821 by an Arapaho war party. Laramai's Point sat at the junction of the trappers' North Platte track to the mountains (a decade later it would be known as the Oregon Trail), and a north-south Indian trade route that predated the coming of the white man.[29] The country belonged to the buffalo and to the Plains Indians who depended on them for their survival.

In early May that year, William Sublette left Independence, Missouri, taking the annual supply caravan to the trappers' rendezvous which was to be held on Ham's Fork of the Green River (in southwestern Wyoming). Nathaniel Wyeth, an eastern entrepreneur who was intent on beating Sublette to the rendezvous and, as a result, capturing the trade, had departed Independence on April 28 (see Fort Hall–Nathaniel Wyeth–about Wyeth's contract to supply the Rocky Mountain Fur Company). Just under two weeks into the journey, Sublette grabbed the lead, and on May 31 when he reached the Laramie River, he was two days ahead.[30] The next morning, Sublette and his clerk Edwin Patton chose the site for a trading post. Sublette and the caravan then rode away, leaving behind Patton and a dozen *engagés* to build a new Fort William.[31]

Sublette won his race to the rendezvous and coerced Tom Fitzpatrick, the managing partner of the Rocky Mountain Fur Company, into repudiating his contract with Nathaniel Wyeth. However, Sublette's victory over the New Englander was bittersweet. Before the rendezvous ended, the Rocky Mountain Fur Company dissolved. Fitzpatrick and Jim Bridger formed a new trapping partnership, then quickly reorganized, joining Lucien Fontenelle and Andrew Drips, former American Fur Company *partisans* who had been cast adrift when Pierre Chouteau, Jr., stopped sending out supply trains. Calling themselves Fontenelle, Fitzpatrick & Company, the partners vowed never again to allow Sublette to furnish their provisions or broker their furs.[32]

Late that summer while Bridger and Drips rode off with the

Fort Laramie Trader's Store

partnership's trapping brigades, Fontenelle and Fitzpatrick started for St. Louis, needing to make arrangements for the following year's supply caravan. On August 20, they reached the Laramie River where Sublette's workmen were putting the finishing touches on the new fort, located a couple of miles upstream from the Laramie's confluence with the North Platte (near the town of Fort Laramie, Wyoming). Sublette's traders were already spreading among the Teton Sioux and Northern Cheyennes, encouraging them to barter their robes and furs at Fort William rather than at the American Fur Company's Fort Pierre on the Missouri River (across from Pierre, South Dakota).

When Fontenelle and Fitzpatrick arrived in St. Louis, they approached Pierre Chouteau, Jr., who with his partner, Bernard Pratte, Sr., had recently bought the American Fur Company's Western Department and Upper Missouri Outfit from John Jacob Astor. Chouteau recognized that Fort William threatened his trade with the Sioux and Northern Cheyennes.[33] What better way to trump Sublette & Campbell than to finance a pack train for Fontenelle, Fitzpatrick & Company?

As soon as William Sublette heard about the agreement between Chouteau and Fontenelle & Fitzpatrick, he realized he was in a box. He could still send a supply caravan to the rendezvous in the hope of buying the independent trappers' pelts, but without having Fontenelle & Fitzpatrick's business in hand, it would be risky. Further, nothing prevented Chouteau from building a competing trading post on the Laramie River next to Fort William. Sublette and Robert Campbell owned a lucrative trading business in St. Louis. By hanging onto Fort William, they would be putting their partnership in jeopardy. Accordingly, Sublette offered to sell the Laramie trading post to Fontenelle & Fitzpatrick.[34]

With funding from Pratte, Chouteau & Company, Fontenelle and Fitzpatrick bought Fort William in early 1835, renaming it Fort Lucien in honor of Fontenelle. Any euphoria that Fontenelle, Fitzpatrick, Drips, and Bridger felt in besting Sublette & Campbell, quickly faded. They soon learned that they had merely swapped one creditor for another. Falling fur prices, brought on by hatters switching from beaver to nutria and silk, compounded their woes. It was impossible for their brigades to

Commissary & Bakery at Fort Laramie

146

trap enough for the partners to climb out of debt. Bowing to the inevitable, the four men ended their partnership in 1836, sold their Laramie River post to Pratte, Chouteau & Company, and joined the firm as employees. Pierre Chouteau, Jr., now added Fort Lucien to his stable of trading houses.[35]

In 1841, a former Army officer named Lancaster P. Lupton built an adobe trading post near the confluence of the North Platte and Laramie rivers (see Fort Platte), prompting Chouteau to replace the aging Fort Lucien. *Engagés* constructed the new facility from adobe, placing it a few hundred yards upstream from the cottonwood original. The whitewashed trading post was named Fort John after John Sarpy, a partner in Chouteau's firm.[36]

During the 1840s, Fort John, which was increasingly called Fort Laramie, served as an important rest stop for emigrants heading to Oregon, California, and Utah. Each night in early summer, thousands of campfires dotted the Laramie landscape, and in the peak years of America's great westering, as many as nine thousand wagons lumbered past the fort in a single day.[37] As the Oregon Trail grew in importance, the need to safeguard its travelers pushed the Army to establish military posts along its length. On June 26, 1849, the US Government bought Fort John for four thousand dollars and officially changed its name to Fort Laramie.[38] The adobe stockade and its buildings were used as temporary quarters until the fall of 1850, when soldiers finished constructing the replacements. Afterwards, the old structure was allowed to rot. The subjugation of the Plains Indians, and the coming of the railroad ended Fort Laramie's importance, and the Army abandoned it in early March 1890.[39]

8   La Saline Post: In 1822, Auguste Pierre Chouteau secured financing from the partnership of his brother, Pierre, Jr.–called Berthold, Chouteau & Pratte, it was renamed Bernard Pratte & Company in 1823–and built a trading post at a salt spring on the Neosho River, about thirty-five miles above its confluence with the Arkansas (in northeastern Oklahoma). Called La Saline Post, the facility was a satellite of Auguste Chouteau's four-post Osage Outfit. The other posts were ten miles south of the new Osage village farther up the Neosho River (near Oswego, Kansas), in the old Indian factory on the Marais des Cygnes River (north of Rich Hill, Missouri), and at Auguste Chouteau's farm on the lower Verdigris River (south of Wagoner, Oklahoma).[40] (See Osage Posts and Fort Osage for more about the Osage Outfit.)

8   **Fort Leavenworth:** In May 1827, the Third US Infantry under the command of Colonel Henry Leavenworth established Cantonment Leavenworth as a replacement for Fort Atkinson at Council Bluffs. Soldiers built the new garrison on the west side of the Missouri, twenty-three miles upstream from its confluence with the Kansas River (north of Kansas City, Kansas). Five years after its founding, the cantonment was renamed Fort Leavenworth.[41]

Although the fort's primary mission was to guard the Santa Fe Trail which passed to the south, the Army required keelboats and steamers ascending the Missouri River to stop at Fort Leavenworth for inspection. US law prohibited the fur companies from trading liquor to the Indians, and government agents had orders to confiscate any alcohol in excess of that allowed for the companies' white employees. Bribes and a liberal interpretation of what could be legally imported ensured that the law was a failure. Despite Fort Leavenworth's inspectors, the fur companies shipped enough alcohol to debauch every Indian who acquired a taste.

5,6   **Leclerc's Posts:** In the early 1830s, Narcisse Leclerc (or LeClerc) operated at least two Missouri River trading posts in opposition to the American Fur Company, one upstream from the mouth of Chouteau Creek (near Greenwood, South Dakota), and a second one near the mouth of the Bad River (in the vicinity of Pierre, South Dakota).[42] Backed by Henry Shaw of St. Louis, Leclerc puffed up his fledgling firm by calling it the Northwest Fur Company.

Leclerc gained a measure of fame in 1832 when American Fur partner, John Cabanné, Sr., confiscated a keelboat-load of alcohol that Leclerc's traders had somehow legally slipped past the government inspectors at Fort Leavenworth. Leclerc screamed to Washington, DC, causing such an uproar that the American Fur Company had to pay him ninety-two hundred dollars in hush money. Outraged that the indiscretion of Cabanné had tarnished the firm's reputation, his fellow partners stripped him of his Council Bluffs command (see Cabanné's Post).[43]

3 **Fort Lewis** (aka Fort Benton): See Fort Benton (formerly known as Fort Clay).

3 **Fort Lisa** (confluence of the Bighorn and Yellowstone rivers) (aka Fort Ramon, Fort Manuel, Manuel's Fort, and variations thereof): See Fort Raymond.

6 **Fort Lisa** (aka Fort Hunt): In 1812, Manuel Lisa, managing partner of the Missouri Fur Company, ordered the construction of Fort Lisa on the west side of the Missouri River near Council Bluffs (about nine miles north of Omaha, Nebraska).[44] His timing was auspicious. During the War of 1812, British agents fueled Indian hostility along the upper Missouri, forcing Lisa to abandon most of his firm's trading posts. Fort Lisa among the Omahas, and Bijou's trading house on Cedar Island, were the only Missouri Fur Company facilities that remained open. After the company dissolved in January 1814, Lisa retained possession of both places.[45]

Needing financing, Manuel Lisa formed a partnership with Theodore Hunt, a relative of Astorian Wilson Price Hunt,[46] and renamed the Council Bluffs stockade Fort Hunt in his partner's honor. With the war threatening the downriver settlements, William Clark, Indian Superintendent for the upper Missouri, enlisted Lisa in a plot to turn the tribes against the British. Taking $1,335 in government-purchased trade goods, Lisa ascended the Missouri in the autumn of 1814 to induce the Indians into joining the Americans' cause. While spending the winter at Fort Hunt, he won the allegiance of the Teton Sioux. Now allied with the United States, the Tetons foiled English attempts at persuading the Santee Sioux to attack American settlers. Among the Omahas, Lisa cemented the loyalty of the tribe by marrying one of its daughters.[47]

Throughout the war, Manuel Lisa worked as an Indian agent as well as a trader. When peace finally came to the frontier, he resigned his government duties and concentrated on traffic with the Omahas and Sioux. At the time, he and Theodore Hunt employed nearly one hundred men.

In June 1817, Lisa and Hunt ended their partnership, although they remained friends. Lisa kept ownership of Fort Hunt, changing its name back to Fort Lisa. During the next two years he continued to trade on the Missouri River, sending his agents as far north as the Mandans. All the while, John Jacob Astor's giant American Fur Company loomed on the horizon, casting its shadow on the Missouri and intimidating the much smaller St. Louis trading firms. Wanting to put together an outfit that could compete with Astor, Lisa formed a partnership—known as Cabanné & Company—with a few of St. Louis's more formidable trading families. However, in June 1819, the company dissolved amid bickering and backbiting.[48]

Lisa immediately sought out new investors and, during the summer, re-established the Missouri Fur Company. That autumn he and Mary Hempstead Lisa, a widow he had married in August 1818, ascended the Missouri, making her the first white woman to go beyond the downriver settlements. The couple wintered at Council Bluffs where Fort Lisa was either being rebuilt or remodeled, for when the Lisas arrived, they had to spend a night in a tepee; their lodgings at the fort were still under construction.[49] The following spring when Lisa and his wife accompanied the season's take of furs to St. Louis, he was ill. Over the next four months his condition deteriorated, and in August 1820, Manuel Lisa died.

Joshua Pilcher became the Missouri Fur Company's new field manager and made his headquarters at Fort Lisa. In the spring of 1823, the Blackfeet decimated a Missouri Fur brigade on the Yellowstone River. Pilcher no sooner received word of that disaster than he became embroiled in Colonel Henry Leavenworth's ill-fated campaign to punish the Arikaras. The resulting debacle closed the Missouri (for details see Fort Henry at the confluence of the Missouri and Yellowstone rivers). Pilcher withdrew his trappers and traders to Council Bluffs, but his company never recovered. During the next five years, retrenchment followed retrenchment until the Missouri Fur Company, like Fort Lisa, faded into oblivion.

4 **Lisa's Post:** See Fort Mandan (St. Louis Missouri Fur Company) and Mandan Villages.

6 **Little Bend Posts:** In the early 1830s, William Laidlaw ran an American Fur Company trading fort on the Cheyenne River, most likely near its confluence with the Missouri (now covered by South Dakota's Lake Oahe).[50] In 1843, Bernard Pratte, Jr., and John Cabanné, Jr., received a license to establish a trading house on the Missouri at Little Bend, near the mouth of the Cheyenne. That fall Pierre Chouteau, Jr., & Company countered with a small post, as did the Union Fur Company (see forts George and Mortimer for more about this opposition firm).[51]

7 **Lock, Randolph & Company's North Platte Post:** In 1841, the undercapitalized partnership of Lock & Randolph erected a log trading house on the North Platte, near the mouth of the Laramie River, a couple of miles upstream from Fort Adams (somewhere between Guernsey and Lingle, Wyoming; the exact sites are unknown).[52] Unable to buck the considerable competition in the region, the partners abandoned their post the following year and retreated to the South Platte, where they had recently purchased Fort Vasquez (see Fort Vasquez endnote 63 about when Lock & Randolph bought Fort Vasquez).

6 **Loisel's Fort:** See Cedar Island.

6 **Fort Lookout** (Berthold, Chouteau & Pratte) (aka Brazeau's or Brassaux's Fort): See Fort Kiowa.

6 **Fort Lookout** (Columbia Fur Company): In the mid-1820s, the Columbia Fur Company constructed a small trading post named Fort Lookout on the west side of the Missouri River, close to the Missouri Fur Company's Fort Recovery (near Chamberlain,

South Dakota).[53] Fort Lookout was probably abandoned in 1828, after the American Fur Company absorbed the Columbia Fur Company as its Upper Missouri Outfit.

7 **Fort Lookout** (South Platte River) (aka Fort George): See Fort St. Vrain.

7 **Fort Lucien** (aka Fort William and Fort John): See Fort Laramie.

7 **Fort Lupton** (aka Fort Lancaster): In 1837, a former US Army lieutenant of dragoons, Lancaster P. Lupton, built an adobe trading post on the right side of the central South Platte River (near Fort Lupton, Colorado, about six miles north of Brighton).[54] Fort Lupton was the southern-most post of four competing trading houses on the South Platte, each separated by a few miles. Lupton's post lasted until late 1840 or early 1841 before succumbing to Bent, St. Vrain & Company. After reaching an accommodation with the Bent brothers and their partner, Ceran St. Vrain, Lupton rode to the North Platte to try his hand competing with Pierre Chouteau, Jr., & Company's Fort John (see Fort Platte).

Fort Madison through Fort Mortimer

8 **Fort Madison** (aka Fort Bellevue): At the time of the Louisiana Purchase in 1803, the Sauk and Fox Indians who lived north of St. Louis (in northeastern Missouri, eastern Iowa, northern Illinois, and southern Wisconsin) were firmly in the grip of North West Company traders operating from posts around Lake Superior. In early November the following year, the US Government hoodwinked some minor chiefs of the tribes into signing away fifteen million acres of their land (a region bounded by the Mississippi, Illinois, and Wisconsin rivers, together with a triangle of country upstream from the Mississippi-Missouri confluence). In exchange

Fort Madison Blockhouse & Mississippi River

for the concession, the government promised the Indians a trader and yearly presents valued at one thousand dollars. Because the United States had not the wherewithal to relocate the tribes immediately, the territorial governor permitted them to live on their own land until it could be parceled out to white settlers. Eventually, the Sauks and Foxes were expected to move west of the Mississippi River. In 1805, the US Army, which supervised the Indian factory system for the Office of Indian Trade, opened a military post and trading store on the south side of the Missouri, about four miles above its mouth (see Fort Bellefontaine). The Sauks and Foxes deemed the post too remote from their principal villages, and too close to the Osages, whose warriors regularly raided the farms between St. Charles and St. Louis. Like their Winnebago allies, the Sauks and Foxes found it more convenient to continue trading with the British.

By 1807, the Army recognized that its trading factory at Fort Bellefontaine was a mistake. Unwilling to surrender the Sauks,

Foxes, and their neighbors to the Nor'Westers, acting Louisiana Territory Governor Frederick Bates dispatched Indian agent Nicholas Boilvin to the Des Moines Rapids (on the Mississippi River, east of Montrose, Iowa) with a boatload of trade goods. Boilvin did enough business to persuade Meriwether Lewis—who replaced Bates in March 1808—to authorize a permanent Indian factory. That summer the Sauks, Foxes, and Ioways sold the government three square miles of riverbank on the right side of the Mississippi, near the top of the rapids.[1]

In late August, Lieutenant Alpha Kingsley of the First US Infantry Regiment led a four- or six-boat flotilla up the Mississippi to erect an Indian factory and military stockade. Early in September, Kingsley and his keelboats negotiated the twelve-mile stretch of rapids above the mouth of the Des Moines River. However, rather than build on the plot that had been purchased by the government agents, the lieutenant continued another ten miles up the Mississippi and began construction at a west bank site (now Fort Madison, Iowa) that could not have been more difficult

Fort Madison Trade Factory & Blockhouse

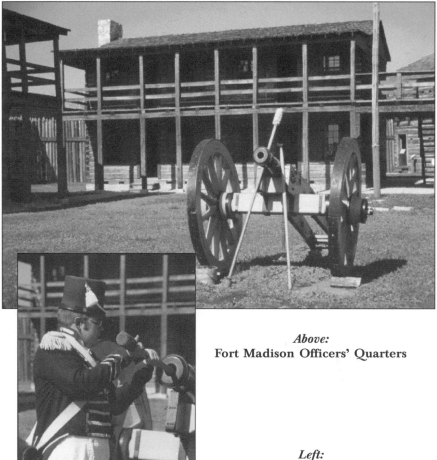

Above:
Fort Madison Officers' Quarters

Left:
**Fort Madison Cannoneer,
D.J. Tripp, Swabbing Bore**

to defend. On one side of the stockade, a high ridge allowed attackers to fire down on the fort, while on another, a deep gully offered cover for Indian fusillades.[2] The local tribes had agreed to exchange the site at the head of the rapids for Kingsley's choice, so the young lieutenant saw no reason to worry.

Initially calling the post Fort Bellevue, Lieutenant Kingsley changed its name the following spring to Fort Madison in honor of

Fort Madison

President James Madison. For several years the Indians did a fair and profitable business with the resident trader, John Johnson, bartering deer, beaver, bear, raccoon, muskrat, and otter skins for goods that Johnson sold at twenty percent above his cost.[3] However, lead soon eclipsed the trade in animal pelts. Indian women dug the ore from mines south of the Wisconsin River (below Prairie du Chien, Wisconsin), and their menfolk transported it down the Mississippi to Fort Madison, where Johnson paid for it in trade goods at the rate of five cents a pound. During the first sixteen months the factory was in operation, the Indians bartered forty-eight thousand pounds of lead ore, an amount they increased to eighty thousand pounds in 1810. By the start of the War of 1812, Fort Madison's lead trade had far outstripped the post's commerce in fur.[4]

After the United States declared war on Great Britain, British agents in the North West Company redoubled their efforts to sway the tribes of the middle and upper Mississippi away from the Americans. Among the Sauks, Foxes, and Winnebagoes, the Nor'Westers found many warriors willing to listen, especially after the Americans surrendered forts Michilimackinac, Dearborn, and Detroit to the redcoats and their Indian allies. In early September 1812, a combined Sauk, Fox, and Winnebago war party laid siege to Fort Madison for four days, killing one dragoon and all of the post's cattle and hogs. Because the trading factory was located outside the stockade, the senior officer ordered it burned to keep it out of Indian hands. Nineteen welcome reinforcements arrived at Fort Madison two months later, encouraging the beleaguered command to hold on.

For the next half year, the soldiers went about their duties with one eye turned toward the nearby ridge and ravine where Indian warriors were continually lurking. Then in July 1813, a band of Sauks and Winnebagoes ambushed a wood-cutting detail, killing two men. A week later the tribes attacked the stockade itself, but grape from a six-pound cannon prevented the Indians from gaining entrance to the fort. When the battle ended, the post adjutant added several more names to the list of Army dead. Over the next couple of months Indian harassment continued, often in the form of flaming arrows shot into the log palisades and buildings from the nearby ravine. That September[5] the current commander, Lieutenant Thomas Hamilton, decided to abandon Fort Madison and withdraw to St. Louis. Before leaving, his soldiers primed the post with gunpowder, then set it ablaze. As the garrison retreated in boats down the Mississippi, Fort Madison burned to the ground.

4 **Fort Makay:** See Jusseaume's Post and Mandan Villages.

4 **Fort Mandan** (Lewis and Clark): See Mandan Villages.

4 **Fort Mandan** (St. Louis Missouri Fur Company) (aka Lisa's Post): In 1809, the St. Louis Missouri Fur Company established a trading post on the south side of the Missouri River, ten or twelve miles upstream from the Hidatsa villages (above the mouth of the Knife River, about midway between Stanton, North Dakota, and the Garrison Dam).[6] Meant to be a forward supply base from which the company could support its trappers and traders on the Yellowstone and at the Three Forks of the Missouri, Fort Mandan also served as a trading center for the Hidatsas and Mandans.[7] The fort was abandoned during the War of 1812 when traders working for the North West and Hudson's Bay companies incited the Indians against the Americans. (For a more in-depth discussion, see Mandan Villages.)

4 **Mandan Villages:** For over three hundred years before their first contact with white traders, the Mandans lived in semi-permanent villages along the Missouri River, near its confluence with the Heart (in the vicinity of Bismarck, North Dakota).[8] Like neighboring tribes, such as the Hidatsas to the north and the Arikaras to the south, the Mandans farmed, as well as hunted buffalo.

In December 1738, French trader Pierre Gaultier de Varennes, the Sieur de la Vérendrye, became the first European to visit the tribe.[9] La Vérendrye approached the upper Missouri from the northeast, his expedition supported by a string of trading forts that stretched along a network of Canadian rivers reaching back to Lake Superior. He traded with the Mandans and left them two men who were to learn their language, but he did not establish a permanent post. The two emissaries remained with the Mandans until the following summer, when they returned to Fort La Reine on Canada's Assiniboine River.[10]

During the 1740s and 1750s, a few other French traders maintained contact with the tribe, even though their government discounted the importance of the upper Missouri because the region's beaver pelts were spare when compared with the thick, rich furs of the far north.[11]

In 1763, France ceded Canada to Great Britain, and the Louisiana Territory to Spain. The country from Lake Superior to Lake Winnipeg and the Assiniboine River was now open to the Hudson's Bay Company; however, access to the Missouri watershed was administered by the Spanish governor-general in New Orleans. In the years 1781–2, a smallpox epidemic spread across the upper Missouri into Canada, decimating Indians who possessed no natural immunity. Among the Mandans, it wiped out nearly half the tribe. The Sioux—who had also suffered from the disease but less so than the Mandans—began harassing the Mandan villages. Deeming their homes beside the Heart River to be unsafe and possessed by an evil spirit, the surviving Mandans moved up the Missouri, settling just below their Hidatsa allies near the mouth of the Knife (in the vicinity of Stanton, North Dakota).

In 1783, Montreal's "Peddlers"—a loose association of merchants who had established a successful trading network across central Canada—organized themselves into the North West Company and began competing in earnest with their Hudson's Bay rival. Their struggle was fierce. Ignoring international boundaries, the North West Company sent its traders to the upper Missouri, opening commerce with the Mandans and Hidatsas in 1785.[12] The Hudson's Bay Company soon followed suit. For the most part, traders from the two firms were transient, traveling from their posts in Canada to the Missouri River for a few months of barter, then journeying north with their bounty of furs. A French-Canadian trader named Pierre Menard was an exception to the norm, having taken up residence with the Mandans around 1776 or 1778, before the tribe had moved north to be near the Hidatsas.[13]

No white men visited the tribes from the south until Jacques D'Eglise did so in 1792.[14] That October when D'Eglise returned to St. Louis with reports of British incursions into the upper Missouri, the merchants, traders, and Spanish authorities pondered the news with a mixture of envy and alarm. The following year D'Eglise launched another trading sortie, intending once more to visit the Mandans; this time his venture failed when either Sioux or Arikara warriors blocked the Missouri. In 1794, he tried again with a similar result.[15]

While D'Eglise was having no luck passing the Sioux and Arikaras, word kept filtering downriver that the British had increased their toehold among the Mandans and Hidatsas by opening a permanent trading post between their villages. Known as Jusseaume's Post, the trading house had been built in early 1794 by the Nor'Wester René Jusseaume (sometimes spelled Jessaume, Jussaume, or Jussome) near the mouth of the Knife River.[16]

Needing to defend Spain's sovereignty, the Spanish governor-general gave Jacques Clamorgan—a St. Louis merchant of possible Portuguese descent[17]—and his associates, a trading monopoly for all the tribes above the Poncas. Clamorgan and the other traders had recently formed the Company of the Discoverers and Explorers of the Missouri River.[18] The Spanish governor-general also charged the company with finding a route to the Pacific Ocean, offering the first member of its expedition to do so, a reward of three thousand *pesos*.[19]

Jean Baptiste Truteau, a former schoolmaster, led the company's first sally up the Missouri, departing St. Louis on June 7, 1794, with an eight-man crew aboard a large pirogue.[20] He planned on trading with the Arikaras, then wintering with the Mandans before seeking a way to the western sea. On August 6, Jacques D'Eglise and a four-man crew caught up with Truteau's pirogue. Truteau wanted the parties to travel together, but his voyageurs could not keep up with D'Eglise's canoe. Two days later near the mouth of the Platte River, D'Eglise grew weary of having to wait on the slower pirogue and struck out on his own. As on his other voyages up the Missouri, he was hounded by bad luck. Sometime after leaving Truteau, D'Eglise encountered a Ponca war party which looted much of his merchandise.[21]

Meanwhile, as Truteau and his crew neared the Missouri's Grand Detour (on South Dakota's Crow Creek Indian Reservation) in late September, a large band of Teton and Yankton Sioux forced them to halt, demanding presents. Upon learning that Truteau intended to visit the Arikaras, the Tetons robbed him and warned him to abandon any idea of trading with their enemies. When the Sioux finally allowed him to leave their camp, Truteau and his men continued up the Missouri, shadowed by a Teton war party on the east bank. Knowing that he could not evade the warriors while on the river, Truteau cached what was left of his trade goods, and sank his pirogue during cover of night, then sneaked overland to the Arikara village. He found it deserted, the tribe having fled up the Missouri to escape Sioux raids.[22]

Desperately needing food and wanting to salvage something from their trading venture, Truteau and his men retrieved their pirogue and cache, then slipped down the Missouri out of Sioux country and constructed a small cabin above the mouth of the Niobrara (see Truteau's Winter Post). Just before winter began in earnest, the notorious Chief Blackbird arrived with a passel of Omaha warriors.[23] Revered by his people, Blackbird held sway because of his ability to predict death. Some years earlier, a French trader had given the chief a measure of arsenic, showing him how to rid himself of his enemies. Blackbird quickly turned its use into a ritual. While his tribe looked on, Blackbird served arsenic-laced food to those he wanted to kill and announced to all that his adversaries would be dead by sunrise. Because the predictions always came true, the Omahas believed that Blackbird possessed magical power.[24]

During the last part of the eighteenth century, Blackbird transformed the Omahas into the villains of the central Missouri, using them to exact tribute from any St. Louis trader who dared come upriver. Over the winter of 1794–5, he directed his warriors to harass Truteau and his men, who were powerless to do anything except feed the chief's greed and pray they would keep their scalps.[25]

Soon after the spring thaw Truteau abandoned the post, sending part of his company to St. Louis with the handful of furs he had managed to accumulate the previous year. Accompanied by the remainder of his men, the trader pushed upstream, avoided the Sioux, and spent a number of months among the Arikaras, who had moved near the mouth of the Grand River (just above Mobridge, South Dakota). After giving up on a relief party that never showed, Truteau returned to St. Louis in early summer 1796, having never reached the Mandans.[26]

While Truteau was busy hanging onto his hair, Jacques Clamorgan and his partners had launched a second expedition up the Missouri in April 1795. This effort was commanded by a trader named Lécuyer who had orders to leave supplies with Truteau at the Arikaras,[27] pass the winter with the Mandans, then explore westward to the Pacific Ocean. The Poncas ended this foray below the point Truteau had reached, sending Lécuyer's men scurrying down the Missouri in fear for their lives.[28]

Four months after Lécuyer left St. Louis, Clamorgan's company dispatched yet another expedition, this one made up of thirty men aboard four pirogues and commanded by James Mackay.[29] As Mackay and his crew *cordelled* and poled their boats up the Missouri, they met Lécuyer's frightened voyageurs fleeing downriver, some of whom Mackay snared for his expedition. In mid-October, Mackay paused among the Otoes and erected a small trading house a mile or two north of the mouth of the Platte (see James Mackay's Otoe Post).[30] On November 11, the flotilla reached the Omahas' main village where Mackay stopped for the winter and had his men construct Fort Charles between the tribe's clustered lodges and the Missouri River (six miles south of Omadi, Nebraska, on the Omaha Indian Reservation).[31]

Now aware that Truteau and Lécuyer had failed in their mission to open trade with the Mandans and find a way to the Pacific, Mackay determined to carry it through by sending his lieutenant, John (or Juan or Jean) Evans, and a handful of *engagés*. The detachment left Fort Charles on November 24, traveling overland since the Missouri was about to freeze. The Sioux frightened Evans's party near the mouth of the White River, and it returned to Fort Charles on January 6, 1796.[32] After a few weeks rest, Evans again went up the Missouri, this time to persuade the Sioux to return with him to Fort Charles for a parley. A month later, four chiefs came to the post and listened to Mackay's pleas for peace. Hopeful that the Sioux would allow Evans to pass through their country, Mackay again dispatched his trusted lieutenant to the Mandans. This time Evans had luck. He departed Fort Charles on June 8, avoided the Sioux, and reached the Mandans on September 23.[33]

Under instructions to drive all foreigners off Louisiana soil, Evans hoisted the Spanish flag at the Nor'Westers' Jusseaume's Post and ordered its handful of traders to keep out of the Mandan and Hidatsa villages. A couple of weeks later, when more Canadian traders approached the Mandans, Evans repeated his warning. Fearful that he might have a large force coming up the Missouri to bolster his demands, the Nor'West and Hudson's Bay men withdrew to their forts above the forty-ninth parallel.[34] That winter Evans courted the Mandans and Hidatsas from Jusseaume's Post, which he renamed Fort Makay [sic] after James Mackay.[35] Though he tried, Evans had too little merchandise to cement the tribes' loyalties. In the spring of 1797, René Jusseaume returned with a huge quantity of goods and quickly regained the trade. After Jusseaume made two attempts on his life, Evans piled his meager take of furs into his pirogues and struck downriver for St. Louis, surrendering the Mandans and Hidatsas to the British and forgetting about his orders to scout a route to the Pacific Ocean.[36]

James Mackay had remained on the central Missouri until the spring of 1797, when he abandoned Fort Charles and returned to St. Louis amid the collapse of the Company of the Discoverers and Explorers of the Missouri River. While the firm was being liquidated, Jacques Clamorgan formed a new partnership with Régis Loisel and, again, sent traders to the Mandan villages. Yet as hard as they worked, Clamorgan & Loisel's agents produced little more than token returns. Each year saw the Nor'West and Hudson's Bay traders becoming more firmly entrenched among the Hidatsas,

Mandans, and other Indians of the upper Missouri (for more about Loisel see Cedar Island).[37]

With President Jefferson's completion of the Louisiana Purchase in 1803, sovereignty of the Missouri watershed passed to the United States. The following year Meriwether Lewis and William Clark undertook their Corps of Discovery expedition, reaching the Mandans in late October. Unable to speak the Mandan language, the two captains enlisted René Jusseaume as their interpreter. On November 3, 1804, Lewis and Clark started their men building a double row of cabins and two storerooms, protected by a stockade and a gate on the side nearest the Missouri. Fort Mandan, as the triangular-shaped winter quarters were called, sat on the river's left bank about seven miles downstream from the Knife, and 1,609 miles above the Missouri's confluence with the Mississippi.[38] A village of earth-domed Mandan huts occupied the opposite shore. On November 27, 1804, a party of Nor'Westers commanded by François Antoine Larocque joined the Corps of Discovery at the Mandan villages, and spent the winter trading.

Fort Mandan (Lewis and Clark Fort)

Although the Nor'Westers were trespassing on United States soil, Lewis and Clark could not stop them from doing so without provoking the Mandans' ire. The tribe had become dependent on the white man's manufactured goods and did not care whether the trade came from the British or Americans.

Over the winter, the twenty-year-old Larocque asked to join the Corps' expedition to the Pacific. Though the captains liked him, they refused his request lest he relay word of the country's trapping potential to his Nor'West bosses. In the spring of 1805, Lewis and Clark departed for the Oregon coast, leaving the young adventurer to propose a similar trek to his superiors. That summer, while the Corps of Discovery was struggling across the Continental Divide, the North West Company permitted Larocque to lead an exploration from the Mandan villages to the Yellowstone country. Traveling by horseback, he meandered to

Mountain Men Bob Southland & Bill Gross at Fort Mandan (Lewis and Clark Fort)

within sight of the Bighorn Mountains (in central Wyoming), then swung north to the Yellowstone River. After wandering down the Yellowstone to the Missouri, Larocque proceeded to Fort Assiniboine on the Assiniboine River (in Manitoba, Canada), having failed to record any useful information.[39]

When the Corps of Discovery returned to St. Louis in September 1806, the town's merchants and traders salivated at the multitude of beaver the explorers reported having seen on the Missouri's tributaries. Over the winter, merchants Manuel Lisa, Pierre Menard, and William Morrison formed a partnership and began organizing a party of trappers and traders to follow in the footsteps of Lewis and Clark.[40] The partners recruited many of the Corps' former members, including George Drouillard. In the spring of 1807, the Lisa, Menard & Morrison expedition sailed up the Missouri on two keelboats. Upon reaching the Mandans in mid-summer, Lisa parleyed with the tribal leaders, seeking permission to pass their villages in peace. Although there is no record of it, some historians think Lisa left behind one or two traders and a small store of goods; assuming he did, they most likely built a trading cabin.[41]

During the winter of 1808–9, Lisa incorporated his firm into the newly established and better capitalized St. Louis Missouri Fur Company. That spring, the partners launched a two-pronged force up the Missouri that totaled three hundred and fifty men supported by thirteen keelboats and mackinaws. Just above the Mandan and Hidatsa villages, Lisa paused to build Fort Mandan (aka Lisa's Post) a few miles upstream from the Missouri's confluence with the Knife.[42]

In 1812, the St. Louis Missouri Fur Company expired, and its partners recapitalized as the Missouri Fur Company. Yet despite the optimism with which it was born, the new concern was short-lived. War between the United States and Great Britain allied many of the upper Missouri tribes to the English, obliging Manuel Lisa to withdraw his traders from every post except those among the Sioux and Omahas. However, these two ventures by themselves were unable to supply enough beaver to stem the company's losses, especially with the fur market plummeting amid wartime financial panic. By January 1814, the Missouri Fur Company was finished.

When the war ended later that year, the price of pelts began to firm. Encouraged, Lisa again sent his traders up the Missouri to the Arikaras, Hidatsas, and Mandans. The tribes had stayed friendly with him despite efforts by British agents working for the Hudson's Bay and North West companies to keep them hostile. In 1819, Lisa resuscitated the defunct Missouri Fur Company, bringing in new investors including Joshua Pilcher and Andrew Drips. On August 12 the following year, Manuel Lisa died unexpectedly, and field command of the company passed to Pilcher. That fall the beaver market took another of its precipitous dives, once more bringing the firm's solvency into question. Still, the Missouri Fur traders among the Mandans and other tribes continued sending enough pelts downriver to enable the company to squeak by.

In 1821, the Hudson's Bay and North West companies merged under the Hudson's Bay name. The combination forced out many former Nor'West employees. Knowing it would be impossible to compete in the Canadian fur business against the British monopoly, a number of them, including Kenneth McKenzie and William Laidlaw, immigrated to St. Louis. Soon after arriving, McKenzie and Laidlaw became partners in the newly formed Columbia Fur Company.

In 1822, John Jacob Astor's American Fur Company created its Western Department and established the headquarters in St. Louis. Realizing that the Columbia Fur Company must act quickly to stay ahead of Astor's firm, McKenzie authorized the construction of Fort Tecumseh (near Pierre, South Dakota) as a headquarters post from which to expand his trading network farther up the Missouri. Then in the late fall, he sent Thomas Jeffries to open trade with the Mandans. The following May, McKenzie's able lieutenants, James Kipp and William Tilton, went to the Knife River country and began erecting a permanent trading fort, completing it in the fall of 1823.[43] Known as Tilton's Fort, the stockade sat on the right side of the Missouri, downstream from the old fort of Lewis and Clark.[44]

While the Columbia Fur Company was launching its trade

Above:
**Tepee Camp Outside
Fort Mandan
(Lewis and Clark Fort)**

Right:
**Fort Mandan
(Lewis and Clark Fort)**

167

with the Mandans, the Blackfeet drove the Missouri Fur Company off the Yellowstone. No sooner did word of this disaster reach Joshua Pilcher, than he learned that the Arikaras had attacked keelboats belonging to William Ashley. That summer, the US Army launched a punitive expedition to punish the Arikaras. The inept campaign proved a disaster (for the details see Fort Henry at the confluence of the Missouri and Yellowstone rivers). The Arikaras escaped, and the Missouri was closed to all traffic. Pilcher had no choice but to pull his trappers and traders downriver.

The departure of Pilcher's people from the Mandans left the Columbia Fur Company alone on the upper Missouri. However, the firm's monopoly among the Mandans soon became a nightmare when the belligerent Arikaras set up camp outside the company's fort.[45] Fearing for their lives, Kipp and the other Columbia Fur employees abandoned their stockade and sought refuge inside the main Mandan village, near which they eventually built a new trading house. The Columbia Fur Company maintained a shaky presence among the Mandans until 1827, when Kenneth McKenzie folded the firm into the American Fur Company and assigned the Mandan post to the Upper Missouri Outfit, which he managed. The acquisition marked the first time John Jacob Astor's company had traders so far up the Missouri.

In 1831, McKenzie commissioned a new trading post for the Mandans, naming it Fort Clark in honor of William Clark. Built that spring by James Kipp, the stockade was located on the right side of the Missouri, about eight miles below the mouth of the Knife.[46] After forts Union and Pierre, Fort Clark was the American Fur Company's most important post on the upper Missouri. Two years later, Sublette & Campbell opened a competing trading house near the old Missouri Fur Company's Fort Mandan site. The tiny post closed the following spring when Sublette sold Fort William (at the mouth of the Yellowstone) and the rest of his fledgling Missouri River trading operation to the American Fur Company. In June 1834, Astor unloaded his majority interest in the firm, and the Upper Missouri Outfit and Western Department passed to Pratte, Chouteau & Company. Nevertheless, little changed at the Missouri trading posts; life and commerce continued as they had before the sale, although the slumping fur market meant that, in importance, buffalo robes were increasingly replaced by beaver.

On June 19, 1837, Pratte & Chouteau's steamboat *St. Peter's* landed at Fort Clark with the annual allotment of trade goods. Excitement at seeing the side-wheeler ran high among the Mandans and the Arikaras, who had recently taken up residence at the Mandan's village. Members of both tribes lined the bank and gawked while the cargo was being off-loaded. The next morning when the *St. Peter's* continued its journey up the Missouri toward Fort Union,[47] none of the spectators from the previous day suspected the lethal consequence of its visit. The steamer had left behind far more than a few boxes of blankets, awls, and beads; it had also left smallpox.

In mid-July, the first Mandan died. Soon the deaths defied counting. Like a vengeful whirlwind, the deadly virus raced through the tribes of the upper Missouri. It broke the back of the Blackfoot Confederation. It destroyed the power of the Arikaras to ever again halt river traffic. It laid low the Hidatsas, Assiniboines, and Crees, but nowhere did it strike with such finality as it did among the Mandans. By the time the epidemic had run its course, the Mandans ceased to exist as a nation.[48]

After the pestilence ended, the handful of Mandans left alive, and the surviving Hidatsas deserted their Knife River villages and moved up the Missouri forty-two miles to Fishhook Bend (see "Old" Fort Berthold).[49]

5   **Fort Manuel** (Arikaras): Between August and October 1812, Manuel Lisa's carpenters constructed a Missouri Fur Company trading post for the Arikaras on the west side of the Missouri River, just above the mouth of Hunkpapa Creek, and twelve miles north of the tribe's villages (about twenty miles above the Missouri's confluence with the Grand River and ten miles south of the North and South Dakota state line).[50] In the spring of 1813, the war between the United States and Great Britain ignited the upper Missouri, as the Hudson's Bay and North West companies turned many of the region's Indians against the Americans. That March, Lisa evacuated Fort Manuel and retreated to St. Louis.[51]

3 **Fort Manuel or Manuel's Fort** (confluence of the Bighorn and Yellowstone Rivers) (aka Fort Ramon, Fort Lisa, and variations thereof): See Fort Raymond.

8 **Marais des Cygnes River Post:** In July 1821, US officials established a satellite post of the Fort Osage government Indian factory on the Marais des Cygnes River, about five miles upstream from its confluence with the Osage (a bit north of Rich Hill, Missouri). The small trading house closed the following year, after the United States Congress ended the factory system.[52]

Between 1823 and 1825, Auguste Pierre Chouteau, financed by his brother Pierre, Jr.'s partnership, opened a trading operation at the old Marais des Cygnes factory for the Little Osages. The post was part of the four-post Osage Outfit that August Chouteau managed for Bernard Pratte & Company (for more about the Osage Outfit, see Osage Posts and Fort Osage).[53]

7,8 **Fort Mason** (aka Camp Holmes) **and Auguste Chouteau's Post:** In June 1835, the First US Dragoons erected Fort Mason on the north side of the Canadian River (near Lexington, Oklahoma). The facility was never intended to garrison troops; rather, the government used it to house Indian representatives during treaty negotiations later that summer. After the parties withdrew, Auguste Pierre Chouteau opened a trading post on a stream–soon named Chouteau Creek–near the deserted fort (see Osage Posts and Fort Osage for more about Auguste Chouteau's trading ventures).[54]

1 **McKay's Fort:** See Umpqua River Posts.

3 **Fort McKenzie** (aka Fort Brulé–the burned fort–after it was destroyed): During the spring of 1832, James Kipp, founder and *bourgeois* of Fort Piegan, the first American Fur Company trading post for the Blackfeet, floated a keelboat of beaver pelts and buffalo robes down the Missouri from the mouth of the Marias River to Fort Union (see Fort Piegan for the details leading up to this journey). Needing Kipp to take command of Fort Clark among the Mandans, Kenneth McKenzie, director of the firm's Upper Missouri Outfit, gave the Blackfoot trade to David Mitchell. In mid-summer, Mitchell labored up the Missouri aboard a keelboat filled with thirty thousand dollars worth of supplies. Somewhere between the Milk and Musselshell rivers, a pre-dawn thunderstorm ripped the boat loose from its lines. While a handful of voyageurs frantically tried to regain control, the current dashed the craft against an *embarra,* smashing its hull. It sank in seconds, taking along its cargo and two of Mitchell's crew.[55]

Although the record is fuzzy, most historians think Mitchell returned to Fort Union for another boat and more trade goods. He eventually reached the Marias River where he found Fort Piegan reduced to ashes. Rather than rebuild at that site, Mitchell chose another seven miles farther up the Missouri (about thirteen miles below Fort Benton, Montana), naming the new post Fort McKenzie after his boss. The following year, *engagés* replaced that facility with a larger one, also called Fort McKenzie.[56]

In 1837, the steamboat *St. Peter's* ascended the Missouri, bringing supplies for the former American Fur trading posts—owned since mid-1834 by Pratte, Chouteau & Company. This year, the *St. Peter's* carried more than cargo; it also carried death. Among its passengers was Jacob Halsey, bound for Fort Union as its temporary *bourgeois.* Traveling with him were his pregnant, mixed-blood wife, and their son. When the steamer landed at Fort Clark, a couple of members of the crew and Halsey's wife were prostrate with high fevers, and rashes that slowly elevated their skin. A day or so later, somewhere above the Mandan and Hidatsa villages, the young woman gave birth to a stillborn daughter, then died herself from smallpox. When the *St. Peter's* reached Fort Union on June 24, Halsey lay wrapped in blankets, his body shivering and racked with pain.[57]

Crewmen unloaded the steamboat's supplies and took aboard packs of beaver and robes, while two *engagés* carried Halsey to the master bedroom in the *bourgeois's* house. Alexander

Fort McKenzie

Harvey was among those who watched the *St. Peter's* arrival, having come down from Fort McKenzie to pick up the annual allotment of trade goods for the Blackfeet. Wanting to escape the smallpox, Harvey had his keelboat quickly filled with stores, and ordered his voyageurs to begin pulling and poling the sluggish craft up the Missouri. At the mouth of the Judith River, an Indian passenger and one of the voyageurs came down with fever. Knowing that they had the dreaded disease, Harvey halted, sending an express to Alexander Culbertson, Fort McKenzie's current *bourgeois,* informing him that he would hold the keelboat at the Judith until the affliction had run its course.

Camped in the bottomland around the fort were thirty-five hundred Blackfeet, all eagerly awaiting the keelboat and its supplies. When Culbertson told the Indians that the boat would be delayed because of a deadly sickness, they accused him of trickery, claiming that the fur company intended to sell the trade goods to the Crows and other enemies of the Blackfeet. The Blackfoot chiefs and elders knew nothing of smallpox. They warned Culbertson that he had better order the boat upriver, or they would burn Fort McKenzie as they had done Fort Piegan. Fearing for the lives of his men, Culbertson sent word for Harvey to continue up the Missouri with all possible haste.

When Harvey arrived at the trading post, the Blackfeet bartered their furs and robes, then drank water-diluted alcohol, danced, and celebrated their coup over the company's keelboat. By the time the Blackfeet finally struck their tepees and rode north for their buffalo hunt, two of Harvey's voyageurs were dead.

That autumn, the virus raced through Fort McKenzie like the black plague. It struck Culbertson, his *engagés,* and their Indian wives. Twenty-seven of the post's residents died, so many that the grave diggers discarded their spades and tossed the corpses into the Missouri.

Among the three tribes of the Blackfoot Confederation, the smallpox destroyed whole bands, indiscriminately killing the old and young, even the strongest and bravest of warriors. Throughout the fall, winter, and into the spring, shamans shook rattles and sang to the spirits, seeking to stem the epidemic. But pestilence raced on . . . and on.

During the summer and fall of 1838, hardly any Indians came to Fort McKenzie. Now recovered and anxious about his trade, Alexander Culbertson rode out searching for his clientele. Everywhere he looked, he found death. He located villages by their stench. Inside he saw men, women, and children, their bodies bloated and rotting, their limbs gnawed by coyotes and rats. The few people he discovered alive were little more than skin-draped, pock-marked skeletons, their hands reaching out, begging for food. By the time the smallpox epidemic of 1837–8 had run its course, the power of the Blackfoot Confederation was forever destroyed. Still, enough Blackfeet lived to keep Fort McKenzie functioning for several more years.

In the winter of 1843–4, two of the most Indian-hating men ever to work for the American Fur Company and its successors were together at the McKenzie fort. Francis Chardon was the *bourgeois,* and Alexander Harvey was his senior trader and clerk. In January, a party of Bloods (one of the three tribes in the Blackfoot Confederation, the others being the Piegans and Blackfeet proper) murdered a black bondman named Reese.[58] Swearing revenge, Chardon hatched a plot with Harvey and Jacob Berger, the post's interpreter, whereby they would kill the tribe's chiefs when they next came to trade.

A month later the Indians gathered beyond the stockade, clamoring for permission to come inside. Before opening the front gate, Harvey loaded the fort's cannon with grape and pointed it at the entrance to the trade room. Once within the fort, the Indians clustered together, awaiting their turn with the traders. As was customary, an *engagé* locked the gate. Then, just when Harvey was ready to fire the cannon, something about his demeanor alerted the chiefs. Screaming a warning, they began clawing their way atop the pickets. Harvey lit the cannon's touchhole as the crowd broke. The blast killed three Indians outright and wounded two more. Chardon fired his pistol at a chief who was attempting to vault the stockade, splintering his thighbone. While the wounded Indians writhed on the ground, Harvey went from one to another, slitting their throats and lifting their scalps. After he finished, he slowly licked the blood off his dirk. The conspirators divided the property the panicked warriors had left behind, and that night, Harvey forced the Indian wives of the fort's *engagés* to dance around the crusted scalps.[59] This wanton murder prompted the tribe to begin harassing the post's traders. By springtime, tensions had risen so high that Chardon burned Fort McKenzie and established a new post at the Judith River (see Fort Chardon–aka Fort F.A.C.). Thereafter, the Blackfeet called the charred remains Fort Brulé.

1 **McKenzie's Post** (aka Clearwater Post): In the summer of 1812, Donald McKenzie, a partner in John Jacob Astor's Pacific Fur Company, built a post on the Clearwater River above its confluence with the Snake (a bit east of Lewiston, Idaho), intending to trade with the Nez Perces.[60]

Soon after finishing the fort, McKenzie began to sour on the entire Fort Astoria undertaking. That autumn, he journeyed to the company's trading house on the Spokane River to consult John Clarke about relocating the Clearwater post. While McKenzie was there, a party of Nor'Westers burst in, shouting that the United States had declared war on Great Britain. In a state of jubilation, they warned that a British frigate was on its way to force the surrender of Fort Astoria. Without telling Clarke of his plans, McKenzie rushed back to his post on the Clearwater, cached what equipment and furs his *engagés* could not carry, and abandoned his command. After returning to Astoria in mid-January 1813, McKenzie began enlisting other officers in a scheme to sell the Pacific Fur Company's forts and retreat to the United States (see Fort Astoria for more details).

4 **Owen McKenzie's Post:** Between August and September 1862, Owen McKenzie–the mixed-blood son of Kenneth McKenzie, former commander of the American Fur Company's Upper Missouri Outfit–founded a trading post for La Barge, Harkness & Company on the north side of the Missouri, midway between the mouths of the Poplar River and Big Muddy Creek (near Brockton, Montana, on the Fort Peck Indian Reservation; see Fort Charles Galpin about the competition between La Barge & Harkness and the Chouteau empire.) Although Indian hostility forced the post's abandonment in 1863, Owen McKenzie did not live to see it.[61]

In late June that year, low water had halted Pierre Chouteau, Jr., & Company's steamboat, *Nellie Rogers,* near the mouth of the Milk River. Unable to continue up the Missouri to Fort Benton, the steamer's crew off-loaded the fort's supplies so the stores could finish their journey via wagon. As the *Nellie Rogers* prepared to return to St. Louis, Owen McKenzie came aboard, requesting passage downriver. He was quite drunk. Also traveling on the boat was Malcolm Clark, a powerfully-built man with piercing eyes, who brooked no insult. When in his twenties, Clark had been expelled from the US Military Academy at West Point for beating one classmate with a whip and another with his fists. After leaving the Academy, Clark went to Texas and fought for the Republic's independence.[62] Sometime later he moved to the upper Missouri and worked for Pierre Chouteau, Jr., & Company, followed by Frost & Todd and then Clark, Primeau & Company, of which he was part owner.[63] When that partnership failed, he rejoined the Chouteau firm.

For some time, a feud had simmered between Owen McKenzie and Malcolm Clark, its origins stemming from Clark's early days in the fur trade. McKenzie had lived his life up-country, far from the settlements and rule of law. He was an expert shot with a rifle, and with the Navy Colt he carried in his belt. Like Clark, he was not a man to let an impertinence pass.

Soon after McKenzie boarded the *Nellie Rogers,* he met Clark. Perhaps it was caused by the liquor, perhaps orneriness, maybe even their festering grudge, but they had words. As their voices and tempers escalated, Clark drew his revolver and repeatedly fired. McKenzie crumpled to the deck, his life spurting from three wounds, his own pistol still in his belt.

Clark pleaded self-defense, but no one believed him. Knowing that McKenzie's friends and kin would never leave the young man's death unavenged, Clark stole away from the steamboat and made his way to Fort Benton. The *Nellie Rogers* took McKenzie's body to Fort Union, where it was buried.

In time, Malcolm Clark founded a Montana cattle ranch; however, he could never escape his hair-trigger temper. During an argument in 1869, his wife's Piegan Blackfoot brother did to him what he had done to Owen McKenzie.[64] As the old fur trappers would have said, it was "mountain justice."

5 **Fort Mitchell:** In 1833, *engagés* for the American Fur Company built a trading post near the confluence of the Missouri and Niobrara Rivers (near Niobrara, Nebraska), naming it for David Mitchell, a long-standing employee, *bourgeois,* and partner of the firm's Upper Missouri Outfit. After Fort Mitchell was abandoned in 1837, passing steamboats burned its buildings and stockade in their fireboxes.[65]

7 **Moncravie House:** Around 1856, John B. Moncravie opened a tiny, makeshift trading post on the Laramie River, twelve miles upstream from Fort Laramie, on land given to him and his Sioux wife by her Ogalala brothers (near Grayrocks Reservoir, south of Guernsey, Wyoming; for more about Moncravie, see Fort John II and other Pierre Chouteau, Jr., & Company Scotts Bluff Trading Posts—endnote 4). Moncravie's post lasted no more than two years.[66]

Montero's Forts (aka The Portuguese Houses): During the 1830s, Portuguese trader and trapper Antonio Montero established a series of small, short-lived trading posts in the Powder River country (central Wyoming). Montero also worked as a brigade *partisan* for Captain Benjamin Bonneville during his brief sojourn in the fur trade.[67]

7 **Morrow's Post** (aka Junction House): In the early to mid-1850s, a trader named Morrow erected a shabby post on the south side of the Platte River at the confluence of its north and south tributaries (a bit southeast of North Platte, Nebraska). Junction House, as it was sometimes called, most likely saw more traffic with the

Oregon and California Trail emigrants than it did with Indians seeking to barter buffalo robes.[68]

4　**Fort Mortimer** (aka Fort William): In 1841, John Ebbetts took a dozen traders among the Sioux and bartered for several hundred packs of buffalo robes. After selling the robes for a tidy profit, Ebbetts traveled to New York City and enlisted Fulton Cutting and Charles Kelsey in a trading venture on the upper Missouri. As an inducement, Ebbetts told his prospective partners that Pierre Chouteau, Jr., & Company had so alienated the Missouri tribes that it was in danger of losing their trade. Needing more capital, Cutting used family ties to entice his cousin, Mortimer Livingston, into investing in the enterprise. Livingston did so through his trading firm, Bolton, Fox, Livingston & Company, which ran cargo ships between the east coast of the United States and Europe.[69]

With Livingston's financial powerhouse behind them, Ebbetts, Cutting, and Kelsey christened their partnership the Union Fur Company and, in the summer of 1842, steamed up the Missouri intending to open posts in direct competition with those of Pierre Chouteau, Jr. Thirty miles below Chouteau's Fort Pierre, the partners paused to construct Fort George (see Fort George–Missouri River). After several days, Cutting and Ebbetts left Kelsey to finish the post, while they continued upriver to the mouth of the Yellowstone and established Fort Mortimer near the ruins of Sublette & Campbell's Fort William (about twenty-two miles southwest of Williston, North Dakota), and five miles downstream from Fort Union. The partners named their cottonwood trading house after their benefactor, Mortimer Livingston.[70]

In 1843, flooding undercut the front of the Fort Mortimer stockade, causing the Union Fur *engagés* to shift the post inland where they rebuilt it from adobe.[71]

The Bolton, Fox & Livingston partners soon regretted having ever heard of John Ebbetts. Far from losing its grip on the fur trade, Pierre Chouteau, Jr., & Company proved a formidable competitor. When the Union Fur Company's traders gave the Indians gifts and liquor, the Chouteau traders countered with richer gifts and more liquor. After three years of red ink, Bolton, Fox, & Livingston decided to cut its losses. In the spring of 1845, the firm sold Fort Mortimer and its other posts to Pierre Chouteau, Jr., and severed its ties with Ebbetts and the Union Fur Company.[72]

Chouteau's *engagés* stripped the stores and other movable property from Fort Mortimer, then left the stockade to the elements and passing steamboat captains who began burning the post's pickets to fire their boilers. In 1846, Alexander Harvey, who for years had murdered and traded his way across the upper Missouri, formed Harvey, Primeau & Company and occupied what was left of Fort Mortimer, changing its name to Fort William.[73]

Following Harvey's death in 1854, ownership of Fort William passed to J. Picotte & Company. Two years later it transferred again, this time to Frost & Todd. By 1858, encroachment by the Sioux from the east had made the Assiniboines reluctant to trade at the post. They felt safer going to Fort Union, though it was only a few miles away. Hoping to win the Assiniboines back from Pierre Chouteau, Jr., & Company, Frost & Todd abandoned Fort William and built Fort Stewart forty miles farther west.

Fort Nez Perces through Fort Owen

1 **Fort Nez Perces:** See Fort Walla Walla (formerly called Fort Nez Perces).

1 **Fort Nisqually** (aka Nisqually House): In 1833, Francis Heron built a Hudson's Bay trading post one-half mile inland from Puget Sound, and about three miles northeast of the mouth of the Nisqually River (near Du Pont, Washington, about midway between Olympia and Tacoma).[1] Named for the local Indians, Fort Nisqually was intended to monopolize the Puget Sound fur trade, cutting it off from American sea captains who had recently been making inroads with the district's tribes.

Fort Nisqually

Interior of Fort Nisqually

Fort Nisqually

In 1839, Governor George Simpson transferred Fort Nisqually to the Puget's Sound Agriculture Company, a Hudson's Bay subsidiary that sought to encourage and regulate farming north of the Columbia River. Simpson hoped to induce mixed-blood families from the Red River Settlement (south of Canada's Lake Winnipeg; see Pembina Posts) to immigrate to the Pacific Northwest and work the land as tenants, giving the Hudson's Bay Company half of their crops in rent. Simpson's plan failed to attract more than a handful of takers because most people wanted to farm their own property rather than slave away as chattels. The few families that came to Fort Nisqually lasted only a couple of years. After watching their stunted crops wither in the sandy soil and their ewes sicken and lose their lambs, the disenchanted colonists moved south to the more fertile Willamette River Valley (Oregon) below Fort Vancouver.

**Bastion of
Fort Nisqually**

In the early 1840s (the exact date is unknown), Fort Nisqually was rebuilt one-third mile due east of the original site. The Hudson's Bay Company continued raising sheep on the land bordering Puget Sound, with the herd numbering nearly eight thousand in 1846.[2] For shepherds, the firm resorted to Indians, Hawaiians, and the few retired white employees who could be persuaded to work on shares. A shortage of dependable labor, coupled with disease, wolf predation, and encroachment by American emigrants, doomed the Nisqually farming venture to operate at a loss. The Hudson's Bay agricultural experiment and Fort Nisqually closed in 1869.

1 **Nisqually House:** See Fort Nisqually.

6,8 **Nishnabotna Posts:** In 1819, Joseph Robidoux III and Alexander Papin built a trading post for the partnership of Bartholomew Berthold and Pierre Chouteau, Jr., near the confluence of the Nishnabotna and Missouri rivers (about ten miles southwest of Rock Port, Missouri).[3] That November, John Zenoni and Joseph Perkins of the Missouri Fur Company erected a competing post nearby, but it failed within three months.[4] The Nishnabotna post of Berthold & Chouteau eventually passed to the American Fur Company which operated it as late as 1833.

2 **Fort Nonsense** (aka Bonneville's Folly): See Fort Bonneville.

1 **Fort Okanagan:** In June 1811, word reached the Pacific Fur Company's post at Fort Astoria that the North West Company had opened a trading house on the Spokane River. Late that summer, Astorian David Stuart built Fort Okanagan in the triangle of land above the confluence of the Okanogan and Columbia rivers (about five miles east of Brewster, Washington; see Fort Astoria endnote 64 about the spelling of Okanagan and Okanogan). It was the first of several forts the Astorians meant to establish, in order to contest British encroachment.[5]

In 1813, war between the United States and Great Britain

unnerved the Pacific Fur Company's shareholders, spurring them to sell Fort Astoria and its satellite posts to the Nor'Westers. After the transfer, Fort Okanagan gained added importance as a way station on the trade line between Fort George–the renamed Fort Astoria–and Fort Alexandria on the Fraser River (in British Columbia). The Okanagan Trail, as the route was called, gradually replaced the more cumbersome east-west route that ran from Montreal to Fort William on the north shore of Lake Superior, to the myriad rivers and portages that connected the company's western-most forts. Supplies could now be off-loaded from company ships in the Columbia River estuary and distributed throughout the Northwest region via the Okanagan Trail.

In 1821, Fort Okanagan changed hands again, going to the Hudson's Bay Company after its merger with the Nor'Westers. The Hudson's Bay Company used the Okanagan Trail until 1846, when the border between the United States and Canada was finally fixed along the forty-ninth parallel.

8 **Osage Posts and Fort Osage** (aka Fort Clark, Fort Sibley, and Fiery Prairie Fort): Roving French traders from posts along the Illinois and Mississippi rivers began penetrating the Osage River country (west-central Missouri) in the second half of the seventeenth century. They quickly created a demand in the Big and Little Osages for European-manufactured goods, especially matchlock and, then, flintlock fusils.[6] The tribes were fierce in battle, making it risky for any white trader to venture into their midst; however, the rewards for doing so were substantial since the Osages had a reputation for producing the finest furs on the lower Missouri.[7] In the mid-1700s, a handful of English traders visited the Osages in an attempt to win their loyalty, but the tribes remained allied with the French.

In 1763, Auguste Chouteau came up the Mississippi River from New Orleans as the fourteen-year-old clerk of his stepfather, Pierre Lacléde Liguest. Their expedition was funded by Maxent, Lacléde & Company which had been granted a trading monopoly on the Missouri and central Mississippi rivers.[8] In mid-February the following year, Lacléde established a trading post and settlement on the west bank of the Mississippi just down from the mouth of the Missouri, naming it for the patron saint of France's Louis XV. The king had recently signed the Treaty of Paris, ceding the western Louisiana Territory to Spain.[9]

During the ensuing years, Laclède's St. Louis settlement prospered,[10] and so did Auguste Chouteau and his younger half brother, Pierre Chouteau, Sr. By the 1790s, the Chouteaus were among the town's leading families, their wealth stemming from land and trade.

Commerce with the Big and Little Osages had always been profitable, if somewhat dangerous. Considered two of the most hostile tribes on the central prairie, the Osages tolerated traders but harassed any who refused to pay tribute. In 1790, their attacks prompted the Spanish governor-general to forbid all traffic with the tribes, hoping the prohibition would induce the chiefs to restrain their warriors. The policy failed. Osage war parties continued to stop Spanish traders on the Missouri River and its tributaries, robbing them or bringing them to their villages for forced barter that was little more than armed extortion.[11] Even the Spanish settlements of Ste. Geneviève and St. Charles were not immune. Bands of Osages routinely killed village farmers as they tended their crops.[12]

In the spring of 1794, Auguste and Pierre Chouteau, Sr., asked the Spanish government for a six-year trading monopoly with the Big Osages. The half brothers proposed building a fort near the Indians' village, and inducing the tribe to sign a peace treaty that would extend from the trading post to the white settlements along the Mississippi River. The governor agreed. That summer, Auguste and Pierre, Sr., went up the Missouri and Osage rivers and began constructing Fort Carondelet on a limestone bluff overlooking the Osage River, just upstream from Panther Creek and a bit below the Big Osage village (in eastern Vernon County, Missouri).[13] The Chouteaus made good on their promise, at long last bringing a measure of tranquillity to the lower Missouri. Their plan worked so well that in 1800, the government extended their monopoly another four years.[14]

In the late 1790s, the Missouri River's fur potential captured the interest of Manuel Lisa, a Spanish trader who for several years had operated in the central Mississippi River drainage between Vincennes and Ste. Geneviève. After moving to St. Louis in 1799, Lisa sought to expand his business up the Missouri, but was thwarted by a government policy that granted certain well-placed men exclusive license to trade with a particular tribe. When his petition for free trade was rejected by the lieutenant governor in St. Louis, Lisa bribed the Spanish governor-general in New Orleans. In June 1802, the governor-general terminated the Osage monopoly of the Chouteaus, transferring it to Manuel Lisa, Benoît & Company.[15]

Until this time, no one in western America knew that on October 1, 1800, Spain had secretly given the Louisiana Territory to France under the Second Treaty of San Ildefonso.[16] No sooner did the citizens of St. Louis learn about the treaty than they received word that France had sold the Louisiana Territory to the United States. As one of his last official acts, the Spanish lieutenant governor recommended to the incoming American officials that the Osage trade be taken away from Manuel Lisa and returned to the Chouteaus.[17] Fortunately for Lisa, the advice was ignored; nonetheless, the lieutenant governor's back-stabbing ploy demonstrated to Lisa the need to cultivate friendships among the incoming American politicians.

In March 1808, Meriwether Lewis arrived in St. Louis having been appointed governor of the Louisiana Territory. Highly critical of the way the Spanish had administered the fur trade, Lewis called for an end to the private trading monopolies which overcharged the Indians and kept them in debt through the onerous extension of credit. Rather, he suggested that the US Army should build a series of forts from the Osages to the Mandans, and that a government trading factory should be located at each site. Congress had approved the factory system in the mid-1790s, hoping to protect the Indians from unscrupulous traders. Eastern lawmakers felt that by licensing private merchants to sell their wares in Army forts, the trade could be controlled and abuses avoided. The first factories were opened at Tellico (eastern Tennessee) and on Georgia's St. Mary's River. However, during the five years since President Jefferson had purchased the Louisiana Territory, the system had not spread west of the Mississippi. In addition to establishing state-owned trading factories, Lewis also proposed opening the country beyond the Mandans to a single, private, American trading conglomerate with the resources to drive out the North West Company, which acted as if the territory belonged to Great Britain instead of the United States.[18]

That fall, a band of the Osage tribe known as the Great Osages gave Lewis an excuse to put his plan into action. All year the band's warriors had raided settlements along the lower Missouri, taking captives and burning homesteads. With Lisa's traders furnishing the Indians a continual supply of fusils and gunpowder, the Osages saw little reason to respect American authority. Needing to curb the war parties, Lewis seized on their attacks as an opportunity to institute the factory system west of the Mississippi. Accordingly, he authorized William Clark to ascend the Missouri with a company of infantry and establish a military fortification and Indian factory. In October, while Clark's troops erected the fort's palisades, Lewis sent Pierre Chouteau, Sr., to negotiate a new peace treaty with the Osages.[19]

Originally named for its founder, Fort Clark sat on a rise immediately south of the Missouri River, forty miles downstream from the mouth of the Kansas (near Sibley, Missouri, about fourteen miles east of Independence).[20] In November, the stockade was formally christened Fort Osage, although it was occasionally referred to as Fort Sibley—after George Sibley, its resident Indian factory trader—and as the Fiery Prairie Fort.[21]

During the winter of 1808–9, Lewis launched the next phase of his plan for the fur trade by helping organize the St. Louis Missouri Fur Company. Under his authority as territorial governor, Lewis granted the firm an exclusive license to trade with the tribes above the Mandans. In addition to William Clark, the company's partners included Manuel Lisa, and many other traders who had been stripped of their monopolies when Lewis inaugurated his Indian factory scheme. Meriwether Lewis's brother, Reuben, also became a partner, and though there is no record of it, Governor Lewis may have been a secret partner. Making it more of a sweetheart deal, Lewis promised to refrain from issuing

185

Fort Osage Exterior Blockhouse & Palisade
Permission to photograph Fort Osage provided by Jackson County, MO, Parks & Recreation

Fort Osage Blockhouse & Barracks

186

any additional trading licenses for tribes between the mouth of the Platte and the Mandans.[22]

On October 11, 1809, Meriwether Lewis committed suicide. Dying with him were his dreams for the organization of the western fur trade. Although the St. Louis Missouri Fur Company sent its traders and trappers to the Yellowstone and upper Missouri rivers, Lewis's plan to open additional government Indian factories above Fort Osage never came to fruition. Except for three years, during which it was left unoccupied in the War of 1812, Fort Osage guarded the lower Missouri until 1819, when the main garrison moved upriver to Council Bluffs and established Fort Atkinson. The government trading house remained at the old fort until lobbying by John Jacob Astor's American Fur Company prompted Congress to end the Indian factory system in 1822. George Sibley, who had managed the trade at Fort Osage since 1808, purchased the government's stock of merchandise and continued trading at the post, in partnership with Paul Baillio and Lilburn Boggs. Troops were occasionally stationed at Fort Osage until Fort Leavenworth opened in 1827.[23]

Despite Lewis's grand designs and the construction of Fort Osage, the Chouteaus had not abandoned their trade with the Osage tribes. Ignoring the legalities of a government license, an A.P. Chouteau had traded with the tribe in 1812. Whether he was Auguste Pierre Chouteau—the older brother of Pierre, Jr.,—or some cousin with the same name, is unknown.[24] Beginning in 1814, Paul Liguest Chouteau, a younger brother of Auguste and Pierre, Jr., traded with the Osages for the partnership of Bartholomew Berthold and Pierre Chouteau, Jr.[25] After the end of the government factory system in 1822, Auguste Chouteau joined his brother Paul—financed by brother Pierre, Jr., and Bartholomew Berthold—and secured an Osage trading license for the Arkansas River. That summer, Auguste Chouteau went to the Great Osage village (in Missouri) and talked some of the tribe into coming with him to the country bounded by the Arkansas, Neosho, and Verdigris rivers (in northeastern Oklahoma). Upon reaching the Neosho, Auguste Chouteau established a trading house at a salt spring known as La Saline (about thirty-five miles above the river's mouth). The Osages looked over the land, then placed their village fifty miles farther up the Neosho (in the vicinity of Oswego, Kansas).[26] Smelling an opportunity, Paul Baillio–of Sibley, Baillio & Boggs–persuaded the trapper "Old Bill" Williams (in early 1823), that they should open a tiny post near the tribe's new home (see "Old Bill" Williams's Post on the Fork of the Grand–aka Neosho–River).[27]

With "Old Bill's" fort close by, the Osages had no reason to frequent the post at La Saline, which August Chouteau had turned over to his cousin, Pierre Melicourt Papin. To regain the Osages' trade, Papin established a satellite post (of the La Saline trading house) ten miles south of the tribe's new village and began to enjoy a profitable return.[28]

Meanwhile, in late 1822, Auguste Chouteau had moved southwest to the Verdigris River and acquired thirty acres of clearing about four miles above the river's confluence with the Arkansas. In addition to a farm and ferry, Chouteau established a trading post for the neighboring tribes. Sometime later, his half

Fort Osage Trading Factory & Blockhouse

brothers, Francis Guesseau and Cyprian, reopened the old government Indian factory on the Marais des Cygnes River, bringing to four the number of posts in Auguste Chouteau's orbit. Brother Pierre Chouteau, Jr., furnished the financing through his various partnerships, calling Auguste's operation the Osage Outfit.[29]

In June 1825, the Osages signed a treaty with the United States, swapping their Missouri and Arkansas homeland for a piece of the Arkansas-Neosho-Verdigris-River-country. Soon thereafter, government agents began pressuring the Creeks, Choctaws, and Cherokees to give up their homes east of the Mississippi, and move to the so-called Indian Territory (Oklahoma).[30] As more and more Indians crowded onto the land around his trading posts, Auguste Chouteau became their benefactor, furnishing them the food and supplies that the government had promised but never delivered.

During the next few years, Auguste Chouteau continued befriending the Osages and other dispossessed tribes, all the while pressing the government to reimburse him for his expenses. In the

Fort Osage Indian Trading Room

meantime, fur-bearing game disappeared from the Indian Territory, frightened away by the hordes of Native American emigrants. With nothing to barter except the promise of their nonexistent government annuities, the tribes were totally beholden to Auguste Chouteau's kindness. The much-needed stores that he dispensed on credit came from the St. Louis warehouse of Pierre, Jr., who was now managing the Western Department of the American Fur Company. By 1833, the debt that Auguste owed his brother and his brother's partners had ballooned out of control.[31]

That June, the Verdigris River flooded, destroying Auguste Chouteau's trading post, as well as the other buildings on his farm. Auguste's indebtedness grew larger. Spring 1834 found him in New York City, representing Pratte, Chouteau & Company in the purchase of the American Fur Company's Western Department and Upper Missouri Outfit from John Jacob Astor. When the negotiations were finished, he journeyed to Washington, DC, and besieged the corridors of Congress, seeking payment of his claims. Citing more pressing needs, the politicians refused to appropriate the funds.[32]

With his brother no longer willing to throw good money after bad, Auguste, in 1835, turned to Siter, Price & Company of Philadelphia. With additional financing in hand, Auguste returned to the Indian Territory in mid-summer and sought to open a trading post among the Cherokees; however, the local Indian agent refused to grant him a license. Meanwhile, the merchandise paid for by Siter & Price sat in boxes, unsold. Auguste's debts expanded even more.

Earlier that year, the Army had constructed a stockade on the north side of the Canadian River, upstream from its confluence with the Arkansas (near Lexington, Oklahoma). Known as Fort Mason, the facility had hosted a number of Indians who gathered in August to negotiate a peace treaty between the "civilized," meaning dispossessed, tribes and those living freely on the plains. When the parley ended, Auguste Chouteau constructed a trading post on a small creek near the site (see Fort Mason—aka Camp Holmes—and Auguste Chouteau's Post).[33]

Two summers later, Chouteau erected a tiny, short-lived

trading house to serve the Kiowas, locating it on Cache Creek below the eastern foot of the Wichita Mountains (three miles south of Oklahoma's Fort Sill Military Reservation).[34] None of these posts earned enough to cover the interest on his mounting debts.

Just after New Year's Day 1838, Auguste Chouteau's financial obligations came crashing down around his head. Siter, Price & Company sued for $40,000.00. Though stunned by the news, Auguste was knocked to his knees two months later when he received word that his brother, Pierre, Jr., had brought suit for $500,000.00.[35] The court's judgment was swift and brutal. All of Auguste's St. Louis property—including two slaves—was forfeit and sold, bringing $26,844.40. Evicted from their home, his white wife and her children were thrown on the mercy of family.

Agents came to the Indian Territory, seeking to return Auguste to face his brother, but he refused to leave. Now deathly sick, Auguste Chouteau determined to spend his final weeks helping the Osages and other tribes he had befriended these last sixteen years. But his health was too far gone for him to carry through on his pledge. Auguste Pierre Chouteau died Christmas Day, 1838, seven months past his fifty-second birthday.

6 **Otoe Posts:** In October 1795, during the third expedition of Jacques Clamorgan's Company of the Discoverers and Explorers of the Missouri River, James Mackay paused among the Otoes and built them a small trading house a couple of miles above the mouth of the Platte River (near Nebraska's Offutt Air Force Base).[36] A year later, company trader Francisco Derouin came up the Missouri with a boat-load of merchandise that included brandy, and traded with the Otoes during the winter of 1796–7. He erected a new trading house a mile or so downriver from the mouth of the Platte.[37] By 1797, Clamorgan's company was falling apart; it lacked the resources to send another trading mission to the Otoes (see Mandan Villages for more detail about Clamorgan's company).[38]

Jacques Clamorgan and Spanish Governor-General François Luis Hector Carondelet had envisioned establishing a string of trading posts, garrisoned with Spanish troops, from the mouth of the Missouri River to its source. They thought such a line of defense would protect Spain's Louisiana Territory from incursions by the North West and Hudson's Bay companies. British traders roamed Spanish soil at will, supported by their posts in Canada and on the Red River of the North (see Pembina Posts).[39] Though the idea was sound, company losses and bureaucratic lethargy saw it die unfulfilled.

In 1799, two years after the demise of Clamorgan's Company of the Discoverers and Explorers of the Missouri River, Spanish Governor-General Carondelet granted the Otoe trade to Jacques Chauvin (or Santiago Chovín) and José Ortiz (or Joseph Hortiz). The following year, a new governor-general, the Marqués de Casa Calvo, returned it to Clamorgan. In 1801, it went to Josef Cruzet (or José Cruzet or Cruzatte) who built a trading post between the Otoe and Omaha villages, a few miles above what would later be known as Council Bluffs (north of Omaha, Nebraska, and a bit upriver from the Fort Atkinson State Historical Park).[40] A year later, the trade again reverted to Clamorgan. Still, the Spanish government did nothing to improve the security of the upper Missouri.

Yet unbeknownst to the Spanish traders and governor-general, in 1800 the secret Second Treaty of San Ildefonso had returned Louisiana to France. In 1803, the United States purchased the Louisiana Territory, leaving the Spanish government to ponder what might have been had it carried through on Clamorgan's dream to fortify the Missouri River with a line of Spanish trading posts.

2 **Fort Owen:** In 1841, Father Pierre Jean DeSmet built a Catholic mission, sawmill, and gristmill on the Bitterroot River, about thirty miles upstream from its confluence with the Clark Fork (near Stevensville, Montana). Nine years later, Major John Owen and his Shoshone wife, Nancy, purchased the mission for $250 and established an independent trading post for the local Indians. Owen had previously worked as a sutler at Fort Leavenworth and had come west with Lieutenant Colonel William Loring's Mounted Riflemen in 1849.

When the fur trade waned in the late 1850s, Owen catered to the miners who were flocking to the region's goldfields. Then, in the 1860s, traders Frank Worden and Christopher Higgins opened a competing post at Hell Gate Ronde (the confluence of the Clark Fork and Bitterroot rivers, just west of Missoula, Montana), siphoning off most of his trade. After the death of his wife in 1868, Owen became an insane alcoholic and was eventually deported from the territory. In 1872, Fort Owen passed to Washington McCormick who allowed it to fall into ruin.[41]

Fort Owen

Papin's House through Roy's House

6 **Papin's House** (aka Teton Post, the French Post, and Cerré's Establishment): See Fort Teton.

5 **Park River Post:** In September 1800, Nor'Wester Alexander Henry the Younger came to the confluence of the Park and Red rivers (about nine miles south of Drayton, North Dakota), meaning to found a headquarters post for a chain of trading houses he intended to establish throughout the Red River Valley. Although he constructed a fort and dispatched traders to the nearby Pembina Mountains, the Park River location soon proved a disappointment. Henry found the water too salty for his taste, and his Ojibwa customers were reluctant to venture so deep into territory patrolled by their Sioux enemies.

The following spring, Henry moved north down the Red and built his headquarters at the mouth of the Pembina River (see Pembina Posts). Henry's traders then spent the next four years erecting subposts on both sides of the forty-ninth parallel.[1]

5 **Fort Paubna:** See Pembina Posts.

Pawnee Posts: By 1700, Spanish traders from Santa Fe were sporadically visiting the Pawnees in the Platte River Valley (Nebraska); however, the trade was haphazard and the Indians received little more than a sampling of European goods.[2] Then in 1702, French traders from the Tamarois Mission (across from St. Louis, Missouri, near Cahokia, Illinois) ventured up the Missouri River and opened a short-lived post for the tribe.[3] In the 1790s, St. Louis traders, such as Benito Vasquez, began frequenting the Pawnees, winning their furs away from the New Mexicans.[4] After the completion of the Louisiana Purchase, American-owned companies established temporary trading posts among the Pawnees, moving them every few seasons as the Indians shifted their villages to stay close to the buffalo.

Despite the strong competition from St. Louis, traders from Santa Fe and Taos continued courting the tribe. During the decade before Mexico won its independence, the Spanish government encouraged the trade, hoping to use the Pawnees as a shield between New Mexico and the expansion-hungry Americans.[5] In 1821, Mexico threw off the Spanish yoke and opened the Santa Fe Trail to what quickly became a flood of American merchandise. By then, the New Mexican traders had lost their influence among the Pawnees, who preferred the better quality goods offered by the more aggressive St. Louis fur companies.

5   **Pembina Posts:** By the mid-1770s, the Red River country on both sides of the forty-ninth parallel was an important fur trading center (the Red River Valley from Winnipeg, Manitoba, into North Dakota and Minnesota). For years, the mixed-blood descendants—Canada's *Métis*—of French and English traders had made this buffalo-rich area their home. Montreal's Scottish merchants, or "Peddlers" as they were called before they coalesced into the North West Company in 1783, relied on the *Métis* to produce the pemmican needed to feed the voyageurs who paddled massive freight canoes over the inland waterways.[6]

In 1793, the Nor'Wester Peter Grant constructed the first Pembina post, locating it on the east side of the Red River across from the Red's confluence with the Pembina (just below the US-Canadian border, near St. Vincent, Minnesota).[7] Grant's small, seasonal trading house lasted but a few years before Sioux hostility persuaded him to withdraw. Still eager to tap the local Ojibwa market, the North West Company ordered Charles Jean Baptist Chaboillez to close his post on Canada's Rat River (east of Sainte-Agathe, Manitoba) in 1797, and construct another at the mouth of the Pembina. He placed Fort Paubna on the west side of the Red River, immediately below the Pembina confluence (near Pembina, North Dakota).[8] During the two seasons that Chaboillez maintained Fort Paubna, he dispatched traders throughout the region, including one named Roy, who operated a trading house at the mouth of the Forest River (near the Forest-Red River confluence, about midway between Drayton, North Dakota, and Oslo, Minnesota).[9] By 1800, Chaboillez had fled north of the forty-ninth parallel where there was less danger from Sioux war parties.

Unwilling to give up on the Pembina trade, the North West Company dispatched Alexander Henry the Younger during the summer of 1800. On September 5, he and his party reached Chaboillez's old post beside the Pembina-Red River confluence. Some days later, Henry's men began building their main Indian factory at the mouth of the Park River (about nine miles south of Drayton, North Dakota; see Park River Post). In May 1801, Henry abandoned his plan to keep his headquarters on the Park and instead directed his senior trader, Michel Langlois, to relocate it on the left bank of the Pembina, just above its merger with the Red.[10] In September, the Hudson's Bay Company started a trading house on the east side of the Red River (St. Vincent, Minnesota), and John Crébassa began one for the XY Company on the west side, both just below (north of) the Red-Pembina confluence.[11] Over the next half dozen years, Henry dispatched traders up and down the Red River Valley, establishing seasonal satellite posts from the Pembina Mountains to Grandes Fourches (Grand Forks, North Dakota) and Red Lake (Minnesota), and into Canada. The North West Company's competitors followed suit, expanding their operations in Henry's wake. Even the Sioux cooperated with the economic boom by temporarily halting their harassment of the companies' traders and their Ojibwa patrons. By late 1805, the Red River country had begun showing the early signs of overtrapping, causing fur company returns to slip. Compounding the pressure on the traders' profits, the Sioux renewed their raids. During the next two and one-half years, Sioux hostility increased, climaxing in July 1808 with an attack on Henry's Pembina headquarters. The next month, Henry received word from Fort William (on Lake Superior), ordering him to withdraw.

After Henry departed Pembina, the Red River Valley beaver trade slid into a malaise as many of the former Ojibwa trappers drifted away, reverting to the life they had known before the arrival of the fur companies. The Nor'Westers soon started directing what remained of their Red River trade from their new base near the mouth of Canada's Assiniboine River (south of Lake Winnipeg). The *Métis,* who had proven to be superb traders, hunters, and trappers, gradually shifted their focus from beaver to buffalo.[12]

In 1811, Thomas Douglas, the Fifth Earl of Selkirk and a senior shareholder in the Hudson's Bay Company, purchased 116,000 square miles of North America's heartland, a territory that reached from Canada's upper Assiniboine River, east to Rainy Lake, and south of the forty-ninth parallel to the source of the Red.[13] Lord Selkirk planned to people the holding—known as the Red River Settlement or Assiniboia—with Scottish and Swiss colonists who would establish farms. The first emigrants arrived in August 1812. That fall, the Hudson's Bay Company built Fort Daer on the south bank of the Pembina River, just above the Red confluence. Before long, friction ignited between the settlers and the *Métis,* who viewed an agricultural colony as a threat to their life as buffalo hunters. Cutting, as it did, across the Nor'Westers' riverine supply lines, the Hudson's Bay settlement also threatened the North West Company's survival. Selkirk's experiment allied two resolute powers who resolved to fight rather than abandon what they considered rightfully theirs. Within two years the *Métis*—with Nor'West support—began burning the colonists' farms. The Red River Valley, especially north of the forty-ninth parallel, erupted into the Pemmican War, a conflict that eventually weakened the North West and Hudson's Bay companies, and in 1821, pushed the British Parliament to call for their merger.[14] With their ally absorbed by their former adversary, the *Métis* had little choice but to make peace with the Red River colonists.[15]

Two years after the Hudson's Bay Company absorbed its chief rival, British and American envoys fixed the international border a couple of miles north of the Pembina-Red confluence, obliging the Hudson's Bay Company to relocate its Pembina trading post north of the forty-ninth parallel.[16] During the 1820s and early 1830s, the American Fur Company's Northern Department operated a post just south of the international boundary, competing with the Hudson's Bay Company's Fort Garry, located seventy miles north, near the confluence of the Assiniboine and Red rivers.

Unwilling to forgo the lucrative trade south of the forty-ninth parallel, the Hudson's Bay Company regularly outfitted independent *Métis* traders from the Red River Settlement above the border, urging them to barter their wares among the Indian tribes living on American soil. To counter this continual drain of robes, the American Fur Company decided to turn its Pembina post over to private operators who would be allowed to run the trade as they saw fit.[17] The prospect of competing against freelance traders who would be backed by John Jacob Astor's money, caused the Hudson's Bay governor to rethink his position. It was one thing for the Hudson's Bay Company to compete against the devil it knew, but quite another to challenge one that might be as unscrupulous about ignoring international boundaries as were its own Red River traders. Consequently, in 1833 the British proposed to Astor's agent that the American Fur Company close its trading posts from Pembina to Lake Superior in return for an annual fee of three hundred pounds. Astor's man agreed, signing a contract that gave the Hudson's Bay Company exclusive trading rights to the Red River country and Mississippi headwaters for the next five years.[18]

In 1834, Astor sold his interest in the American Fur Company. Ramsay Crooks bought control of the Northern Department and the American Fur Company name; Bernard Pratte, Sr., and Pierre Chouteau, Jr., purchased the firm's Western Department and Upper Missouri Outfit. Three years later the United States slid into a depression that seemed destined to last forever. Teetering on bankruptcy in 1842,[19] Crooks sold his interest in the Red River and upper Mississippi watersheds to Pierre Chouteau, Jr., & Company. Determining that the 1833 non-compete agreement with the Hudson's Bay Company applied to Crooks and not to him, Pierre Chouteau, Jr., decided to re-establish a trading presence at Pembina and snare the Red River trade.

In 1843, Norman Kittson established a trading house for Pierre Chouteau, Jr., & Company on the upper Pembina River

(Walhalla, North Dakota), a few miles above the post of independent trader Antoine Gingras (see Gingras's Trading Post), which opened about the same time. The following year, Kittson built a Chouteau post on the Red River, just below the forty-ninth parallel.[20] The Hudson's Bay Company countered by dispatching Henry Fisher, an American citizen in British employ, to construct a trading house alongside Kittson's; however, Fisher's stay was short-lived. When American authorities protested his selling whiskey to the Indians, the Hudson's Bay Company withdrew him rather than see the border-country overrun by the US Army.[21] Kittson's traders were so successful in threatening the Hudson's Bay Red River operations, in 1846 the British Sixth Royal Regiment of Foot sent 340 soldiers to Fort Garry in order to deter the Americans from invading Canada en masse.

Despite the regiment, Kittson cracked the Hudson's Bay monopoly north of the border. By offering higher prices than the company men at Fort Garry would pay, Kittson induced the independent, mixed-blood traders in Canada to sell their furs and robes to him. To keep from losing all of the Red River trade, the Hudson's Bay Company finally raised its prices at Fort Garry. This, in turn, induced Canadian Indians from outside the Garry district to trade their furs at that post rather than at Hudson's Bay trading factories that were closer to their homeland. As can be imagined, the practice had a decidedly negative impact on Hudson's Bay profits.

By the early 1850s, settlements in the Pembina Mountains had eclipsed those along the Red River, prompting Kittson to shift his headquarters to his trading post on the upper Pembina where the village of St. Joseph (today's Walhalla, North Dakota) had grown up around it.[22] The former headquarters post at Pembina now became a satellite, commanded by Joseph Roulette, Jr. In 1854, Kittson transferred the entire Pembina operation to Roulette, who continued the commercial warfare, forcing the Hudson's Bay Company to match his prices or see its business go south of the border.

The 1860s saw the demise of the great buffalo herds and the subsequent collapse of the Pembina robe trade. North of the forty-ninth parallel the Hudson's Bay Company relinquished its Red River lands to the Dominion of Canada, while south of the border the Homestead Act brought waves of foreign-born settlers onto the North Dakota plains. For a time the proud *Métis* struggled for independence, but it was not to be.

In July 1870, the US Army established Fort Thomas on the west side of the Red River, a bit upstream (south) from its confluence with the Pembina. Two months later, the post's name was changed to Fort Pembina. After a fire burned many of the facility's main buildings, the Army abandoned it in 1895.[23]

3 **Fort Piegan:** During the early part of the nineteenth century, the Blackfoot Confederation[24] dominated the upper Missouri. Highly protective of its territory—which stretched across central Montana from the Yellowstone River to the Continental Divide, and north into Canada—the confederation challenged anyone who dared trespass. In 1808, the Blackfeet stripped the mountain man John Colter naked and made him run for his life. Two years later, they drove Andrew Henry from the fort he had built at the Three Forks of the Missouri. The trapping brigades of William Ashley and his successors, Smith, Jackson & Sublette and the Rocky Mountain Fur Company, fought them continually. Although traders of the Hudson's Bay Company maintained a shaky truce with the confederation's three tribes, the Blackfeet refused to allow the firm to set a trap on tribal land.

By 1830, the Utah country and huge sections of the Green and Yellowstone River drainages had been stripped of their beaver. Increasingly, the virgin streams of the Blackfeet lured the trapping brigades north. Determined to defend its sovereignty, the confederation met each incursion with arrows and lead. Every season saw the scalps of more and more trappers decorating Blackfoot lodgepoles.

Wanting to ally the Blackfeet to the American Fur Company, as well as tap the resources of their country, Kenneth McKenzie, the head of the firm's Upper Missouri Outfit and *bourgeois* of Fort Union, hatched a bold plan. Living at Fort Union in the fall of 1830 was Jacob Berger, a former Hudson's Bay Company interpreter who spoke the Blackfoot language. At McKenzie's behest, Berger agreed to visit the Blackfeet and ask several of their chiefs to return with him to Fort Union. McKenzie hoped the sight of the fort would impress the chiefs with the American Fur Company's power, and would persuade them to allow the firm to open a trading post on tribal territory.[25]

Accompanied by four or five *engagés,* Berger headed up the Missouri. Few of his friends at Fort Union expected him to keep his hair. As Berger's party approached the Marias River, several dozen shrieking warriors came galloping across the sagebrush plain. Waving an American flag, Berger shouted in Blackfoot that he was a friend.

To his *engagés'* relief, the Indians remembered the interpreter from his days on Canada's South Saskatchewan River. With great fanfare the warriors escorted the interpreter and his party to their village, which was located farther up the Marias. For some weeks, the tribe listened as Berger described the strength of the American Fur Company and the benefits that a trading post would bring. The elders and chiefs debated the proposal, finally agreeing to send forty of their countrymen to meet with Kenneth McKenzie at Fort Union.[26]

Berger and the Blackfoot legation began their journey in early December, a time of wind, sleet, and snow on the upper Missouri. Each morning as the Indians awakened and glanced at the heavy gray clouds, they groused about the cold and the days they were spending away from their wives and warm lodges. Despite Berger's assurance that Fort Union was just a bit farther, they began to fear that he might be leading them into a trap. After all, they murmured among themselves, the confluence of the Yellowstone and Missouri rivers belonged to the Assiniboines, perennial enemies of the Blackfeet.

At last the Indians refused to go on. Claiming that Berger spoke with a forked tongue, they jeered his promise that Fort Union was but one sleep away. Desperate to keep them from deserting, the interpreter told them that if they did not reach the trading post by dusk the following day, they could have his party's horses and his scalp. Vowing to hold him to his word, the warriors agreed to continue. The next afternoon about two hours before sunset, Berger and the Blackfeet drew rein before Fort Union's massive stockade.

Kenneth McKenzie lavished the delegation with food, tobacco, and other presents. He cajoled and bribed the chiefs, promising them that the American Fur Company would strike better bargains than its Hudson's Bay rival. He told them that an American Fur trading post would provide them a steady supply of gunpowder and fusils. In truth, he told them everything they wanted to hear. As a result, it was no surprise when, before returning to their homes sometime after the New Year, the Blackfeet granted McKenzie permission to build his fort.

In July 1831, James Kipp (having just returned from building Fort Clark for the Mandans) went up the Missouri with *engagés,* voyageurs, and a keelboat-load of trade goods. Reaching the Marias in mid-October, the American Fur men began chopping logs and building the palisade for Fort Piegan on the left side of the Missouri River, immediately above the Marias confluence (about eleven miles northeast of Fort Benton, Montana).[27]

The Hudson's Bay Company quickly countered Kipp's post by sending envoys to the Blackfeet, begging them for their trade. It was all for naught. The tribe brought its fur to the Americans, bartering twenty-four hundred beaver pelts in the first week and a half Fort Piegan was open.

Still, the British were determined. The Blackfeet had been customers of the Hudson's Bay Company for decades, and Dr. John McLoughlin, its chief factor at Fort Vancouver on the lower Columbia River, swore to do whatever it took to win them back. During the winter of 1831–2, McLoughlin's agents persuaded the Bloods–the Blackfoot Confederation's most bellicose tribe–to send a war party against the Marias River fort. Tipped off to the plot, James Kipp pulled his men inside the gate before the Indians arrived. The Bloods screamed threats and futilely fired their arrows and fusil balls at the stockade, but to no avail. The warriors were not strong enough to breach the fort's walls, and they did not have the temperament for a prolonged siege, especially in winter.

A few days after the attack began, the Indians called it quits and started home.

Hoping to turn the tables on the Hudson's Bay Company, Kipp caught up with the Bloods, assured them that he had no hard feelings, and gave them copious quantities of mountain whiskey. The liquor won over the tribe completely. During the next few months, a continual line of Indians awaited admission into Fort Piegan's trade room, their arms filled with furs and buffalo robes, their bodies longing for another sip of Kipp's firewater.

When the Missouri's pack ice finally broke that spring, Kipp had exhausted the fort's supply of trade goods. Because his *engagés* were too frightened to remain at the post while he floated the cargo of skins to Fort Union and obtained more stores, he closed Fort Piegan and took everyone with him downriver.[28]

Egged on by the Hudson's Bay Company and angered that the Americans had left, the Blackfeet attacked the vacant fort, this time reducing it to a smoking rubble.

6 **Fort Pierre** (known officially as Fort Pierre Chouteau): During the spring runoff of 1831, the Missouri severely undercut the bank in front of the American Fur Company's Fort Tecumseh (on the Missouri's right side, across from Pierre, South Dakota). Although *engagés* relocated the post's main warehouse on higher ground to prevent it from washing downstream, it was apparent that the river would eventually destroy the entire stockade. In June, Pierre Chouteau, Jr., manager of the company's Western Department, journeyed to Fort Tecumseh on the maiden voyage of the firm's new steamboat *Yellow Stone*. During his visit Chouteau authorized the post's *bourgeois,* William Laidlaw, to construct a new trading post away from the bottomland that was so susceptible to flooding. In keeping with Fort Tecumseh's role as a depot for support of the Sioux trade, Chouteau decided that the new facility should be substantial, larger even than Fort Union, headquarters of the company's Upper Missouri Outfit, of which Fort Tecumseh was a part. Laidlaw soon picked a suitable site about three miles above the Missouri's confluence with the Bad River, and two miles upstream from Fort Tecumseh. Construction began that fall, supervised by Fort Tecumseh's senior clerk, Jacob Halsey.[29] Although Laidlaw christened the post Fort Pierre Chouteau, convention shortened the name to Fort Pierre. When the work was completed in early 1833, the stockade enclosed over one hundred thousand square feet.[30]

In June 1834, John Jacob Astor sold the American Fur Company's Missouri assets to Pratte, Chouteau & Company. The following year, Chouteau carved the Sioux Outfit from territory that had traditionally been part of the Upper Missouri Outfit and administered by William Laidlaw. The move so angered the Fort Pierre *bourgeois,* who resented having his authority snipped, that he sold his interest in the Upper Missouri Outfit to Jacob Halsey and went to work for Powell, Lamont & Company, competing with Pratte & Chouteau.[31] After Kenneth McKenzie retired as the senior manager of the Upper Missouri Outfit in 1837, Pratte, Chouteau & Company shifted the enterprise's headquarters from Fort Union to Fort Pierre.

By the mid-1850s, Fort Pierre was showing its age. In St. Louis, Pierre Chouteau, Jr., and his son, Charles, debated whether it made economic sense to invest in its repair. Before they could come to a decision, Sioux unrest necessitated garrisoning troops on the central Missouri plain. Seeing a chance to unload the old post for a profit, the Chouteaus *persuaded* the Army's quartermaster general to buy it for forty-five thousand dollars. Title transferred in April 1855, and in July the current *bourgeois,* Charles Galpin, moved the fort's trading store to a temporary camp about nineteen miles upriver.[32]

The Army abandoned Fort Pierre two years later because the neighboring countryside lacked sufficient grazing lands and timber. Many of the fort's buildings were dismantled and their materials taken 150 miles downriver to the new military reservation of Fort Randall (just above the South Dakota-Nebraska state line).

While the Army was salvaging Fort Pierre's lumber, Charles Galpin founded a trading post—called both Fort Galpin and Galpin's Post—on the right side of the Missouri, a couple of miles above the old Fort Pierre stockade. In 1859, he replaced this tiny trading house with a larger one a half mile downriver, naming the new facility in memory of the original: Fort Pierre II. Galpin ran the trading post for the Chouteaus until the winter of 1861–2, when he quit to help organize the opposition firm of La Barge, Harkness & Company. The Chouteaus abandoned Fort Pierre II in 1863.[33]

6   **Fort Pierre II:** See Fort Pierre (known officially as Fort Pierre Chouteau).

7   **Fort Platte:** In 1841, Lancaster P. Lupton built an adobe trading post on the right side of the North Platte River, about three-quarters of a mile above its confluence with the Laramie (twenty miles west of Torrington, Wyoming).[34] Lupton had been discharged from the US Army for publicly criticizing President Andrew Jackson. At his new Fort Platte, the former lieutenant resorted to whiskey to win the Indian trade from nearby Fort John (aka Fort Laramie). However, his early success quickly evaporated when the traders at Fort John trumped his use of alcohol by pouring it copiously themselves.

After a year, Lupton sold Fort Platte to Sibille, Adams & Company which had been operating a small log trading house in the vicinity for about the same amount of time (see Fort Adams).[35] The new owners continued to dispense liquor but fared no better than Lupton in competing with Fort John. In 1843, Sibille & Adams sold Fort Platte to John Cabanné, Jr., and Bernard Pratte, Jr. Cabanné was the nephew of Pierre Chouteau, Jr., whose company owned Fort John. Pratte, besides being Chouteau's former partner, was the son of Bernard, Sr., who until his death had helped Chouteau build one of the most powerful trading companies in the United States.[36] Despite these ties, a quarrel with Chouteau had turned the junior Pratte and Cabanné into fierce competitors. Yet as much as they tried, they were unable to best Fort John. Hoping that a different location would give them an advantage, Pratte and Cabanné abandoned Fort Platte in 1845 and constructed Fort Bernard about eight miles farther east. The tactic failed, for the partners fared no better with their new post than they had with Fort Platte (see Fort Bernard and the Sarpy's Point Posts).

4 **Poplar River Post:** In the autumn of 1860, Charles Larpenteur and Robert Lemon established a trading post for their new firm of Larpenteur, Smith & Company, locating it at the confluence of the Missouri and Poplar rivers (near Poplar, Montana). Hoping to finally wrest the upper Missouri from the grip of Pierre Chouteau, Jr., Robert Campbell had financed Larpenteur's portion of the enterprise.[37]

In a way, Campbell's action was natural, since it brought his relationship with the French-born Larpenteur full circle. Larpenteur had gone west in 1833 as a member of Sublette & Campbell's supply caravan. After the Green River rendezvous, he helped escort the Rocky Mountain Fur Company's cargo of beaver pelts across South Pass and down the Bighorn and Yellowstone rivers to the Missouri, where Sublette & Campbell's *engagés* were erecting the log pickets for Fort William. That fall, William and Milton Sublette floated the furs downstream to St. Louis, leaving Robert Campbell to finish the trading post and begin competing with Kenneth McKenzie, *bourgeois* of nearby Fort Union. Larpenteur remained behind in Campbell's employ.[38]

When Sublette & Campbell sold Fort William to the American Fur Company in early 1834, McKenzie hired Larpenteur as a clerk at Fort Union. Unassuming but dependable, Larpenteur stayed up-country for many years, working for the Upper Missouri Outfit through its transfer from the American Fur Company to Pratte, Chouteau & Company, and then Pierre Chouteau, Jr., & Company. In the 1850s, he tried his hand at farming but quit after an Omaha war party murdered his Assiniboine wife.

In 1859, he joined Clark, Primeau & Company and became the *bourgeois* of Fort Stewart (ten miles west of Culbertson, Montana). The following year the firm sold out to the Chouteaus, leaving Larpenteur without a job.[39] His prospects dim, he dropped down the Missouri and, at Fort Berthold (in west-central North Dakota), met Jefferson Smith, an old unemployed trader who had accumulated a nest egg of four thousand dollars. The two of them decided to go to St. Louis, put together an outfit, and reopen Fort Stewart which had been abandoned after Pierre Chouteau, Jr., &

Company acquired Clark & Primeau. Before leaving Fort Berthold, they enlisted another former clerk and trader named Henry Boller, who said that his father would contribute two thousand dollars to the enterprise.[40]

After reaching St. Louis, Larpenteur went to Robert Campbell to secure his own share of the financing and, in the process, recruited Campbell's clerk, Robert Lemon, to the venture.[41] By mid-August when the four partners had assembled their supplies, the upper Missouri was too low for steamboats. Not wanting to lose the winter trading season, Larpenteur and the others shipped their stores by steamer, up the Mississippi River to St. Paul, Minnesota, then headed overland in wagons. At the Souris River (in north-central North Dakota), Smith and Boller turned south toward the Hidatsa-Mandan village at Fishhook Bend. That fall, they built a sod trading post beside the Missouri and began competing with nearby Fort Berthold.[42]

Meanwhile, Larpenteur and Lemon pressed on to Fort Stewart which they found in ashes; it and neighboring Fort Kipp had been burned by Indians soon after the Chouteau traders abandoned them. With no choice but to build anew, Larpenteur and Lemon directed their *engagés* to cut cottonwood trees for the palisades. Work had hardly begun when Malcolm Clark, the current *bourgeois* at Fort Union, arrived offering to buy out Larpenteur and his partners. Larpenteur declined, prompting Clark to open a satellite trading post twenty-five miles farther up the Missouri at an Assiniboine wintering camp near the mouth of the Poplar River (see Malcolm Clark's Fort). Knowing that the tribe would never ride downstream to trade if it had another post close at hand, Larpenteur countered Clark's gambit by also constructing his and Lemon's fort at the mouth of the Poplar.[43]

The next spring, Henry Boller came upriver from Fishhook Bend and reported that he and Jefferson Smith had not had much success trading. Seeing the packs of buffalo robes that Larpenteur and Lemon had accumulated, Boller asked Larpenteur to let him take them to St. Paul in the partnership's wagons. When Larpenteur refused, Boller became angry and persuaded Lemon to go with him downriver. Paddling a canoe, the two men descended the Missouri, stopping at Fort Berthold to pick up Smith. Soon after the threesome reached St. Louis, Smith quit the partnership and joined Pierre Chouteau, Jr., & Company. Wanting to reap something for the time and money he had invested, Lemon bade good-bye to the fuming Boller, booked passage on a steamboat, and, that June, returned to Larpenteur at Poplar River Post. The two of them then loaded their robes on a mackinaw that Larpenteur had acquired and floated them to market in St. Louis.[44]

Financed by Robert Campbell, Larpenteur and Lemon formed another partnership–without Henry Boller–and again trekked overland from St. Paul with trade goods. Although they had intended to spend the winter of 1861–2 at their Poplar River Post, at the last minute they nailed together a trading house–more likely a shack–near the ruins of forts Stewart and Kipp. By the spring thaw, they were at each other's throats. After selling their equipment and stores to the La Barge brothers, the latest challengers to tilt with the Chouteau empire, Larpenteur and Lemon dissolved their partnership. Lemon departed for St. Louis, while Larpenteur went to work for the La Barges at their new Missouri River trading post above the mouth of the Milk (see Fort Charles Galpin).[45] Meanwhile, Pierre Chouteau, Jr., & Company continued to operate its trading fort at the Poplar River.

5   **Ponca House:** See Truteau's Winter Post.

5   **Ponca Posts** (not to be confused with Truteau's Winter Post which was sometimes called Ponca House): Juan Munier (or Jean Meunier) ascended the Missouri to the mouth of the Niobrara River (on the Nebraska-South Dakota border) in 1789, claiming to be the first European to visit the Poncas, who lived just above the confluence.[46] Eager to extend Spain's influence up the Missouri, the Spanish governor-general readily granted him and his partner, Jacques Rolland, a Ponca trading monopoly, and Munier soon opened a small trading house near the Poncas' village. During the winter of 1794–5, another St. Louis trader named Solomon Petit built a trading post for the Poncas, disregarding Munier's exclusive license.[47] Jacques Clamorgan's Company of the Discoverers and

Explorers of the Missouri River (for more about this firm see Mandan Villages) probably acquired Munier's post and license in 1796, a short time before the firm fell apart.[48] In the late 1790s, British traders from the North West and Hudson's Bay companies pushed down the Missouri River from their Canadian posts and also established trading houses among the Poncas.[49] Meanwhile, from 1799 through 1803, the Spanish governor-general of Louisiana rotated the Ponca trade among no fewer than three different St. Louis traders.[50]

Sometime after 1820, Pascal Cerré, who worked for Berthold & Chouteau (reorganized as Bernard Pratte & Company in 1823), established a Ponca trading post on the Missouri, placing it a bit downstream from the Niobrara (near Nebraska's Santee Sioux Indian Reservation).[51] About six years later, the Columbia Fur Company also constructed a Ponca trading house.[52] With the absorption of Bernard Pratte & Company and the Columbia Fur Company into the American Fur Company, the Ponca trade transferred to the Upper Missouri Outfit in 1827.

In 1829, Pierre Papin formed a partnership with a few other French traders, intending to compete with Astor's enterprise. Officially known as P. D. Papin & Company, the upstart firm was more often called the French Fur Company because of the heritage of its investors.[53] Papin's company lasted a little over a year, selling out to the American Fur Company on October 16, 1830. In addition to its Ponca Post, the French Fur Company also sold Fort Teton (across from Pierre, South Dakota) and its Sioux trading post on the White River (southwest of Chamberlain, South Dakota).[54]

By 1833, the Poncas were reeling from their forty-four years of commerce with white traders. Encroachment by settlers in Minnesota and Iowa had steadily pressured the Sioux onto the Missouri River plains, propelling indigenous tribes such as the Poncas into a nearly continual state of war. Unable to best the numerically-superior Sioux or to fight white diseases for which they had no natural immunity, the Poncas watched helplessly as their warriors died in battle, and their children perished from measles and cholera. Struggling to survive as a people, the tribe eventually abandoned its fixed villages and adopted the nomadic ways of its Sioux enemies.[55] Because the Poncas could not escape their dependence on the white man's trade goods, they continued bringing their buffalo robes to the American Fur Company's post near the mouth of the Niobrara.

In the summer of 1851, a trader named Schlegel had a tiff with Pierre Chouteau, Jr., & Company over his selling liquor to the tribes around the Vermilion River. Wanting to strike back at the firm, Schlegel boarded the steamboat *St. Ange* and sailed upstream to the mouth of the Niobrara where he founded yet another trading house for the Poncas.[56] Charles Larpenteur ran a Ponca post for Peter Sarpy from the spring of 1852 through the following winter, when it was closed because of scant trade.[57]

Powder River Posts and The Portuguese Houses: See Montero's Forts.

6 Pratte and Vasquez's Omaha Post: Around 1819, Sylvestre Pratte and Antoine François (*dit* Baronet) Vasquez built a trading post for Berthold & Chouteau at the Omaha village on the west side of the Missouri River, about forty-five miles above Council Bluffs (a bit north of Decatur, Nebraska).[58]

4 Fort Primeau (aka Primeau's Post): In the late 1840s, Harvey, Primeau & Company opened Fort Primeau for the Arikara trade atop a high bank on the right side of the Missouri River, about three hundred yards upstream from Pierre Chouteau, Jr., & Company's Fort Clark (a few miles southeast of Stanton, North Dakota; see Fort Defiance for more about the competition between the Chouteau firm and its opposition.) Following the death of Alexander Harvey in 1854, a succession of new partnerships operated Fort Primeau until 1860, when the latest one—Clark, Primeau & Company—finally succumbed to the Chouteaus' superior financial strength and sold out. Soon thereafter, fire damaged Fort Clark, prompting its traders to shift into Fort Primeau.[59]

The next year the Arikaras moved up the Missouri to Like-A-Fishhook Village (see "New" Fort Berthold), and the Chouteau employees abandoned Fort Clark and Fort Primeau, leaving their stockades and buildings to be burned by passing steamboats.[60]

7   **Fort Pueblo:** In 1842, George Simpson, J.B. Doyle, and Alexander Barclay established a trading house near the confluence of Fountain Creek and the Arkansas River (now Pueblo, Colorado). Known as Fort Pueblo, the post quickly attracted other independent traders, including the notorious liar and former beaver trapper James Beckwourth.[61] The liberal and illegal sale of alcohol to the neighboring tribes allowed the Pueblo traders to compete successfully with Bent's Fort, located some miles down the Arkansas. Although the Pueblo stockade sat on American soil, the closest Army troops were stationed too far east to enforce the law. On Christmas Day 1854, a Ute war party destroyed Pueblo, massacring nearly every one of the fort's inhabitants.[62]

3   **Fort Ramon** (aka Fort Manuel, Fort Lisa, Manuel's Fort, and variations thereof): See Fort Raymond.

7   **Rawhide Butte Post:** See Bordeaux's Post.

3   **Fort Raymond** (aka Fort Ramon, Fort Manuel, Fort Lisa, Manuel's Fort, and variations thereof): During the autumn of 1807, Manuel Lisa of Lisa, Menard & Morrison founded a trading post in the triangle of land above the confluence of the Bighorn and Yellowstone rivers, naming it Fort Raymond in honor of his son.[63] That winter, while *engagés* completed the fort's cabins, Lisa sent Edward Rose, John Colter, and George Drouillard to encourage the Crows to trade their furs at the Bighorn post. Of mixed Indian, white, and black ancestry, Rose—with his justly earned reputation for bravery and his knowledge of the tribe's language—should have been a top-rate ambassador; however, he lazed away his days in a warm tepee at a nearby Indian camp, doing little to make Fort Raymond a success. In contrast, the Virginia-born Colter and the Shawnee-French-blooded Drouillard, both veterans of the Lewis and Clark Corps of Discovery, did Lisa's bidding with zest. Colter crossed the Continental Divide in his search for Crows and was

211

the first white man to enter what would become Yellowstone National Park, a journey that covered about five hundred miles. Drouillard made two excursions, initially traveling south to visit Indian bands in the Bighorn Basin, then heading for the country cut by the Little Bighorn, Rosebud, and Tongue rivers.[64] It was most likely spring when Colter and Drouillard completed their rounds and returned to Fort Raymond.

Meanwhile, Manuel Lisa bartered with the Indian bands that trickled in to trade and sent his trappers to work the beaver ponds that were in a several-day radius from the Yellowstone-Bighorn confluence. As summer hit full bloom and the pelts began to grow thin, Lisa boarded his keelboat and floated down the Yellowstone to the Missouri, and on to St. Louis, carrying the season's harvest of furs.

Around the time Lisa departed, John Colter went up the Yellowstone River and over Bozeman's Pass with orders to find more Indians and encourage them to trade at Fort Raymond. Somewhere during the circuit, he fell in with a band of Flathead warriors. As they approached the lower Gallatin River, they crossed trails with a Blackfoot war party. Lifelong enemies, the two tribes attacked, leaving Colter no choice but to defend himself alongside the Flatheads. During the fray he received a leg wound, but, more ominously, the Blackfeet recognized him as white. When the battle ended, Colter returned to Fort Raymond to mend. Little did he suspect how his presence at that fight would unleash thirty years of bloodshed. Seeing no difference between one white man and another, the Blackfeet now sought revenge on all American trappers.[65]

After reaching Lisa's trading post at the mouth of the Bighorn River, Colter quickly healed. Wary of the Blackfeet, yet unwilling to ignore the rich beaver country that he had seen near the Three Forks, he joined with Fort Raymond's other trappers to hunt the headwaters of the Missouri. In early autumn, the party journeyed up the Yellowstone and crossed over to the Missouri's forks where Colter teamed with John Potts—another alumnus of the Corps of Discovery—to work a tributary of the Jefferson River. One morning while retrieving their traps, they were surprised by several hundred Blackfeet. The Indians killed Potts outright, but challenged Colter to race for his life. Stripped naked and without moccasins, Colter evaded the tribe's swiftest runners and eventually made it back to Fort Raymond.[66]

While Colter was sprinting to save his scalp, Lisa and his partners in St. Louis folded their firm into the newly organized St. Louis Missouri Fur Company which took possession of the Lisa, Menard & Morrison assets, including Fort Raymond. Lisa and the other owners then put together a 350-man expedition supported by thirteen keelboats and mackinaws. The first section of this riverine armada shoved off in May 1809, with the second one starting a month later.[67]

Just above the Hidatsas' village at the mouth of the Knife River (near Stanton, North Dakota), the cavalcade paused to build Fort Mandan. With the yellow cottonwood leaves announcing the approach of winter, company partner Andrew Henry took forty men on horses to Fort Raymond, while fellow shareholder Pierre Menard followed with the supply boats. Just before the spring thaw in 1810, John Colter guided Henry, Menard, and a company of trappers from Fort Raymond to the Three Forks of the Missouri, where they built Fort Henry.[68] Two months later after continual harassment by the Blackfeet, they abandoned the post (for details see Fort Henry—aka Fort Three Forks—and Fort Henry on Henry's Fork of the Snake River). Menard returned to St. Louis, while Henry and a party of volunteers crossed the Continental Divide to the North Fork of the Snake River (Idaho's Henry's Fork).

Menard reached St. Louis that summer, bringing word of the Three Forks disaster, and news that many of the company's supply caches had been pilfered. He told Lisa that Henry expected to return to Fort Mandan in August or September the following year. Adding to the partners' woes, the price of beaver pelts had plummeted to $2.50 per pound.[69] Further, the St. Louis Missouri Fur Company had failed to send a supply expedition to the mountains that spring, forcing its trappers to live off the land. Over the winter of 1810–11, the firm's partners, after much hemming and hawing, finally agreed to assemble a relief party for Andrew Henry.[70]

Fort Raymond

Manuel Lisa set out with a keelboat-load of supplies in early April. (See Fort Astoria about the famous boat race that Lisa had with Wilson Price Hunt's Astorians during this voyage up the Missouri.) Lisa reached the Mandans around the beginning of July. Two months later Henry arrived, looking much thinner than the last time Lisa had seen him. Grinning with satisfaction, Henry presented the senior partner several hundred pounds of prime pelts. That fall, Lisa and Henry returned to St. Louis and a fur market that had swung sharply higher.

Over the winter, the partners of the St. Louis Missouri Fur Company gained confidence in their prospects but felt their company needed an infusion of capital to fully exploit the bounty of the upper Missouri. In January 1812, they reorganized as the Missouri Fur Company, allowing the St. Louis Missouri Fur Company to expire. The new partnership acquired the assets of the old, including the trading posts.[71]

In May, Lisa again ascended the Missouri with a boatload of trade goods. The growing tension between the United States and Great Britain worried him about the future of his partnership should war be declared. In June, it began. That summer the Missouri Fur Company's *engagés* built a trading house for the Sioux (see Cedar Island), and transferred its Arikara operations to a new post a dozen miles upriver (see Fort Manuel). The firm still had traders at Fort Mandan, but it most likely had no presence at Fort Raymond.

Over the winter of 1812–13, the Missouri Fur partnership's outlook dimmed as the market price for beaver crashed in St. Louis, while on the Missouri and Yellowstone rivers, the British incited the tribes to attack the company's trappers.[72] From his quarters at Fort Manuel (on the Missouri River, ten miles south of the North and South Dakota state line), Lisa alerted his traders that they should withdraw. In early March, he abandoned the Arikara post and dropped down to Bijou's Cedar Island trading house among the Sioux (in South Dakota, above the Missouri's Grand Detour), and in May, he retreated to St. Louis.[73] Like the company's other up-country outposts, Fort Raymond was left to rot.

6 **Fort Recovery** (aka Cedar Fort and Fort aux Cédres): In 1820 or 1821, the Missouri Fur Company established Fort Recovery on a mile-long, cedar-covered island near the west side of the Missouri, about ten miles above its confluence with the White River (near Chamberlain, South Dakota).[74] Intended for the Sioux trade, the fort was also used as a forward supply point from which the firm launched its trapping brigades toward the upper Missouri and Yellowstone rivers. After Fort Kiowa opened in 1822 (built by rival Berthold, Chouteau & Pratte and located thirteen miles farther up the Missouri), Fort Recovery's trade steadily declined.

Meanwhile, downstream at Council Bluffs, the Missouri Fur Company faced more competition. Continuing a retrenchment that had begun after Colonel Henry Leavenworth's inept campaign against the Arikaras the year before, the Missouri Fur Company abandoned Fort Recovery in 1824.[75] Several months later, the partnership dissolved. Then, like the phoenix it had always been, the firm found new life and a new name as its owners reorganized as Pilcher & Company. For the next two years, Joshua Pilcher and his partners reoccupied the Missouri Fur Company's old forts as they struggled to compete with the Columbia Fur Company, Bernard Pratte & Company (formerly Berthold, Chouteau & Pratte), and the American Fur Company. The effort failed.

In 1827, in a final, desperate gamble for survival, Pilcher & Company took a trapping brigade to the mountains. Bad luck was its only reward. A year later, the partners called it quits. Joshua Pilcher and nine trappers rode to the Flathead country north of the Clark Fork River (in western Montana), gamely trying to give their crumbling enterprise a last chance. Stolen horses and a hard winter dashed the party's spirit. Eager to leave the mountains, Pilcher accompanied a Hudson's Bay Company trader to Fort Colvile (ten miles west of Colville, Washington), and from there traveled to Canada. Journeying from one Hudson's Bay post to another, Pilcher worked his way east along the firm's supply line, eventually returning to St. Louis in June 1830.[76]

Later, Pilcher joined the American Fur Company, managing its trading operations around Council Bluffs. On February 28,

1839, he became the Indian Superintendent for the Upper Louisiana Territory, replacing William Clark who had passed away the year before. Pilcher held the post for two and a half years and died June 5, 1843.

2   **Fort Robidoux** (Green River): In 1837, Antoine Robidoux (occasionally spelled Robideaux, Robidou, and variations thereof) opened a small trading house near the confluence of the Green and White rivers (a mile or so south of Ouray, Utah). The adobe post operated as a satellite of Fort Uintah which was located about thirty-five miles north. In addition to these establishments, Robidoux also had a trading post on the Gunnison River (see Fort Uncompahgre), and trading stores in Taos, Santa Fe, and at the Santa Rita copper mines in southwest New Mexico. Robidoux abandoned his Green River post in 1844.[77]

2   **Robidoux's   Post**   (Gunnison   River):   See   Fort Uncompahgre.

7   **Robidoux's Posts near Scotts Bluff:** Between 1849 and the late 1850s, Joseph Robidoux III held a trading license for a series

Robidoux's Post

216

Robidoux's Post

of posts that he and his brothers and their offspring operated in the vicinity of Scotts Bluff (near the Scotts Bluff National Monument in western Nebraska). Like nearby Fort John II of Pierre Chouteau, Jr., & Company, the Robidoux posts trafficked in buffalo robes, though their primary business was catering to the westering emigrants.[78] The first Robidoux post, which consisted of a store and blacksmith shop under the same roof, was located beside the Oregon Trail-California Road, near two springs about midway up the east side of Robidoux Pass (spelled Roubadeau on modern maps); it lasted from 1849 until at least mid-1851. The Robidoux had a second, somewhat larger post in Carter Canyon (southwest of Gering, Nebraska) which they ran from late 1850 or early 1851 until perhaps 1853. In the closing months of 1851, the Robidoux brothers opened another post a few miles farther east and nearer the Platte River (about halfway between Gering and Melbera, Nebraska), and yet another one on the right side of Horse Creek, a mile or so upstream from its mouth (about three miles northeast of Lyman, Nebraska). These posts survived into the late 1850s.[79]

217

4 **Roulette's Post:** In late 1862 or early 1863, Joseph Roulette, Jr., working for Pierre Chouteau, Jr., & Company, constructed a small trading house on the north side of the Missouri River among the ruins of Fort Kipp (about ten miles west of Culbertson, Montana). During the post's early months of operation, Roulette routinely cheated his Indian customers, causing a number of them to demand his scalp. Fearing for his life, the trader barricaded himself inside his post, praying he would live until a company steamboat stopped to take on his buffalo robes. In late June, the *Nellie Rogers* put in to shore, enabling Roulette to slip aboard, undetected by the Assiniboines camped on the surrounding plain.

A night or so later, after learning that Roulette had escaped, warriors sacked and burned his post, murdering the seven company employees he had left behind.[80]

5 **Roy's House:** See Pembina Posts.

Fort St. Vrain through Vermilion Post

7 **Fort St. Vrain** (aka Fort Lookout and Fort George): In 1837, Charles and William Bent sent their younger brother George to the South Platte to oppose three new trading posts that were siphoning the Arapaho and Cheyenne trade from the Bents' adobe fort on the Arkansas River. Charles and William Bent, together with their partner, Ceran St. Vrain, had earned the South Platte robe trade through years of sweat and blood, and they had no intention of allowing three upstarts to wrest it from their control. Stretching from south to north (in north-central Colorado), forts Lupton, Jackson, and Vasquez stood as a competitive gauntlet that the mighty Bent, St. Vrain & Company could not afford to ignore.

That autumn, George Bent's *engagés* constructed Fort St. Vrain on a bluff overlooking the South Platte River (about fourteen miles southwest of Greeley, Colorado), adding a fourth post to the line of trading houses that now reached across fifteen miles of prairie. Over the next few years, Bent & St. Vrain relentlessly drove one after another of the would-be usurpers from the field. After they were gone, the firm shut down Fort St. Vrain in early 1845.[1]

During the next four years until Bent & St. Vrain dissolved, its traders used the post intermittently. Then in 1850, numerous bands of Arapahos and Cheyennes collected around the South Platte, prompting William Bent to fix the fort's decaying buildings and staff it with a permanent trader.[2] After a few seasons, the nomadic tribes drifted away, and Fort St. Vrain was again closed. By 1859, it lay in ruin.

2 **Salish or Saleesh House:** See Flathead Post.

7 **Fort Sarpy** (North Platte River): See Fort Bernard and the Sarpy's Point Posts.

3 **Fort Sarpy** (aka Fort Alexander and Fort Alexander Sarpy): In the summer of 1850, Pierre Chouteau, Jr., & Company's *engagés* built the first Fort Sarpy on the north side of the Yellowstone River, a bit downstream from its confluence with Rosebud Creek (near Cartersville, Montana), and not far from old Fort Van Buren. Named for John Sarpy, a St. Louis merchant and partner of Pierre Chouteau, Jr., Fort Sarpy replaced Fort Alexander (twenty miles west near Forsyth, Montana) and was often called by that alias or Fort Alexander Sarpy.[3]

During the early 1850s, Fort Sarpy gained a notorious reputation. Regarding the post as his own private fiefdom, the *bourgeois* encouraged drunken brawls and Indian prostitution. Because security was nearly nonexistent, stores regularly disappeared from the warehouse and trade room. Finally deciding to cut its losses, the company removed everything of value from Fort Sarpy and in May 1855, ordered it burned.[4]

A few years later, Pierre Chouteau, Jr., and his son, Charles, tried to revive the Crow trade by establishing Fort Sarpy II on the south side of the Yellowstone River near its confluence with Sarpy Creek (close to Sanders, Montana). After buying out Clark,

Primeau & Company, their latest competitor on the upper Missouri, the Chouteaus abandoned the second Fort Sarpy and gave up having fixed posts among the Crows.

7 **Sarpy's Point Posts:** See Fort Bernard and the Sarpy's Point Posts.

6 **Sarpy's Trading Post** (Bellevue): See Fort Bellevue (in later years known as Sarpy's Trading Post).

8 **Fort Sibley** (aka Fort Clark and Fiery Prairie Fort): See Osage Posts and Fort Osage.

5,8 **Big Sioux Post:** In the mid-1820s, a trader, possibly Joseph LaFramboise, constructed a post near the confluence of the Big Sioux and Missouri rivers (western Iowa).[5] The American Fur Company acquired it in 1827. During the late 1840s and early 1850s, settlers spread across the new state of Iowa staking out farms and pushing the Yankton Sioux west of the Big Sioux River. Merchants, saloonkeepers, and other purveyors of civilization naturally gravitated to Big Sioux Post, and in 1855, the area around the old fort officially became Sioux City.[6]

2 **Smith's Fort** (aka Big Timbers Trading Post): In 1827, mountain man Thomas L. Smith earned the nickname "Peg-leg" while trapping in North Park on the upper North Platte River (in northern Colorado). At camp one morning, an Indian shot Smith from ambush, shattering the bones in his lower left leg. With the aid of his friend Milton Sublette, Smith cut through the skin and tendons with a butcher knife, amputating his foot just above the ankle joint. Tougher than meat jerked from an old bull buffalo, Smith survived the ordeal and eventually returned to trapping, hobbling into the creeks on a wooden leg.[7]

With the decline of the beaver trade in the late 1830s, Peg-leg Smith turned to stealing horses from the Spanish rancheros in southern California. Then in 1844, seeing the early success that Jim Bridger was having with his trading post on Black's Fork of the

Green River (see Fort Bridger), Smith also established a small trading house for the Oregon Trail emigrant traffic. He located it on the Bear River in the Bear Lake Valley, northeast of Bear Lake (a few miles south of Montpelier, Idaho), about midway between Bridger's place and Fort Hall. By mid-1849, Smith was earning one hundred dollars a day, swapping fresh horses for the exhausted stock of the passing wagon trains, especially those rushing to the gold diggings in California.[8] A year later, the lure of gold caused the old trapper to give up his lucrative business and join the tide of prospectors hoping to strike it rich.

1 **Snake Fort** (aka Big Wood Fort): See Fort Boisé and other Boise River Posts.

1 **Spokane House:** In 1809 or 1810, David Thompson built Spokane House for the North West Company near the confluence of the Spokane and Little Spokane rivers (northwest of Spokane, Washington).[9] In June 1811, when the Pacific Fur Astorians were constructing their headquarters at the mouth of the Columbia River, they received word of the Nor'Westers' fort on the Spokane. Determined to contest it, the Astorians sent John Clarke to establish a competing facility nearby. Clarke built his Spokane River trading post in the late summer of 1812.[10]

Sixteen months after the War of 1812 erupted between the United States and Great Britain, the Pacific Fur Company's field commanders sold their Spokane fort and their other trading posts to the North West Company (See Fort Astoria). In 1821, Spokane House passed to the Hudson's Bay Company when it merged with the Nor'Westers. As the North West Company had done, the Hudson's Bay Company used the post as a central supply base for its smaller inland trading houses such as Flathead Post on the Clark Fork River. The company abandoned Spokane House in 1826, transferring its operations to the new Fort Colvile (ten miles west of Colville, Washington).[11]

In October 1880, the US Army built Camp Spokane (called Fort Spokane after 1881) on the left side of the Columbia, immediately below the mouth of the Spokane River (near Miles,

Washington). The military reservation closed in 1899, and its facilities were converted into a school for Indian children.[12]

4 **Fort Stewart:** In the summer of 1858, Malcolm Clark constructed Fort Stewart for Frost, Todd & Company—a consortium of investors backed by Robert Campbell—on the left side of the Missouri, five miles above its confluence with Big Muddy Creek (about nine miles west of Culbertson, Montana). Intended for the Assiniboine trade, Fort Stewart replaced old Fort William at the mouth of the Yellowstone (in western North Dakota; see Fort Mortimer—aka Fort William) and competed with Pierre Chouteau, Jr., & Company's Fort Union.[13]

The following spring, Chouteau traders opened Fort Kipp, two hundred yards away from Stewart. The competition was immediate and brutal. From his counting room in St. Louis, Robert Campbell watched with dismay as Frost & Todd hemorrhaged red ink. Needing to stem the losses, he agreed when the firm's partners proposed selling out. That November, Fort Stewart passed to Charles Primeau and Malcolm Clark who purchased the post with Campbell's blessing, but not his money. Having had his fill of financing losing causes, Campbell declined to back the fort's newest owners. Primeau and Clark lasted less than a year. In 1860, they turned the keys to Fort Stewart over to a Chouteau agent and ended their partnership. Pierre Chouteau, Jr., & Company promptly closed forts Kipp and Stewart, transferring their operations to Fort Union. A short time later, Indians torched the abandoned stockades.[14]

6 **Sublette & Campbell's Post at the Bad River:** During the early autumn of 1833, Sublette & Campbell *engagés* built a small trading post near the mouth of the Bad River, not far from the site of old Fort Tecumseh (across the Missouri from Pierre, South Dakota). Wanting to challenge the American Fur Company on its home ground, William Sublette and Robert Campbell intended for the post to compete with nearby Fort Pierre, just as their Fort William at the mouth of the Yellowstone was going to oppose Fort Union. By the next spring, losses at the Sublette & Campbell trading houses pushed William Sublette to sell out to his rival (for more detail, see Fort William–Sublette & Campbell). The Bad River post was abandoned and, presumably, burned as firewood by passing steamboats.[15]

5,6 **Tabeau's Arikara Post:** In 1802, the former Nor'Wester Pierre-Antoine Tabeau went up the Missouri as a clerk of Régis Loisel and helped establish a trading fort on Cedar Island (in South Dakota, above the Missouri's Grand Detour). After the Sioux forced the post's abandonment in the spring of 1804, Loisel sent Tabeau to open trade with the Arikaras. Meanwhile, Loisel returned to St. Louis. Upon reaching the Arikaras' three-mile-long island near the confluence of the Grand and Missouri rivers (a bit north of Mobridge, South Dakota, and now covered by Lake Oahe), Tabeau moved into the earthen lodge of Chief Kakawita (The Male Crow), eventually erecting a wall of stakes and a door to separate his quarters and trading stock from the Indian occupants. About two thousand Arikaras lived in the tribe's three villages (one village occupied the island, and the other two sat four miles upriver).[16]

On October 8 that year, Lewis and Clark camped across from the Arikaras' island and parleyed with the tribe, employing Joseph Gravelines, Tabeau's interpreter, as their own. The Arikaras had harried Tabeau from the moment he opened his trade, and he had little to show for his effort.

After taking leave of Tabeau and the Arikaras, the Corps of Discovery continued up the Missouri and wintered among the Mandans. The following spring, Lewis and Clark sent a portion of their command to St. Louis with letters and specimens of flora and fauna that the captains had collected during the expedition's first year. Traveling via keelboat and canoe, the party stopped at the Arikaras' island where Tabeau begged passage for himself and four of his *engagés*. Having had his fill of the tribe's hostility, the clerk desperately wanted to retreat to the settlements while he was still wearing his hair.[17]

6 **Fort Tecumseh:** In 1822, Columbia Fur Company *engagés* constructed Fort Tecumseh on the west side of the Missouri, one and a half miles upstream from its confluence with the Bad River (across the Missouri from Pierre, South Dakota).[18] Determined to capture the Sioux trade away from nearby Fort LaFramboise, William Laidlaw, Fort Tecumseh's *bourgeois,* bid up the price of pelts, confident that he could withstand the resulting losses longer than his competitor. The tactic worked. The LaFramboise post closed within the year.

Fort Tecumseh quickly became the Columbia Fur Company's central supply hub on the upper Missouri, supporting traders among seven different Indian tribes. By the mid-1820s, the firm's promising future caught the attention of John Jacob Astor. His powerful American Fur Company had opened its Western Department in 1822, but so far its St. Louis agent, David Stone & Company, had done little to penetrate the upper Missouri. That region was dominated by the Columbia Fur and Bernard Pratte companies. Deciding to buy what he could not defeat competitively, Astor authorized his trusted lieutenant, Ramsay Crooks, to seek a merger with the two rivals. In 1827, Crooks dismissed the Stone firm, giving charge of the Western Department to Bernard Pratte & Company. Crooks saw in the Pratte partnership the perfect man to manage the American Fur Company's Missouri trade: Pierre Chouteau, Jr.

That same year, Crooks persuaded the Columbia Fur Company's senior partner, Kenneth McKenzie, to join his organization with Astor's colossus. The Columbia Fur Company was renamed the Upper Missouri Outfit, and McKenzie became its managing partner. Title to Fort Tecumseh passed to the American Fur Company in December, together with its inventory of trade goods and equipment valued at $14,453.[19] McKenzie used the post as his headquarters until 1829, when he shifted his office to newly opened Fort Union at the mouth of the Yellowstone. Afterwards, Fort Tecumseh continued functioning as a depot, supplying satellite trading operations between the Mandans and Sioux.

Flooding by the Missouri River and the subsequent erosion was a continual problem for the fort. In June 1830, *engagés* relocated its blacksmith shop to higher ground, and the next spring they moved a double-story warehouse. Even so, it was obvious that the

Missouri would eventually undercut the entire stockade. During a visit in June 1831, Pierre Chouteau, Jr., authorized William Laidlaw to build a replacement post about two miles farther north. By the time Fort Pierre was finished in 1833, Fort Tecumseh had been reduced to a single decaying building.[20]

6 **Fort Teton** (aka Teton Post, Papin's House, the French Post and Cerré's Establishment): In the late 1820s–most likely 1828– P.D. Papin & Company (aka the French Fur Company) opened a trading post on the west side of the Missouri, just below its confluence with the Bad River and about two miles south of the American Fur Company's Fort Tecumseh (across from Pierre, South Dakota).[21] Wishing to rid itself of a competitor, John Jacob Astor's firm absorbed the Papin partnership on October 16, 1830, gaining control of Fort Teton, as well as a post for the Poncas (near Niobrara, Nebraska), and one for the Sioux at the mouth of the White River (southwest of Chamberlain, South Dakota). Fort Teton was probably dismantled for its logs or burned.[22]

6 **Teton Post** (aka Papin's House, the French Post, and Cerré's Establishment): See Fort Teton.

2 **Fort Three Forks:** See Fort Henry.

4 **Tilton's Fort:** See Mandan Villages.

5,6 **Truteau's Winter Post** (aka Ponca House, not to be confused with Ponca Post): In late 1794, Jean Baptiste Truteau (sometimes spelled Trudeau; see Mandan Villages endnote 17) constructed a winter trading house for the Company of the Discoverers and Explorers of the Missouri River on the left side of the Missouri, about thirty-seven miles above the mouth of the Niobrara River (just below the Fort Randall Dam in southeastern South Dakota). Truteau and his men abandoned the post the following spring.[23] (For details about Truteau's expedition, see Mandan Villages.)

3 **Tulloch's Fort:** See Fort Cass.

5 **Turtle River Post:** In September 1802, the Nor'Wester Alexander Henry the Younger dispatched John Cameron and eight *engagés* to establish a satellite post of Pembina on the Turtle River (north of Grand Forks, North Dakota; see Pembina Posts for more about Henry's operations).[24]

2 **Fort Uintah** (sometimes spelled Uinta) (aka Fort Robidoux): In 1832,[25] Antoine Robidoux built a trading post on the right side of the Uinta River, near its confluence with the Whiterocks (on the Uintah and Ouray Indian Reservation in northeastern Utah). Robidoux's traders ran the fort until the spring of 1845 when it was abandoned. Ute warriors then burned the deserted post in 1846 or 1847.[26]

1 **Umpqua River Posts:** In 1820 or 1821, Thomas McKay opened a trading house on the right bank of the Umpqua River above the mouth of Elk Creek (upstream from Elkton, Oregon).[27] Known as McKay's Fort, the Hudson's Bay post probably saw intermittent use until the end of the decade.

In 1832, the Hudson's Bay Company built Fort Umpqua on the south bank of the Umpqua River, three miles downstream from its confluence with Elk Creek (three miles west of Elkton, Oregon). The company hoped the tiny fort would induce the local tribes to stop trading with American sea captains who plied the coastal waters, seeking furs. Four years later, the firm replaced this "Old Fort Umpqua" with a new one farther upriver.[28] That post survived until the late 1840s when the declining fur market made it unprofitable.[29]

In 1856, the US Army founded its own Fort Umpqua, locating it near the Oregon coast, a couple of miles above the mouth of the Umpqua River (near Reedsport, Oregon). Intended for Indian control, the post lasted until 1862.

1 **Fort Umpqua:** See Umpqua River Posts.

2 **Fort Uncompahgre** (aka Robidoux's Post): Antoine Robidoux began trading in the Gunnison River Valley as early as 1825. Seeing a need for a permanent post, he established Fort Uncompahgre in 1828. Made from adobe, the fort sat beside the Gunnison River, just below its confluence with the Uncompahgre (about two miles west of Delta, Colorado).[30] Four years later, Robidoux built Fort Uintah, several days ride farther west (see Fort Uintah–sometimes spelled Uinta; aka Fort Robidoux). Forts Uncompahgre and Uintah gave trappers in the southern Rocky Mountains another market for their furs, rather than having to sell them at the annual rendezvous or pack them to Taos. During the early 1840s when the summer trade fairs were no longer held and trappers operated in small groups instead of large brigades, Robidoux's forts hung on, catering to mountain men such as Kit Carson, who desperately clung to a dying way of life.[31] Still, Antoine Robidoux could not ignore the laws of economics forever. The beaver market was finished, and his posts were too far from the buffalo herds and Plains Indians for him to compete successfully in the robe trade. Forts such as Hall and Boisé survived

Interior Fort Uncompahgre

227

Dan Deuter, Fort Uncompahgre Trader

Trader's Quarters at Fort Uncompahgre

by catering to travelers on the Oregon Trail, but no wagon trains lumbered by Robidoux's forts. Like the mountain men, their time had passed.

On September 8, 1844, the New Mexican territorial governor murdered a Ute warrior during a parley in the governor's Santa Fe office. Later that month, a Ute war party retaliated by raiding Fort Uncompahgre while Antoine Robidoux was away; the warriors killed the traders and carried off their Indian wives (see Fort Uintah endnote 24 concerning whether this attack took place at Fort Uintah or Fort Uncompahgre). Shortly afterwards, the Utes sent word to Robidoux that they wanted him to reopen the fort, now that they had avenged their brother's death. Robidoux refused.

In the spring of 1845, Antoine Robidoux quit the Rocky Mountains and headed to his family's enclave in St. Joseph, Missouri. The Utes burned Fort Uncompahgre in 1846 or 1847, but by then Robidoux was in California, serving as an interpreter for General Stephen Kearny in the Mexican War.[32]

Ed Maddox, Fort Uncompahgre Blacksmith

4 **Fort Union:** In September 1828, an American Fur Company trading party set out from the Mandan villages in the keelboat *Otter* to open a post for the Assiniboines at the mouth of the Yellowstone River.[33] Upon reaching the Yellowstone-Missouri confluence later that fall, the crew continued another five miles up the Missouri and erected a small cabin on the river's north side (in western North Dakota, a few steps from the Montana state line and twenty-four miles southwest of Williston, North Dakota).[34]

Wanting to expand his command to the far reaches of the Missouri River, Kenneth McKenzie, senior partner in the Upper Missouri Outfit of the American Fur Company, decided to shift his headquarters from Fort Tecumseh (across from Pierre, South Dakota) to the mouth of the Yellowstone. In the fall of 1829, company carpenters began constructing a large trading post on the gravel bench near where the 1828 wintering house was located. McKenzie christened the new facility Fort Union.

When it was finished in 1830, Fort Union's cottonwood stockade enclosed 52,800 square feet, making it the biggest trading post on the upper Missouri until the completion of Fort Pierre. Early morning, February 3, 1832, a fire destroyed the sleeping quarters on the west side of Fort Union's courtyard. By mid-June, when the *Yellow Stone* became the first steamboat to reach the post, most of the damage had been repaired.[35]

In 1833, McKenzie imported a distillery in an effort to circumvent the government cargo inspectors at Fort Leavenworth, who checked all riverboats to ensure that they carried no contraband liquor.[36] That summer, Sublette & Campbell began building Fort William a few miles east of Fort Union, intending to vie with the American Fur Company for the Assiniboine trade. When the trappers' mountain rendezvous ended a short time later, Robert Campbell floated down the Bighorn and Yellowstone rivers with several bull-boat loads of beaver pelts. Accompanying him were his partner's brother, Milton Sublette, and Nathaniel Wyeth. Milton was going east to seek treatment for an infected foot, while Wyeth was returning to Massachusetts after a fruitless stab at the fur trade. Upon reaching the Missouri, the three men visited Fort Union where McKenzie proudly showed them his still. When

Above:
Fort Union

Right:
Entrance to
Fort Union

Wyeth asked to purchase some liquor for his journey to St. Louis, McKenzie refused, lest Wyeth trade it to the mid-river tribes to the detriment of the American Fur Company. The decision rankled Wyeth. From Fort Union, Wyeth, Campbell, and Milton Sublette descended to the Missouri-Yellowstone confluence where William Sublette was supervising Fort William's construction. After a short stay, Wyeth continued downstream in a pirogue. The Sublettes followed a few days later in a keelboat, leaving Campbell to finish Fort William and serve as its *bourgeois*.[37]

At the Army's Fort Leavenworth, either Wyeth or William Sublette, who was less than a week behind, reported McKenzie's distillery to Henry Ellsworth, the resident Indian agent. History has given Wyeth the blame, although Sublette had more to gain by making trouble for the American Fur Company. When Ellsworth sent word of the distillery to Washington, DC, the Indian Commissioner threatened to revoke the American Fur Company's trading license. Because of its high-placed friends— including Lewis Cass, Secretary of War, and Senator Henry Clay— the company retained its license; however, McKenzie was eventually forced to dismantle the still.

Meantime, during the fall and winter of 1833 while the furor over Fort Union's liquor production was slowly escalating, McKenzie paid unheard-of prices to keep the fur trade away from Fort William. Pierre Chouteau, Jr., the managing partner of the American Fur Company's Western Department, watched with alarm as the Upper Missouri Outfit's losses mounted. For Sublette & Campbell, the situation was worse. Expresses from Fort William to Sublette's counting room in St. Louis told about the fierce competition and how Robert Campbell had acquired only a handful of pelts. Even then, Campbell had been forced to pay more than the furs would bring at market. Knowing that the American Fur Company could withstand the red ink longer than his partnership, Sublette offered to sell Fort William and the other trading houses he and Campbell had opened on the Missouri. In early 1834, Chouteau accepted, reasoning that it was the least costly way for the American Fur Company to rid itself of a competitor. As part of the agreement, Sublette abandoned his plans to build more posts

Bourgeois's House at Fort Union

on the Missouri, and Chouteau stopped sending supply caravans to the trappers' annual rendezvous.

Word of the sale reached Fort Union about the time the distillery trouble was at its height. Annoyed that Chouteau had bought Fort William without consulting him, and eager to escape the controversy over his still, McKenzie departed for a European vacation. In the summer of 1834, while McKenzie sailed across the Atlantic Ocean and John Jacob Astor sold the Upper Missouri Outfit and Western Department of the American Fur Company to Pratte, Chouteau & Company, *engagés* dismantled the stockade at Fort William, using its lumber to build a horse corral at Fort Union.[38]

McKenzie returned to the mouth of the Yellowstone in the fall of 1835. In the spring of 1837, he retired and moved to St. Louis.[39] That summer when the steamboat *St. Peter's* came upriver with the annual supplies, it carried smallpox. At Fort Clark, it infected the Mandans, Hidatsas, and visiting Arikaras, and at Fort Union, the disease attacked the Assiniboines. Over the next year, the epidemic raced like an August wildfire across the plains of the upper Missouri, decimating Indians by the thousands. Fearing retaliation from the neighboring tribes, Jacob Halsey, the temporary *bourgeois* at Fort Union, had his carpenters build a second gate inside the main one, thereby walling off the trade room from the post's interior. In addition, they installed a wicket in the stockade so if it became necessary, the Indians could be kept outside when they came to trade. When the deadly virus finally ran its course, tribal hegemony on the upper Missouri had been changed forever.

By the 1840s, the trade in buffalo robes had eclipsed that of beaver. Despite the government's injunction against liquor, it continued to be the mainstay of the trade goods, smuggling having

Southwest Bastion of Fort Union

replaced McKenzie's distillery. In 1856, smallpox again struck the Missouri tribes, but the death toll was far less terrible than it had been nineteen years before.

The early 1860s saw white settlers flooding into Iowa and Minnesota, lured by the Homestead Act's offer of free land. Farmers destroyed the game, ripped the prairie with steel plows, and pressured the Sioux westward onto the territory of their traditional enemies. The upper Missouri plains ignited with Indian warfare, bringing anxious calls for Army troops to restore the peace. In the summer of 1864, while waiting for the politicians in Washington to authorize a permanent military installation on the Missouri, the Army positioned several steamboat-loads of supplies at Fort Union, sending a detachment from the Thirtieth Wisconsin Infantry as a guard.[40]

Downriver in St. Louis, old Pierre Chouteau, Jr., and his son, Charles, saw that the encroaching settlements spelled the end of their company. Beaver pelts, buffalo robes, and a keen business sense had made theirs one of the richest families on the Mississippi. Yet, the Civil War threatened their wealth and their freedom. Suspicioned to be rebel sympathizers,[41] the Chouteaus continually battled the lies of their competitors as they strove to prove themselves loyal to the Union. Although they managed to defend their reputations, they were unable to protect their fur business from the changing times.

The Civil War had reduced the demand for robes, making their trade unprofitable. The Chouteaus now earned their money by distributing Indian annuities and hauling freight in their company's steamboats. Of all their posts, only Fort Benton prospered, kept healthy by supplying the gold and silver mines in the Idaho and western Montana territories.[42] Like Fort Union, the Chouteaus' other trading houses were falling apart, succumbing to weather and age. The upper Missouri fur trade had been good to the Chouteaus, but its time had waned. Vowing to salvage what he could, Charles Chouteau began searching for a buyer.

In June 1865, a steamboat landed at Fort Union with the news that Pierre Chouteau, Jr., & Company had sold its trading operations to the Northwest Fur Company (not to be confused with the old North West Company of Montreal).[43] The soldiers departed the post the end of August, leaving the government provisions for the new owners who arrived in mid-September, two weeks after the death of Pierre Chouteau, Jr. The following June, the Army dusted off its plans for a permanent base on the upper Missouri and began building Fort Buford a few miles east of Fort Union at the Yellowstone-Missouri confluence. In the summer of 1867, declining trade and Sioux war parties compelled the Northwest Fur Company to sell Fort Union to the Army. Troops soon tore down the old trading post and used its materials to enlarge Fort Buford.[44]

3 **Fort Van Buren:** In the autumn of 1835, Samuel Tulloch established Fort Van Buren for Pratte, Chouteau & Company, locating the Crow trading post on the north side of the Yellowstone River across from the mouth of Rosebud Creek (east of Cartersville, Montana).[45] Intended to replace Fort Cass near the mouth of the Bighorn, Fort Van Buren was named in honor of Martin Van Buren when he was Vice President of the United States under Andrew Jackson. After a short tour as the fort's *bourgeois,* Charles Larpenteur burned it in the summer of 1842, then built Fort Alexander (west of Forsyth, Montana) as its replacement.[46]

1 **Fort Vancouver:** As 1824 began, the Northern Department governor of the Hudson's Bay Company, George Simpson, was worried. The source of his concern lay in the disputed ownership of the Oregon Territory (the states of Washington, Oregon, and Idaho, in addition to the portions of Wyoming and Montana lying west of the Continental Divide), a squabble that had begun the previous century.

On May 11, 1792, Boston merchant-captain Robert Gray had sailed into the mouth of a large river on the northwest Pacific coast. Before returning to sea, Gray determined the river's latitude and longitude and named it after his ship, *Columbia.*[47] Following Gray's departure, English explorer George Vancouver sent a scouting party 110 miles up the Columbia River to the mouth of the Sandy, creating a British claim on the Oregon country's interior.[48] In 1803, the Louisiana Purchase gave the United States title to all land in the western half of the Mississippi River drainage. Although the drainage ended at the Missouri's headwaters along the Continental Divide, President Jefferson expanded it in his own mind, and eventually, in the mind of the American public, to include the Oregon Territory. However, the British crown maintained otherwise.

The exploratory expedition of Lewis and Clark provided useful information about Oregon but did little to bind the region to the United States. Then in the spring of 1811, the contested ownership tilted toward the Americans when John Jacob Astor's Pacific Fur Company established Fort Astoria on the south bank of the Columbia River estuary. Yet while Astor's men were constructing their stockade, the Nor'Wester David Thompson was mapping the Columbia from its source to its mouth.[49] At the confluence of the Snake and Columbia rivers (about two miles east of Pasco, Washington), Thompson raised the Union Jack and posted a letter claiming the country north of the forks for Great Britain.

In June 1812, the United States and Great Britain went to war for a second time. When word of the conflict reached the men at Fort Astoria, they decided to salvage what they could of Astor's investment and sell their enterprise to the North West Company, rather than wait for a British frigate to capture it as a spoil of war. On October 23, 1813, Fort Astoria and the Pacific Fur Company's inland trading houses officially passed to the Nor'Westers. Seven weeks later, the twenty-six-gun HMS *Raccoon* dropped anchor in the Columbia estuary, and its captain claimed Fort Astoria for his king, renaming the post Fort George.[50]

In 1814, the Treaty of Ghent ended the War of 1812, requiring the return of all territories captured by force of arms. The Nor'West directors refused to give Fort George back to Astor, arguing that his agents had sold the post before the *Raccoon's* captain ever set foot on Oregon soil. The dispute simmered until 1818 when the United States and Great Britain agreed to joint occupancy of the Oregon country, making the controversy over Fort George's ownership moot.

By 1821, decades of struggle with its Hudson's Bay rival had brought the North West Company to its knees. Adding to its weakness was a shortage of capital, aggravated by its partners' insistence that the firm's earnings be paid as dividends instead of being reinvested in the company. In London, the British Colonial Office recognized that the Hudson's Bay and North West companies were the only mechanism that Great Britain could employ, short of another war, to prevent the United States from eventually expanding its borders to the Pacific Ocean, and possibly into western Canada. Yet with the fur companies continually at each other's throats, neither had the strength to block an American onslaught. As the Colonial Office ministers studied the dilemma, they concluded that a single, well-capitalized firm with an army of traders and a host of outlying posts might have the muscle to hold the Americans at bay. Armed with the ministers' recommendation, the British government pressured the Hudson's Bay and North West companies to merge.[51] The amalgamated firm took the Hudson's Bay name.

In the years that followed, American trading companies again began pushing west from St. Louis, creeping ever closer to the land that Governor George Simpson considered his exclusive domain. Being a political realist, Simpson knew that the Hudson's Bay Company would most likely lose Fort George. It sat on the south side of the Columbia River, and English logic assumed that if Oregon were ever divided, it would be along the Columbia. To Simpson, giving up territory seemed far worse than forfeiting Fort George. The company spent a small fortune every year, furnishing the post's personnel with food that had to be shipped from England via Cape Horn. Perhaps, Simpson reasoned, if he established a new trading factory inland from the coast where the weather was more temperate, the locale might be conducive to farming.[52] And if the site was on the north shore of the Columbia River, the risk of losing the post to the Americans would be reduced. Accordingly, Simpson decided to quit spending resources on Fort George and began planning its replacement. With an eye toward denying the American trappers any cause to venture west of the Continental Divide, Simpson ordered the Columbia Department's new chief factor, Dr. John McLoughlin, to turn the land into a beaver desert. The Hudson's Bay Company might well lose much of the Oregon Territory, but it made little sense to let the Americans have its furs. Besides, if the company's trapping brigades stripped the Pacific Northwest of its beaver, the Americans might stay away[53]—or so Simpson hoped.

Simpson's order to empty the Oregon country of its beaver heralded a marked change in the Hudson's Bay Company's fur-gathering policies. From its earliest days, the firm had primarily relied on Indians to do its trapping; so, too, had its chief competitor, the North West Company. Outfitted by the two rivals and tutored by their French-Canadian and Iroquois agents, native hunters trapped beaver, otters, muskrats, and other fur-bearing mammals, then bartered the pelts to the companies' roving traders or at the companies' trading factories. Rather than deplete an area of its game, the Indians trapped lightly, thereby conserving the animals as a renewable resource.

In 1818, the North West Company launched its first large-scale trapping brigade, sending the former Astorian, Donald McKenzie, to the Snake River country (Idaho and western Wyoming; for more about the Snake River brigades, see Flathead Post—aka Salish or Saleesh House—and Fort Walla Walla—formerly called Fort Nez Perces). Although the experiment proved successful, the company confined its future trapping sorties to land that would eventually become the United States. Across its Canadian territory and among the Blackfeet, it continued using Indian hunters. At the time of their consolidation in 1821, the Hudson's Bay and North West companies maintained a series of trading posts—seventy-six for the Hudson's Bay Company and ninety-seven for the North West Company—that stretched from their supply depots at York Factory on Hudson Bay and Lachine (near Montreal) on the St. Lawrence River, to the Pacific coast.[54] All but a handful of these forts were located above the forty-ninth parallel, where after the merger, the Hudson's Bay Company enjoyed a fur-trading monopoly. Simpson revived the Snake River brigades in 1822, but until he decided to replace Fort George, he had not ordered their *partisans* to kill every beaver down to the last kit. That mandate fell to John McLoughlin.

Fort Vancouver Blacksmith Shop

McLoughlin seemed the perfect man to carry out Simpson's command to denude Oregon of its beaver. A medical doctor by training, McLoughlin had joined the North West Company in the early nineteenth century to escape punishment for having taught a British Army officer some manners. Legend has it that young Dr. McLoughlin was escorting a lady through the streets of Quebec City when their way was blocked by a stretch of muddy water. A narrow plank walkway had been laid over the muck, so they started across. Coming toward them staggered a drunken redcoat officer, his cheeks flushed the color of his blouse. Upon meeting them in the center of the walkway, the officer refused to yield and instead pushed McLoughlin's lady, sending her stumbling backwards into the mire. Enraged, the six-foot-four-inch McLoughlin grabbed the officer by his belt and collar, hurling him into the ankle-deep goo.[55]

Knowing that the British Army would never allow a civilian to treat one of its own so roughly, especially an officer, John McLoughlin quickly departed the city and offered his services to the North West Company. Sent to Fort William on the north shore of Lake Superior as its resident physician, McLoughlin became a company partner by 1814 and, subsequently, served as the fort's factor. After the unification of the North West and Hudson's Bay companies, McLoughlin's administrative abilities gained the notice of George Simpson. In 1824, Simpson promoted McLoughlin to chief factor of the firm's Columbia Department, which encompassed 670,000 square miles of North America's Pacific Northwest.[56] That autumn, McLoughlin and his family arrived with Simpson at Fort George, the department's headquarters, and the two men immediately began searching for a suitable location for the fort's replacement. They soon found it at Belle Vue Point on the north side of the Columbia River (across from Portland, Oregon), three-quarters of a mile up from the water's edge, and about six miles above the Columbia's confluence with

**Flag Staff &
Fur Store
(in background)
at Fort Vancouver**

the Willamette.[57] Construction began at once and continued throughout the winter. On March 19, 1825, Governor Simpson dedicated Fort Vancouver—named in honor of English explorer George Vancouver—to King George IV, and a month later, McLoughlin moved his family into its new home inside the unfinished post.[58]

Four years later, Governor Simpson directed McLoughlin to rebuild Fort Vancouver closer to the river. In the spring of 1829, workmen broke ground for a ninety thousand-square-foot stockade that was to be constructed on a long flat bench, two hundred yards from the Columbia.[59] After its completion, the new Fort Vancouver was the grandest post ever owned by the Hudson's Bay Company below the forty-ninth parallel. Its wooden palisades stood fifteen feet high; they enclosed numerous buildings, including the chief factor's two-story house which McLoughlin occupied until the 1840s. In time, the fort boasted crops of wheat, corn, barley, and oats, as well as a multitude of vegetables from a large garden. Fort Vancouver also had an apple orchard and grape vineyard. Its *engagés* raised cattle, hogs, goats, and chickens, all in

Chief Factor's House at Fort Vancouver

**Bastion of
Fort Vancouver**

all, enough bounty to make the post self-sustaining. In addition to developing Fort Vancouver's successful agriculture program, McLoughlin supervised his department's fur brigades. During the late 1820s and early 1830s, Fort Vancouver annually shipped over thirty thousand beaver pelts and lesser quantities of sea otter, fox, mink, and other animal skins.

Despite shipments such as these, McLoughlin's boss, Governor Simpson, had little reason to smile. By the end of the mountain man era, the Oregon Territory had, as he had wished, been trapped into a beaver desert. Yet Americans still came to the Pacific Northwest, lured not by fur as Simpson had feared, but by land, free for the taking. Beginning in 1840, a trickle of west-bound wagons soon expanded to a deluge.

Known today as the "Father of Oregon," John McLoughlin repeatedly offered succor to the growing tide of emigrants, many of whom arrived destitute at the gates of Fort Vancouver.[60] As Simpson (he became Sir George Simpson in 1841) watched increasing numbers of Americans stream into the Hudson's Bay domain, he became exasperated with McLoughlin for playing the Good Samaritan. Eventually facing the possibility that the company could lose the Oregon country on both sides of the Columbia River, Simpson established Fort Victoria on Vancouver Island in 1843. A year later, he and his London partners stripped McLoughlin of command of the Columbia Department, transferring its seat to the new fort.

His pride mortally wounded, the old doctor resigned from the Hudson's Bay Company and moved to Oregon City. On June 15, 1846, the United States and Great Britain settled the US-Canadian boundary along the forty-ninth parallel, placing Fort Vancouver firmly on American soil. McLoughlin applied to become a US citizen, but his adopted countrymen turned on him, denying his claim for land around his home. Compounding McLoughlin's woes, Simpson pressed him to reimburse the company for the food and equipment he had sold on credit to the needy emigrants. Most had refused to repay the loans which stood as uncollected debits on Fort Vancouver's ledgers.

In May 1849, the US Army made Fort Vancouver a military reservation (named Columbia Barracks) but allowed the Hudson's Bay Company to continue its trading operation. The following year, the American government leased some of the firm's buildings and constructed barracks and other facilities outside the stockade. In 1853, the Army post was officially named Fort Vancouver.

Meanwhile, John McLoughlin sat in his Oregon City home, detested by those he had helped, as well as by those to whom he had devoted his life's service. Having grown more bitter with each passing year, McLoughlin died on September 3, 1857.[61]

The Hudson's Bay Company maintained a trading store at

Fort Vancouver until 1860. Eleven years later, the Army changed the post's name to Vancouver Barracks, occupying it until 1947. Today the facility is home to the Army Reserve and National Guard.[62]

4 **Fort Vanderburgh:** In the late summer of 1822, Joshua Pilcher, the Missouri Fur Company's managing field partner, established Fort Vanderburgh on the Missouri River, twelve miles above its confluence with the Knife (north of Stanton, North Dakota).[63] Intended for the Mandan and Hidatsa trade, the post was named for company partner, William Henry Vanderburgh.

After the Blackfeet attacked a Missouri Fur Company brigade on the Yellowstone in the spring of 1823 and killed its *partisans,* Michael Immell and Robert Jones, Pilcher ordered Fort Vanderburgh abandoned.[64] That summer, the Missouri Fur Company joined Colonel Henry Leavenworth's campaign against the Arikaras in order to punish the tribe for having attacked William Ashley's expedition earlier in the year. The colonel's inept command allowed the Arikaras to escape and led to the closing of the upper Missouri (for details see Fort Henry at the confluence of the Missouri and Yellowstone rivers). By the time white traders could again safely ascend the river, Fort Vanderburgh had rotted away.

7 **Fort Vasquez:** In 1835, Louis Vasquez and Andrew Sublette, a younger brother of William and Milton Sublette, built Fort Vasquez on the South Platte River (about midway between Brighton and Greeley, Colorado). William Sublette provided most of the financing. Fort Vasquez was one of four competing trading posts located along a fifteen-mile line. Fort Lupton anchored the line's south end, followed by Fort Jackson, Fort Vasquez, and Fort St. Vrain. By 1840, Bent, St. Vrain & Company's Fort St. Vrain had cornered the region's robe trade, prompting Louis Vasquez and Andrew Sublette to sell their adobe post to Lock, Randolph & Company. At the time, Lock & Randolph's partners were floundering in their attempt to trade on the North Platte and hoped they

Fort Vasquez

would have better luck on the South. But it was not to be. The new owners lasted until 1842 before calling it quits. Within a year, Fort Vasquez was a crumbling ruin.[65]

8 **Verdigris River Post:** In late 1822, Auguste Pierre Chouteau opened a trading post on the left side of the Verdigris River, four miles above its confluence with the Arkansas (south of Wagoner, Oklahoma). The post was part of a larger complex that included a ferry and a thirty-acre farm. As with most other A.P. Chouteau ventures, Auguste's younger brother, Pierre, Jr., furnished the funding (see Osage Posts and Fort Osage for more about Auguste Chouteau and his Osage Outfit).[66]

5,8 **Vermilion Post:** See Dickson's Post and other trading houses near the mouths of the James and Vermilion rivers.

Wallace House through Big Wood Fort

1 **Wallace House:** In the fall of 1812, Astorians William Wallace and J.C. Halsey built Wallace House for the Pacific Fur Company, locating it east of the Willamette River in the heart of the Willamette Valley (about fourteen miles north of Salem, Oregon).[1] The following year the North West Company countered Wallace House by establishing Willamette Post about thirty miles north on what soon became known as French Prairie. That fall, the firms' competition ended when the Astorians sold out to the Nor'Westers (for details see Fort Astoria).

1 **Fort Walla Walla** (formerly called Fort Nez Perces): In the summer of 1818, the Nor'Wester Donald McKenzie built Fort Nez Perces on a sandy bench overlooking the left bank of the Columbia River, immediately above its confluence with the Walla Walla (about two miles south of Wallula, Washington).[2] Most historians consider McKenzie to be the father of the trapping brigades that were later refined by William Ashley and Smith, Jackson & Sublette. A former Astorian, McKenzie had joined the North West Company after it bought out John Jacob Astor's Pacific Fur Company in 1813. During the two years before he founded Fort Nez Perces, McKenzie supervised Nor'West trading on the Columbia River. Between 1818 and mid-1821, he led three trapping expeditions. His men harvested beaver from the Snake River to the Bear, proving the efficiency of free and company trappers over Indians, who hunted sporadically.

Fort Nez Perces passed to the Hudson's Bay Company following its merger with the Nor'Westers in 1821. Sometime afterwards, the Walla Walla name began to replace Nez Perces in company correspondence.[3] The post's primary commodity was horses rather than pelts. The factor maintained a breeding program, supplementing it with stock purchased from the neighboring

Cayuse and Nez Perce tribes which were famous for their large herds. Fort Walla Walla regularly furnished the Hudson's Bay trapping brigades and other company trading houses with mounts.

In its later years, the trading post helped Dr. Marcus Whitman and Henry Spalding establish their missions in the Oregon Territory. Marcus Whitman and his new bride, Narcissa, had left western New York on March 3, 1836, en route to bring Christianity to the northwestern Indians. In Pittsburgh, Pennsylvania, the Whitmans boarded a steamboat and proceeded down the Ohio River. Henry Spalding and his wife, Eliza, came aboard in Cincinnati. After a short stay in St. Louis, the Whitmans and Spaldings sailed up the Missouri River to Liberty, Missouri, then raced overland to join an American Fur Company supply caravan on the Platte. Tom Fitzpatrick, the pack train's *partisan,* escorted them to the trappers' rendezvous on the Green River. During the journey, Narcissa and Eliza became the first white women to cross South Pass.[4]

After the rendezvous ended, the missionaries continued their trip in company with a Hudson's Bay trapping brigade commanded by John McLeod. Their travel took them past forts Hall and Boisé, and on September 1, brought them to Fort Walla Walla. Needing to replenish their supplies, the missionaries descended the Columbia River for a brief stay at Fort Vancouver.

Late that fall, Marcus Whitman built his and Narcissa's Cayuse mission at Waiilatpu, about twenty-five miles up the Walla Walla River from Fort Walla Walla. At the same time, Henry and Eliza Spalding opened their Nez Perce mission on Lapwai Creek, two miles above its confluence with the Clearwater River (about ten miles east of Lewiston, Idaho). Because Fort Walla Walla was the closest of any trading post to the two missions, the Whitmans and Spaldings relied on the fort and Pierre Pambrun, its factor, for companionship and influence over the neighboring Indians.

In the mid-1840s, streams of passing emigrants introduced the surrounding country to measles. As the death rate among the Cayuses approached half of the tribe, the survivors blamed Marcus Whitman. Although the doctor treated the Indians with the same care that he gave the children from the wagon trains, only the whites recovered. Suspecting him of using an evil magic to destroy their people, Cayuse warriors attacked the Waiilatpu Mission on November 29, 1847, murdering nearly a dozen men and women, including Marcus and Narcissa Whitman. A few of the mission's Indian and mixed-blood residents escaped the massacre by slipping downriver to Fort Walla Walla, and safety. The Hudson's Bay Company abandoned the fort on October 16, 1855, during another period of prolonged Indian unrest.

In 1856, the US Army established Fort Walla Walla (now the city of Walla Walla, Washington) about eight miles east of the Whitmans' mission. Intended for Indian pacification, the garrison was used intermittently until it closed in 1911.[5]

4 **White Earth River Post** (aka Kipp's Post): See Fort Floyd.

4 **White Earth River Post of Owen McKenzie:** During the 1840s, Pierre Chouteau, Jr., & Company established a trading post on the left side of the Missouri, immediately above its confluence with the White Earth River (beneath North Dakota's Lake Sakakawea). Owen McKenzie, the mixed-blood son of Kenneth McKenzie, served as the post's *bourgeois* in 1847.[6]

6 **White River Post of P. D. Papin & Company:** In the late 1820s, P. D. Papin & Company (aka the French Fur Company) constructed a trading post near the confluence of the White and Missouri rivers (southwest of Chamberlain, South Dakota) to compete with nearby Fort Kiowa. The post was one of three the firm established in opposition to the American Fur Company. As with P. D. Papin & Company's Ponca trading house and Fort Teton, its White River post was also short-lived. On October 16, 1830, Pierre Papin and his partners bowed to John Jacob Astor's superior financial strength and sold the three posts to the American Fur Company. Papin joined the firm's Upper Missouri Outfit which assigned him to the Sioux trade on the White River until 1834.[7]

6 **White River Post of Sublette & Campbell:** In 1833, *engagés* of William Sublette and Robert Campbell erected a small trading house near the mouth of the White River (downstream from Chamberlain, South Dakota), intending to compete with the American Fur Company's Fort Kiowa.[8] Sublette & Campbell abandoned its White River post the following year after selling its Missouri River trading facilities to the American Fur Company. The post's buildings and palisades probably became fuel for passing steamboats.

8   **Wigwam Neosho:** In the early 1830s, Sam Houston joined the exile of his Cherokee friends in the Indian Territory, opening a tiny log trading cabin near the Verdigris River post of Auguste Pierre Chouteau (south of Wagoner, Oklahoma). Houston evidently devoted more time to the whiskey bottle than trading, because the Osages nicknamed him "Big Drunk." Soon tiring of his life in commerce, Houston gave the post to his Cherokee "country wife" and headed to Texas and eventual glory.[9]

7   **Fort William** (Bent's log stockade): William Bent probably built his log trading post in the fall of 1831, locating it on the north bank of the Arkansas River in the vicinity of Fountain Creek (near Pueblo, Colorado).[10] After the completion of his adobe post in 1834 (see Bent's "Old" Fort), Bent transferred his headquarters and the Fort William name to the new facility.

7   **Fort William** (aka Bent's "Old" Fort): See Bent's "Old" Fort (known officially as Fort William).

4   **Fort William** (Ebbetts, Cutting & Kelsey): See Fort Mortimer.

4   **Fort William** (Harvey & Primeau): See Fort Mortimer.

7   **Fort William** (Laramie River) (aka Fort Lucien and Fort John): See Fort Laramie.;

4   **Fort William** (Sublette & Campbell): Between late August and Christmas, 1833, Sublette & Campbell *engagés* erected Fort

William on the north bank of the Missouri River, across from the mouth of the Yellowstone and about three land-miles east of the American Fur Company's Fort Union (twenty-one miles southwest of Williston, North Dakota). The stockade measured 150 by 130 feet, and its cottonwood pickets extended fifteen feet above the ground. During the fort's construction, the partnership established a dozen other small trading houses on the Missouri near those of its American Fur rival. Sublette & Campbell also sent traders to the Wind River country in order to win the Crows away from Fort Cass (northeast of Billings, Montana, at the Yellowstone-Bighorn confluence).[11]

Immediate and ruthless competition from Kenneth McKenzie at Fort Union soon convinced William Sublette and Robert Campbell to withdraw from the Missouri River. In early 1834 during a visit to New York, Sublette sold Fort William and his firm's other upper Missouri posts to Pierre Chouteau, Jr., managing partner of the American Fur Company's Western Department.[12]

After the transfer was completed, McKenzie's work crews removed Fort William's log pickets, using them to build corrals at Fort Union.[13] During the following two years, various American Fur employees and their mixed-blood families occupied Fort William's deserted cabins. In the summer of 1836, a feud between two of these clans, the Deschampses and Remses, escalated into a gun battle. When the Deschampses took cover at Fort William, some of their attackers kept them pinned down with rifles, while others set its buildings ablaze. Like the Deschampses, Fort William came to a fiery end.[14]

1 **Fort William** (Nathaniel Wyeth): Nathaniel Wyeth left the 1834 mountain rendezvous on Ham's Fork of the Green River (in southwestern Wyoming) enraged that Tom Fitzpatrick had repudiated Wyeth's contract to supply the Rocky Mountain Fur Company. Vowing revenge, Wyeth took his men to the Snake River and began constructing Fort Hall (in eastern Idaho; see Fort Hall–Nathaniel Wyeth–for the circumstances leading up to these events). The stockade quickly took shape and, in early August,

Wyeth deemed the work sufficiently progressed that he could continue to the Columbia River to meet the brig *May Dacre* which was coming from Boston via Cape Horn. Leaving a dozen *engagés* to complete the fort, Wyeth headed into the heart of Hudson's Bay country.

He reached Fort Vancouver in mid-September, and the next day the *May Dacre* sailed up the Columbia—exactly three months behind schedule. The brig had successfully rounded the Horn, but while coming up the coast of Chile, it had been severely damaged by lightning and forced to lay over for repairs in Valparaiso.[15] In addition to trade goods, the ship's holds were filled with empty wooden barrels, containers that Wyeth had hoped would now be brimming with salted salmon that the *May Dacre* could carry to the fish markets of Massachusetts. But lightning had dashed his plan. The salmon run had passed.

Vowing to salvage what he could of his trading scheme, the energetic Wyeth established a trading post at Warrior Point on the narrow, northern end of Sauvie Island (near Portland, Oregon), which sat at the confluence of the Columbia and Willamette rivers, a few miles below Fort Vancouver.[16] During the late fall, Wyeth filled the *May Dacre* with lumber and, in December, dispatched it to peddle the cargo in the Hawaiian Islands. Over the winter while the ship was gone, Wyeth led his trappers up the Willamette Valley and to the Deschutes River country east of the Cascade Mountains. The following April 1835, the *May Dacre* returned to Fort William, having swapped the lumber for sheep, cattle, pigs, and goats.[17] Sometime that year, carpenters rebuilt the post on the west side of Sauvie Island beside the Multnomah Channel.

Despite Wyeth's energy, the bold plans he had hatched in the comfort of his Cambridge, Massachusetts home, failed. By that summer, fourteen of his trappers had perished from drowning or tomahawks. Dr. John McLoughlin, chief factor of the Hudson's Bay Company's Columbia Department, outbid him for tribal furs and saw to it that the Indians refused to help him fish during the annual salmon migration. Feeling no loyalty to the enterprise, Wyeth's employees stole traps, trade goods, and horses.

Compounding the New Englander's woes, a fever struck him in August, nearly taking his life.

Although Wyeth recovered his health, his business teetered on bankruptcy. He spent the winter of 1835–6 at Fort Hall, seeing if he could salvage some portion of that post's operation, but it too was beyond hope. In the spring, he returned to his trading house on Sauvie Island, sold its equipment and stores to the Hudson's Bay Company for a few cents on the dollar, and placed Fort William in the hands of a caretaker, instructing him to lease it if possible.

During the summer, Nathaniel Wyeth started home for good, going by way of Fort Hall and the mountain rendezvous which was held on the upper Green River, near the mouth of Horse Creek (a few miles west of Pinedale, Wyoming). Delighted to be shedding a competitor, the Hudson's Bay Company agreed to purchase Fort Hall, finalizing the sale the following year;[18] however, the British monopoly had no interest in Fort William. Wyeth retained ownership of the post but found Massachusetts too distant for him to monitor its use. After Wyeth returned to Cambridge, the Hudson's Bay Company began grazing cattle on Sauvie Island, converting his fort into a dairy.[19]

1   **Willamette Post:** In the spring or summer of 1813, the North West Company established Willamette Post on the right side of the Willamette River, about seventeen miles upstream from Willamette Falls (near Champoeg State Park, south of Portland, Oregon; Oregon City is located at Willamette Falls).[20] The Nor'Westers intended the post to counter the Pacific Fur Company's Wallace House, about thirty miles farther south.

In 1821, after its merger with the Nor'Westers, the Hudson's Bay Company acquired Willamette Post. During the next forty years, the structure served as a trading center for the Willamette River Valley. Settlers began moving into the region during the late 1820s, many of them former Hudson's Bay and Nor'West French-speaking employees.[21] In 1841, the Hudson's Bay Company constructed a granary at French Prairie, which was two miles downriver from Willamette Post, followed by a warehouse two years later. In the 1850s, a small village took root near the Hudson's Bay facilities, and the population seemed destined to continue expanding. Then in 1861, the Willamette River flooded, destroying the fledgling town and the Hudson's Bay buildings.[22] The town and Willamette Post were never rebuilt, and today the French Prairie is farmland.

8 **"Old Bill" Williams's Post on the Fork of the Grand (Neosho) River:** In early 1823, "Old Bill" William Sherley Williams and Paul Baillio opened a trading post for the Osage Indians on the lower Neosho River, near a noted confluence of creeks known as the Fork of the Grand (in the vicinity of Oswego, Kansas; the Neosho was formerly the Grand River).[23] Financed by Sibley, Baillio & Boggs, the partnership between Williams and Baillio ended after a few months when "Old Bill" left for the mountains and joined Jedediah Smith's trapping brigade, journeying with it to Flathead Post on the Clark Fork River (in western Montana).[24] Even compared to Smith, who had a well-earned reputation for long, fast travel, "Old Bill" covered some ground. After leaving Smith's brigade in the early spring of 1825, Williams skipped the first mountain man rendezvous and returned to his family on the Neosho, arriving in late May. Paul Baillio was probably still running the post, since a one-year trading license had been issued for it twelve months earlier. On August 1, Williams departed again, embarking on a remarkable, twenty-four-year odyssey that ended with his death at the hands of the Utes, when he was just shy of his sixty-second birthday.[25]

Sometime between 1823 and early 1825, Pierre Melicourt Papin opened a satellite trading house for his cousin, Auguste Pierre Chouteau, about ten miles down the Neosho from the Osages' village. Papin's establishment most likely siphoned away enough business from the Williams post to spell its doom, because Paul Baillio showed up in Santa Fe on April 27, 1825.[26]

1 **Big Wood Fort** (aka Snake Fort): See Fort Boisé and other Boise River Posts.

A Visitor's Guide to Trading Post Replicas

Readers are encouraged to contact the replica forts about visiting times. Some facilities are closed during the winter and on certain holidays.

Fort Astoria: A facade of a Fort Astoria blockhouse has been constructed in the city of Astoria, Oregon. The front piece is located at the corner of 15th and Exchange streets near the center of town. For more information, contact: Clatsop County Historical Society, 1618 Exchange Street, Astoria, OR 97103.

Fort Atkinson: Administered by the Nebraska State Game and Parks Commission, the Fort Atkinson replica is located one mile east of the town of Fort Calhoun, Nebraska. From Interstate 680, north of Omaha, drive nine miles north on US 75 to Fort Calhoun, then follow the signs to the Fort Atkinson State Historical Park. Mailing address: Fort Atkinson State Historical Park, P.O. Box 240, Fort Calhoun, NE 68023–0240.

Fort Benton: Administered by the Fort Benton Museum Association, the Fort Benton replica is located in the town of Fort Benton, Montana, off US 87, northeast of Great Falls. The replica and the Fort Benton Museum are in the historic district near the edge of the Missouri River. The keelboat *Mandan*, which was built for the 1952 Howard Hawks movie *The Big Sky,* sits across from the

BLM office, about a block away from the museum. Mailing address: Fort Benton Museum Association, Fort Benton, MT 59442.

Bent's "Old" Fort: Administered by the National Park Service, Bent's Old Fort National Historic Site is located eight miles east of La Junta, Colorado, and fifteen miles west of Las Animas, on Colorado State Highway 194. Mailing address: Superintendent, 35110 Highway 194 East, La Junta, CO 81050–9523.

Fort Boisé: Administered by the Old Fort Boisé Historical Society, the Fort Boisé replica is located beside US 20/26/95 on the southeastern outskirts of Parma, Idaho. The original fort sat near the confluence of the Boise and Snake rivers, about five miles northeast. Mailing address: Old Fort Boisé Historical Society, P.O. Box 942, Parma, ID 83660.

Bordeaux's Post: Administered by the Museum of the Fur Trade, the Bordeaux's Post replica is located behind the museum on US 20, three miles east of Chadron, Nebraska. Mailing address: Museum of the Fur Trade, P.O. Box 1276, Chadron, NE 69337.

Fort Bridger: Administered by the Wyoming Division of State Parks and Historic Sites, the restored Fort Bridger Army post and Bridger & Vasquez trading post replica are located near the town of Fort Bridger in the southwestern corner of Wyoming. The site can be accessed from Interstate 80, exits 34 or 39. Mailing address: Fort Bridger State Historic Site, P.O. Box 35, Fort Bridger, WY 82933.

Fort Buenaventura: Administered by Utah State Parks, the Fort Buenaventura replica is located in Ogden, Utah, beside the Weber River, two miles south of its confluence with the Ogden River. From Interstate 15 in Ogden, if southbound, take Exit 344B to 31st Street; if northbound, take Exit 346. From the exits, follow the Fort Buneaventura State Park signs to the entrance on A Avenue.

Mailing address: Fort Buenaventura State Park, 2450 A Avenue, Ogden, UT 84401–2203.

Fort Clatsop: Administered by the National Park Service, the Fort Clatsop National Memorial and replica are located about seven miles southwest of Astoria, Oregon. From Astoria, cross Youngs Bay on US 101, turning east at the sign for the Fort Clatsop Memorial. Mailing address: Superintendent, Fort Clatsop National Memorial, Route 3, Box 604-FC, Astoria, OR 97103.

Fort Connah: Administered by the Fort Connah Restoration Society, one building of the original post (constructed in 1846, it is one of Montana's oldest buildings) is located north of St. Ignatius, Montana, one-half mile east of US 93 between Post Creek and McDonald Lake roads, and just south of the Ninepipe Reservoir. Although the structure is not presently accessible to the public, it is visible from a signed turnout on US 93. Plans call for the Restoration Society to reconstruct Fort Connah's other two buildings, a museum, and visitor center sometime in the future. Mailing address: Fort Connah Restoration Society, c/o George Knapp, 2445 Blue Mountain Road, Missoula, MT 59804.

Gingras's Trading Post: Administered by the North Dakota State Historical Society, this historic trading post is located one mile north of Walhalla, North Dakota, just off North Dakota Highway 32. Cabins built by Norman Kittson for Pierre Chouteau, Jr., & Company are located in Walhalla. Mailing address: Gingras's Trading Post, Route 1, Box 55, Walhalla, ND 58282.

Fort Hall: Administered by the Pocatello Parks and Recreation Department, Nathaniel Wyeth's Fort Hall replica is located in Upper Ross Park, off 4th Avenue in south Pocatello, Idaho. The actual Fort Hall site is in the Fort Hall Indian Reservation near the village of Fort Hall, between Pocatello and Blackfoot. Mailing address: Old Fort Hall, P.O. Box 4169, Pocatello, ID 83205.

Fort Laramie: Administered by the National Park Service, the restored Fort Laramie is located three miles southwest of the town of Fort Laramie, Wyoming. This historic fort looks as it did during its later years, after the US Army replaced the old Fort William and Fort John stockades. From US 26 near the town of Fort Laramie, turn west on Wyoming Highway 160 and follow the signs to the Fort Laramie National Historic Site. Mailing address: Superintendent, Fort Laramie National Historic Site, Fort Laramie, WY 82212.

Old Fort Madison: Administered by the City of Fort Madison, Iowa, the Fort Madison replica is located off US 61 in River View Park, beside the Mississippi River in the town of Fort Madison, Iowa. The site of the original fort is two blocks away from the replica. Mailing address: Old Fort Madison, 811 Avenue E, P.O. Box 240, Fort Madison, IA 52627.

Fort Mandan: Administered by the Lewis and Clark Foundation, the Lewis and Clark Fort Mandan replica is located on the north side of the Missouri River, three miles west of Washburn, North Dakota. The original Fort Mandan is thought to have been ten miles upstream. From US 83 near Washburn, turn south on North Dakota Highway 200, then immediately swing west on the county road that passes the Lewis and Clark Interpretive Center. Signs lead to the Fort Mandan replica in the forest about a mile away. Mailing address: McLean County Historical Society, P.O. Box 124, Washburn, ND 58577.

Fort Nisqually: Administered by the Metropolitan Park District of Tacoma, the Fort Nisqually replica is located in Point Defiance Park in Tacoma, Washington. The replica contains two original Hudson's Bay Company buildings, the granary, and the factor's house. The actual Fort Nisqually site is one-half mile from Puget Sound, a bit northeast of the Nisqually River, near Du Pont, Washington. Mailing address: Fort Nisqually Historical Site, 5400 N. Pearl Street, #11, Tacoma, WA 98407.

Fort Osage: Administered by Jackson County Parks and

Recreation, the Fort Osage replica is located near Sibley, Missouri. From US 24 in Buckner, Missouri (fourteen miles northeast of Independence), turn north on Sibley Street, driving toward the Missouri River and the replica, a distance of about three miles. Mailing address: Jackson County Parks and Recreation, Heritage Museum and Programs, 22807 Woods Chapel Road, Blue Springs, MO 64015.

Fort Owen: Administered by Montana Fish, Wildlife & Parks, Fort Owen State Park is located near Stevensville, Montana, twenty-five miles south of Missoula. From the Stevensville Junction of US 93, turn east on Secondary Road 269 for eight-tenths of a mile. The park contains the fort's original east barracks, root cellar foundation, and reconstructed well house. Mailing address: Montana Fish, Wildlife & Parks, 3201 Spurgin Road, Missoula, MT 59801.

Robidoux's Post: Administered by the North Platte Valley Historical Association, the 1851 Robidoux trading post replica is located in Carter Canyon, south of the Scotts Bluff National Monument near Scottsbluff, Nebraska. From the junction of Nebraska State Highways 71 and 92, drive south three miles on Highway 71, turning west on Carter Canyon Road for another nine miles. Although the grounds are open year-round, the replica is open to tours by appointment only. Mailing address: North Platte Valley Historical Association, P.O. Box 435, Gering, NE 69341–0435.

Fort Uncompahgre: Administered by the City of Delta, the Fort Uncompahgre replica is located at 502 Gunnison River Drive in Delta, Colorado. The original Fort Uncompahgre sat beside the Gunnison River, just below its confluence with the Uncompahgre, about two miles west of Delta. Mailing address: Fort Uncompahgre, 502 Gunnison River Drive, Delta, CO 81416.

Fort Union: Administered by the National Park Service, the Fort Union replica is located beside the North Dakota-Montana border, twenty-four miles southwest of Williston, North Dakota. From US 2, two miles west of Williston, turn southwest on North Dakota State Highway 1804, following the signs to the Fort Union Trading Post National Historic Site. Mailing Address: Superintendent, Fort Union National Historic Site, Buford Route, Williston, ND 58801.

Fort Vancouver: Administered by the National Park Service, the Fort Vancouver replica is located in Vancouver, Washington. In Vancouver, take the Mill Plain Boulevard Exit from Interstate 5, following the signs to the Fort Vancouver National Historic Site Visitor Center on East Evergreen Boulevard. The Fort Vancouver replica is located one-quarter mile down the hill on East 5th Street. Mailing address: Superintendent, Fort Vancouver National Historic Site, 612 East Reserve St., Vancouver, WA 98661.

Fort Vasquez: Administered by the Colorado Historical Society, the Fort Vasquez replica and museum are located on US 85, one mile south of Platteville, Colorado. Mailing Address: 13412 US Highway 85, Platteville, CO 80651.

Endnotes

PART I
America's Weath: Beaver and Buffalo

America's Fur Trading Century

1 David J. Wishart, *The Fur Trade of the American West, 1807–1840: A Geographical Synthesis* (Lincoln, NE: University of Nebraska Press, Bison Book Edition, 1992; republished from the University of Nebraska Press Edition, 1979), pp. 20–1, 67–70. Also see Washington Irving, Edgeley W. Todd, ed., *The Adventures of Captain Bonneville USA. in the Rocky Mountains and the Far West* (Norman, OK: University of Oklahoma Press, 1961, 1986; reprinted from *The Rocky Mountains; or Scenes, Incidents, and Adventures in the Far West, digested from the Journal of Captain B.L.E. Bonneville, USA., and Illustrated from various other sources*, 2 vols., published by Carey, Lea, and Blanchard, Philadelphia, PA, 1837), p. 279 for an example of Indians killing a bull buffalo for sport.

2 Annie Heloise Abel, ed., *Chardon's Journal at Fort Clark, 1834–1839* (Lincoln, NE: University of Nebraska Press, Bison Book Edition, 1997; reprinted from the edition published by Lawrence K. Fox, Superintendent, Department of History, State of South Dakota, Pierre, SD, 1932), p. li.

3 Hiram Martin Chittenden, *The American Fur Trade of the Far West,* 2 vols. (Lincoln, NE: University of Nebraska Press, Bison Book Edition, 1986; republication of a 2 vol. edition published by Press of the Pioneers, NY, 1935; originally published in 3 vols. by Francis P. Harper, NY, 1902), 1:45.

4 Merrill J. Mattes, *The Great Platte River Road: The Covered Wagon Mainline Via Fort Kearny To Fort Laramie* (Lincoln, NE: University of Nebraska Press, Bison Book Edition, 1987; republished from the Nebraska State Historical Society Edition, Lincoln, NE, 1969), pp. 112–13.

5 Charles E. Hanson, Jr., and Veronica Sue Walters, "The Early Fur Trade in Northwestern Nebraska," *Nebraska History* 57, no. 4 (fall 1976), 1985 reprint, p. 15.

6 John Sunder, *The Fur Trade on the Upper Missouri, 1840–1865* (Norman, OK: University of Oklahoma Press, 1965), p. 17.

7 Robert G. Athearn, *Forts of the Upper Missouri* (Englewood Cliffs, NJ: Prentice-Hall, Inc., 1967), pp. 31–2 and Bernard DeVoto, *Across the Wide Missouri* (Boston, MA: Houghton Mifflin Company, 1947), p. 40.

8 Wishart, *op. cit.,* p. 3.

261

Perseverance: The Life of a Fur Trader

1 The French-Canadians of the North West and Hudson's Bay companies applied the term *mangeur de lard* to the lowest caste of voyageurs, "the goers and comers," who paddled the companies' heavy freight canoes. American fur traders and trappers applied it to greenhorns who had never spent a winter above the mouth of the Platte River.

2 Abel, ed., *op. cit.,* p. 11.

3 LeRoy R. Hafen, ed., *Fur Traders, Trappers, and Mountain Men of the Upper Missouri* (Lincoln, NE: University of Nebraska Press, Bison Book Edition, 1995; reprinted from *The Mountain Men and the Fur Trade of the Far West,* 10 vols., published by Arthur H. Clark Company, Glendale, CA, 1965–72), p. 24.

4 Erwin N. Thompson, *Fort Union Trading Post: Fur Trade Empire on the Upper Missouri* (Medora, ND: Theodore Roosevelt Nature and History Association, 1986; originally published as *Fort Union Trading Post Historic Structures Report, Part I,* by the National Park Service, 1968), p. 62.

5 Hafen, ed., *op. cit.,* p. 49.

6 LeRoy R. Hafen, ed., *Mountain Men and Fur Traders of the Far West* (Lincoln, NE: University of Nebraska Press, Bison Book Edition, 1982; reprinted from *The Mountain Men and the Fur Trade of the Far West,* 10 vols., published by Arthur H. Clark Company, Glendale, CA, 1965–72), p. 175.

7 Harold H. Schuler, *Fort Pierre Chouteau* (Vermilion, SD: University of South Dakota Press, 1990), p. 65.

8 Abel, ed., *op. cit.,* p. l.

9 Hafen, ed., *Fur Traders, Trappers, and Mountain Men of the Upper Missouri,* pp. 42–3.

10 Abel, ed., *op. cit.,* p. 18. Francis Chardon's journal entry for December 25, 1834, is most telling: "Christmas comes but once a year, and when it comes it brings good cheer. But not here! As every thing *[sic]* seems the same, No New faces, No News, and worst of all No Cattle [buffalo]. . . ."

11 *Ibid.,* p. 193.

12 Peter C. Newman, *Caesars of the Wilderness, Company of Adventurers,* vol. II (NY: Penguin Books, 1988; republished from the Viking Penguin Edition, 1987), pp. 259–60. After the merger of the Hudson's Bay and North West companies in 1821, George Simpson became governor of the combined firm's Northern Department which reached from Canada's Hudson Bay to the coast of Oregon. In 1826, his authority was expanded to include the smaller Southern Department and the company's posts at Montreal; see Glyndwr Williams, "The Hudson's Bay Company and the Fur Trade: 1670–1870," *The Beaver* (autumn 1983), reprinted, 1991, pp. 51–2.

13 Abel, ed., *op. cit.,* p. 240 n. 145.

14 *Ibid.,* p. xvii.

The Cycle of Trade

1 Abel, ed., *op. cit.,* p. xlix reports that Bernard Pratte, Sr., and John Cabanné, Sr., opposed the company's use of steamers, arguing that it was a waste of money.

2 Sawyers were trees that had toppled into the river and were held fast by their roots. Many times, high water caused by up-country thunderstorms sucked them free, then bore them downstream like battering rams intent on disemboweling any keelboat or steamer whose lookouts wavered in their vigilance. Often the branches of a cotton-wood ripped from a bank on the Milk or Judith rivers would anchor themselves in the Missouri's muddy bottom, leaving the trunk to bob at the surface, ready to skewer the next unsuspecting pilot. It was not unusual for these mountain streams to tear off chunks of shoreline—miniature islands, really—and hurl them along as though they were inland icebergs. *Embarra* was the name French-Canadian voyageurs gave

to logs that a river piled against the upstream side of sandbars and islands. These jumbles of debris constricted the channel, speeding the current and making passage treacherous.

3 Abel, ed., *op. cit.,* pp. 109–10.

4 The nutria is a large South American rodent whose fur has properties similar to a beaver. Because the cost of nutria pelts was a fraction of that of beaver pelts, hatters found them to be economical substitutes; Exhibit, Museum of the Mountain Man, Pinedale, WY.

5 Sunder, *The Fur Trade on the Upper Missouri,* pp. 16–17.

6 Abel., ed., *op. cit.,* pp. 224–5 n. 77. Readers wishing to study the effects of alcohol on Native Americans are encouraged to peruse the journal of Alexander Henry the Younger in Elliott Coues, ed., *The Manuscript Journals of Alexander Henry, Fur Trader of the Northwest Company, and of David Thompson, Official Geographer and Explorer of the same Company,* 2 vols. (Minneapolis, MN: Ross & Haines, Inc., 1897; reprinted in 1965), paying special attention to 1:209 where Henry discusses the evils of liquor.

7 Charles Larpenteur, *Forty Years a Fur Trader on the Upper Missouri* (Lincoln, NE: University of Nebraska Press, Bison Book Edition, 1989; originally edited by Elliott Coues and published in two vols., NY, 1898; then re-edited by Milo M. Quaife and published as a Lakeside Classic by R. R. Donnelley & Sons, Chicago, IL, 1933), pp. 137–8, 150, 201, and Abel, ed., *op. cit.,* pp. 257–8 n. 246, 378. John James Audubon, ed. by Maria R. Audubon, with notes by Elliott Coues, *Audubon and His Journals,* 2 vols. (NY: Dover Publications, Inc., 1960; originally published by Charles Scribner's Sons, 1897), 2:109 describes a band of Crees demanding whiskey from the traders at Fort Union; when it was not forthcoming, the Indians threatened go to a Hudson's Bay Company post above the forty-ninth parallel.

8 A. P. Nasatir, ed., *Before Lewis and Clark: Documents Illustrating the History of the Missouri, 1785–1804,* 2 vols. (Lincoln, NE: University of Nebraska Press, Bison Book Edition, 1990; originally published by the St. Louis Historical Documents Foundation, St. Louis, MO, 1952), 1:190.

9 Abel, ed., *op. cit.,* p. 248 n. 195.

10 Abel, ed., *op. cit.,* p. 204 n. 27. Congress first attempted to restrain the sale of liquor to Indians by passing the Act of March 30, 1802. Twenty years later the legislators added an amendment to the law, strengthening the penalties for non-compliance.

11 *Ibid.,* p. 261 n. 247, and Audubon, *op. cit.,* 1:478–9, n. 1. Near Council Bluffs during an 1843 voyage up the Missouri aboard the steamboat *Omega,* the captain, Joseph Sire, employed the famed naturalist John James Audubon to divert government inspectors from the liquor stock that the steamer was smuggling to the trading posts of Pierre Chouteau, Jr., & Company.

12 Hafen, ed., *Fur Traders, Trappers, and Mountain Men of the Upper Missouri,* p. 49.

PART II
Forts, Factories, and Posts of America's Fur Trade

Fort Adams through Fort Atkinson

1 Hanson, Jr., and Walters, *op. cit.,* p. 7.

2 David Lavender, *Bent's Fort* (Lincoln, NE: University of Nebraska Press, Bison Book Edition, 1972; republished from the Doubleday & Company, Inc., Dolphin Book Edition, NY, 1954), pp. 264, 434–5 n. 10.

3 *Ibid.,* pp. 332, 442 n. 8. During the winter of 1849–50, independent trader Dick Wootton traded with the Comanches at the burned-out adobe fort, garnering twelve Conestoga wagon-loads of buffalo robes and other skins; LeRoy R. Hafen, ed., *Fur*

Trappers and Traders of the Far Southwest (Logan, UT: Utah State University Press, 1997; republished from *Mountain Men and the Fur Trade of the Far West*, 10 vols., LeRoy R. Hafen, ed., Arthur H. Clark Company, Glendale, CA, 1965–72), p. 296.

4 Hafen, ed., *Mountain Men and Fur Traders of the Far West*, p. 188 puts the figure at three thousand, more than seven times the number of troops and scouts in Carson's command.

5 Thelma S. Guild and Harvey L. Carter, *Kit Carson: A Pattern for Heroes* (Lincoln, NE: University of Nebraska Press, Bison Book Edition, 1988; republished from the University of Nebraska Edition, 1984), pp. 250–5.

6 Texas state historical marker at the Adobe Walls site.

7 Chittenden, *op. cit.*, 2:939 states that Fort Alexander was built on or before 1839, citing its name on Pierre Chouteau, Jr., & Company's trading license for that year. Chittenden mistakenly places Fort Alexander across from the mouth of the Rosebud, the location given by Larpenteur, *op. cit.*, p. 138 for Fort Van Buren. Sunder, *The Fur Trade on the Upper Missouri*, pp. 59–60 agrees with Larpenteur. For my part, it seems unlikely that Larpenteur would have made a mistake about the location of Fort Van Buren, since it was his first command. For a reference to the Union Fur Company's unnamed post at the mouth of the Little Bighorn, see Sunder, *The Fur Trade on the Upper Missouri*, p. 55.

8 Larpenteur, *op. cit.*, pp. 148–9.

9 *Ibid.*, pp. 239–40.

10 Chittenden, *op. cit.*, 2:939, and Sunder, *The Fur Trade on the Upper Missouri*, p. 126. In 1851, the artist Rudolph Kurz wrote that Alexander Culbertson was supervising "Fort Union, Fort Benton, and Fort Alexander"; Thompson, *op. cit.*, p. 62. Because Fort Sarpy was often called both Fort Alexander and Fort Alexander Sarpy, Kurz was undoubtedly referring to the new post; also see Sunder, *The Fur Trade on the Upper Missouri*, p. 126.

11 Sunder, *The Fur Trade on the Upper Missouri*, p. 240.

12 Donald J. Lehmer, *Selected Writings of Donald J. Lehmer*, Reprints in Anthropology, vol. 8 (Lincoln, NE: J & L Reprint Company, 1977), pp. 106–7 use this number, whereas Roy W. Meyer, *The Village Indians of the Upper Missouri: The Mandans, Hidatsas, and Arikaras* (Lincoln, NE: University of Nebraska Press, 1977), p. 14 puts the Arikara population at nine thousand. Other estimates range as high as thirty thousand.

South Dakota's Bad River was formerly named the Teton. Adding to the confusion, the Teton was sometimes called the Little Missouri even though another Little Missouri River empties into the main Missouri in North Dakota.

Nasatir, ed., *op. cit.*, 2:379. In 1796, Zenon Trudeau, the Spanish commandant of St. Louis and lieutenant governor of Spanish Illinois, reported that the Arikara villages were "two leagues"–about six to ten miles–below the mouth of the Cheyenne River.

13 *Ibid.*, 1:28.

14 Stephen E. Ambrose, *Undaunted Courage: Meriwether Lewis, Thomas Jefferson, and the Opening of the American West* (NY: Simon & Schuster, 1996), p. 178.

15 Bernard DeVoto, *The Course of Empire* (Boston, MA: Houghton Mifflin Company, 1952), p. 366, and Alvin M. Josephy, Jr., *The Indian Heritage of America* (Boston, MA: Houghton Mifflin Company, 1968, Revised Edition, 1991), pp. 118–19. The Ojibwas lived west of Lake Superior and were often called Chippewas by the whites; Josephy, *op. cit.*, pp. 82–3.

16 Nasatir, ed., *op. cit.*, 2:418.

17 *Ibid.*, 1:91; 2:441, 527–8.

18 Ambrose, *op. cit.*, p. 178 places all three Arikara villages on the three-mile-long island

at the mouth of the Grand River, whereas Meyer, *op. cit.*, pp. 37–8 locates them as I have indicated. According to Meyer, the Arikaras deserted their island village between 1806 and 1811, but retained the other two.

19 Richard Edward Oglesby, *Manuel Lisa and the Opening of the Missouri Fur Trade* (Norman, OK: University of Oklahoma Press, 1963), pp. 84, 130.

20 Hafen, ed., *Mountain Men and Fur Traders of the Far West,* p. 31.

21 Dale L. Morgan, *Jedediah Smith and the Opening of the West* (Lincoln, NE: University of Nebraska Press, Bison Book Edition, 1964; republished from the Bobbs-Merrill Company Edition, Indianapolis, IN, 1953), pp. 37, 51. Although Morgan places the Arikara villages six or eight miles above the Grand, it is probable that he meant the two villages mentioned by Meyer, *op. cit.*, p. 38, which were four miles above the Grand.

22 Chittenden, *op. cit.*, 1:273; 2:947, and Harrison Clifford Dale, *The Explorations of William H. Ashley and Jedediah Smith, 1822–1829* (Lincoln, NE: University of Nebraska Press, Bison Book Edition, 1991; reprinted from *The Ashley-Smith Explorations and the Discovery of a Central Route to the Pacific, 1822–1829,* published by Arthur H. Clark Company, Glendale, CA, 1941), p. 164 n. 324. On p. 182 n. 380, Dale intimates that Ashley's Fort was established in 1826 rather than 1825.

23 Washington Irving, *Astoria* (Portland, OR: Binfords & Mort, Publishers, Clatsop Edition, 1967; reprinted from *Astoria, or Anecdotes of an Enterprise beyond the Rocky Mountains,* 2 vols., published by Carey, Lea, and Blanchard, Philadelphia, PA, 1836), pp. 13–15, Newman, *op. cit.*, pp. 94–7, and Chittenden, *op. cit.*, 1:164–6.

24 Newman, *op. cit.*, pp. 97–8.

25 Ambrose, *op. cit.*, p. 37. Boston captain Robert Gray sailed into the river's estuary on May 11, 1792, determined its latitude and longitude, and christened it for his bark, the *Columbia.* For more about Captain Gray and the *Columbia* see Fort Vancouver, endnote 47.

26 Chittenden, *op. cit.*, 1:167 asserts that New York State issued the American Fur Company's charter on April 6, 1808. Irving, *Astoria,* p. 16 uses 1809.

27 Irving, *Astoria,* p. 22, and Hafen, ed., *Mountain Men and Fur Traders of the Far West,* pp. 58–9.

28 Irving, *Astoria,* pp. 24–5, and Chittenden, *op. cit.*, 1:168.

29 Newman, *op. cit.*, pp. 4, 28, 33–7, and Williams, *op. cit.*, p. 43.

30 Newman, *op. cit.*, p. 91.

31 Hafen, ed., *Mountain Men and Fur Traders of the Far West,* p. 61.

32 Chittenden, *op. cit.*, 1:169, 171, and Newman, *op. cit.*, p. 99.

33 Chittenden, *op. cit.*, 1:171. The *Tonquin* reached the open sea two days later and picked up an escort from the frigate USS *Constitution,* lest a British warship attempt to press any of the *Tonquin's* passengers or crew into service; see Irving, *Astoria,* pp. 33–5.

34 Newman, *op. cit.*, p. 100.

35 Irving, *Astoria,* pp. 41–3, and Chittenden, *op. cit.*, 1:172–3.

36 Newman, *op. cit.*, p. 100. Twenty-four Hawaiians joined the Astorian enterprise and sailed aboard the *Tonquin;* Chittenden, *op. cit.*, 2:887.

37 Newman, *op. cit.*, p. 102. The second sounding boat, like the first, held five crewmen, including two Hawaiian islanders. In the second crew, two men drowned when their boat capsized. Stephen Weekes and the Hawaiians eventually righted the boat and made for shore, but before they reached safety, one of the Hawaiians died from exposure. He was later buried on land; Irving, *Astoria,* pp. 60–3. The historian Hiram Martin Chittenden includes the dead Hawaiian among those drowned crossing Peacock Bar; Chittenden, *op. cit.*, 2:887.

38 Chittenden, *op. cit.*, 1:175.

39 *Ibid.*, 1:175–9, and Irving, *Astoria,* pp. 85–93. Except where noted, my sources for the *Tonquin* disaster are Irving and Chittenden. My version differs slightly from the May 15, 1813, Missouri Gazette report reprinted in Chittenden, *op. cit.*, 2:892–4.

40 Hafen, ed., *Fur Traders, Trappers, and Mountain Men of the Upper Missouri,* p. 2.

41 Hafen, ed., *Mountain Men and Fur Traders of the Far West,* pp. 60, 62.

42 *Ibid.*, pp. 62, 64.

43 Oglesby, *op. cit.*, p. 105.

44 Chittenden, *op. cit.*, 1:184.

45 Oglesby, *op. cit.*, p. 109.

46 Hafen, ed., *Mountain Men and Fur Traders of the Far West,* p. 65.

47 Oglesby, *op. cit.*, p. 110.

48 *Ibid.*, p. 112.

49 Hafen, ed., *Mountain Men and Fur Traders of the Far West,* p. 65. Of John Hoback, Edward Robinson, and Jacob Reznor, sixty-six-year-old Robinson probably made the greatest impression on Wilson Hunt, especially when the grizzled mountain man removed the bandanna from atop his head. Years earlier, Indians had lifted his scalp, and he used the kerchief to protect his white skull; Burton Harris, *John Colter: His Years in the Rockies* (Lincoln, NE: University of Nebraska Press, Bison Book Edition, 1993; republished from the Charles Scribner's Sons Edition, NY, 1952), p. 160, and Irving, *Astoria,* p. 151.

50 Oglesby, *op. cit.*, p. 112. Hunt's voyageurs must have also benefited from the upriver wind that allowed Lisa to cover seventy-five miles in twenty-four hours. Otherwise, Lisa would have caught Hunt before June 2.

51 *Ibid.*

52 *Ibid.*, pp. 112–13 report that Lisa caught Hunt on June 2 and that their parties reached the Arikara villages ten days later. Hafen, ed., *Mountain Men and Fur Traders of the Far West,* p. 66 concurs. Irving, *Astoria,* p. 162 mistakenly places the Lisa-Hunt overtaking in July; however, on p. 169 Irving corrects himself.

53 Irving, *Astoria,* p. 180, and Oglesby, *op. cit.*, p. 114.

54 Irving, *Astoria,* p. 189, and Chittenden, *op. cit.*, 2:887. As the Astorian party journeyed west, Wilson Hunt acquired additional horses from various Indian bands with whom he crossed trails.

Irving never gives Pierre Dorion's Indian wife a first name. Other historians call her Marie or Marguerite, either one of which could have been fiction or her husband's pet name for her. Rather than cumbersomely referring to this remarkable woman as "the wife of Pierre Dorion," I have chosen to call her Marie.

55 *Ibid.*, p. 240, and Hafen, ed., *Mountain Men and Fur Traders of the Far West,* pp. 67–8.

56 Irving, *Astoria,* pp. 238, 241–2, and Chittenden, *op. cit.*, 2:887.

57 Chittenden, *op. cit.*, 1:190.

58 Hafen, ed., *Fur Traders, Trappers, and Mountain Men of the Upper Missouri,* p. 9.

59 Cort Conley, *Idaho for the Curious: A Guide* (Cambridge, ID: Backeddy Books, 1982), pp. 233–4. Some historians claim that Antoine Clappine's canoe overturned in Caldron Linn rather than above it; see Hafen, ed., *Fur Traders, Trappers, and Mountain Men of the Upper Missouri,* p. 9 n. 8. Irving, *Astoria,* p. 249 disputes this, reporting that the party's lead canoe safely passed the rapid where Clappine, in the second canoe, capsized. A close reading of Irving reveals that the accident occurred above Caldron Linn. Anyone who thinks that the first dugout could have gone through this cataract should visit the two closely spaced waterfalls that compose Caldron Linn (located a few miles from Murtaugh, Idaho). Taking a dugout through them would be equivalent to playing Russian roulette with all of the chambers loaded.

60 Irving, *Astoria,* pp. 257–67.

61 *Ibid.*, pp. 271–87, 291, Hafen, ed., *Mountain Men and Fur Traders of the Far West,* pp.

71–2, and Hafen, ed., *Fur Traders, Trappers, and Mountain Men of the Upper Missouri,* p. 10.

62   Chittenden, *op. cit.,* 1:200–1.

63   Newman, *op. cit.,* p. 90.

64   Coues, ed., *op. cit.,* 2:783 n. 5, and Irving, *Astoria,* p. 83. The Okanogan River is spelled Okanagan in Canada.

65   Chittenden, *op. cit.,* 1:201–2 are unclear whether David Stuart established the She-Whaps Post in the late fall of 1811 or early 1812. James R. Gibson, *Farming the Frontier: The Agricultural Opening of the Oregon Country, 1786–1846* (Seattle, WA: University of Washington Press, 1985); the flyleaf map dates the founding of "Shewaps" Post as 1812, the same year the North West Company countered with nearby Fort Kamloops.

66   Chittenden, *op. cit.,* 1:193–4, 204.

67   Hafen, ed., *Fur Traders, Trappers, and Mountain Men of the Upper Missouri,* p. 10, and Hafen, ed., *Mountain Men and Fur Traders of the Far West,* p. 73.

68   Chittenden, *op. cit.,* 1:217–18.

69   *Ibid.,* 1:219–20, Irving, *Astoria,* pp. 424–7, 430–3, and Hafen, ed., *Mountain Men and Fur Traders of the Far West,* p. 73.

70   Chittenden, *op. cit.,* 1:220–1, and Newman, *op. cit.,* p. 104. Some texts spell HMS *Raccoon* with one "c."

71   Chittenden, *op. cit.,* 1:221–2.

72   *Ibid.,* 1:222–3, 225 n. 2, and Coues, ed., *op. cit.,* 2:770.

73   Hafen, ed., *Mountain Men and Fur Traders of the Far West,* p. 75.

74   Newman, *op. cit.,* pp. 106–7.

75   Chittenden, *op. cit.,* 2:935.

76   Abel, ed., *op. cit.,* p. 298 n. 363, 373.

77   *Ibid.,* pp. 31, 298 n. 363.

78   *Ibid.,* pp. 37, 301 n. 375, and pp. 376 n. 381.

79   Chittenden, *op. cit.,* 2:935 reports that the post was abandoned on April 2, 1835, shortly after the *Assiniboine's* departure. However, Abel, ed., *op. cit.,* p. 380 quotes a December 1835 letter from Kenneth McKenzie wherein he mentions a "new equipment" being sent to Fort Assiniboine for the coming trading season; also see p. 378.

80   Robert W. Frazer, *Forts of the West: Military Forts and Presidios and Posts Commonly Called Forts West of the Mississippi River To 1898* (Norman, OK: University of Oklahoma Press, 1965), p. 79.

81   Frazer, *op. cit.,* pp. 84–5, and "Fort Atkinson, 1820–1827" Brochure, Nebraska Game and Parks Commission, 1996.

82   Mattes, *op. cit.,* p. 122. Lewis and Clark referred to the site of their parley as "Council-bluff" (singular); see Audubon, *op. cit.,* 1:483 n. 1.

83   Morgan, *op. cit.,* pp. 112–13 place Tom Fitzpatrick's bull boat mishap at Devil's Gate on the Sweetwater River (in central Wyoming, about five miles west of Independence Rock), whereas Robert M. Utley, *A Life Wild and Perilous: Mountain Men and the Paths to the Pacific* (NY: Henry Holt and Company, Inc., 1997), pp. 328–9 n. 14 argue for the North Platte Canyon, a number of miles farther east and below the mouth of the Sweetwater; so, too, does Dale, *op. cit.,* p. 91, and LeRoy R. Hafen, *Broken Hand, The Life of Thomas Fitzpatrick: Mountain Man, Guide, and Indian Agent* (Lincoln, NE: University of Nebraska Press, Bison Book Edition, 1973; reprinted from the Old West Publishing Company Edition, Denver, CO, 1931), pp. 39–40. Utley, Dale, and Hafen base their arguments on Fitzpatrick's comment to John Frémont after Frémont's boat capsized on the North Platte. According to Frémont, Fitzpatrick claimed to have lost his bull boat in the same rapid which is now beneath the Pathfinder Reservoir. To have reached that point, Fitzpatrick would have had to

run the Sweetwater through Devil's Gate, line his boat through, or portage around. None of these options would have been particularly attractive. To understand my point, I invite adventurous readers to examine Devil's Gate from the wooden sluiceway that snakes along its left edge. Hafen assumes that Fitzpatrick, upon seeing Devil's Gate, decided to cache his boat-load of furs at Independence Rock rather than risk them in another cataract.

84 Frazer, *op. cit.*, p. 85.

Fort Barclay through Buzzards' Roost

1 LeRoy R. Hafen, ed., *French Fur Traders and Voyageurs in the American West* (Lincoln, NE: University of Nebraska Press, Bison Book Edition, 1997; reprinted from *The Mountain Men and the Fur Trade of the Far West,* 10 vols., published by Arthur H. Clark Company, Glendale, CA, 1965–72), p. 187, Marc Simmons, *Following the Santa Fe Trail, A Guide for Modern Travelers* (Santa Fe, NM: Ancient City Press, 1984), p. 165, and Hafen, *Broken Hand,* p. 256.

2 Mattes, *op. cit.*, pp. xxxii–xxxiii, 263, 270, 279.

3 Donald Jackson, *Old Fort Madison, 1808–1813* (Fort Madison, IA: The Old Fort Commission, 1990; originally published as an article in *The Palimpsest* 47, no. 1, January, 1966): pp. 5–6, 43, and Frazer, *op. cit.*, pp. 68–70.

4 Hafen, ed., *Mountain Men and Fur Traders of the Far West,* p. 333. Mattes, *op. cit.*, p. 121 states that traders had established the first post near the site by 1810.

5 Chittenden, *op. cit.*, 1:151.

6 Hafen, ed., *Fur Traders, Trappers, and Mountain Men of the Upper Missouri,* p. 101, and Lavender, *Bent's Fort,* pp. 47, 83, 88.

7 LeRoy R. Hafen, ed., *Trappers of the Far West* (Lincoln, NE: University of Nebraska Press, Bison Book Edition, 1983; reprinted from *The Mountain Men and the Fur Trade of the Far West,* 10 vols., published by Arthur H. Clark Company, Glendale, CA, 1965–72), p. 130.

8 *Ibid.*, p. 133.

9 Hafen, ed., *French Fur Traders and Voyageurs in the American West,* p. 298 speculates that by the late 1830s, either Pierre Chouteau, Jr., & Company or Fort Bellevue's *bourgeois,* Peter Sarpy, may have acquired the post.

10 DeVoto, *Across the Wide Missouri,* p. 271, and Hafen, ed., *Trappers of the Far West,* p. 141.

11 Hafen, ed., *French Fur Traders and Voyageurs in the American West,* pp. 298–9.

12 According to Abel, ed., *op. cit.*, p. lix, Alexander Culbertson wanted to call the post Fort Honoré after Honoré Picotte; however, Picotte recommended that it be named for Meriwether Lewis.

13 Chittenden, *op. cit.*, 2:937 erroneously state that Fort Lewis was relocated on the left side of the Missouri River in 1846. Sunder, *The Fur Trade on the Upper Missouri,* pp. 98–9 report that the priest Nicholas Point saw the old post dismantled and the new one built while he was on the upper Missouri in May 1847, a date also used by *Highlights of the Upper Missouri National Wild & Scenic River Lewis & Clark National Historic Trail* (Lewiston, MT: Bureau of Land Management, 1993), p. 9.

14 An historical site interpretive sign at Fort Benton, Montana states that the adobe construction ended in 1858; Sunder, *The Fur Trade on the Upper Missouri,* p. 127 n. 47 says 1860.

15 R. G. Robertson, "Mullan Road: A Feat of 624 Miles," *Idaho Spokesman-Review* (Coeur d'Alene, ID), 29 July 1996, sec. A, p. 10.

16 Sunder, *The Fur Trade on the Upper Missouri,* pp. 212–13. Although Fort Benton was thought to be the limit of steamboat navigation on the Missouri River, an 1866 floodsurge allowed the steamer *Peter Balen* and, possibly, two other boats to pass over the rock shelf and continue another thirty–or more–miles upstream.

17 Interpretive signs at historical Fort Benton mistakenly state that the sale occurred in 1865, the year the Northwest Fur Company acquired Fort Union and Pierre Chouteau, Jr., & Company's other facilities. William E. Lass, "The History and Significance of the Northwest Fur Company, 1865–1869," *North Dakota History, Journal of the Northern Plains* 61, no. 3 (summer 1994): p. 24 reports that when Charles Chouteau sold the firm's Missouri River trading operations to the Northwest Fur Company in March 1965, Fort Benton was not included because the Northwest partners had not yet secured a trading license for the western Montana Territory. The Northwest Fur Company was also known as Hawley, Hubbell & Company.

18 Historians disagree over the date of Fort Benton's founding. Morgan, *op. cit.*, pp. 45, 378–9 n. 5 argue for 1822, citing Joshua Pilcher's Congressional Report of December 1, 1831. Wishart, *op. cit.*, p. 48 says that Michael Immell and Robert Jones went up the Missouri in 1821 and built Fort Benton that fall, which would put them one year ahead of the Andrew Henry expedition of Ashley & Henry; like Morgan, Wishart also cites Pilcher's 1831 Congressional Report. John E. Sunder, *Joshua Pilcher: Fur Trader and Indian Agent* (Norman, OK: University of Oklahoma Press, 1968), p. 36 states that Pilcher sent a trapping brigade commanded by Immell and Jones from Council Bluffs to the Yellowstone country in 1821, and that they built Fort Benton that fall. Chittenden, *op. cit.*, 1:147 says that Joshua Pilcher constructed Fort Benton in the autumn of 1821, while 2:938 says that the Missouri Fur Company built it in 1922. In a letter to Lewis Cass, Secretary of War, William Gordon states that he went to the mountains with Immell and Jones in 1822; see Abel, ed., *op. cit.*, p. 343. Finally, Athearn, *op. cit.*, pp. 6–7 say that the two brigade leaders ascended the Missouri in 1822, after Andrew Henry had built Fort Henry at the mouth of the Yellowstone River; however, Athearn makes no mention of Fort Benton.

19 Lavender, *Bent's Fort,* pp. 145–8, 333–4.

20 *Ibid.*, pp. 338–9.

21 *Ibid.*, p. 347.

22 *Ibid.*, pp. 369–70.

23 Frazer, *op. cit.*, pp. 41–2.

24 Lavender, *Bent's Fort,* pp. 375–6.

25 Frazer, *op. cit.*, pp. 39–40, 41–2.

26 Hafen, ed., *French Fur Traders and Voyageurs in the American West,* p. 288. Peter Sarpy's baptismal name was Pierre Sylvester Gregoire Sarpy.

27 Charles E. Hanson, Jr., "James Bordeaux," *The Museum of the Fur Trade Quarterly* 2, no. 1 (spring 1966), "James Bordeaux Issue," p. 6.

28 Fort Lucien was rebuilt in 1841 and renamed Fort John. A successor to the old American Fur Company, Pratte, Chouteau & Company became Pierre Chouteau, Jr., & Company in 1839.

29 Sunder, *The Fur Trade on the Upper Missouri,* p. 10.

30 Hafen, ed., *French Fur Traders and Voyageurs in the American West,* p. 46 states that the post burned in late 1846. Hanson, Jr., *op. cit.*, p. 6. says that in 1847, passing Oregon-bound emigrants reported the post had burned to the ground. However, Hanson, Jr., and Walters, *op. cit.*, p. 13 says that John Richard ran Fort Bernard until at least 1849. Either Richard rebuilt the post or the emigrants were mistaken.

31 Hafen, ed., *French Fur Traders and Voyageurs in the American West,* p. 48.

32 *Ibid.,* and Hanson, Jr., and Walters, *op. cit.*, p. 15.

33 Virginia L. Heidenreich, ed., *The Fur Trade In North Dakota* (Bismarck, ND: State Historical Society of North Dakota, 1990), p. 22.

34 Abel, ed., *op. cit.*, p. lix.

35 *Ibid.*, p. 250 n. 205.

36 Sunder, *The Fur Trade on the Upper Missouri,* p. 195. The principal shareholders in

Frost, Todd & Company were D. M. Frost and John B. S. Todd, who was a cousin of Mary Todd Lincoln. A former Army captain, Todd had left the military in September 1856 to become partners with Frost. Later, during the Civil War, Todd used the influence of President Lincoln's wife to win a commission as a brigadier general. He served only four days before learning that the Dakota Territory had elected him to Congress; Athearn, *op. cit.*, pp. 56–7, 76.

37 Sunder, *The Fur Trade on the Upper Missouri,* pp. 208, 213–14.
38 Frazer, *op. cit.*, pp. 109–10.
39 Lass, *op. cit.*, p. 24.
40 Frazer, *op. cit.*, p. 110.
41 Hanson, Jr., and Walters, *op. cit.*, p. 13.
42 Hafen, ed., *French Fur Traders and Voyageurs in the American West,* p. 48 says that their partnership lasted about one year. In contradiction, Hanson, Jr., and Walters, *op. cit.*, p. 15 reports that the two partners purchased six thousand dollars worth of trade goods in 1851.
43 Irving, *Captain Bonneville,* p. 320 n. 27, and Mattes, *op. cit.*, pp. 112–13.
44 Coues, ed., *op. cit.*, 2:886–7 n. 7, Chittenden, *op. cit.*, 1:224–5, Conley, *op. cit.*, pp. 245–6, Irving, *Astoria,* pp. 446–8, and Utley, *op. cit.*, p. 37. Historians have recorded several versions of Reed's massacre and Marie Dorion's escape; my account is but one of them.
45 Conley, *op. cit.*, pp. 545–6, and Leonard J. Arrington, *History of Idaho,* 2 vols. (Moscow, ID: University of Idaho Press, 1994), 1:112. Arrington spells McKenzie's name as Mackenzie.
46 Gibson, *op. cit.*, p. 58 gives Fort Boisé's founding as 1835. Carlos A. Schwantes, *In Mountain Shadows: A History of Idaho* (Lincoln, NE: University of Nebraska Press, 1991), p. 33 makes the date August 1834. Bernard DeVoto, *Across the Wide Missouri,* p. 207 also uses 1834. James Clyman, *Journal of a Mountain Man,* Linda M. Hasselstrom, ed. (Missoula, MT: Mountain Press Publishing Company, 1984 by Winfred Blevins; originally published as *James Clyman; American Frontiersman, 1792–1881,* California Historical Society Special Publication No. 3, California Historical Society, San Francisco, CA, c1928), p. 147 places the fort on the right side of the Snake River, "a few miles below the mouth of the Boise." Other travelers have described it as being as much as eight miles north (downstream) of the Boise; Gregory M. Franzwa, *The Oregon Trail Revisited* (St. Louis, MO: Patrice Press, 1972), pp. 334–5. Charles Preuss, on his "Topographical Map of the road from Missouri to Oregon commencing at the mouth of the Kansas in the Missouri River and ending at the mouth of the Wallah-Wallah in the Columbia, in VII Sections, from the field notes and journal of Capt. J. C. Frémont, and from sketches and notes made on the ground by his assistant Charles Preuss, by order of the Senate of the United States" (Baltimore, MD: E. Weber & Company, Lithography, 1846), Section VI, places Fort Boisé on the right side of the Snake River, one mile downstream from the mouth of the Boise.

    Over the years, floods have changed the channels of the Boise and Snake rivers so they are far different today than they were during the fur era. Although the State of Idaho commemorates the site of Fort Boisé with a lion's head marker, the land on which the post stood has long since been washed downstream; Conley, *op. cit.*, p. 548.

    Fort Boisé's founder, Thomas McKay, was the son of the Astorian Alexander McKay who died aboard the Pacific Fur Company's sailing ship *Tonquin* (see Fort Astoria). A Nor'Wester before he became an Astorian, the elder McKay had abandoned his half-Cree "country wife," Marguerite, prior to joining the Pacific Fur Company. When Dr. John McLoughlin married Marguerite, her son, Thomas, became McLoughlin's stepson.

47 Conley, *op. cit.*, p. 548.
48 Irving, *Captain Bonneville,* pp. xxvi–xxix, li, 13. Some historians think that Bonneville's trapping venture was a ruse intended to fool the British, who shared joint occupancy of the Oregon Territory with the United States. It is speculated that Bonneville's primary purpose was to spy on the Hudson's Bay Company which projected the British presence in the northwest. See DeVoto, *Across the Wide Missouri,* pp. 59–60, and Hafen, ed., *Mountain Men and Fur Traders of the Far West,* p. 275 n. 9.
49 Hafen, ed., *Mountain Men and Fur Traders of the Far West,* p. 276. This was the first time anyone took wagons over South Pass.
50 Irving, *Captain Bonneville,* p. 49 n. 10, Edith Haroldsen Lovell, *Benjamin Bonneville, Soldier of the American Frontier* (Bountiful, UT: Horizon Publishers & Distributors, Inc., 1992), p. 57, and Wyoming state historical marker at the Fort Bonneville site, off Wyoming State Highway 354, four miles west of Daniel Junction.
51 DeVoto, *Across the Wide Missouri,* p. 58.
52 Irving, *op. cit.,* pp. xxxvii, liii, and Lovell, *op. cit.,* pp. 89, 97.
53 Irving, *op. cit.,* pp. 79, 80 n. 1, and Lovell, *op. cit.,* pp. 60, 260 n. 21.
54 Irving, *op. cit.,* p. 104 n. 1 put Bonneville's final winter camp on the North Fork of the Salmon. Hafen, ed., *Mountain Men and Fur Traders of the Far West,* p. 277 concurs. Lovell, *op. cit.,* p. 61 argues that because the camp was in a narrow valley beneath towering cliffs, it had to have been south of Bonneville's wintering post; Lovell places it some distance upstream from the mouth of the Lemhi River (south of Salmon, ID). Irving's opinion relies on Bonneville's manuscript, whereas Lovell's is based on the physical nature of the Salmon River and North Fork valleys.
55 Oral Interview with James Hanson, Curator, Museum of the Fur Trade, Chadron, NE, 10 June 1997.
56 Hanson, Jr., "James Bordeaux," pp. 4–6.
57 Hafen, ed., *French Fur Traders and Voyageurs in the American West,* p. 45.
58 Hanson, Jr., *op. cit.,* pp. 6–9.
59 Museum of the Fur Trade interpretive sign at the Bordeaux's Post replica.
60 Chittenden, *op. cit.,* 2:938.
61 Robert S. Ellison, *Fort Bridger–A Brief History* (Cheyenne, WY: Wyoming State Archives, Museums and Historical Department, Second Edition, 1981; Historical Landmark Commission of Wyoming, Original Edition, 1931), pp. 7–8, and Utley, *op. cit.,* p. 182.
62 DeVoto, *Across the Wide Missouri,* p. 378.
63 Ellison, *op. cit.,* pp. 14, 25.
64 Hafen, ed., *Mountain Men and Fur Traders of the Far West,* pp. 263–5.
65 Ellison, *op. cit.,* pp. 21–3.
66 *Ibid.,* p. 26, and Hafen, ed., *Mountain Men and Fur Traders of the Far West,* p. 270.
67 Frazer, *Forts of the West,* p. 178.
68 DeVoto, *Across the Wide Missouri,* pp. 246, 249–50.
69 Bernard DeVoto, *The Year of Decision, 1846* (Boston, MA: Houghton Mifflin Co., 1942), pp. 46–7, and Allen Kent Powell, ed., *Utah History Encyclopedia* (Salt Lake City, UT: University of Utah Press, 1994), pp. 227–8.
70 Hafen, ed., *French Fur Traders and Voyageurs in the American West,* pp. 183–6, and Hafen, *Broken Hand,* p. 256.

Cabanné's Post through Cruzet's Post
 1 Aka the French Company, this partnership among Bartholomew Berthold, Pierre Chouteau, Jr., Bernard Pratte, Sr., and John Cabanné, Sr., was reorganized in 1823, becoming Bernard Pratte & Company; see Hafen, ed., *Fur Traders, Trappers, and Mountain Men of the Upper Missouri,* p. 17.

2 Chittenden, *op. cit.*, 2:925–6 say that John Cabanné, Sr., built the trading post between 1822 and 1826, which is too late. Hafen, ed., *Mountain Men and Fur Traders of the Far West*, pp. 32–3 state that Cabanné "took over" the Council Bluffs trading house for Bernard Pratte & Company in 1823, indicating that the post was already in existence. Hafen, ed., *Fur Traders, Trappers, and Mountain Men of the Upper Missouri*, p. 17 says that Cabanné accepted command of the French Company's Council Bluffs post in 1819, which is too early. In the next sentence, Hafen's text reports that the post was founded by 1823, the year that Cabanné became its *bourgeois*.

3 Chittenden, *op. cit.*, 2:926.

4 Sunder, *The Fur Trade on the Upper Missouri*, p. 94.

5 *Ibid.*, p. 214.

6 Oral Interview with James Hanson, Curator, Museum of the Fur Trade, Chadron, NE, 10 June 1997.

7 Abel, ed., *op. cit.*, p. 207 n. 33.

8 Sunder, *The Fur Trade on the Upper Missouri*, p. 107.

9 John Joseph Mathews, *The Osages: Children of the Middle Waters* (Norman, OK: University of Oklahoma Press, 1961), pp. 283, 362, Hafen, ed., *French Fur Traders and Voyageurs in the American West*, pp. 97, 100, Nasatir, ed., *op. cit.*, 1:343, 2:486, and Oglesby, *op. cit.*, p. 16.

10 Guild and Carter, *op. cit.*, pp. 61, 305 n. 8, and Hafen, *Broken Hand*, p. 50.

11 Irving, *Captain Bonneville*, p. 308, and Larpenteur, *op. cit.*, p. 38 n. 23.

12 DeVoto, *Across the Wide Missouri*, pp. 125–7.

13 Chittenden, *op. cit.*, 2:938 gives the date of Fort Cass's abandonment as 1835. Sunder, *The Fur Trade on the Upper Missouri*, p. 59 states that Fort Cass "was abandoned seven years" after it was built which would make the date 1839. Chittenden is probably correct, since Pratte, Chouteau & Company (successor to the American Fur Company) established Fort Van Buren in 1835, locating it close enough to Fort Cass that if both posts were open, it would have been wastefully redundant.

14 Historians disagree on the location of Gantt's Fort. Guild and Carter, *op. cit.*, pp. 50–1 place it near the confluence of the Arkansas River and Fountain Creek, the site of modern Pueblo, CO. David J. Weber, *The Taos Trappers: The Fur Trade in the Far Southwest, 1540–1846* (Norman, OK: University of Oklahoma Press, 1968 [in microfilm], published 1970, revised 1971), p. 203, and Hafen, ed., *Trappers of the Far West*, pp. 208–9 locate it at the mouth of the Purgatoire River, near Las Animas, while Hafen, ed., *Trappers of the Far West*, p. 211 n. 24 puts it in Baxter, CO, six miles east of Pueblo. See Fort William (Bent's log stockade) endnote 10 for the controversy concerning whether Bent's log post–the first Fort William–was erected before or after Gantt's Fort.

15 Hafen, ed., *Trappers of the Far West*, pp. 211–12, 226.

16 Nasatir, ed., *op. cit.*, 1:114; 2:636–8.

17 *Ibid.*, 1:114 states that Régis Loisel established the Cedar Island post around 1800, while Oglesby, *op. cit.*, p. 34 says 1802. Loisel's petition to Charles Dehault Delassus, the Spanish Louisiana lieutenant governor in St. Louis, for a trading license was dated March 20, 1800; Nasatir, ed., *op. cit.*, 2:611–12.

   Confusion arises over the name Cedar Island which was appended to at least three wooded islands on the southern South Dakota stretch of the Missouri. In the 1843 log of the steamboat *Omega*, Captain Joseph Sire noted passing Little Cedar Island on May 22, another on May 25, and Grand Cedar Island on May 28; Chittenden, *op. cit.*, 2:963–5. Jean Baptiste Truteau wrote about camping on an island in mid-September 1794, about twenty leagues upriver from the mouth of the Niobrara, and fifteen leagues downriver from that of the White which would put it somewhere near the State Highway 44 bridge; Nasatir, ed., *op. cit.*, 1:266–7. Bernard

DeVoto, ed., *The Journals of Lewis and Clark* (Boston, MA: Houghton Mifflin Company, 1953), p. 30 quotes from William Clark's journal that the Corps of Discovery went through the Missouri's Grand Detour on September 21, 1804. The entry for September 22 (pp. 30–1), describes passing "Ceder *[sic]* Island" on which a "Mr. Louiselle" *[sic]* had built a trading post. This clearly puts Loisel's Cedar Island above the Grand Detour. DeVoto, *The Course of Empire,* p. 439 also places Loisel's Cedar Island trading post upstream from the Grand Detour. Wishart, *op. cit.*, p. 44 fig. 5 erroneously shows Cedar Island at the mouth of the White River, west of Chamberlain, SD, which is below the Grand Detour. Wishart dates the establishment of the Cedar Island post as 1809, which is the year the St. Louis Missouri Fur Company opened their trading house in Régis Loisel's old fort. However, Wishart errs by placing the post where Fort Recovery was located. The confusion is understandable since Fort Recovery was also known as Cedar Fort and Fort aux Cédres. "A New Map of Texas, Oregon and California and the regions adjoining compiled from the most recent authorities," (Philadelphia, PA: S. Augustus Mitchell, Publisher, 1846) shows "Old Ft. Aux Cédres"–Fort Recovery–just above the Missouri-White River confluence. Nasatir, ed., *op. cit.*, 1:114 places Loisel's post near the northern Lyman, SD, county line, which is above the Grand Detour. Finally, Chittenden, *op. cit.*, 2:928–9 apply the "Fort aux Cédres" name to Loisel's post.

18 Nasatir, ed., *op. cit.*, 2:737. In October 1804, a few months after returning to St. Louis, Régis Loisel died of natural causes; he was thirty-one.

19 Oglesby, *op. cit.*, pp. 83, 97.

20 *Ibid.*, pp. 128–9.

21 *Ibid.*, pp. 141, 151.

22 Berthold & Chouteau was a partnership between Pierre Chouteau, Jr., and his brother-in-law, Bartholomew Berthold, which began in 1813; see Hafen, ed., *Mountain Men and Fur Traders of the Far West,* pp. 27, 31.

23 Chadron Creek derives its name from Louis B. Chartran who, in the winter of 1841–2, worked for Pierre Chouteau, Jr., & Company, trading among the Ogalala Sioux. Chartran joined Sibille, Adams & Company in 1842.

24 Hanson, Jr., and Walters, *op. cit.*, p. 6.

25 Sunder, *The Fur Trade on the Upper Missouri,* pp. 61–2.

26 *Ibid.*, pp. 63, 81.

27 *Highlights of the Upper Missouri National Wild and Scenic River Lewis and Clark National Historic Trail,* p. 9 states that Alexander Culbertson set fire to Fort Chardon in the spring of 1846, whereas Abel, ed., *op. cit.*, p. lix asserts that Culbertson burned the fort in late 1845, and Larpenteur, *op. cit.*, p. 207 is ambiguous.

28 Sunder, *The Fur Trade on the Upper Missouri,* pp. 236, 249.

29 Nasatir, ed., *op. cit.*, 1:98, 362, and DeVoto, *The Course of Empire,* pp. 375–6, 379.

30 Nasatir, ed., *op. cit.*, 1:143–4.

31 *Ibid.*, 2:597, 615. Also see Pawnee Posts endnote 4.

32 *Ibid.*, 2:591–2. "Monsieur Bernal" listed for the Kansas license in 1800 is Bernal or Beral Sarpy. The Marqués de Casa Calvo replaced Governor-General François Luis Hector Carondelet in 1800; *ibid.*, 2:611 n. 3.

33 Hafen, ed., *Mountain Men and Fur Traders of the Far West,* pp. 25–6.

34 Chittenden, *op. cit.*, 2:923–4.

35 Hafen, ed., *French Fur Traders and Voyageurs in the American West,* p. 292.

36 Abel, ed., *op. cit.*, pp. xvi, 197 n. 1.

37 *Ibid.*, p. 118.

38 DeVoto, *Across the Wide Missouri,* pp. 287, 418 n. 2 say that contemporary survivor estimates ranged from 40 to 125, whereas William R. Swagerty in his introduction to Abel, ed., *op. cit.*, p. ix, makes the count 138.

39 Abel, ed., *op. cit.*, p. x.

40 Heidenreich, ed., *op. cit.*, p. 24.

41 *Ibid.*, "Fort Clark State Historic Site" Brochure, State Historical Society of North Dakota, and Fort Clark Site, North Dakota state historical marker. The Arikaras actually spent the winter of 1861–2 in a camp above Like-A-Fishhook Village, moving opposite "New" Fort Berthold the following March. As the Arikaras built their lodges, the Sioux descended, driving them across the Missouri to live among the Hidatsas and Mandans for security.

42 Sunder, *The Fur Trade on the Upper Missouri,* p. 218.

43 "Fort Clatsop" Official Map and Guide, National Park Service, GPO, 1996; reprint 1991.

44 Ambrose, *op. cit.*, pp. 313, 320, and Harris, *op. cit.*, p. 27.

45 Ambrose, *op. cit.*, pp. 314, 320–1, and "Fort Clatsop" Official NPS Map and Guide.

46 Ambrose, *op. cit.*, pp. 208, 298, 328–9, 336–7, 339.

47 Many historians have written about the Corps of Discovery's epic exploration. My short summary relies on Stephen Ambrose's *Undaunted Courage* and the edited version of Bernard DeVoto's *The Journals of Lewis and Clark,* referenced above.

48 Unlike Fort Colvile, the town of Colville, WA, is spelled with three l's. The date for the founding of Fort Colvile is sometimes given as 1827; however, in 1825, a local Indian chief presented the land for the post to the Hudson's Bay Company which makes 1826 a more probable date for its construction. Gibson, *op. cit.*, p. 18 uses 1825–6 for Fort Colvile's establishment, whereas p. 43 cites 1825, as does the flyleaf map.

49 Hafen, ed., *Mountain Men and Fur Traders of the Far West,* p. 105, and Hafen, *Broken Hand,* p. 78 report that Jedediah Smith met David Jackson in Montana's Flathead River Valley. Morgan, *op. cit.*, p. 290 presumes they linked up on the Flathead. Dale, *op. cit.*, p. 292 says that a detachment from Jackson's brigade located Smith in Pierre's Hole (near Driggs, ID), and John E. Sunder, *Bill Sublette, Mountain Man* (Norman, OK: University of Oklahoma Press, 1959), p. 81 agrees with Dale. This difference is most likely brought on by the recollections of the trapper Joe Meek when he was an old man; see Hafen, *Broken Hand,* p. 81–2.

50 Frazer, *op. cit.*, pp. 172–3, 174.

51 F. Lee Graves, *Montana's Fur Trade Era* (Helena, MT: Montana Magazine and American & World Geographic Publishing, 1994), p. 59, and "Fort Connah" Brochure, Fort Connah Restoration Society, St. Ignatius, MT.

52 "Fort Connah" Brochure and Oral Interview with George Knapp, Fort Connah Restoration Society, Missoula, MT, 28 April and 7 May 1997.

53 Hafen, ed., *Fur Traders, Trappers, and Mountain Men of the Upper Missouri,* pp. 84 n. 9, 85 n. 12.

54 Sunder, *The Fur Trade on the Upper Missouri,* pp. 55, 63, 81.

55 Guild and Carter, *op. cit.*, p. 88 calls him "Prewett Sinclair." Carter's essay, "Kit Carson," in Hafen, ed, *Mountain Men and Fur Traders of the Far West,* p. 173 spells it "Prewitt." Chittenden, *op. cit.*, 2:945 spells his last name "St. Clair," whereas DeVoto, *Across the Wide Missouri,* p. 380 spells it "Sinclair." A plaque at the fort site gives its founding as 1837.

56 Chittenden, *op. cit.*, 2:945, and Hafen, *Broken Hand,* p. 208.

57 Chittenden, *op. cit.*, 1:160–1, and Oglesby, *op. cit.*, pp. 51, 53–4.

58 Chittenden, *op. cit.*, 1:161–3, and Oglesby, *op. cit.*, pp. 99–100.

59 Prior to 1822, Michilimackinac was the field headquarters for John Jacob Astor's fur empire. After Astor divided the American Fur Company into the Northern and Western Departments, Michilimackinac became the supply depot for the Northern Department.

60 Hafen, ed., *Fur Traders, Trappers, and Mountain Men of the Upper Missouri*, p. 8.

Fort Daer through Fort Hunt

1 John S. Galbraith, *The Hudson's Bay Company as an Imperial Factor, 1821–1869* (Berkeley, CA: University of California Press, 1957), p. 100.
2 Abel, ed., *op. cit.*, p. 295 n. 345.
3 *Ibid.*, p. 290 n. 320.
4 Sunder, *The Fur Trade on the Upper Missouri*, p. 188.
5 *Ibid.*, p. 92.
6 *Ibid.*, pp. 92–3.
7 *Ibid.*, pp. 93–4.
8 *Ibid.*, p. 94.
9 *Ibid.*, p. 111.
10 *Ibid.*, p. 144.
11 *Ibid.*, pp. 164–5.
12 *Ibid.*, p. 184.
13 *Ibid.*, pp. 200, 208. John B. S. Todd and D. M. Frost established the Upper Missouri Land Company in February 1858; Athearn, *op. cit.*, p. 57.
14 Sunder, *The Fur Trade on the Upper Missouri*, p. 213.
15 Abel, ed., *op. cit.*, pp. 328 n. 522, and Hafen, ed., *Fur Traders, Trappers, and Mountain Men of the Upper Missouri*, p. 23.
16 Hafen, ed., *French Fur Traders and Voyageurs in the American West*, p. 259.
17 Abel, ed., *op. cit.*, pp. 228 n. 83, 292 n. 332, 294–5 n. 343. Chittenden, *op. cit.*, 2:927 places one of Dickson's early posts midway between the James and Vermilion rivers.
18 Audubon, *op. cit.*, 1:493–4 n. 1, and Chittenden, *op. cit.*, 2:927 place Vermilion Post just below the mouth of the Vermilion River. During Audubon's return voyage down the Missouri in the autumn of 1843, the naturalist recorded in his journal that he had camped "a few miles above the Vermilion River" on September 26; Audubon, *op. cit.*, 2:168. The next morning his mackinaw "passed the Vermilion River at half-past seven." He then reached the "Fort of Vermilion" at noon and stopped. Sometime that morning *before* landing at Vermilion Post, Audubon and his party paused alongside a "barge" that was heading upstream; for how long, his journal does not say (see entry for September 27, pages 168–9). Despite the encounter with the "barge," the four and one-half hours that went by from the time Audubon's mackinaw passed the mouth of the Vermilion River until it reached the trading house, seems much too long if Vermilion Post sat immediately below the Vermilion-Missouri confluence. One logical conclusion is that Audubon erred in naming the river the Vermilion, and that he possibly meant the James or some stream between the James and the Vermilion. However, this is speculation.
19 Larpenteur, *op. cit.*, p. 120.
20 *Ibid.*, pp. 248–9, 258.
21 Sunder, *The Fur Trade on the Upper Missouri*, p. 200.
22 Hafen, ed., *Mountain Men and Fur Traders of the Far West*, p. 344, and Hafen, ed., *Fur Traders, Trappers, and Mountain Men of the Upper Missouri*, p. 78.
23 Coues, ed., *op. cit.*, 2:606 n. 5, Dale, *op. cit.*, p. 40, and DeVoto, *The Course of Empire*, p. 536. Thompson named his post and its river after the Salish Indians, spelling their name "Saleesh."
24 Newman, *op. cit.*, p. 93 (n.n.).
25 Chittenden, *op. cit.*, 1:204.
26 Gibson, *op. cit.*, flyleaf map shows "Saleesh" House immediately downstream from Flathead Post and attributes their foundings to the North West Company in 1809. Graves, *op. cit.*, p. 59 states that Alexander Ross established Flathead Post for the

Hudson's Bay Company in 1823, locating it about five miles east of Thompson Falls on the Clark Fork River.

27 Morgan, *op. cit.*, pp. 120–1.

28 *Ibid.*, pp. 122–5.

29 *Ibid.*, pp. 125–7.

30 *Ibid.*, p. 128.

31 For these events I rely on *ibid.*, pp. 128–9, and Utley, *op. cit.*, pp. 66–7. Dale, *op. cit.*, pp. 93–4 give a slightly different version.

32 Morgan, *op. cit.*, p. 133.

33 Hafen, ed., *Mountain Men and Fur Traders of the Far West*, pp. 121–2.

34 These figures come from Morgan, *op. cit.*, pp. 134–5. Hafen, ed., *Mountain Men and Fur Traders of the Far West,* p. 123 reports different numbers.

35 Morgan, *op. cit.*, p. 139.

36 *Ibid.*, p. 142, and Hafen, ed., *Mountain Men and Fur Traders of the Far West,* p. 124.

37 Morgan, *op. cit.*, pp. 148–9 say that most of the Americans were free trappers hunting in Weber's brigade; Johnson Gardner was their ringleader. Also, see Hafen, ed., *Mountain Men and Fur Traders of the Far West,* pp. 125–6, and Sunder, *Bill Sublette,* pp. 56–8.

38 Morgan, *op. cit.*, pp. 152–3.

39 Fort Floyd's record is murky, at best. William J. Hunt, Jr., "Fort Floyd: An Enigmatic Nineteenth-Century Trading Post," *North Dakota History, Journal of the Northern Plains* 61, no. 3 (summer 1994): pp. 7–20 refute the long-held opinion among many fur trade historians that Fort Floyd somehow metamorphosed into Fort Union, a theory put forth by Chittenden, *op. cit.*, 2:932–3. DeVoto, *Across the Wide Missouri,* p. 69 obviously follows Chittenden's lead when stating that Fort Union "was first called Fort Floyd."

40 Hunt, Jr., *op. cit.*, p. 10 cites 1826 as the probable construction date, whereas Abel, ed., *op. cit.*, pp. 309–10 n. 421 uses the winter of 1825–6.

41 Hunt, Jr., *op. cit.*, p. 12. Acceptance of Hunt's scenario dictates that James Kipp must have abandoned the first White Earth trading post after one season.

42 *Ibid.*, pp. 14, 20, and W. Raymond Wood, "An Introduction to the History of the Fur Trade on the Northern Plains," *North Dakota History, Journal of the Northern Plains* 61, no. 3 (summer 1994): p. 4.

43 Heidenreich, ed., *op. cit.*, p. 38.

44 Chittenden, *op. cit.*, 2:944 mistakenly says that Fraeb's Post was located on "St. Vrain's Fork of Elkhead River, itself a branch of Yampah River, Colorado." In 1:257, he correctly states that St. Vrain's Fork is a tributary of the Yampah, not the Elkhead. A "Map of a Reconnaissance between Fort Leavenworth on the Missouri River and the Great Salt Lake in the Territory of Utah made in 1849 and 1850 by Captain Howard Stansbury of the Corps of Topographical Engineers" (on display at the Fort Bridger, WY, state historical site) shows St. Vrain's Fork as a tributary of the Little Snake River, which is a tributary of the Yampah. (Alfred Glen Humpherys in his essay, "Thomas L. [Peg-leg] Smith," Hafen, ed., *Fur Trappers and Traders of the Far Southwest,* p. 214 contradicts this, stating that the Little Snake River was formerly known as St. Vrain's Fork.) Stansbury's map has the Elkhead River flowing into the Yampah, upstream from the mouth of the Little Snake and nowhere near the modern-day St. Vrain's Creek which is in north-central Colorado. The *Wyoming Atlas and Gazetteer* (Freeport, ME: DeLorme Mapping, 1992), p. 21 places Battle Creek approximately where Stansbury locates his St. Vrain's Fork. Battle Creek rises in southern Wyoming's Medicine Bow Mountains and empties into the Little Snake just inside the Colorado border.

Adding to the confusion, DeVoto, *Across the Wide Missouri,* p. 375 states that Fraeb and "John" Sarpy had a post on St. Vrain's Fork. DeVoto is probably referring to Fort Jackson, which Henry Fraeb and Peter Sarpy (not John) established on the South Platte River. The modern-day St. Vrain Creek flows into the South Platte River southwest of Greeley, CO, and downstream from the site of Fort Jackson.

Fraeb's Post was most likely located on Battle Creek (Chittenden's and Stansbury's St. Vrain's Fork), since Chittenden, *op. cit.*, 1:257–8 say that Fraeb was killed near his trading post, and DeVoto, *Across the Wide Missouri*, p. 375 reports that he died on Battle Creek, as does Hafen, ed., *Mountain Men and Fur Traders of the Far West*, p. 303. Adding to the uncertainty, Utley, *op. cit.*, pp. 177–8 assert that the post was located on the right side of the Green River, a bit downstream from its confluence with the Big Sandy. However, Hafen, *Broken Hand*, p. 194 n. 13 calls the Green River post a forerunner of Fort Bridger.

Fort Galpin through Fort Hunt

1 Sunder, *The Fur Trade on the Upper Missouri*, p. 219.
2 *Ibid.*, p. 240.
3 *Ibid.*, pp. 37–8, 40.
4 *Ibid.*, p. 56. Audubon, *op. cit.*, 1:520 places Fort George roughly thirty miles downriver from Fort Pierre.
5 Sunder, *The Fur Trade on the Upper Missouri*, p. 57, and Chittenden, *op. cit.*, 1:369–70.
6 Abel, ed., *op. cit.*, p. 245 n. 173.
7 Heidenreich, ed., *op. cit.*, pp. 8–9.
8 "Walhalla, North Dakota, 'Valley of the Gods,'" Information Booklet of Walhalla, ND (n.d.), p. 1. In 1871, the name of St. Joseph was changed to Walhalla.
9 Hafen, ed., *Fur Trappers and Traders of the Far Southwest*, pp. 43–4.
10 DeVoto, *Across the Wide Missouri*, p. 107, and Sunder, *Bill Sublette*, pp. 108–9.
11 Hafen, ed., *Mountain Men and Fur Traders of the Far West*, pp. 320–1.
12 DeVoto, *Across the Wide Missouri*, pp. 118–9, 122, Irving, *Captain Bonneville*, p. 315 n. 20, and Sunder, *Bill Sublette*, p. 129. DeVoto mistakenly asserts that Wyeth floated down the Missouri to St. Louis in his bull boat, whereas Irving and Sunder report that he acquired a "twenty-foot sailing canoe"–or pirogue–from Kenneth McKenzie.
13 Hafen, ed., *Mountain Men and Fur Traders of the Far West*, pp. 321–2, Irving, *Captain Bonneville*, pp. 374–5, and DeVoto, *Across the Wide Missouri*, pp. 181–5.
14 DeVoto, *Across the Wide Missouri*, p. 190 says that William Sublette captured the lead after thirteen days, whereas David Lavender, *Fort Laramie and the Changing Frontier* (DC: Division of Publications, National Park Service, 1983), p. 24, says twelve.
15 Exhibit, Fort Hall replica, Pocatello, ID.
16 Hafen, ed., *Mountain Men and Fur Traders of the Far West*, p. 244.
17 Conley, *op. cit.*, p. 509.
18 DeVoto, *Across the Wide Missouri*, p. 258.
19 Hafen, ed., *op. cit.*, pp. 244–5.
20 John D. Unruh, Jr., *The Plains Across: The Overland Emigrants and the Trans-Mississippi West, 1840–60* (Urbana, IL: University of Illinois Press, Illini Books Edition, 1982), p. 202.
21 Conley, *op. cit.*, p. 510.
22 Frazer, *op. cit.*, p. 44.
23 *Ibid.*, p. 45.
24 Sunder, *The Fur Trade on the Upper Missouri*, p. 188.
25 Chittenden, *op. cit.*, 2:927 mentions the post but gives no details. For more about Fort Randall, see Athearn, *op. cit.*, p. 50, and Frazer, *op. cit.*, pp. 136–7.
26 Nasatir, ed., *op. cit.*, 1:114, 2:936–8, and DeVoto, *The Course of Empire*, p. 440.
27 Lewis and Clark met Hugh Heney in December 1804 at their winter post among the

Mandans. Heney delivered a letter to the captains from the North West Company factor in charge of Fort Assiniboine, at the confluence of Canada's Souris and Assiniboine rivers in southern Manitoba. During the Corps of Discovery's return from the Pacific coast in 1806, Lewis wrote Heney, requesting that he persuade several Sioux chiefs to visit Washington, DC. Lewis hoped the chiefs would be awed by the power of the United States and, as a result, convince their people to remain friendly toward American traders.

As partial payment for his services, Heney was to be given command of a government-owned Indian trading factory that would be built on the Cheyenne River. Lewis's plan called for Nathaniel Pryor and two privates to deliver the proposal to Heney at either the Mandan villages or Fort Assiniboine, depending on where he happened to be. Knowing that Heney would need to give presents to the Sioux chiefs in order to win their cooperation, Lewis sent the Corps' horses with Pryor so he could barter them to the Mandans in return for trade goods for Heney. However, the elaborate scheme fell apart when Pryor lost the entire remuda to a Crow war party.

For more about Hugh Heney and Lewis and Clark, see Ambrose, *op. cit.*, pp. 366–8, and DeVoto, ed., *The Journals of Lewis and Clark,* pp. 446, 450.

28 Oglesby, *op. cit.*, p. 75 n. 22.
29 *Ibid.*, p. 90.
30 The nearby merger of the Gallatin River with the combined Jefferson and Madison rivers forms the start of the Missouri and gives the locale its name. The Three Forks confluence is a shade under three thousand river-miles west of St. Louis.
31 Oglesby, *op. cit.*, p. 96, and Utley, *op. cit.*, p. 23.
32 *Egin* is a Shoshone word meaning cold.
33 Conley, *op. cit.*, p. 162.
34 Some months later, a detachment from Wilson Hunt's Astorian expedition found Archibald Pelton near the Snake River and took him to Fort Astoria. However, his trials were far from finished. In 1814, Pelton lost his hair and his life to an Indian war party; Hafen, ed., *Mountain Men and Fur Traders of the Far West,* pp. 72, 75 n. 98.
35 Oglesby, *op. cit.*, pp. 103, 109.
36 *Ibid.*, p. 114.
37 *Ibid.*, pp. 115–17.
38 *Ibid.*, pp. 117, 145.
39 Morgan, *op. cit.*, p. 27.
40 *Ibid.*, pp. 28–9, 33–4, 40.
41 *Ibid.*, p. 42.
42 *Ibid.*, pp. 50–1. Dale, *op. cit.*, p. 8 cites the Arikaras' concern about losing control of the Missouri fur traffic as another reason for the tribe's hostility.
43 Morgan, *op. cit.*, p. 52, and Sunder, *Bill Sublette,* p. 39.
44 Morgan, *op. cit.*, p. 53.
45 *Ibid.*, p. 56.
46 *Ibid.*, p. 59.
47 *Ibid.*, reports that Colonel Leavenworth initiated the campaign against the Arikaras without authority from his superiors. Athearn, *op. cit.*, p. 10 states that Leavenworth's plan was approved by Western Department commander, General E. P. Gains. Since Leavenworth launched his campaign within four days of learning about the Arikaras' assault on William Ashley, there was no time for the colonel to have received authorization from Gains's headquarters in Kentucky.
48 Morgan, *op. cit.*, p. 62.
49 *Ibid.*, pp. 68–9, 71–2, 75, and Sunder, *Bill Sublette,* pp. 42–5.
50 Morgan, *op. cit.*, pp. 79–80, 101.

51 *Ibid.*, pp. 101, 392 n. 7. Historians are uncertain whether the fort was set in the triangle of land just above the confluence (the site of Fort Raymond) or on the high ground a bit downstream.

52 *Ibid.*, p. 113.

53 Graves, *op. cit.*, p. 59, and Dale, *op. cit.*, p. 30. Dale spells Howse's name "Howes."

Fort Jackson through Fort Lupton

1 Abel, ed., *op. cit.*, pp. liii, 239 n. 138 correctly place Fort Jackson near the mouth of the Milk River. Chittenden, *op. cit.*, 2:935 mistakenly locates it at the confluence of the Missouri and Poplar rivers. See Sunder, *Bill Sublette*, p. 127 n. 21 about Sublette & Campbell's competing post.

2 Hafen, ed., *French Fur Traders and Voyageurs in the American West*, pp. 291–2.

3 *Ibid.*, p. 296, and Lavender, *Bent's Fort*, pp. 193–5.

4 Abel, ed., *op. cit.*, p. 238 n. 127 gives his name as Jean Baptiste Moncrèvier, the same spelling used by Audubon, *op. cit.*, 2:146.

5 Hafen, ed., *Fur Traders, Trappers, and Mountain Men of the Upper Missouri*, p. 77. Formerly called *Me-a-pa-te* ("hill that is hard to go around") by the local Indians, Scotts Bluff acquired its Anglo name when the fur trapper Hiram Scott died in the vicinity in 1828; "Scotts Bluff National Monument," Official Map and Guide, National Park Service, GPO, 1996. For more on the Hiram Scott legend, see Sunder, *Bill Sublette*, p. 77, and Mattes, *op. cit.*, pp. 426–35.

6 Mattes, *op. cit.*, pp. 464, 468–9; Mattes cites the three Pierre Chouteau, Jr., & Company posts listed in my narrative. Hafen, ed., *Fur Traders, Trappers, and Mountain Men of the Upper Missouri*, pp. 77–8 mistakenly place the first Chouteau post at Robidoux Pass, the second eight miles farther south—which is correct—and the third somewhere "closer to the Oregon Trail."

7 Hafen, ed., *Fur Traders, Trappers, and Mountain Men of the Upper Missouri*, p. 78.

8 Mattes, *op. cit.*, p. 471.

9 Abel, ed., *op. cit.*, pp. 93, 313 n. 451.

10 Nasatir, ed., *op. cit.*, 1:331.

11 Wood, *op. cit.*, pp. 3–4.

12 On July 19, 1823, William Ashley wrote a letter from "Fort Brassaux," which has caused some historians to conclude that Brazeau's Fort was a separate trading post located somewhere between Fort Kiowa and Fort Recovery. However, Morgan, *op. cit.*, pp. 376–7 n. 22 conclude that Brazeau's Fort and forts Kiowa and Lookout are one and the same, reasoning that the Kiowa name came from Joseph Brazeau's possible nickname, Young Cayewa. (See Fort Lookout–Columbia Fur Company, endnote 53.) Wishart, *op. cit.*, p. 49 fig. 6 mistakenly places Fort Kiowa, which the map calls Fort Lookout, above the Missouri's Grand Detour.

   Around the time that Brazeau established Fort Kiowa, Bartholomew Berthold and Pierre Chouteau, Jr., reorganized their partnership, bringing in Bernard Pratte, Sr. Then in early 1823, John Cabanné, Sr., joined the firm, and the owners changed its name to Bernard Pratte & Company. All of the partners were related by either blood or marriage. See Hafen, ed., *Mountain Men and Fur Traders of the Far West*, pp. 30–2.

13 Morgan, *op. cit.*, pp. 79–80.

14 *Ibid.*, pp. 80, 385–6 n. 7. Morgan numbers Jedediah Smith's brigade between eleven and sixteen.

15 *Ibid.*, pp. 376–7 n. 22.

16 Hafen, ed., *French Fur Traders and Voyageurs in the American West*, p. 119.

17 Sunder, *The Fur Trade on the Upper Missouri*, p. 206.

18 *Ibid.*, pp. 214, 240, 249.

19 Coues, ed., *op. cit.*, 2:606 n. 5, Dale, *op. cit.*, p. 40, and DeVoto, *The Course of Empire*, pp. 534–5 place the first "Kootanae" House in British Columbia. David Thompson reached the Columbia River above the fifty-first parallel. Not realizing that he was on the true Columbia, he named the river the "Kootanae," after a local Indian tribe, then went upstream—meaning south, up the Columbia—and established "Kootanae" House. Continuing south, Thompson came to the river that modern maps call the Kootenay (spelled Kootenai in the United States, it rises in Canada's Kootenay National Park) and named it the McGillivray River. Eventually Thompson realized that his "Kootanae" River was actually the upper Columbia and corrected his maps. Later cartographers then changed the McGillivray River's name to the Kootenay; see Coues, ed., *op. cit.*, 2:694 n. 10.

20 Gibson, *op. cit.*, flyleaf map shows a North West Company "Kootenay Ft." south of the forty-ninth parallel on the lower Kootenai River. This is most likely the 1808 trading post that Thompson erected near the mouth of the Tobacco River (just south of the US-Canadian border); see Coues, *op. cit.*, 2:707 n. 3. For Finan McDonald's post, see Graves, *op. cit.*, p. 59.

21 Conley, *op. cit.*, pp. 680–2, and Newman, *op. cit.*, pp. 85–94.

22 Conley, *op. cit.*, pp. 680–2 correctly place Kullyspell House at Memaloose Point, agreeing with Coues, ed., *op. cit.*, 2:672–3 n. 22, which states that Thompson built it on a peninsula called Hodgkin's Point (not on modern maps) that jutted into Lake Pend d'Oreille near the mouth of the Clark Fork River. DeVoto, *The Course of Empire*, p. 536 mistakenly says that the post was located above the mouth of the Clark Fork River.

23 Sunder, *The Fur Trade on the Upper Missouri*, p. 238. The buffalo robe trade was secondary to Fort La Barge's main business, which was to compete with nearby Fort Benton in supplying the Montana Territory's gold mines.

24 *Ibid.*, p. 251.

25 Schuler, *op. cit.*, pp. 8–9.

26 Sunder, *op. cit.*, p. 240. Sunder spells LaFramboise's Christian name "Françoise."

27 Hafen, ed., *Mountain Men and Fur Traders of the Far West*, pp. 42–3. Sunder, *Bill Sublette*, p. 134 reports that the American Fur Company agreed to cease supplying the mountain rendezvous for only one year.

28 Lavender, *Fort Laramie*, p. 19 uses these spellings, whereas Hafen, ed., *French Fur Traders and Voyageurs in the American West*, pp. 192, 193 n. 6 give his name as "Baptiste Laramée."

29 DeVoto, *Across the Wide Missouri*, p. 190.

30 Mattes, *op. cit.*, p. 481 quotes from the diary of William Anderson, which says that he and Sublette's pack train arrived at the Laramie Fork on May 31. Lavender, *Fort Laramie*, p. 18 states that they arrived on May 30. DeVoto, *Across the Wide Missouri*, p. 190 places their arrival on June 1.

31 Historians disagree about Fort William's location. Mattes, *op. cit.*, p. 483 argues that it was at the confluence of the Laramie and North Platte rivers, whereas National Park Service rangers at the Fort Laramie National Historic Site point to an empty field just downstream from the Visitor Center as the most likely place. So far, archaeological digs have failed to provide an answer.

32 Lavender, *Fort Laramie*, p. 28. For a different interpretation of these events, see Sunder, *Bill Sublette*, p. 142.

33 Lavender, *Fort Laramie*, p. 29.

34 *Ibid.*, p. 30.

35 Hafen, *Broken Hand*, p. 159, and Hafen, ed., *Mountain Men and Fur Traders of the Far West*, pp. 244–5.

36 Mattes, *op. cit.*, p. 483. The "Fort Laramie," Official Map and Guide, National Park

Service, GPO, 1996; reprint, 1995 places Fort John at the west end of the Fort Laramie National Historic Site.

37 Unruh, Jr., *op. cit.*, p. 86, table 3.

38 Mattes, *op. cit.*, p. 494.

39 Frazer, *op. cit.*, p. 182.

40 Hafen, ed., *French Fur Traders and Voyageurs in the American West*, p. 106.

41 Frazer, *op. cit.*, p. 56. The fort is still an active military reservation.

42 In Hafen, ed., *Fur Traders, Trappers, and Mountain Men of the Upper Missouri*, p. 97, Charles E. Hanson, Jr.'s essay, "William Gordon," places the lower Leclerc post near "Fort Lookout" (Fort Kiowa), which would put it close to Chamberlain, SD. However, in Audubon, *op. cit.*, 1:503–4, the famed naturalist reports that his steamboat *Omega* stopped at the deserted trading post of "Monsieur Le Clerc" on May 21, 1843, soon after passing Chouteau Creek. Early the following morning, the steamer chugged past "Grand Town," a noted village of prairie dogs, which Audubon editor Elliott Coues puts between Yankton and Fort Randall, SD; see 1:506 n. 2. Because Audubon saw Leclerc's post firsthand, his account must be taken as true. Still, it is possible that Hanson is also correct about a Leclerc trading post near Fort Kiowa since Leclerc may have operated more than two.

43 Hafen, ed., *Fur Traders, Trappers, and Mountain Men of the Upper Missouri*, p. 97, and Hafen, ed., *Mountain Men and Fur Traders of the Far West*, p. 42.

44 Chittenden, *op. cit.*, 2:926, and Wishart, *op. cit.*, p. 44 fig. 5.

45 Oglesby, *op. cit.*, pp. 141, 151.

46 Hafen, ed., *Mountain Men and Fur Traders of the Far West*, p. 77 states that Theodore Hunt was Wilson Price Hunt's cousin, whereas Oglesby, *op. cit.*, p. 150 claims that they were brothers.

47 Hafen, ed., *Mountain Men and Fur Traders of the Far West*, pp. 20–1. Indian hostility persisted for some time after the United States and Great Britain signed the Treaty of Ghent, ending the war.

48 *Ibid.*, p. 22.

49 Oglesby, *op. cit.*, p. 174.

50 Hafen, ed., *Fur Traders, Trappers, and Mountain Men of the Upper Missouri*, p. 96. During an 1843 voyage up the Missouri, Joseph Sire, master of the steamboat *Omega*, reported stopping for the evening a bit upstream from "old Fort George," located just below the mouth of the Cheyenne River. The post may have been a seasonal trading house for the Sioux or Cheyennes since nothing more is known about it; see Chittenden, *op. cit.*, 2:931, 966.

51 Sunder, *The Fur Trade on the Upper Missouri*, pp. 58, 71.

52 Hanson, Jr., and Walters, *op. cit.*, p. 7.

53 Chittenden, *op. cit.*, 2:928 places the Columbia Fur Company's Fort Lookout near Fort Kiowa, also called Fort Lookout. After Kenneth McKenzie joined the American Fur Company and reorganized his Columbia Fur Company as the Upper Missouri Outfit, the Columbia's Fort Lookout was most likely abandoned. On April 22, 1836, William Clark, Superintendent of Indian Affairs, mentioned a Fort Lookout in the trading license that he issued to Pratte, Chouteau & Company, although the license probably referred to Fort Kiowa.

54 After Lancaster Lupton resigned from the US Army in March 1836, he headed for the South Platte with a few wagon-loads of trade goods. Wishart, *op. cit.*, p. 73 says that he founded Fort Lupton that summer. Lavender, *Bent's Fort*, pp. 184–5 state that although Lupton had begun trading in 1836, in the spring of 1837 he had not yet built his fort. Lupton may have erected a temporary wooden post in 1836, replacing it with a permanent adobe structure the following year.

Fort Madison through Fort Mortimer

1 Jackson, *op. cit.*, pp. 5–10, map following p. 32.

2 *Ibid.*, pp. 12–13.

3 *Ibid.*, p. 45.

4 *Ibid.*, p. 46.

5 *Ibid.*, pp. 60–2 question whether Lieutenant Hamilton abandoned Fort Madison in September 1813 as is generally accepted, or some months afterwards, perhaps as late as mid-November.

6 Hafen, ed., *Mountain Men and Fur Traders of the Far West*, p. 12, and Wood, *op. cit.*, p. 4. Also, see Mandan Villages, endnote 42.

7 Oglesby, *op. cit.*, p. 84.

8 DeVoto, *The Course of Empire*, p. 77.

9 Wood, *op. cit.*, p. 2.

10 La Vérendrye had hoped to discover a water route to the Pacific Ocean, but the French government refused to finance such a costly venture. Deciding to pay for it himself, the resourceful explorer secured a trading monopoly for all the lands he would visit. Supported by Montreal merchants, he established a line of trading posts along a riverine highway leading west from Lake Superior and paid his investors in beaver. When he reached the Mandans, he was certain that the Pacific lay but a short distance away. Now hopeful of receiving government assistance, la Vérendrye returned to Montreal and reported his findings to France. Although admitting that the information was interesting, the Crown's ministers refused to help. Disheartened by the news, la Vérendrye determined to press ahead with his exploration; however, business affairs prevented him from doing so until 1742. Even then, he could not go himself and had to send his sons, Louis-Joseph and François.

Accompanied by Mandan guides, the two young men left the Missouri River in the spring of 1742, heading west by southwest. For the next fifteen months they wandered about North America's heartland, seeking word about a vast sea that always seemed to lie just beyond the next range of hills. Each tribe they met suggested they visit a neighboring tribe that certainly would know of such a splendid sight. Eventually becoming discouraged, the Frenchmen abandoned their quest and returned to Fort La Reine on Canada's Assiniboine River. See Meyer, *op. cit.*, pp. 18–23, Nasatir, ed., *op. cit.*, 1:32–4, and DeVoto, *The Course of Empire*, pp. 213–16.

11 Heidenreich, ed., *op. cit.*, p. 4.

12 *Ibid.*

13 Pierre Menard lived with the Mandans until 1803 when he was killed by the Assiniboines. See Nasatir, ed., *op. cit.*, 1:82, 331; 2:381, and Meyer, *op. cit.*, pp. 28, 31–2, 271 n. 34 .

14 Nasatir, ed., *op. cit.*, 1:160–1 report that D'Eglise visited the Mandans in 1790; however, DeVoto, *The Course of Empire*, p. 601 n. 13 gives a more convincing argument for 1792. Also see Meyer, *op. cit.*, p. 272 n. 41.

15 Nasatir, ed., *op. cit.*, 1:82–3, 87–8, 233. In 1806, Jacques D'Eglise sought to make his fortune in New Mexico. This time his luck ran out when he was killed near Santa Fe; Weber, *op. cit.*, p. 38.

16 Nasatir, ed., *op. cit.*, 1:331, and Wood, *op. cit.*, p. 3.

17 Hafen, ed., *French Fur Traders and Voyageurs in the American West*, p. 124.

18 *Ibid.*, p. 129, and Oglesby, *op. cit.*, p. 17 use this title, which is a translation of its French name, given by Dale, *op. cit.*, p. 22 as *"La Compagine de Comerce pour la Decouverte des Nations du haut du Missouri."* DeVoto, *The Course of Empire*, p. 363 calls the partnership the "Commercial Company for the Discovery of the Nations of the Upper Missouri" or "Missouri Company" for short. Nasatir, ed., *op. cit.*, 1:86 calls it the "Company of Explorers of the Upper Missouri," listing its founding as October

15, 1793; see pp. 217–26 for the company's articles of incorporation. In correspondence about the company, Spanish officials called it (after translation) everything from the "Company of Commerce of the Mandan nation" to the "Company of the Upper Missouri"; see Nasatir, ed., *op. cit.*, 1:"Documents 1785–1808," pp. 119–375.

19 Nasatir, ed., *op. cit.*, 2:388.

20 *Ibid.*, 1:87, 260. DeVoto, *The Course of Empire*, p. 365 mistakenly says that Truteau took two pirogues. Dale, *op. cit.*, p. 22 spells Truteau's name "Trudeau," reporting that he was related to Lieutenant Governor Zenon Trudeau, Commandant of St. Louis.

21 See Nasatir, ed., *op. cit.*, 1:259–311 for a translation of Truteau's Journal. Except where noted, my account of the 1794–5 expedition up the Missouri comes from this source.

22 DeVoto, *The Course of Empire*, p. 366.

23 *Ibid.*, p. 367.

24 Oglesby, *op. cit.*, p. 111.

25 Chief Blackbird died in 1802 (some sources say 1800) during the smallpox scourge that swept the Missouri. The epidemic decimated the Omahas, ending their ability to terrorize St. Louis traders; *ibid.,* and Audubon, *op. cit.*, 1:485–6 n. 2.

26 Nasatir, ed., *op. cit.*, 1:88–90, and DeVoto, *The Course of Empire*, p. 368.

27 Nasatir, ed., *op. cit.*, 2:441.

28 *Ibid.*, 1:91–2, 351, and DeVoto, *The Course of Empire*, pp. 372–3.

29 DeVoto, *The Course of Empire*, p. 374. Also, see Nasatir, ed., *op. cit.*, 1:351 n. 2 for the controversy about the date James Mackay left St. Louis.

Mackay had visited the Mandans from the north in 1787, before moving from Canada to St. Louis; see DeVoto, *The Course of Empire*, p. 373, and Nasatir, ed., *op. cit.*, 2:494.

30 Nasatir, ed., *op. cit.*, 1:356.

31 *Ibid.*, 1:98, 362; 2:489.

32 *Ibid.*, 1:99, 362; 2:494–5.

33 Readers of Bernard DeVoto and A. P. Nasatir will notice differences between my version of Evans' attempts to reach the Mandans and theirs. DeVoto, *The Course of Empire*, p. 376 states that Evans made his unsuccessful foray to the Mandans in February 1796, followed by a successful one the following June. Nasatir, ed., *op. cit.*, 1:99–101 argue that he made his first try between November 1795 and January 6, 1796, and that he began his second trip a few weeks later, reaching the Mandans on September 23. James Mackay's journal entry for January 18, 1796, reveals that Mackay planned to send Evans "within a few days"; Nasatir, ed., *op. cit.*, 1:364. In his letter to Evans, written February 19, 1796, at Fort Charles, Mackay says that he has "found the time tedious since you [Evans] left," which leads to the conclusion that Evans had already departed; Nasatir, ed., *op. cit.*, 2:415–16. From this, Nasatir surmises that Evans had begun his second–successful–journey to the Mandans; Nasatir, ed., *op. cit.*, 1:101. Yet if Evans made only one try in 1796–leaving Fort Charles around the beginning of February–his trip to the Mandans would have taken seven and a half months, an inordinately long time. Debunking this theory is Evans' note in his own journal that his successful push to the Mandans began from Fort Charles on June 8; Nasatir, ed., *op. cit.*, 2:495. Nasatir read this and wondered if Evans made two tries in 1796: one starting in late January or early February, which was unsuccessful, and another beginning on June 8, which was successful; Nasatir, ed., *op. cit.*, 1:101 n. 71. A more logical answer is found in James Mackay's journal which is the basis of my narrative; Nasatir, ed., *op. cit.*, 2:494–5. By assuming that Evans led the winter trek inviting the Sioux to parley at Fort Charles, there is an explanation for his absence from the post during February when Mackay wrote that

he missed him. This assumption also jives with Evans's assertion that he began his successful trip to the Mandans on June 8.

34 DeVoto, *The Course of Empire*, pp. 377–8, and Nasatir, ed., *op. cit.*, 1:102; 2:496.

35 Wood, *op. cit.*, p. 4.

36 Nasatir, ed., *op. cit.*, 1:105–6; 2:463–4, 496–7, and DeVoto, *The Course of Empire*, p. 379.

37 Nasatir, ed., *op. cit.*, 1:111. Clamorgan and Loisel may have begun their partnership as early as 1796.

38 The site of Fort Mandan, which lay across the river from where Fort Clark was built in 1831, is now covered by the Missouri. In 1972, the McLean County, North Dakota Historical Association constructed a replica of the Lewis and Clark post ten miles east of the original. Also, see Abel, ed., *op. cit.*, pp. 310–11 n. 432.

39 DeVoto, *The Course of Empire*, pp. 529, 532–3 map 33, and Harris, *op. cit.*, p. 41. DeVoto assumes that Larocque returned to Fort Assiniboine (near the Souris-Assiniboine confluence in southern Manitoba) after his western odyssey, whereas Harris states that it was Fort de La Bosse (on the Assiniboine River, fifty miles upstream from the mouth of the Souris). Coues, ed., *op. cit.*, 1:301 n. 17 refers to the North West Company's "La Bosse" post as Fort Montagne à la Bosse. As Coues points out, Larocque traveled from Fort Assiniboine to the Mandans in November 1804, returning to the North West Company post in February 1805. With permission to explore the upper Yellowstone River in hand, he departed Fort Assiniboine on June 3, 1805. When he finished his unsuccessful adventure, Larocque–in the words of Coues–"returned to his post," meaning Fort Assiniboine. If Larocque went to Fort Montagne à la Bosse, it was after he reported in at Fort Assiniboine.

40 Oglesby, *op. cit.*, p. 39.

41 *Ibid.*, pp. 49–50.

42 Wood, *op. cit.*, pp. 4–5. Oglesby, *op. cit.*, p. 84 needlessly muddles the location of Fort Mandan by stating that Lisa built it "ten or twelve miles above the Gros Ventres." Rather than referring to the Gros Ventre of the Prairie–aka the Atsinas, who were allies of the Blackfeet and lived in central Montana–Oglesby means the Hidatsas. French traders named the Atsinas the Gros Ventres–meaning Big Bellies–after misinterpreting the Mandan sign for the tribe, which really signified hunger. Because the Mandans referred to the Hidatsas as the Minetaree (or Minnetaree), meaning Crossing-the-Water, early white traders called them that rather than by their true name. Lewis and Clark confused the Hidatsas with the Atsinas, labeling the Hidatsas the Gros Ventres. All of this has prompted some historians to refer to the Hidatsas as Minetarees and Gros Ventres, but never as Hidatsas.

43 Morgan, *op. cit.*, p. 385 n. 2 reports that James Kipp and William Tilton arrived at the Mandan villages in the spring of 1823 but did not finish the construction of their trading post until November. Chittenden, *op. cit.*, 1:326 also uses the 1823 date; however, 2:932 says that Kipp and Tilton established their Mandan fort a year earlier. Heidenreich, ed., *op. cit.*, p. 11 states that they built their post in the spring of 1822. Abel, ed., *op. cit.*, p. 197 n. 1 gives the post's construction as between May and November 1822. Morgan's dates are probably correct, since on pp. 374–5 n. 9 he reports that Indian Superintendent William Clark issued Tilton's trading license for the Mandans on July 17, 1822, at which time Tilton told Clark he intended going to the Mandans via the Columbia Fur Company's depot post at Lake Traverse on the upper St. Peter's–now Minnesota–River; see Abel, ed., *op. cit.*, p. 333. Hafen, ed., *Fur Traders, Trappers, and Mountain Men of the Upper Missouri*, p. 22 says that Clark issued the license on June 17, 1822, and that Thomas Jeffries began trading with the Mandans during the winter of 1822–3, adding that James Kipp began building a formal fort in May 1823.

44 Abel, ed., *op. cit.*, p. 289 n. 313 places it one and one-half to two miles below the larger Mandan village. Also see Meyer, *op. cit.*, pp. 276–7 n. 64.

45 Hafen, ed., *Fur Traders, Trappers, and Mountain Men of the Upper Missouri,* p. 35.

46 At the time Fort Clark was established, the Mandans lived in two villages. Named *Mitutanka, Matootonha,* or *Mih-tutta-hang-kush,* the larger one sat a couple of hundred yards upriver from the new post, while *Roop-tar-hee* or *Ruhptare,* as the smaller village was called, sat on the Missouri's left shore; Abel, ed., *op. cit.*, pp. 274–5 n. 271, and Meyer, *op. cit.*, map opposite p. 38.

47 Abel, ed., *op. cit.*, p. 118.

48 The "Fort Clark" State Historic Site Brochure, State Historical Society of North Dakota estimates that out of the 1,600 members of the tribe who were alive in the spring of 1837, 1,500 died before year-end. William R. Swagerty in his introduction to Abel, ed., *op. cit.*, pp. ix–x state that out of the 1,600 to 2,000 Mandans who were living before the *St. Peter's* arrived, only 138 survived.

49 Heidenreich, ed., *op. cit.*, p. 22. Today, few ethnologists think that there are any full-blooded Mandans.

50 Oglesby, *op. cit.*, pp. 130, 133–4.

51 Hafen, ed., *Mountain Men and Fur Traders of the Far West,* pp. 19–20.

52 *Ibid.*, pp. 196, 198.

53 Hafen, ed., *French Fur Traders and Voyageurs in the American West,* p. 108.

54 *Ibid.*, p. 119 and Frazer, *op. cit.*, p. 122.

55 Chittenden, *op. cit.*, 1:335.

56 Hafen, ed., *Fur Traders, Trappers, and Mountain Men of the Upper Missouri,* p. 41, and Audubon, *op. cit.*, 2:189.

57 My narrative about the smallpox epidemic of 1837 draws on DeVoto, *Across the Wide Missouri,* pp. 280–301, as well as my own research concerning the medical properties of the disease. In all the sources I have read about the *St. Peter's* 1837 voyage, only DeVoto's mentions Jacob Halsey's pregnant wife and young son. I have included them—even though I cannot confirm their existence—on the strength of DeVoto's reputation as a historian.

58 Abel, ed., *op. cit.*, p. xx.

59 The date and events of this dreadful episode have long since evolved from fact to legend. My account is paraphrased from Larpenteur, *op. cit.*, pp. 187–9. For more, see Abel, ed., *op. cit.*, p. 246 n. 186, and Chittenden, *op. cit.*, 2:685–6.

60 Irving, *Astoria,* p. 393 calls the Clearwater River the Shahaptan, stating that McKenzie located his post "some distance" above the mouth. The "Nez Perce" National Historical Park Brochure, National Park Service, GPO, 1994, places his trading post on the north side of the Clearwater, reporting that the precise site is unknown. Also see Chittenden, *op. cit.*, 1:205. McKenzie's name is sometimes spelled MacKenzie.

61 Sunder, *The Fur Trade on the Upper Missouri,* p. 240.

62 Hafen, ed., *Fur Traders, Trappers, and Mountain Men of the Upper Missouri,* pp. 69–70.

63 Sunder, *The Fur Trade on the Upper Missouri,* pp. 88, 185, 196, 208.

64 *Ibid.*, pp. 250–1.

65 Chittenden, *op. cit.*, 2:927 states that Narcisse Leclerc (Chittenden spells his name LeClerc) established Fort Mitchell, which seems unlikely since, at the time, Leclerc was in competition with the American Fur Company. Mattes, *op. cit.*, p. 464 places Fort Mitchell near the mouth of the Niobrara. Joseph Sire, master of the steamboat *Omega,* reported stopping at the abandoned trading post to salvage firewood in 1843; see Chittenden, *op. cit.*, 2:963.

66 Hafen, ed., *Fur Traders, Trappers, and Mountain Men of the Upper Missouri,* pp. 78–9.

67 Hafen, ed., *Mountain Men and Fur Traders of the Far West,* p. 284, Irving, *Captain*

Bonneville, pp. 300–1 n. 3, 365–6 n. 1, and Wishart, *op. cit.,* p. 189. Montero is some-times spelled Montaro.

68 Mattes, *op. cit.,* pp. xxviii–xxix, 263.
69 Sunder, *The Fur Trade on the Upper Missouri,* pp. 52–4.
70 *Ibid.,* p. 54.
71 Thompson, *op. cit.,* p. 47, and Audubon, *op. cit.,* 2:53.
72 Sunder, *The Fur Trade on the Upper Missouri,* pp. 81–2.
73 *Ibid.,* p. 94, and Thompson, *op. cit.,* pp. 59–60.

Fort Nez Perces through Fort Owen
1 Some historians credit Archibald McDonald with constructing Fort Nisqually; how-ever, McDonald, who at the time was in command of Fort Langley (near the mouth of the Fraser River above the forty-ninth parallel), merely chose the site for the post. Francis Heron came up from Fort Vancouver to supervise the actual building. See Galbraith, *op. cit.,* pp. 200–1. According to Gibson, *op. cit.,* p. 67, McDonald became Fort Nisqually's first factor.
2 Gibson, *op. cit.,* p. 97.
3 Hafen, ed., *Mountain Men and Fur Traders of the Far West,* p. 31.
4 Oglesby, *op. cit.,* p. 175.
5 Galbraith, *op. cit.,* p. 80 places Fort Okanagan near the confluence of the Spokane and Columbia rivers which is an error. Newman, *op. cit.,* pp. 102–3 locate the fort in the Okanogan Valley, near the mouth of the Okanogan River, as does Gibson, *op. cit.,* p. 58. Irving, *Astoria,* p. 83 puts it in the gore above the Okanogan-Columbia confluence.
    British and Canadian cartographers spell the Okanagan River as such, whereas those in the United States spell it Okanogan. I follow the British and Canadian spelling for Fort Okanagan and the American spelling for the river and its valley.
6 Mathews, *op. cit.,* pp. 98, 131.
7 Nasatir, ed., *op. cit.,* 1:13, 18, 42–3.
8 *Ibid.,* 1:55, 60.
9 Chittenden, *op. cit.,* 1:100–3.
10 Nasatir, ed., *op. cit.,* 1:64 reports that Lacléde exercised his trading monopoly on the Missouri River, permitting other traders to work the Missouri's lower tributaries and central Mississippi.
11 *Ibid.,* 1:133–4, 158–60.
12 *Ibid.,* 1:199; 2:526.
13 Mathews, *op. cit.,* pp. 283, 362, Hafen, ed., *French Fur Traders and Voyageurs in the American West,* pp. 97, 100, and Nasatir, ed., *op. cit.,* 1:343; 2:486, 526.
14 Nasatir, ed., *op. cit.,* 1:320; 2:526–7, and Hafen, ed., *Mountain Men and Fur Traders of the Far West,* p. 4.
15 Nasatir, ed., *op. cit.,* 2:592, 688, 716, and Hafen, ed., *Mountain Men and Fur Traders of the Far West,* p. 4. Gregoire Sarpy and Charles Sanguinet were also partners in Lisa's firm.
16 Under the terms of the Second Treaty of San Ildefonso, Spain returned Louisiana to France with the stipulation that France not transfer it to any other country but Spain. Although Napoleon broke the agreement by selling Louisiana to the United States, Spain was too weak to protest.
17 Oglesby, *op. cit.,* p. 31.
18 Ambrose, *op. cit.,* pp. 432–4.
19 *Ibid.,* p. 447.
20 *Ibid.,* pp. 440, 447 mistakenly say that William Clark built Fort Osage on the Osage River. The fort was actually located in western Missouri, about a mile or so north-west of Sibley.

21 Frazer, *op. cit.*, pp. 75–6. In total, the US Government established twenty-eight Indian factories.

22 Ambrose, *op. cit.*, pp. 444, 451.

23 Weber, *op. cit.*, p. 101 and Frazer, *op. cit.*, pp. 75–6.

24 Mathews, *op. cit.*, p. 300 and Hafen, ed., *French Fur Traders and Voyageurs in the American West,* pp. 100, 101 n. 17.

25 Hafen, ed., *French Fur Traders and Voyageurs in the American West,* p. 105 n. 26 and Hafen, ed., *Mountain Men and Fur Traders of the Far West,* p. 31.

26 Hafen, ed., *French Fur Traders and Voyageurs in the American West,* pp. 105–6 and Hafen, ed., *Mountain Men and Fur Traders of the Far West,* p. 198.

27 Weber, *op. cit.*, p. 101. Also, see "Old Bill" Williams's Post on the Fork of the Grand River, endnote 23.

28 This may have forced the closing of "Old Bill's" fort because Paul Baillio, who probably ran it after Williams went wandering in the latter part of 1823, showed up in Santa Fe on April 27, 1825; see Weber, *op. cit.*, p. 134.

29 Hafen, ed., *French Fur Traders and Voyageurs in the American West,* pp. 106–11.

30 After Andrew Jackson became President in 1829, this policy escalated into the shameful Trail of Tears; for more see Josephy, *op. cit.*, pp. 323–4.

31 Hafen, ed., *French Fur Traders and Voyageurs in the American West,* p. 116.

32 *Ibid.*, p. 117.

33 *Ibid.*, pp. 118–9 and Frazer, *op. cit.*, p. 122.

34 Hafen, ed., *French Fur Traders and Voyageurs in the American West,* p. 119.

35 *Ibid.*, p. 121 reports that the actual amount owed was sixty-six thousand dollars.

36 Nasatir, ed., *op. cit.*, 1:356 quotes from James Mackay's journal which states that his men built a winter trading house one-half league above the mouth of the Platte.

37 *Ibid.*, 2:516–7; on p. 489 Nasatir cites Mackay's 1797 survey of the Missouri River in which Mackay places the Otoe post one league below the Platte, indicating that the post was moved between 1795 and 1797.

38 *Ibid.*, 2:519–20.

39 *Ibid.*, 1:337; 2:389–93. Governor-General Carondelet had a far greater worry than losing a few furs to British traders. England and Spain were at war, which meant that the Louisiana Territory was in danger of a British invasion from Canada; see *ibid.*, 2:586–7 n. 5.

40 DeVoto, ed., *The Journals of Lewis and Clark,* p. 17. Peter Cruzatte (or Cruzet), the son or younger brother of Josef Cruzet, worked at the trading post before joining the Corps of Discovery. In his journal entry of August 4, 1804, William Clark noted passing the fort's "rimains" *[sic]*. Nasatir, ed., *op. cit.*, 2:592, citing Lieutenant Governor Delassus, shows the 1801 Otoe trade going to Sarpy & Cabanné, but this disputes 2:617 n. 1 and 629 n. 3, which indicate that it went to Cruzet.

41 Roberta Carkeek Cheney, *Names on the Face of Montana: The Story of Montana's Place Names* (Missoula, MT: Mountain Press Publishing Company, 1983, revised 1984), p. 101, Rick Newby, *Great Escapes: Montana State Parks* (Helena, MT: Falcon Press Publishing Co., Inc., 1989), pp. 39–42, and "Fort Owen State Park" Brochure, Montana Fish, Wildlife & Parks, Helena, MT.

Papin's House through Roy's House

1 Coues, ed., *op. cit.*, 1:90, 93–5, 123–4, and Heidenreich, ed., *op. cit.*, pp. 36, 38.

2 Nasatir, ed., *op. cit.*, 1:6, and Hanson, Jr., and Walters, *op. cit.*, p. 3.

3 Nasatir, ed., *op. cit.*, 1:8 n. 17.

4 Hafen, ed., *French Fur Traders and Voyageurs in the American West,* p. 303. During this time, the Pawnee trade, as well as the rest of the Louisiana trade, fell under the authority of the Spanish governor-general in New Orleans and his lieutenant

governor in St. Louis. License to traffic with the Pawnee and Kansas Indians was determined by lot. The governor-general granted trading monopolies for the other Missouri tribes, giving Auguste and Pierre Chouteau, Sr., the Osages; Juan Munier the Poncas; and the Company of the Discoverers and Explorers of the Missouri River the Otoes, Omahas, and all the tribes above the Poncas. However, Spain had neither the military resources nor the will to stop the encroachment of British and New Mexican freebooters. See Nasatir, ed., *op. cit.*, 2:477 n. 2; also see pp. 590–2 for the division of the trade from 1799 through 1803.

5 Weber, *op. cit.*, pp. 28–30, 35.

6 Newman, *op. cit.*, pp. 158–9.

7 Coues, ed., *op. cit.*, 1:79–81 n. 2, and Heidenreich, ed., *op. cit.*, pp. 35, 45. The name Pembina evolved from the French pronunciation of the Ojibwa word *anepeminan*, meaning redberry, a term the tribe applied to the high bush cranberry that grew with profusion along the Pembina River. The Ojibwas called the Pembina the *Anepeminan Sipi*, meaning Redberry Water.

8 Heidenreich, ed., *op. cit.*, pp. 35, 45.

9 Coues, ed., *op. cit.*, 1:137 n. 18. Coues speaks of Roy's Trading House being located at the mouth of the Salt River; the Salt is now the Forest River.

10 *Ibid.*, 1:181, and Heidenreich, ed., *op. cit.*, p. 36.

11 Coues, ed., *op. cit.*, 1:79–81 n. 2, pp. 187–8, and Heidenreich, ed., *op. cit.*, p. 38. Founded in 1798, the XY Company was officially known as the New North West Company, its partners being former North West Company employees. The XY firm took its nickname from the initials it used to mark its trade goods and furs. In 1804, its partners rejoined the North West Company; see Newman, *op. cit.*, pp. 73, 75.

12 Heidenreich, ed., *op. cit.*, p. 44.

13 Newman, *op. cit.*, p. 148, and Williams, *op. cit.*, p. 44. Lord Selkirk's grant included sections of Minnesota, and North and South Dakota.

14 Newman, *op. cit.*, pp. 169–71, 193, 203–4. Coues, ed., *op. cit.*, 1:81 n. 2 places Fort Daer on the north side of the Pembina River, whereas Peg Moll and Larry Wilwant, eds., "Pembina: North Dakota's Oldest Settlement" Information Booklet, 1992, p. 5 puts it on the river's south side where Chaboillez's Fort Paubna had stood.

15 Heidenreich, ed., *op. cit.*, p. 45.

16 Coues, ed., *op. cit.*, 1:81 n. 2, and Heidenreich, ed., *op. cit.*, p. 55.

17 Galbraith, *op. cit.*, pp. 56–7. The American Fur Company's change of policy was to have applied to the entire Rainy Lake district, which reached from Pembina to Lake Superior.

18 *Ibid.*, p. 59. The agreement was eventually extended until 1847.

19 Abel, ed., *op. cit.*, p. 256 n. 242.

20 See "Walhalla, North Dakota, 'Valley of the Gods,'" Information Booklet of Walhalla, ND, p. 1 for facts about the upper Pembina trading posts. For Kittson's post below the forty-ninth parallel, Newman, *op. cit.*, p. 333 gives the date as 1843; Galbraith, *op. cit.*, p. 62 uses the year 1844 for the post's construction, although p. 61 states that Norman Kittson visited the Pembina region in the fall of 1843.

21 American officials seem to have turned a blind eye to Norman Kittson's similar use of liquor.

22 Heidenreich, ed., *op. cit.*, p. 59.

23 Frazer, *op. cit.*, pp. 112–13.

24 The Blackfoot Confederation *(Nitzitapi)* consisted of the Piegans *(Pikuni),* Bloods *(Kainai),* and Blackfeet-proper *(Siksika).*

25 Except where noted, this narrative relies on Chittenden, *op. cit.*, 1:331–5.

26 *Highlights of the Upper Missouri National Wild and Scenic River Lewis and Clark National Historic Trail* (n.p., n.d.), p. 6.

27 An interpretive wall map in the Fort Benton, MT, BLM office places Fort Piegan on a delta island at the confluence of the Marias and Missouri rivers.

28 *Highlights of the Upper Missouri National Wild and Scenic River Lewis and Clark National Historic Trail,* p. 6 states that three of Kipp's men who had married Blackfoot women remained behind.

29 Schuler, *op. cit.,* pp. 29–36. Before cartographers settled on the name Bad River, this tributary was called the Little Missouri (not to be confused with the modern Little Missouri which flows into the main Missouri in North Dakota), and then the Teton River.

30 During his visit in the spring of 1833, Alexander Philipp Maximilian, Prince of Wied-Nuwied, determined the outer stockade to be 324 feet by 342 feet; *ibid.,* p. 35.

31 Hafen, ed., *Mountain Men and Fur Traders of the Far West,* p. 43.

32 Schuler, *op. cit.,* pp. 131–6, and Frazer, *op. cit.,* p. 136.

33 Sunder, *The Fur Trade on the Upper Missouri,* pp. 172, 260.

34 DeVoto, *Across the Wide Missouri,* p. 319 gives the date as 1840, and pp. 420–1 place the post on the North Platte. Wishart, *op. cit.,* p. 73 dates the fort from 1841. David Lavender, *Fort Laramie,* p. 40 uses the years 1841–2, putting the fort in the gore at the confluence of the North Platte and Laramie rivers. A Wyoming state historical marker at the site says the post was established in 1841, placing it fifty yards north of State Highway 160, just upstream from the North Platte's merger with the Laramie. Hanson, Jr., and Walters, *op. cit.,* p. 5 states that Lupton traded from a wagon at the mouth of the Laramie in 1838; on p. 7 the authors report that Lupton operated some sort of trading post at the mouth of the Laramie in 1839. If he did, this was most likely a seasonal cabin, primitive when compared with the adobe fort he constructed two years later.

35 Hanson, Jr., and Walters, *op. cit.,* p. 5.

36 Hafen, ed., *Fur Traders, Trappers, and Mountain Men of the Upper Missouri,* p. 15 states that John Cabanné, Sr., married Julia Gratiot, making him the brother-in-law of Pierre Chouteau, Jr., which would make John Cabanné, Jr., Chouteau's nephew.

37 Sunder, *The Fur Trade on the Upper Missouri,* p. 218, and Larpenteur, *op. cit.,* pp. 271–4.

38 Larpenteur, *op. cit.,* pp. 42–3.

39 Hafen, ed., *Fur Traders, Trappers, and Mountain Men of the Upper Missouri,* p. 117.

40 Larpenteur, *op. cit.,* p. 264.

41 *Ibid.,* p. 265.

42 Sunder, *The Fur Trade on the Upper Missouri,* p. 218.

43 Larpenteur, *op. cit.,* pp. 268–73.

44 Sunder, *The Fur Trade on the Upper Missouri,* p. 218.

45 *Ibid.,* p. 219.

46 Nasatir, ed., *op. cit.,* 1:266 quotes Jean Baptiste Truteau's journal, which places the Ponca village beside the Missouri River, "a league above" the mouth of the Niobrara. In 2:378, Truteau puts it two leagues above the mouth. On p. 490, James Mackay's 1797 survey locates it on the "south bank, at a league and a half from the Missouri," while the notes of French traveler Perrin du Lac place it three miles above the Niobrara; p. 710.

Munier's assertion that he was the first European to visit the Poncas was later disproved; *ibid.,* 1:81, 82 n. 18.

47 *Ibid.,* 1:88.

48 *Ibid.,* 1:82 n. 18 cites the license transfer but does not give the date. In 2:490, James Mackay, writing in 1797, mentions a Ponca post belonging to the "company" on the north side of the Missouri, six and two-third leagues above the Ponca village, and on p. 531, Lieutenant Governor Zenon Trudeau reports that Clamorgan's company owned the Ponca trading license in 1796.

49 *Ibid.*, 1:111–12.
50 *Ibid.*, 2:590–2.
51 Hafen, ed., *Mountain Men and Fur Traders of the Far West*, p. 31, and Chittenden, *op. cit.*, 2:927.
52 Hafen, ed., *Fur Traders, Trappers, and Mountain Men of the Upper Missouri*, p. 23.
53 Hafen, ed., *French Fur Traders and Voyageurs in the American West*, p. 243.
54 Abel, ed., *op. cit.*, pp. 202–3 n. 20. In Irving, *Captain Bonneville*, p. 320 n. 27, editor Edgeley W. Todd reports that Nathaniel Wyeth–during his 1833 voyage down the Missouri River–stopped at "the Ponca Post" on September 11, which was a two-day float past Fort Pierre. Wyeth did not reach the Ponca village until five days later, indicating that unless Wyeth paused for a layover at the American Fur Company's Ponca Post, it had to have been some distance above the Ponca village.
55 Wishart, *op. cit.*, p. 67.
56 Sunder, *The Fur Trade on the Upper Missouri*, p. 139.
57 Larpenteur, *op. cit.*, pp. 255–8.
58 Hafen, ed., *Mountain Men and Fur Traders of the Far West*, p. 31, and Chittenden, *op. cit.*, 2:926.
59 Heidenreich, ed., *op. cit.*, p. 24. Some years before forming Harvey, Primeau & Company, Charles Primeau ran a small trading fort for the Sioux just below Little Beaver Creek (about twenty miles west of Strasburg, ND); at the time, Primeau probably worked for Pierre Chouteau, Jr., & Company. Joseph Sire, master of the steamer *Omega*, reported scavenging wood from the deserted post–which he called Primeau's Fort–when he stopped there on June 4, 1843; Chittenden, *op. cit.*, 2:967. John James Audubon and his party were passengers on the *Omega*, intending to visit Fort Union for the summer. When Audubon descended the Missouri on a mackinaw boat three months later, he noted passing a winter trading house of Charles Primeau, several miles above the mouth of the Cannonball River (in the vicinity of Fort Rice, ND); Audubon, *op. cit.*, 2:159. David Mitchell and Anthony Bouis also managed Chouteau winter trading houses upstream from the Cannonball; Chittenden, *op. cit.*, 2:967.
60 Heidenreich, ed., *op. cit.*, p. 24, "Fort Clark State Historic Site" Brochure, State Historical Society of North Dakota, and Fort Clark Site, North Dakota state historical marker.
61 Twenty years before Simpson, Doyle, and Barclay founded Fort Pueblo, trapper Jacob Fowler erected a temporary stockade and horse corral near the same site. Fowler was the co-leader–with Hugh Glenn–of a trapping expedition to the upper Arkansas River and Sangre de Cristo Mountains (see Glenn's Trading Post); Hafen, ed., *Fur Trappers and Traders of the Far Southwest*, p. 47.

The George Simpson who founded Pueblo is different from Sir George Simpson who was the North American governor of the Hudson's Bay Company. Most authorities dismiss James Beckwourth's claim that he founded the fort. Beckwourth soon gave up his Pueblo trading house and headed for California on a horse-stealing venture.
62 Hafen, ed., *French Fur Traders and Voyageurs in the American West*, p. 73.
63 Harris, *op. cit.*, pp. 69–71, Oglesby, *op. cit.*, p. 54, and Utley, *op. cit.*, p. 12. Pierre Menard and William Morrison were successful merchants from Kaskaskia, IL, and Menard was related by marriage to the Chouteaus.
64 Harris, *op. cit.*, pp. xvi–xvii, map opposite p. 1, pp. 72–4, 88–9, 98, 103, 107, 110, 112–14, Oglesby, *op. cit.*, p. 55, and Utley, *op. cit.*, p. 16. Dale, *op. cit.*, p. 28 and n. 22 cast doubt on Colter ever entering Yellowstone National Park.
65 Harris, *op. cit.*, pp. 121–24, and Utley, *op. cit.*, p. 16.
66 Harris, *op. cit.*, pp. 124–31, and Oglesby, *op. cit.*, pp. 86–8.

67 Oglesby, *op. cit.*, pp. 75–6.
68 Hafen, ed., *Mountain Men and Fur Traders of the Far West*, p. 14.
69 Oglesby, *op. cit.*, p. 97 n. 85.
70 Hafen, ed., *Mountain Men and Fur Traders of the Far West*, p. 15.
71 *Ibid.*, pp. 117–18.
72 Hafen, ed., *French Fur Traders and Voyageurs in the American West*, p. 177.
73 Hafen, ed., *Mountain Men and Fur Traders of the Far West*, p. 20.
74 Morgan, *op. cit.*, p. 62 gives the general location of Fort Recovery; while stating that
    the post's founding date is unknown, on p. 376 n. 22 Morgan asserts that it could have
    been as early as April 1820. Utley, *op. cit.*, p. 44 states that it was established in 1821.
    Audubon, *op. cit.*, 1:512 n. 2 places the trading post on the mile-long, cedar-covered
    island that Lewis and Clark visited on September 18, 1804. See Cedar Island, end-
    note 17 about the confusion caused by the name Fort aux Cédres.
75 Morgan, *op. cit.*, p. 113.
76 *Ibid.*, pp. 298–301.
77 Oral Interview with Dan Deuter, Curator, Fort Uncompahgre replica, Delta, CO, 3
    and 4 November 1997.
78 Mattes, *op. cit.*, pp. 40, 46, 50.
79 *Ibid.*, pp. xxxvi–xxxvii, 439–44.
80 Sunder, *The Fur Trade on the Upper Missouri*, pp. 240, 249–50.

Fort St. Vrain through Vermilion Post
1 Hafen, ed., *French Fur Trappers and Voyageurs in the American West*, p. 284.
2 Lavender, *Bent's Fort*, p. 341.
3 Sunder, *The Fur Trade on the Upper Missouri*, p. 126.
4 *Ibid.*, p. 162.
5 Chittenden, *op. cit.*, 2:927, and Wishart, *op. cit.*, pp. 54, 55 fig. 7.
6 Sunder, *The Fur Trade on the Upper Missouri*, p. 161.
7 Hafen, ed., *Fur Trappers and Traders of the Far Southwest*, pp. 212–16.
8 *Ibid.*, pp. 217–19, and Unruh, Jr., *op. cit.*, pp. 202, 216.
9 Newman, *op. cit.*, p. 92, (n.n.).
10 Chittenden, *op. cit.*, 1:204–5, and Coues, ed., *op. cit.*, 2:767 n. 32.
11 Newman, *op. cit.*, p. 278.
12 Frazer, *op. cit.*, p. 174.
13 Sunder, *The Fur Trade on the Upper Missouri*, pp. 196–7.
14 *Ibid.*, p. 214.
15 Wishart, *op. cit.*, pp. 71, 150–1, and Sunder, *Bill Sublette*, p. 127 n. 21.
16 Daniel J. Rogers, *Objects of Change: The Archaeology and History of Arikara Contact with
    Europeans* (DC: Smithsonian Institution Press, 1990), pp. 59, 67, DeVoto, *The Course
    of Empire*, p. 440, and DeVoto, ed., *The Journals of Lewis and Clark*, pp. 33–4, 49.
17 DeVoto, ed., *The Journals of Lewis and Clark*, p. 91.
18 Abel, ed., *op. cit.*, p. 204 n. 25 places Fort Tecumseh two miles above the mouth of
    the Bad (Teton) River, while Schuler, *op. cit.*, p. 9 places it one mile above.
19 Schuler, ed., *op. cit.*, p. 13.
20 Abel, ed., *op. cit.*, p. 229 n. 84.
21 Chittenden, *op. cit.*, 2:930 places the fort south of the Bad (Teton) River, giving its
    founding as either 1828 or 1829, whereas Schuler, *op. cit.*, p. 28 locates it above the
    mouth of the Bad. Hafen, ed., *French Fur Traders and Voyageurs in the American West*, p.
    243 states that P. D. Papin & Company was established during the summer of 1829,
    which would lead to the conclusion that the fort was most likely constructed that fall;
    however, p. 244 n. 21 cites evidence putting the fort's location just below the Bad
    River and marking its founding in 1828.

22 Chittenden, *op. cit.*, 1:348, and Abel, ed., *op. cit.*, p. 203 n. 20.
23 Nasatir, ed., *op. cit.*, 2:388 n. 17.
24 Coues, ed., *op. cit.*, 1:204, and Heidenreich, ed., *op. cit.*, p. 38.
25 Historians disagree on the date of Fort Uintah's establishment. Hafen, ed., *Trappers of the Far West,* p. 42 says that the winter of 1837–8 is the most likely time. On *ibid.*, p. 254, Janet Lecompte in her essay, "Charles Autobees," asserts that Antoine Robidoux had constructed Fort Uintah and Fort Uncompahgre (in western Colorado) by 1837. On *ibid.*, p. 276 n. 23, Lyman C. Pedersen, Jr., in his essay, "Warren Angus Ferris," cites 1832 and 1837 as possible founding dates; in addition, on p. 276, he places Fort Uintah on the Whiterocks River rather than the Uinta. Rufus Sage, *Rocky Mountain Life* Selected Quotations, *The Museum of the Fur Trade Quarterly* 20, no. 2 (summer 1984): p. 13 puts the fort on the Uinta's right bank, which is probably accurate, since Sage visited the trading post in October 1842. Guild and Carter, *op. cit.*, pp. 304–5 n. 7 say that the post was opened in the early 1830s. Most of these sources state that Fort Uintah and Fort Uncompahgre were established around the same time; however, Hafen, ed., *French Fur Traders and Voyageurs in the American West,* pp. 272–3 place Fort Uintah's founding in the early 1830s and Fort Uncompahgre's in the mid-'20s. During oral interviews on November 3 and 4, 1997, Dan Deuter, curator of the Fort Uncompahgre replica in Delta, CO, cleared up the uncertainty, stating that Fort Uintah was built in 1832 and Fort Uncompahgre in 1828.
26 An editor's note to the selected quotations of *Rocky Mountain Life* by Rufus Sage, referenced in endnote 25 above, says that Sage visited Fort Uintah in 1842, two years before it was razed by Indians. Hafen, ed., *French Fur Traders and Voyageurs in the American West,* pp. 280–1 report that during Robidoux's absence in the late spring or early summer of 1844, a Ute war party sacked Fort Uintah, massacring the traders and carrying off their Indian wives. Weber, *op. cit.*, p. 216 says that the attack happened at Robidoux's Fort Uncompahgre. Dan Deuter, curator of the Fort Uncompahgre replica, agrees with Weber, stating that the raid occurred at Fort Uncompahgre in September 1844. According to Deuter, both forts were burned in either 1846 or 1847, some months after they had been abandoned.
27 Gibson, *op. cit.*, p. 59 places the first Fort Umpqua upstream from the mouth of Elk Creek. Dale, *op. cit.*, p. 274 n. 538 mistakenly puts it within a few miles of the coast, having confused it with the US Army's Fort Umpqua which was established in 1856; see Lewis A. McArthur, *Oregon Geographic Names* (OR: The Press of the Oregon Historical Society, Fifth Edition, 1982), pp. 253, 292, and Frazer, *op. cit.*, pp. 132–3.
28 Gibson, *op. cit.*, p. 59.
29 Hafen, ed., *French Fur Traders and Voyageurs in the American West,* pp. 253–5 give a good description of the fort, although the text makes no mention of the "new" Fort Umpqua.
30 As they do about Fort Uintah, historians disagree about the date Fort Uncompahgre was founded. Hafen, ed., *French Fur Traders and Voyageurs in the American West,* pp. 272–3 argue that Antoine Robidoux most likely built the post in the mid-1820s, citing the 1825 survey that mapped the Santa Fe Trail to the Arkansas River. (Mexican officials refused to allow the Americans to carry the survey to Santa Fe until the following year.) Robidoux certainly would have known about the improved route, which was expected to increase trade between St. Louis and Santa Fe, because in early 1824 he traveled up the Missouri River to Fort Atkinson and received permission to take a pack train of trade goods through Indian country to New Mexico; Weber, *op. cit.*, p. 74. On p. 214 Weber states that Robidoux built Fort Uncompahgre about the same time he did Fort Uintah, although Weber thinks that the Whiterocks post was established during the winter of 1837–8; see p. 213. Dan

Deuter, curator of the Fort Uncompahgre replica in Delta, CO, stated during oral interviews that although Robidoux was in the Gunnison River Valley as early as 1825–a fact confirmed by Dale, *op. cit.*, p. 152 n. 292–he did not build Fort Uncompahgre until 1828. As further evidence that the post was up and running before the mid-1830s, Orral Messmore Robidoux reported that a party of trappers stopped there during the winter of 1832–3; Hafen, ed., *Mountain Men and Fur Traders of the Far West,* p. 257.

31 Weber, *op. cit.*, p. 215.

32 The information about the cause of the Ute attack on Fort Uncompahgre comes from oral interviews on November 3 and 4, 1997, with Dan Deuter, curator of the Fort Uncompahgre replica, Delta, CO. Hafen, ed., *French Fur Traders and Voyageurs in the American West,* p. 281 states that Antoine Robidoux returned to St. Joseph, MO, in late 1844 or early 1845, whereas Deuter says that he moved after closing Fort Uintah in the spring of 1845.

33 See Chittenden, *op. cit.*, 2:932–3, and Hunt, Jr., *op. cit.*, pp. 12–14. Chittenden argues that American Fur *engagés* built Fort Floyd on the Missouri River a few miles above its confluence with the Yellowstone. Hunt makes a more compelling argument that the company established a wintering post above the Yellowstone in the autumn of 1828, and that Fort Floyd was located 105 miles down the Missouri, near the mouth of the White Earth River. Also see Fort Floyd (aka White Earth River Post and Kipp's Post), endnote 39.

34 Although the record is far from clear, this wintering post may have been called Fort Union; see Hunt, *op. cit.*, p. 14.

35 Thompson, *op. cit.*, pp. 17–18. For a description of Fort Union as it appeared in 1843, see Audubon, *op. cit.*, 2:180–8.

36 Hafen, ed., *Fur Traders, Trappers, and Mountain Men of the Upper Missouri,* p. 27.

37 DeVoto, *Across the Wide Missouri,* pp. 118–20.

38 Thompson, *op. cit.*, pp. 32–3.

39 *Ibid.*, pp. 45–6.

40 *Ibid.*, pp. 80–2, and Frazer, *op. cit.*, p. 115.

41 Larpenteur, *op. cit.*, p. 309.

42 Sunder, *The Fur Trade on the Upper Missouri,* p. 260.

43 *Ibid.*, pp. 262–3, and Larpenteur, *op. cit.*, p. 309.

44 Lass, *op. cit.*, p. 33.

45 Chittenden, *op. cit.*, 2:938–9 place the post on the right side of the Yellowstone River near its confluence with the Tongue, which is wrong. Abel, ed., *op. cit.*, p. 315 n. 469 makes the same mistake; however, on p. 378, Kenneth McKenzie's letter of December 10, 1835, states that "Mr. Tulloch was putting up his new fort near the mouth of the Rosebud. . . ." Larpenteur, *op. cit.*, p. 138 states that Fort Van Buren was located at the mouth of the Rosebud, as does Hafen, ed., *Fur Traders, Trappers, and Mountain Men of the Upper Missouri,* p. 114. For more, see Fort Alexander, endnote 7.

46 This disputes Chittenden's claim that Fort Van Buren was deserted in 1843.

47 DeVoto, *The Course of Empire,* p. 323 gives the full name of Captain Gray's ship as *Columbia Rediviva.* Two years before Gray entered the mouth of the Columbia River, he took command of the *Columbia* in mid-voyage while the vessel was on the northwest Pacific coast. The ship had reached the Pacific Ocean via Cape Horn. After leaving the Columbia River estuary, Gray sailed to Vancouver Island and on to China, then around Africa and across the Atlantic Ocean to Boston, making the *Columbia* the first American ship to circumnavigate the globe.

48 Because Vancouver's ship HMS *Discovery* was too large to pass over the treacherous sandbar that guarded the Columbia River's entrance, Lieutenant W. Broughton sailed the smaller HMS *Chatham* into the estuary and anchored on October 19,

1792. Leaving his brig at the river's mouth, Broughton surveyed upstream in a longboat.

49 Newman, *op. cit.*, p. 85.
50 Chittenden, *op. cit.*, 1:223.
51 Newman, *op. cit.*, pp. 203–4.
52 Morgan, *op. cit.*, p. 270.
53 *Ibid.*, pp. 272–3, Newman, *op. cit.*, p. 278, and Williams, *op. cit.*, pp. 63–4.
54 Newman, *op. cit.*, p. 224.
55 *Ibid.*, p. 206.
56 Hafen, ed., *Mountain Men and Fur Traders of the Far West*, p. 109.
57 "Fort Vancouver" National Historic Site Brochure, National Park Service, GPO, 1995.
58 Hafen, ed., *Mountain Men and Fur Traders of the Far West*, p. 116.
59 Over the years, the stockade was repeatedly enlarged and, by 1845, encompassed five and one-third acres; "Fort Vancouver" National Historic Site Brochure, National Park Service, GPO, 1995.
60 Hafen, ed., *Mountain Men and Fur Traders of the Far West*, pp. 118–19.
61 Newman, *op. cit.*, p. 296.
62 Frazer, *op. cit.*, pp. 176–7.
63 Wood, *op. cit.*, pp. 4–5, and Morgan, *op. cit.*, p. 60 give 1822 as Fort Vanderburgh's founding date. Hafen, ed., *Fur Traders, Trappers, and Mountain Men of the Upper Missouri*, pp. 99–100 use 1821, as does Utley, *op. cit.*, p. 44.
64 Morgan, *op. cit.*, pp. 67, 78, 385 n. 2, and Meyer, *op. cit.*, p. 276 n. 62.
65 There is some question about when Lock & Randolph acquired Fort Vasquez. Lavender, *Bent's Fort*, pp. 197–8 are not definitive, although Lavender hints at 1840. Hanson, Jr., and Walters, *op. cit.*, p. 7 states that Lock and Randolph purchased Fort Vasquez after abandoning their post on the North Platte, which they built in 1841. Hanson, Jr., and Walters agree with Lavender that Lock & Randolph went bust in 1842, which leads to the conclusion that the partners obtained Fort Vasquez in either late 1841 or early 1842. Lavender makes the stronger argument, which leads me to think that Lock & Randolph acquired Fort Vasquez before giving up their trade on the North Platte. Hafen, *Broken Hand*, p. 191 reports that, in 1843, John Frémont saw the deserted post falling into ruin.
66 Hafen, ed., *French Fur Traders and Voyageurs in the American West*, pp. 107–8.

Wallace House through Big Wood Fort

1 Coues, ed., *op. cit.*, 2:752 n. 9, Hafen, ed., *French Fur Traders and Voyageurs in the American West*, p. 149, and Irving, *Astoria*, p. 399.
2 Irving, *Captain Bonneville*, p. 258 n. 1, and Morgan, *op. cit.*, p. 117.
3 Morgan, *op. cit.*, p. 284 quotes an 1829 letter from Hudson's Bay governor George Simpson to Jedediah Smith, informing Smith that it would be ". . . imprudent to attempt a Journey from Walla Walla to Salt Lake. . . ."
4 R. G. Robertson, "The Delightful Narcissa Whitman and Three Island Crossing," *The Idaho State Journal* (Pocatello, ID), 17 July 1997, sec. E, p. 8.
5 Frazer, *op. cit.*, p. 177.
6 Hunt, *op. cit.*, pp. 14–15 n. 39.
7 Abel, ed., *op. cit.*, pp. 202–3 n. 20, and Hafen, ed., *French Fur Traders and Voyageurs in the American West*, pp. 243–3.
8 Sunder, *Bill Sublette*, p. 127 n. 21.
9 Hafen, ed., *French Fur Traders and Voyageurs in the American West*, pp. 112–14.
10 Lavender, *Bent's Fort*, pp. 138–9 place the log stockade where Pueblo, CO, is now located, giving its founding as 1831. Hafen, ed., *Trappers of the Far West*, p. 211 says

that it was probably established in 1833; p. 211 n. 24 cites an interview with Tom Autobees that puts the post on the north side of the Arkansas River, a bit east of Devine, CO, and about ten miles east of Pueblo. Hafen, ed., *Trappers of the Far West,* p. 226 says that the log post was set three miles east of the mouth of Fountain Creek, and that Bent constructed it in the spring of 1833 in a competitive response to John Gantt's Fort Cass. Hafen, ed., *Mountain Men and Fur Traders of the Far West,* p. 155 places it on the Arkansas River, nine miles downstream from the mouth of Fountain Creek which is close to Devine.

For my part, it seems unlikely that William Bent would have started constructing his large adobe fort a few months after completing the log post, which makes me think that Lavender is correct and the log post was built in late 1831.

Acceptance of my reasoning dictates that John Gantt founded his first trading house after Bent had established his log post, a theory that agrees with Lavender, *Bent's Fort,* pp. 138–9, 418–9 n. 2, but is at odds with Samuel P. Arnold's essay "William Bent" in Hafen, ed., *Traders of the Far West,* p. 225 n. 14, p. 226. Arnold argues that Gantt built his first trading post at the confluence of the Arkansas and Purgatoire, an area known as Big Timbers because of the abundant cottonwoods. Lavender and Arnold agree that Chief Yellow Wolf of the Hairy Rope band of Cheyennes recommended Big Timbers for a trading post site (Lavender, *Bent's Fort,* pp. 141–2 and Arnold in Hafen, ed., *Traders of the Far West,* p. 225). If Gantt had placed his first fort where the Cheyennes wanted, it seems illogical that Bent, in 1833, would have begun constructing his adobe fort thirty miles west of the favored site, thereby forfeiting one of the Cheyennes' prime camping spots to Gantt. In the same vein, it seems equally improbable that, in 1834, Gantt would have left Big Timbers in order to build Fort Cass farther upriver than Bent had placed his adobe fort.

11 Thompson, *op. cit.,* p. 22, and Sunder, *Bill Sublette,* pp. 127 n. 21, 128–30.

12 Hafen, ed., *Mountain Men and Fur Traders of the Far West,* pp. 42–3.

13 Thompson, *op. cit.,* pp. 32–3.

14 Larpenteur, *op. cit.,* pp. 80–4.

15 DeVoto, *Across the Wide Missouri,* p. 208.

16 McArthur, *op. cit.,* pp. 652–3. Sauvie Island was formerly called Wappatoo, Wapato, and Multnomah Island.

17 DeVoto, *Across the Wide Missouri,* p. 211.

18 *Ibid.,* p. 258.

19 During oral interviews on April 21 and 29, 1997, Scott Langford, National Park Service ranger and historian, Fort Vancouver National Historic Site, Vancouver, WA, stated that Wyeth was not compensated for the use of Fort William; however, Hafen, ed., *Mountain Men and Fur Traders of the Far West,* p. 328 asserts that Wyeth "leased" the post to the Hudson's Bay Company.

20 An Oregon State historical sign near the site of the Willamette Post credits the Pacific Fur Company with its construction in 1811. Harriet D. Munnick in her essay "Etienne Lucier" in Hafen, ed., *French Fur Traders and Voyageurs in the American West,* p. 198 states that the Astorians established Willamette Post which was later called Henry's House. However, Kenneth L. Holmes, in his essay "Joseph Gervais" on p. 148 of the same volume, reports that whereas the Astorian Donald McKenzie explored the Willamette River Valley in the spring of 1812, he did not build a trading house at French Prairie–the location of Willamette Post. Gibson, *op. cit.,* p. 130, and the "Champoeg" Oregon State Heritage Brochure, Oregon State Parks, 1996, agree that the North West Company opened the Willamette Post in 1813. Without evidence to the contrary, it would appear that Munnick and the Oregon state historical sign are mistaken.

21 Hafen, ed., *French Fur Traders and Voyageurs in the American West,* pp. 24–5.

22 *Ibid.,* p. 204.

23 Hafen, ed., *Mountain Men and Fur Traders of the Far West,* p. 198 n. 3. Williams's trading license authorized him to trade with the Osage and Kickapoo Indians at the "Fork of the Grand River." During those years, the Neosho River was known as the Grand. Weber, *op. cit.,* p. 101 states the Paul Baillio ran a Fort Osage satellite post—probably the Marais des Cygnes River Post—until the government ended the Indian factory system in 1822. Afterwards, Baillio formed a partnership with George Sibley and Lilburn Boggs for the Osage trade, with Sibley continuing to manage Fort Osage as he had done the previous fourteen years. At the time, "Old Bill" Williams lived among the Osages, so when a portion of the tribe moved to the lower Neosho River, it was—in my opinion—easy for his friend Baillio to talk Williams into opening a trading post there, backed by Sibley, Baillio & Boggs's money.

24 Hafen, ed., *Mountain Men and Fur Traders of the Far West,* p. 199 puts "Old Bill" Williams with Jedediah Smith's party. Hafen, *Broken Hand,* p. 23 n. 3 questions whether or not Williams accompanied Smith's brigade. The evidence that he did comes from the recollections of Thomas Eddie—another member of the company—when Eddie was an old man.

25 Hafen, ed., *Mountain Men and Fur Traders of the Far West,* pp. 198, 200–20.

26 Weber, *op. cit.,* p. 134.

Glossary of Terms

Avant: Bowsman for a *canot de maître,* whose main responsibility was to watch for obstacles in the water.

Bourgeois: The title given to a trading post commander who worked for an American fur company. The *bourgeois* was often a company partner. The singular and plural forms are spelled the same.

Brig: A two-masted, square-rigged sailing vessel.

Bull Boat: A light-weight boat, usually made from green buffalo skins stretched over a willow frame. Indian bull boats were small, tub like craft, normally fashioned from a single hide and unable to carry more than two or three passengers. Those built by mountain men often measured twenty or thirty feet long and a dozen feet wide. Large boats such as these required the skins of fifteen or twenty buffalo that were stitched together and sealed with pitch. Even when loaded with two men and over two thousand pounds of beaver pelts, the boats drew only a few inches of water. Although bull boats could descend shallow rivers such as the Platte, they needed to be unloaded every couple of hours so their hulls could be dried and the seams resealed.

Canot de maître: A large birch-bark canoe (thirty-six to forty feet long with a five-foot beam) that was usually manned by a steersman, bowsman, and ten paddlers. A *canot de maître* could carry up to three tons of cargo. Because of its size, a *canot de maître* was restricted to the lakes and major rivers between Lachine (near Montreal) and the northwestern end of Lake Superior. Supplies destined for trading posts on smaller waterways had to be transshipped aboard the shorter *canot du nord*.

Canot du nord: A birch-bark freight canoe (twenty-four feet long with a four-foot beam) that was usually manned by a steersman, bowsman, and six paddlers. A *canot du nord* could carry three thousand pounds of cargo and was able to ply rivers too small to accomodate the larger *canot de maître*.

Cantonment: A temporary fort or quarters for troops. During the early 1800s, the US Army called many of its facilities cantonments even though they were permanent installations. The practice ended in 1832 when Army General Orders No. 11 specified that cantonments be renamed forts.

Clerk: In the hierarchy of trading post employees, the clerk occupied the next rung down from the *bourgeois* or factor. In larger posts having more than one clerk, their rankings were determined by seniority within the company. Clerks occasionally became minor shareholders in their companies.

Cordelle: A long rope used to tow keelboats upriver.

Country Marriage: A British colloquialism referring to the marriage of a fort employee into a native family. The employee enjoyed companionship and strengthened ties with his wife's tribe, while the native woman acquired the white man's riches. Fur companies on both sides of the forty-ninth parallel encouraged the practice because it was good for business. Polygamy was also condoned. Some traders regularly took wives for a season or two to cement a relationship with one tribe, then wed other women when they wanted to trade with different bands.

Doughboys: Spanish-style adobe bricks.

Dragoon: A mounted rifleman, the precursor of the cavalryman.

Egin: A Shoshone word meaning "cold."

Embarra: A river-formed logjam at the upstream side of a sandbar or

298

island. These jumbles of debris often constricted the channel, speeding the current and making passage treacherous.

Engagé: Least among the trading post hierarchy, a manual laborer who chopped wood, sawed planks, pressed robes, dug graves, and did other toilsome tasks.

Factor: The title given to a trading post commander who worked for Hudson's Bay, North West, or other Canadian/British fur companies. A chief factor managed an entire region. Many of these officials were also company partners.

Firewater: The Indian term for alcohol. Traders often gave free, water-diluted liquor to the Indians to dull their wits and induce them to barter their furs for more liquor. As the Indians became intoxicated, traders sometimes added more water to the alcohol to reduce its potency and save the fur company money. An Indian who suspected such deceit would spit a mouthful of "mountain whiskey" into a fire to test whether it would burn.

Foofuraw: Beads, ribbons, cloth, bells, or any other gewgaws used by trappers and traders to buy sexual favors from Indian women or to keep Indian wives happy.

Furry Bank Notes: Beaver pelts.

Fusil: A smooth-bore, light-weight, flintlock musket. Although fusils and rifles looked similar, fusil bores were not rifled. In other words, they did not have the spiraled "lands" and "grooves" that caused a lead ball or modern bullet to spin when fired. As a result, a fusil could shoot neither as far nor as accurately as a rifle. Indians generally preferred fusils to rifles because fusils could fire shot (for killing birds), as well as balls, something a rifle could not do. Also, fusils were less expensive than rifles.

Gouvernail: A steersman or coxswain on a *canot de maître.*

Headquarters Posts: A large post, such as Fort Union or Fort Pierre, that served as a supply depot to support outlying regional posts, such as Fort Piegan and Fort Berthold.

Hivernan: A winterer; the French name given to trappers and trading post employees who had spent at least one winter in the wilderness.

Hollow Woods: Small wooden kegs designed to be packed on horses and mules and used to transport alcohol to the trappers' annual rendezvous.

Indian Factory: A trading house for Indians, run by a government-licensed trader who was supervised by the US Army. Factories were usually located at military forts. America's factory trading system began in the mid-1790s while George Washington was president and continued until March 1822. The term "factory" comes from the factor—another name for trader—who brokered furs and trade goods between the Indians and eastern merchants and fur companies.

Indian Telegraph: A term applied to the often uncanny way information quickly passed from tribe to tribe over great distances.

Keelboat: A riverboat with a full-length keel that typically measured sixty to seventy-five feet from bow to stern and had a beam of fifteen to eighteen feet and a hold that was three or four feet deep. A shoulder-high, roofed cargo box occupied the center of the deck, with narrow, fifteen-inch-wide walkways (aka *passe avants*) running along each side. The boat supported a single mast and sail for those occasions when the wind was at its stern. Direction was controlled by a large tiller. When heading upriver, the voyageurs rowed through deep, slow-moving water, using oars that were located near the bow. More often, twenty or thirty men waded the shallows, pulling the boat against the current by means of a *cordelle,* a long rope that was attached to the mast. At the same time, five or six other voyageurs trudged fore and aft along each of the *passe avants,* muscling the boat forward with iron-tipped setting poles that were pushed against the riverbed.

Mackinaw: An inexpensive, flat-bottomed boat that was used to float buffalo robes and other cargo from outlying trading posts to Council Bluffs or St. Louis. Many mackinaws were burned as firewood at journey's end.

Mangeur de lard: French-Canadians in the North West and Hudson's

Bay companies applied this term to the lowest caste of voyageur who paddled the firms' heavy freight canoes. American fur traders and trappers applied it to a greenhorn who had never spent a winter above the mouth of the Platte River. The French term means literally, "eater of pork."

Métis: A non-derogatory Canadian term for people of mixed white and Indian ancestry.

Milieux: Rowers who knelt two abreast in the *canots de maître* and *canots du nord.*

Mountain Whiskey: Trade liquor–typically pure grain alcohol–that was diluted with water and sometimes flavored with cloves and other spices.

Nankeen: A buff-colored cotton cloth originally imported from Nanking, China.

On the Prairie: A commodity, usually liquor, that was given free of charge.

Pemmican: Although recipes varied, pemmican always included powdered meat (buffalo jerky that had been pounded to a pulp) mixed with melted tallow. Indian women often added fresh or dried berries to the mixture, which they put up in large skin bags that held fifty or sixty pounds. Their husbands traded pemmican to the fur companies, where it was stored for times when the buffalo were scarce and the larders were running low of jerked meat.

Piastre: The Spanish dollar.

Pirogue: A canoe-shaped boat that could be built in any number of sizes.

Plew: A beaver pelt.

Regional Post: A smaller trading post, such as Fort Clark or Fort McKenzie, that was supported by a larger headquarters post.

Sawyer: A tree that had toppled into a river and was held fast by its roots. High water caused by thunderstorms often sucked sawyers free, propelling them downstream like battering rams intent on skewering any keelboat or steamer whose lookouts were not vigilant.

Side-wheeler and Stern-wheeler: A side-wheeler was a steamboat with two paddle wheels set amidships on opposite sides of the vessel. A stern-wheeler had a single, large paddle wheel located at its stern.

Sutler: Running an officially sanctioned store at a military installation, a sutler sold provisions to civilians and Indians, as well as to Army troops.

Trapping Brigade: A group of trappers who traveled together for security. A brigade could be made up of free trappers, or company-employed trappers and camp tenders, or a combination thereof. Trapping brigades numbered as few as ten men or upwards of one hundred. When wanting to trap, a brigade split into two- to four-man parties, worked a region's streams for several days, then regrouped and moved to a new area. Trappers were most vulnerable to Indian attack while in these dispersed teams.

Voyageur: A general term applied to any man who worked on the various boats (other than steamboats) of the fur trade.

Wampum: An Algonquian Indian word for strings of small beads (made from shells) that were used by the Indians for money and ornament. Wampum came in both white and, the more valuable, black.

Bibliography

Abel, Annie Heloise, ed. *Chardon's Journal at Fort Clark, 1834–1839*. Lincoln, NE: University of Nebraska Press, Bison Books Edition, 1997. Reprinted from the edition published by Lawrence K. Fox, Superintendent, Department of History, State of South Dakota, Pierre, SD, 1932.

_____, ed. *Tabeau's Narrative of Loisel's Expedition to the Upper Missouri*. Norman, OK: University of Oklahoma Press, 1939.

Alvord, Jack and Dr. Richard Howard. "Old Fort Hall, Gateway to the Pacific Northwest," Pocatello, Idaho, Parks & Recreation Department Brochure to the replica of Old Fort Hall, (n.d.).

Ambrose, Stephen E. *Undaunted Courage: Meriwether Lewis, Thomas Jefferson, and the Opening of the American West*. NY: Simon & Schuster, 1996.

Arrington, Leonard J. *History of Idaho*. 2 Vols. Moscow, ID: University of Idaho Press, 1994.

Athearn, Robert G. *Forts of the Upper Missouri*. Englewood Cliffs, NJ: Prentice-Hall, Inc., 1967.

Audubon, John James. *Audubon and His Journals*. 2 Vols. Ed. by Maria R. Audubon, with notes by Elliott Coues. NY: Dover Publications, Inc., 1960. Originally published by Charles Scribner's Sons, 1897.

"Bent's Old Fort." National Historic Site Brochure. National Park Service. GPO, 1993. Reprint, 1988.

Catlin, George. *Letters and Notes on the Manners, Customs, and Conditions of the North American Indians, Written during Eight Years' Travel (1832–1839) amongst the Wildest Tribes of Indians in North America*. 2 Vols. NY: Dover Publications, 1973. First published in Philadelphia 1841. Republished in London in 1844.

"Chadron Creek Trading Post." Nebraska Historical Marker on US 385, six miles south of Chadron, NE.

"Champoeg." Oregon State Heritage Area Brochure. Oregon State Parks, 1996.

Cheney, Robert Carkeek. *Names on the Face of Montana: The Story of Montana's Place Names*. Missoula, MT: Mountain Press Publishing Company, 1983. Revised, 1984.

Chittenden, Hiram Martin. *The American Fur Trade of the Far West*. 2 Vols. Lincoln, NE: University of Nebraska Press, Bison Book Edition, 1986. Republication of a 2 vol. ed. published by the Press of the Pioneers, NY, 1935. Originally published in 3 vols. by Francis P. Harper, NY, 1902.

_____. *History of Early Steamboat Navigation on the Missouri River: Life and Adventures of Joseph La Barge.* 2 Vols. NY: Francis P. Harper, 1903.

Clyman, James. *Journal of a Mountain Man.* Ed. by Linda M. Hasselstrom. Missoula, MT: Mountain Press Publishing Company, 1984, Winfred Blevins. Originally published as *James Clyman, American Frontiersman, 1792–1881,* California Historical Society Special Publication No. 3, California Historical Society, San Francisco, CA, c1928.

Colorado Atlas and Gazetteer. Freeport, ME: DeLorme Mapping, 1991.

Conley, Cort. *Idaho for the Curious: A Guide.* Cambridge, ID: Backeddy Books, 1982.

Coues, Elliott., ed. *The Manuscript Journals of Alexander Henry, Fur Trader of the Northwest Company, and of David Thompson, Official Geographer and Explorer of the same Company.* 2 Vols. Minneapolis, MN: Ross & Haines, Inc., 1897. Reprint, 1965.

Dale, Harrison Clifford. *The Explorations of William H. Ashley and Jedediah Smith, 1822–1829.* Lincoln, NE: University of Nebraska Press, Bison Book Edition, 1991. Republished from *The Ashley-Smith Explorations and the Discovery of a Central Route to the Pacific, 1822–1829.* Arthur H. Clark Company, Glendale, CA, 1941.

Deuter, Dan, Curator. Oral interviews by author. Fort Uncompahgre replica, Delta, CO. 3 and 4 November 1997.

DeVoto, Bernard. *Across the Wide Missouri.* Boston, MA: Houghton Mifflin Co., 1947.

_____. *The Course of Empire.* Boston, MA: Houghton Mifflin Co., 1952.

_____, ed. *The Journals of Lewis and Clark.* Boston, MA: Houghton Mifflin Co., 1953.

_____. *The Year of Decision, 1846.* Boston, MA: Houghton Mifflin Co., 1942.

Drury, Clifford Merrill ed. *First White Women Over the Rockies: Diaries, Letters, and Biographical Sketches of the Six Women of the Oregon Mission Who Made the Overland Journey in 1836 and 1838.* Vol. 1. Glendale, CA: Arthur H. Clark Co., 1963.

Eckberg, Scott B. "Artist, Clerk, Chronicler: Rudolf F. Kurz and His Fort Union Sojourn." *North Dakota History, Journal of the Northern Plains* 61, no. 3 (summer 1994): 41–52.

Ellison, Robert S. *Fort Bridger–A Brief History.* 2d ed. WY: State Archives, Museums, and Historical Department, 1981. WY: Historical Landmark Commission. Original ed., 1931.

Ewers, John C. *The Blackfeet: Raiders on the Northwestern Plains.* Norman, OK: University of Oklahoma Press, 1958.

"Explore the Past at Fort Mandan." Lewis and Clark Campsite 1804–5 Brochure. McLean County Historical Society.

"Fort Atkinson, 1820–1827." Brochure. Nebraska Game and Parks Commission, 1996.

"Fort Clark State Historic Site." Brochure. State Historical Society of North Dakota, (n.d.).

"Fort Clatsop." National Memorial Official Map and Guide. National Park Service. GPO, 1996. Reprint, 1991.

"Fort Clatsop, The Fort Replica." National Memorial Brochure. National Park Service, (n.d.).

"Fort Connah." Brochure. Fort Connah Restoration Society, St. Ignatius, MT, (n.d.).

"Fort Laramie." Official Map and Guide. National Park Service. GPO, 1992. Reprint, 1991.

"Fort Owen State Park." Brochure. Montana Fish, Wildlife and Parks, Helena, MT, (n.d.).

"Fort Union." Official Map and Guide. National Park Service. GPO, 1990.

"Fort Vancouver." National Historic Site Brochure. National Park Service. GPO, 1995.

Franzwa, Gregory M. *The Oregon Trail Revisited.* St. Louis, MO: Patrice Press, 1972.

Frazer, Robert W. *Forts of the West.* Norman, OK: University of Oklahoma Press, 1965.

Friedman, Ralph. *Oregon for the Curious.* Revised 3d ed. Caldwell, ID: The Caxton Printers, Ltd., 1972.

Galbraith, John S. *The Hudson's Bay Company as an Imperial Factor, 1821–1869.* Berkeley, CA: University of California Press, 1957.

Gibson, James R. *Farming the Frontier: The Agricultural Opening of the Oregon Country, 1786–1846.* Seattle, WA: University of Washington Press, 1985.

Graves, F. Lee. *Montana's Fur Trade Era.* Helena, MT: Montana Magazine and American & World Geographic Publishing, 1994.

Guild, Thelma S. and Harvey L. Carter. *Kit Carson: A Pattern for Heroes.* Lincoln, NE: University of Nebraska Press, Bison Book Edition, 1988. Republished from the University of Nebraska Press Edition, 1984.

Hafen, LeRoy R. *Broken Hand, The Life of Thomas Fitzpatrick: Mountain Man, Guide and Indian Agent.* Lincoln, NE: University of Nebraska Press, Bison Book Edition, 1973, 1981. Reprinted from the Old West Publishing Company Edition, Denver, CO, 1931.

_____, ed. *French Fur Traders and Voyageurs in the American West.* Lincoln, NE: University of Nebraska Press, Bison Book Edition, 1997. Republished from *Mountain Men and the Fur Trade of the Far West.* 10 Vols. Ed. by LeRoy R. Hafen. Glendale, CA: Arthur H. Clark Co., 1965–72.

_____, ed. *Fur Traders, Trappers, and Mountain Men of the Upper Missouri.* Lincoln, NE: University of Nebraska Press, Bison Book Edition, 1995. Republished from *Mountain Men and the Fur Trade of the Far West.* 10 Vols. Ed. by LeRoy R. Hafen. Glendale, CA: Arthur H. Clark Co., 1965–72.

_____, ed. *Fur Trappers and Traders of the Far Southwest.* Logan, UT: Utah State University Press, 1997. Republished from *Mountain Men and the Fur Trade of the Far West.* 10 Vols. Ed. by LeRoy R. Hafen. Glendale, CA: Arthur H. Clark Co., 1965–72.

_____, ed. *Mountain Men and Fur Traders of the Far West.* Lincoln, NE: University of Nebraska Press, Bison Book Edition, 1982. Republished from *Mountain Men and the Fur Trade of the Far West.* 10 Vols. Ed. by LeRoy R. Hafen. Glendale, CA: Arthur H. Clark Co., 1965–72.

_____, ed. *Trappers of the Far West.* Lincoln, NE: University of Nebraska Press, Bison Book Edition, 1983. Republished from *Mountain Men and the Fur Trade of the Far West.* 10 Vols. Ed. by LeRoy R. Hafen. Glendale, CA: Arthur H. Clark Co., 1965–72.

Hanson, Jr., Charles E. "James Bordeaux." *The Museum of the Fur Trade Quarterly* 2, no. 1 (spring 1966): 2–12.

_____. *The Hawken Rifle: Its Place in History.* Chadron, NE: The Fur Press, 1979.

_____, and Veronica Sue Walters. "The Early Fur Trade in Northwestern Nebraska." *Nebraska History* 57, no. 4 (fall 1976). Reprint, 1985.

Hanson, James, Curator. Oral interview by author. Museum of the Fur Trade, Chadron, NE, 10 June 1997.

Harris, Burton. *John Colter: His Years in the Rockies.* Lincoln, NE: University of Nebraska Press, Bison Book Edition, 1993. Republished from the Charles Scribner's Sons Edition, NY, 1952.

Heidenreich, Virginia L., ed. *The Fur Trade in North Dakota.* Bismarck, ND: State Historical Society of North Dakota, 1990.

Highlights of the Upper Missouri National Wild and Scenic River Lewis and Clark National Historic Trail. Lewiston, MT: Bureau of Land Management, 1993.

Hunt, William J. "Fort Floyd: An Enigmatic Nineteenth-Century Trading Post." *North Dakota History, Journal of the Northern Plains* 61, no. 3 (summer 1994): 7–20.

Idaho Atlas and Gazetteer. Freeport, ME: DeLorme Mapping, 1992.

Irving, Washington. *Astoria.* Portland, OR: Binfords & Mort, Publishers, Clatsop Edition, 1967. Reprinted from *Astoria, or Anecdotes of an Enterprise beyond the Rocky Mountains.* 2 Vols. Published by Carey, Lea, and Blanchard, Philadelphia, PA, 1836.

_____. Edgeley W. Todd, ed. *The Adventures of Captain Bonneville, USA. in the Rocky Mountains and the Far West.* Norman, OK: University of Oklahoma Press, 1961, 1986. Reprinted from *The Rocky Mountains; or Scenes, Incidents, and Adventures in the Far West, digested from the Journal of Captain B.L.E. Bonneville, USA., and Illustrated from various other sources.* 2 Vols. Published by Carey, Lea, and Blanchard, Philadelphia, PA, 1837.

Jackson, Donald. *Old Fort Madison–1808–1813.* Fort Madison, IA: The Old Fort Commission, 1990. Originally published as an article in *The Palimpsest* 47, no. 1, January 1966.

Josephy, Jr., Alvin M. *The Indian Heritage of America.* Boston, MA: Houghton Mifflin Company, 1968. Revised ed., 1991.

Knapp, George. Oral interviews by author. Fort Connah Restoration Society, Missoula, MT. 28 April and 7 May 1997.

"Knife River Indian Villages." National Historic Site Brochure. National Park Service. GPO, 1992.

Langer, William L., ed. *An Encyclopedia of World History.* Boston, MA: Houghton Mifflin Company, 1968.

Langford, Scott, National Park Service Ranger and Historian. Oral interviews by author. Fort Vancouver National Historic Site. 21 and 29 April 1997.

Larpenteur, Charles. *Forty Years a Fur Trader on the Upper Missouri: The Personal Narrative of Charles Larpenteur, 1833–1872.* Lincoln, NE: University of Nebraska Press, Bison Book Edition, 1989. Originally edited by Elliott Coues and published in 2 vols., New York, 1898; then re-edited by Milo M. Quaife and published as a Lakeside Classic by R. R. Donnelley & Sons, Chicago, IL, 1933.

Lass, William E. "The History and Significance of the Northwest Fur Company, 1865–1869." *North Dakota History, Journal of the Northern Plains* 61, no. 3 (summer 1994): 21–40.

Lavender, David. *Bent's Fort.* Lincoln, NE: University of Nebraska Press, Bison Book Edition, 1972. Republished from the Doubleday & Company, Inc., Dolphin Book Edition, 1954.

_____. *Fort Laramie and the Changing Frontier,* Handbook 118. Washington, DC: Division of Publications, National Park Service, 1983.

Lehmer, Donald J. *Selected Writings of Donald J. Lehmer.* Reprints in Anthropology, Vol. 8. Lincoln, NE: J & L Reprint Company, 1977.

"Lewis and Clark Trail." National Historical Trail Brochure. National Park Service, GPO, 1991.

Lovell, Edith Haroldsen. *Benjamin Bonneville: Soldier of the American Frontier.* Bountiful, UT: Horizon Publishers & Distributors, Inc., 1992.

Mathews, John Joseph. *The Osages: Children of the Middle Waters.* Norman, OK: University of Oklahoma Press, 1961.

Mattes, Merrill J. *The Great Platte River Road: The Covered Wagon Mainline Via Fort Kearny To Fort Laramie.* Lincoln, NE: University of Nebraska Press, Bison Book Edition, 1987. Republished from Nebraska State Historical Society Edition, Lincoln, 1969.

McArthur, Lewis A. *Oregon Geographic Names.* 5th ed. revised and enlarged by Lewis L. McArthur. OR: The Press of the Oregon Historical Society, 1982. Lewis A. McArthur First Edition Copyright, 1928.

McGuire, Mike. Education Programmer. Oral interview by author. Fort Nisqually Historic Site. 24 April 1997.

Meyer, Roy W. *The Village Indians of the Upper Missouri: The Mandans, Hidatsas, and Arikaras.* Lincoln, NE: University of Nebraska Press, 1977.

Mitchell, S. Augustus, Publisher. "A New Map of Texas, Oregon, and California with the regions adjoining compiled from the most recent authorities." Philadelphia, PA, 1846.

Moll, Peg and Larry Wilwant, eds. "Pembina: North Dakota's Oldest Settlement." Information Booklet, 1992.

Montana Atlas and Gazetteer. Freeport, ME: DeLorme Mapping, 1994.

Morgan, Dale L. *Jedediah Smith and the Opening of the West.* Lincoln, NE: University of Nebraska Press, Bison Book Edition, 1964. Republished from the Bobbs-Merrill Company Edition, Indianapolis, IN, 1953.

Nasatir, A.P., ed. *Before Lewis and Clark, Documents Illustrating the History of the Missouri 1785–1804.* 2 Vols. Lincoln, NE: University of Nebraska Press, Bison Books Edition, 1990. Originally published by the St. Louis Historical Documents Foundation, St. Louis, MO, 1952.

Newby, Rick. *Great Escapes, Montana State Parks.* Helena, MT: Falcon Press Publishing Co., Inc., 1989.

Newman, Peter C. *Caesars of the Wilderness, Company of Adventurers,* Vol. II. NY: Penguin Books, 1988. Republished from the Viking Penguin Inc. Edition, 1987.

"Nez Perce." National Historical Park Brochure. National Park Service, GPO, 1994.

"Nez Perce, Spalding Site." National Historical Park Information Sheet. National Park Service, (n.d.).

1995 Information Please Almanac, Atlas and Yearbook, 48th ed. Boston, MA: Houghton Mifflin Company, 1995.

Oglesby, Richard Edward. *Manuel Lisa and the Opening of the Missouri Fur Trade.* Norman, OK: University of Oklahoma Press, 1963.

"Oregon Trail." Oregon National Historic Trail-Missouri to Oregon Map. National Park Service, GPO, 1993.

"Parma's Old Fort Boise." Brochure. *The Parma Review,* (n.d.).

Powell, Allen Kent, ed. *Utah History Encyclopedia.* Salt Lake City, UT: University of Utah Press, 1994.

Preuss, Charles. "Topographical Map of the Road from Missouri to Oregon commencing at the mouth of the Kansas in the Missouri River and ending at the mouth of the Wallah-Wallah in the Columbia, in VII Sections, from the field notes and journal of Capt. J. C. Frémont, and from sketches and notes made on the ground by his assistant Charles Preuss, by order of the Senate of the United States." Baltimore, MD: E. Weber & Company, Lithography, 1846.

Robertson, R.G., "Mullan Road: A Feat of 624 Miles." *Idaho Spokesman-Review* (Coeur d'Alene, ID), 29 July 1996.

_____, "The Delightful Narcissa Whitman and Three Island Crossing." *Idaho State Journal* (Pocatello, ID), 17 July 1997.

Rogers, J. Daniel. *Objects of Change: The Archaeology and History of Arikara Contact with Europeans.* DC: Smithsonian Institution Press, 1990.

Rollings, Willard H. *The Osage: An Ethnohistorical Study of Hegemony on the Prairie-Plains.* Columbia, MO: University of Missouri Press, 1992.

Rozwenc, Edwin C. *The Making of American Society,* Vol. I to 1877. Boston, MA: Allyn and Bacon, Inc., 1972.

Russell, Carl P. *Firearms, Traps, and Tools of the Mountain Men.* Albuquerque, NM: University of New Mexico Press, 1977. NY: Alfred A. Knopf, Inc. Edition, 1967.

Sage, Rufus. *Rocky Mountain Life* Selected Quotations. *The Museum of the Fur Trade Quarterly* 20, no. 2 (summer 1984): 13–14.

Schuler, Harold H. *Fort Pierre Chouteau.* Vermillion, SD: University of South Dakota Press, 1990.

Schwantes, Carlos A. *In Mountain Shadows: A History of Idaho.* Lincoln, NE: University of Nebraska Press, 1991.

"Scotts Bluff National Monument." Official Map and Guide. National Park Service, GPO, 1996.

Simmons, Marc. *Following the Santa Fe Trail: A Guide for Modern Travelers.* 2d ed. Santa Fe, NM: Ancient City Press, 1984, 1986.

Stansbury, Howard, Captain, Corps of Topographical Engineers. "Map of a Reconnaissance between Fort Leavenworth on the Missouri River and the Great

Salt Lake in the Territory of Utah, made in 1849 and 1850, under orders of Col. J. J. Abert, Chief of the Topographical Bureau."

Sunder, John E. *Bill Sublette, Mountain Man*. Norman, OK: University of Oklahoma Press, 1959.

_____. *The Fur Trade on the Upper Missouri, 1840–1865*. Norman, OK: University of Oklahoma Press, 1965.

_____. *Joshua Pilcher, Fur Trader and Indian Agent*. Norman, OK: University of Oklahoma Press, 1968.

The New International Atlas. Chicago, IL: Rand McNally & Company, 1980.

The North American Indian Portfolios from the Library of Congress. Paintings by George Catlin, Karl Bodmer, Thomas L. McKenney, and James Hall. NY: Abbeville Publishing Group, 1993.

Thompson, Erwin N. *Fort Union Trading Post, Fur Trade Empire on the Upper Missouri*. Medora, ND: Theodore Roosevelt Nature and History Association, 1986. Originally published as *Fort Union Trading Post Historic Structures Report, Part I*. National Park Service, 1968.

Unruh, Jr., John D. *The Plains Across: The Overland Emigrants and the Trans-Mississippi West, 1840–60*. Urbana, IL: University of Illinois Press, Illini Books Edition, 1982. Republished from the University of Illinois Press Edition, 1979.

Urdang, Lawrence, ed. *The World Almanac Dictionary of Dates*. New York, NY: Longman, Inc., 1982.

Utah Atlas and Gazetteer. Freeport, ME: DeLorme Mapping, 1993.

Utley, Robert M. *A Life Wild and Perilous: Mountain Men and the Paths to the Pacific*. NY: Henry Holt and Company, Inc., 1997.

_____, and Wilcomb E. Washburn. *Indian Wars*. Boston, MA: Houghton Mifflin Company, 1987. American Heritage Edition, 1977.

Vestal, Stanley. *Jim Bridger, Mountain Man*. Lincoln, NE: University of Nebraska Press, 1946. Bison Book Edition, 1970.

_____. *Joe Meek, The Merry Mountain Man*. Lincoln, NE: University of Nebraska Press, Bison Book, 1963. Caxton Printer, Ltd., 1952.

"Walhalla, North Dakota, 'Valley of the Gods.'" Information Booklet of Walhalla, ND, (n.d.).

Weber, David. J. *The Taos Trappers: The Fur Trade in the Far Southwest, 1540–1846*. Norman, OK: University of Oklahoma Press, 1968 (in microfilm). Published, 1970. Revised, 1971.

Williams, Glyndwr. "The Hudson's Bay Company and the Fur Trade: 1670–1870." *The Beaver* (autumn 1983). Reprint, 1991.

Wishart, David J. *The Fur Trade of the American West, 1807–1840: A Geographical Synthesis*. Lincoln, NE: University of Nebraska Press, Bison Book Edition, 1992. Republished from the University of Nebraska Press Edition, 1979.

Wood, W. Raymond. "An Introduction to the History of the Fur Trade on the Northern Plains." *North Dakota History, Journal of the Northern Plains* 61, no. 3 (summer 1994): 2–6.

Wyoming Atlas and Gazetteer. Freeport, ME: DeLorme Mapping, 1992.

Index

INDEXER NOTE: Entries such as Missouri River, Yellowstone River, St. Louis, etc. have been omitted. Because of their importance during this era, the entries appear on almost every page of text.

About the Author and Photographer

A native of Michigan, R.G. Robertson has a BA and MBA from the University of Michigan. He was a US Marine Corps officer in the Vietnam War and, afterwards, worked as a stockbroker in San Francisco and as a Pacific Stock Exchange options market maker. His first book, *Idaho Echoes in Time* (1998), has been a successful regional title, going through two printings in the first six months. He now spends his time researching and writing books and articles, as well as traveling, skiing, backpacking, and mountain climbing. R.G. Robertson is also a member of Western Writers of America. He presently lives in Sun Valley, Idaho.

Born and raised in Oregon, Karen Robertson earned BS degrees in history and political science from Portland State University. After a career in the investment business in Oregon and California, she moved to Sun Valley with her husband. Her photographs have been published with R.G.'s articles and in *Idaho Echoes in Time*. In addition to photography, Karen's interests include travel and wilderness adventure.

The author welcomes comments and suggestions for subsequent editions of *Competitive Struggle*. Please write c/o Tamarack Books, PO Box 190313, Boise, ID 83719–0313.

Additional copies of *Competitive Struggle* can be found in fine bookstores nationwide or directly from the publisher.

If ordering direct, please include a check for $23.95 (book @ $18.95 plus a shipping/handling charge of $5.00). Idaho residents should send $24.90 (book @ $18.95, shipping/handling $5.00, and Idaho tax $.95).

Send your name, address, and check to:

Competitive Struggle Orders
Tamarack Books, Inc.
PO Box 190313
Boise, ID 83719–0313

To place orders using MasterCard or Visa, please call 1–800–962–6657.

If you liked this book, you might enjoy these other Tamarack titles:
Mountain Men of the American West by James A. Crutchfield
Give Your Heart to the Hawks by Winfred Blevins

For information on these or other Tamarack titles please call 1–800–962–6657.

Ask for our free catalog!